THE EUROPEAN UNION

The New Europe: Interdisciplinary Perspectives
Stanley Hoffmann, Series Editor

The European Union: Politics and Policies
John McCormick

An Imperfect Union: The Maastricht Treaty and
the New Politics of European Integration
Michael J. Baun

The European Sisyphus: Essays on Europe, 1964–1994
Stanley Hoffmann

France, Germany, and the Western Alliance
Philip H. Gordon

FORTHCOMING

Integrating Social Europe: The International Construction
of a Democratic Policy
Wolfgang Streeck

THE
EUROPEAN UNION

—

Politics and Policies

—

John McCormick
Indiana University—Purdue University Indianapolis

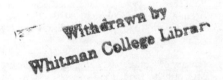

WestviewPress
A Division of HarperCollinsPublishers

The New Europe: Interdisciplinary Perspectives

Copyright 1996 by Westview Press, Inc., A Division of HarperCollins Publishers, Inc.

Published in 1996 in the United States of America by Westview Press, Inc., 5500 Central Avenue, Boulder, Colorado 80301-2877, and in the United Kingdom by Westview Press, 12 Hid's Copse Road, Cumnor Hill, Oxford OX2 9JJ

Library of Congress Cataloging-in-Publication Data
McCormick, John, 1954–
  The European Union : politics and policies / John McCormick.
    p. cm. — (The new Europe : interdisciplinary perspectives)
  Includes bibliographical references and index.
  ISBN 0-8133-2232-4 (hc.) —ISBN 0-8133-2233-2 (pbk.)
  1. European Union. I. Title. II. Series: New Europe (Boulder,
  Colo.
  JN30.M37 1996
  341.24'2—dc20   95-49744
                                                               CIP

The paper used in this publication meets the requirements of the American National Standard for Permanence of Paper for Printed Library Materials Z39.48-1984.

10   9   8   7   6   5   4   3   2   1

Contents

PART TWO: INSTITUTIONS

Illustrations

Boxes

Tables

Maps

Figures

Preface and Acknowledgments

The European Union (EU) is the world's latest superpower, a major actor in the global economic system, and the possible foundation of a European political union. Yet for most people it remains a mystery and an enigma. Most Americans know it exists, but few know how it works or what it means. Even Europeans are perplexed: Most will tell pollsters they support integration as an idea, but—if pushed—they would find it hard to say exactly how the EU works, who makes all the decisions, or why the EU has brought so many changes to their lives.

There are several reasons for the confusion. First, the EU is new and unusual. There has never been anything quite like it, and it fits few of the conventional ideas about the ways in which people govern themselves. Second, much of its work is shrouded in secrecy. Many of its decisions are made behind closed doors by unelected officials, and the average European has little direct impact on those decisions. Third, it is constantly evolving. Its powers, reach, character, and appearance are always changing, and its emergence has even redefined the meaning of the words *Europe* and *European*.

But there is another, more mundane explanation for the confusion: Clear and accessible guides through the EU maze are rare. Amid the torrent of excellent new books and articles European integration has generated since the mid-1980s, few explain how the EU works from first principles. Most assume readers already know their way around the labyrinthine EU bureaucracy, can tell the difference between the European Council and the Council of Ministers, and won't choke on words like *subsidiarity* or *cohesion*. In the absence of explanatory life preservers, the unwary are left floundering in a sea of acronyms and jargon.

I have taught classes on European integration for several years, and I've heard this concern from students and colleagues alike; they find most of the existing texts to be dry and dense and have been looking for a book that really *introduces* the politics and policies of the EU in a real, exciting, and approachable way. Their concerns prompted this book. It is aimed mainly at upper-division undergraduate students, but I hope it will also help researchers, people in business and government, or anyone who wants to learn more about the EU.

My goal has been to help answer five fundamental questions: What is the EU, how and why did it evolve, what does it do, how does it work, and what difference does it make? I don't claim to be comprehensive or exhaustive; instead, I have tried to include all the basic factual material and to put that material in context by trying to explain and assess the goals and motives behind European integration, the significance of the EU for both its member states and the rest of the world (particularly North America), the changes the EU has made in the lives of Europeans, and the long-term implications of the European experiment. Above all, I want to demystify the European Union, to help readers come to grips with this strange new economic and political entity, and—most important—to do all this as clearly and as briefly as possible.

A Note on the Approach. Unlike almost all its predecessors, this book is written specifically for North Americans and addresses the kinds of questions readers on this side of the Atlantic are likely to have about the EU. For that reason, I have made frequent comparisons between the EU and the United States. The book follows the basic model of several other texts by covering the history, institutions, and policies of the EU, but it also includes a chapter on regional integration theory, a chapter that tries to come to grips with the character of the EU, and a chapter that assesses the EU policy process.

To help the intellectual digestion process, I have broken up the text with boxes drawing attention to key events, concepts, processes, and institutions. Every chapter begins with an overview and ends with a summary, a brief set of conclusions, and a (deliberately) brief list of recommended sources of further information that has a bias toward the most recent, readable, and enlightening Anglo-American sources. Much of the best current research on the EU is coming out of continental Europe, but until that work is translated into English, it will only be available to the multilingual. The book ends with a glossary of key terms, a chronology of events, short descriptions of key institutions, and recommended sources of further information.

A Note on Terminology. The European Union has undergone several changes of identity and several changes of name. It began life as the European Coal and Steel Community, but with the creation of the European Economic Community (EEC) in 1958, it became more widely known as the "common market," "the European Economic Community," or "the EEC" and by the 1980s was generally known simply as "the EC" or "the Community." Just as everyone was becoming used to the new label, the Maastricht treaty created a new entity known as the European Union.

Strictly speaking, the European Community still exists as one of three pillars of the European Union (the other two are foreign and security policy and justice and police cooperation). So although it is still correct to use the term *European Community* in describing the Community itself, the broader process of European integration falls under the label *European Union*.

Although no universally agreed convention existed as this book went to press, there has been a steady shift toward the label *European Union*. I have used *European Union* for the broad process of integration and *European Community* when writing specifically about the EC or about events before 1992. For convenience, I have also converted figures in European Currency Units (ECUs) into U.S. dollars at a rate of $1.20 to the ECU.

This book took about eighteen months to complete, but the idea behind it had been brewing in my mind for several years and was prompted mainly by the needs of the students in my European integration classes at IUPUI. I want to thank them for their influence and for being the unwitting guinea pigs for my approach and for much of the material in this book.

For the time they gave to help search for documents, I would also like to thank the staffs at the European Commission and the European Parliament in Brussels and Strasbourg (although I appeal to them to make it easier to get through the front doors of their respective libraries) and the staff of the EU Depository Library at Indiana University in Bloomington. A grant from the Faculty Development Office at IUPUI made it possible for me to travel to eight EU states in the summers of 1992 and 1993, and the West European Studies National Resource Center in Bloomington gave me a research grant in summer 1994.

For their help and their suggestions on early drafts of the book, I would like to thank Stanley Hoffmann, Andrew Moravcsik of Harvard University, and Andrew Appleton of Washington State University. The editing and production team at Westview Press did an excellent job on the project; for their hard work and professionalism I'd particularly like to thank Susan McEachern, Jennifer Knerr, and Shena Redmond. Finally, my thanks and love to Leanne for her moral support and much else besides.

John McCormick

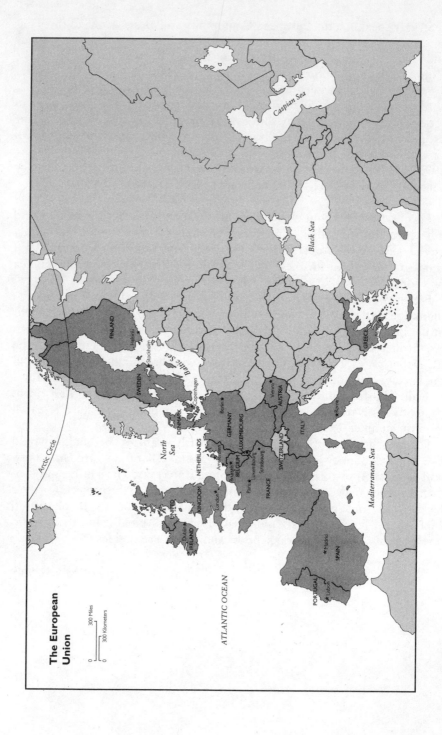

The European Union

ATLANTIC OCEAN

Arctic Circle

FINLAND
Helsinki

SWEDEN
Stockholm

North Sea

Baltic Sea

DENMARK
Copenhagen

NETHERLANDS
Amsterdam

UNITED KINGDOM
London

IRELAND
Dublin

BELGIUM
Brussels

GERMANY
Berlin

LUXEMBOURG
Luxembourg

FRANCE
Paris

Strasbourg

SWITZERLAND

AUSTRIA
Vienna

ITALY
Rome

SPAIN
Madrid

PORTUGAL
Lisbon

GREECE

Mediterranean Sea

Black Sea

Caspian Sea

300 Miles

300 Kilometers

THE EUROPEAN UNION

Introduction

The sovereign nations of the past can no longer solve the problems of the present.

I am certain that the passing seasons will lead us inevitably towards greater unity; and if we fail to organize it for ourselves, democratically, it will be thrust upon us by blind force.

Jean Monnet, *Memoirs*

The emergence of the European Union has been one of the defining events of the twentieth century. It has changed the political, economic, and social landscapes of Western Europe, changed the balance of power in the world by helping Europeans reassert themselves on the world stage, and helped to bring the longest uninterrupted spell of peace in European recorded history.

Until the beginning of the twentieth century, Europe was a continent of competing powers that repeatedly fought with each other on their own soil and took their mutual hostilities to other continents in their competition to build colonial empires. The tragic costs of nationalism were finally confirmed by two world wars, fought largely on European soil and leaving the European powers devastated and drained. If Europeans had not learned of the barbarism and futility of war in the trenches of northern France and Belgium in 1914–1918, the horrors of the period 1939–1945 finally brought home the need to cooperate and to build the kind of society that would eliminate the seeds of conflict.

The idea of European unity is not new. Many have wanted to unify Europe, sometimes in the interests of building peace and prosperity but sometimes for narrower reasons. The first serious thoughts about a peaceful and voluntary union came after World War I, but the concept really matured following World War II. The idea cannot be credited to any one person, but among the first specific suggestions for cooperation was Winston Churchill's proposal in 1946 for a United States of Europe, which led in 1949 to the creation of the Council of Europe. The United States made its most notable contribution to the new atmosphere of cooperation with the

1

Marshall Plan of 1948–1951 and with the security umbrella provided by the North Atlantic Treaty Organization (NATO).

The more serious Europeanists wanted a body that would replace national governments and become something like a European federation. The best-known federalists were French entrepreneur Jean Monnet and French foreign minister Robert Schuman. They began talking about pulling down tariffs between states and eventually removing frontiers, their primary motives being the promotion of peace (especially between France and Germany) and the creation of a new market to offset the growth of the United States as an economic power.

Euroskeptics have long doubted the possibility of overcoming narrow nationalist interests, but since World War II the idea of European unity has developed an irresistible momentum. The European Union has its own institutions and body of laws, and its fifteen member states have found themselves agreeing (sometimes unwillingly, sometimes unwittingly) to give up power and sovereignty to this new central authority. The national economies of Western Europe have grown and become more integrated, and it is steadily becoming less realistic to think of Western European states in isolation; we must think of them instead as elements in a growing European Union. Many problems and obstacles remain, but—if present trends continue—political union of some kind is inevitable, and the place of Europe in the world will have undergone a revolutionary shift.

This book is about the European Union and the changing relationship between North America and Western Europe. It is divided into three parts.

Part One describes and attempts to explain the history of European integration since 1945. The process began in 1951 with the signing of the Treaty of Paris. When the treaty came into force in 1952, it created the European Coal and Steel Community (ECSC), a limited economic association among France, West Germany, Italy, Belgium, the Netherlands, and Luxembourg. Its job was to coordinate the production and distribution of coal and steel, eliminate duplication of effort, and improve the efficiency of European industry.

The process went a step further in 1957 with the Treaty of Rome, which created the European Economic Community (EEC) and the European Atomic Energy Community (Euratom) in 1958. With the same six members as the ECSC, the EEC set out to build an integrated multinational economy among its members, achieve a customs union within twelve years, encourage free trade, and harmonize standards, laws, and prices among its members. To a large extent, the EEC succeeded: Its member states witnessed greater productivity, channeled new investment into industry and agriculture, and became more competitive in the world market.

By the late 1960s, the ECSC, the EEC, and Euratom had become the European Community, which had all the trappings of a new level of government. It had its own executive and bureaucracy (the European Commission), its own proto-legislature (the European Parliament), its own judiciary (the Court of Justice), and its own set of laws (which often superceded those of the member states).

It seemed obvious to many in the 1950s that the biggest power in Europe—Britain—should be a part of the Community. Britain initially preferred to pursue an independent foreign policy, however, placing more value on its relationship with its colonies and with the United States and setting up a looser alternative to the EEC, the European Free Trade Association (EFTA). But it soon changed its mind and joined the EEC in 1973, along with Ireland and Denmark. A second round of expansion came in the 1980s with the accession of Greece (1981) and Spain and Portugal (1986). The third expansion came in 1990 with the adoption of East Germany and in 1995 with the accession of Austria, Sweden, and Finland.

Major boosts to integration came in 1987 with the Single European Act and in 1993 with the Maastricht Treaty on European Union. The first led to the elimination of all remaining barriers to the movement of people, goods, money, and services among the twelve member states. It was now possible to travel almost anywhere in Western Europe without going through time-consuming border controls, and a citizen of one state could move to, live in, and work in another with few restrictions. The Maastricht treaty committed the EC to the creation of a single currency, a common citizenship, and a common foreign and security policy, and it won new powers for the EC institutions. It also made the EC part of a broader new entity called the European Union.

The EU now has its own flag (a circle of twelve gold stars on a blue background) and its own anthem (the "Ode to Joy" from Beethoven's Ninth Symphony). National passports have slowly been replaced with a uniform EU passport, and in many ways Brussels has become the new capital of Europe. The European Union enters the closing years of the twentieth century as the largest economic bloc in the world, accounting for 42 percent of global trade and one-third of global gross domestic product (GDP).

Part Two looks at the institutions of the European Union and describes how they work and how they relate to each other. The development of the European Union has many similarities to the evolution of the United States. The United States set out as a group of separate colonies that came together first under a confederation and then in 1789 became a federation. Skeptics doubted that the union would work, and the framing of the U.S. Constitution was surrounded by concerns over the balance of powers between the states and the federal government. The union has worked, though, and a tolerable balance has been achieved between state and federal powers. The European Union is not yet a political federation or even a confederation, but it has created intergovernmental and supranational institutions that have steadily accumulated authority since the 1950s, changing the balance of power in Western Europe.

There are five main institutions:

The European Commission. Based in Brussels, this is the central executive and administrative branch of the EU. It is responsible for initiating and overseeing the implementation of EU laws and policies.

The Council of Ministers. Also based in Brussels, this is the major decisionmaking body of the EU and is the real center of political power to date. The Council makes most of the key policy decisions and takes the votes that turn Commission proposals into law.

The European Parliament. Split among Strasbourg, Luxembourg, and Brussels, the European Parliament represents the people of the EU; since 1979, it has been directly elected to five-year terms by the voters of the member states. Although it cannot introduce or pass new laws, it is slowly winning the powers of a conventional legislature.

The Court of Justice. Much like the U.S. Supreme Court, the Court of Justice interprets EU law. The Court sits in Luxembourg and bases its decisions mainly on the treaties of Paris and Rome, the Single European Act, and the Maastricht treaty.

The European Council. This is less a physical institution than a forum, consisting of the individual heads of government of the EU member states. The Council meets once every six months and makes broad decisions on policy, the details of which are worked out by the European Commission and the Council of Ministers.

As the powers and reach of the EU have grown, new institutions have been created to deal with more specialized issues, such as job creation, environmental protection, and crime control. These institutions are described in Chapter 10.

Part Three focuses on the policies pursued by the European Union, analyzing what integration has meant for the member states and for Europeans themselves. Economic, agricultural, regional, environmental, social, foreign, and security policies are emphasized. This section examines the EU policymaking process, identifies the key influences on that process, and looks at the consequences and implications of EU policy.

Because European integration is still a work in progress, the relative balance of power among national governments and EU institutions is still evolving. That balance will continue to change as more countries join the EU and as integration reaches further into the lives of Europeans. Why should Americans care about all this, and what impact will these changes have on our lives?

The Changes Have Economic Implications.   The EU and the United States do about one-fifth of their trade with each other; the EU is the market for 22 percent of U.S. exports and is the source of about 18 percent of U.S. imports. Foreign direct investment in the United States grew by 2,500 percent in 1970–1991, with most of that increase coming from the EU, which now accounts for more than one-third of all such investment (most of it from Britain, the Netherlands, and Germany). Subsidiaries of European companies in the United States employ nearly 3 million Americans—more than the affiliates of all other countries combined—and account for 7 percent of all manufacturing jobs in the United States. U.S. corporations, meanwhile, have made their biggest overseas investments in the EU.

All this means bigger profits and more jobs, but it also means more competition. As barriers to internal trade in the EU have fallen, the number of cross-border corporate mergers has grown, and so have the European consumer market and European corporate power. The growing reach of European corporations is best exemplified by Airbus Industrie, which has captured 26 percent of the world market for commercial airliners, and by Arianespace, which has won nearly half of the market for commercial satellites. This new European assertiveness is providing unprecedented levels of competition for U.S. corporations, which have been forced to rethink their commercial strategies.

The Changes Have Security Implications.   The United States, long used to shaping most world events more or less to its liking, is increasingly having to respond to the demands of a newly resurgent Europe and to amend its foreign policy to fit Europe's needs and priorities. As the balance of power in the world enters a new era of fluidity and uncertainty, the rise of the European Union as an economic superpower could also presage its evolution into a military superpower. The EU still relies on the United States for its defense, lacks a unified military, and is working on developing coordinated foreign policies, but the relative balance of power between the two sides is changing, something U.S. policymakers cannot afford to ignore.

There Is Much We Could Learn from the European Experiment.   As barriers to global trade come down under the auspices of the World Trade Organization, the idea of regional economic integration is winning more adherents (but is also raising fears among some). The global economy is already here, and some commentators argue that the world is moving toward a future in which economics and politics will revolve around several major economic blocs (rather than around the nearly two hundred separate nation-states we have today). The European Union has been an important pioneer, and we have much to learn from its experience as we take the first steps toward building a North American free-trade area.

In short, we cannot ignore the European Union, nor can we understand the world today without understanding how the EU has altered the balance of global power. The process of global political and economic change is accelerating, and the problems and possibilities of the European experiment could be a valuable indication of the way the world may look by the middle of the twenty-first century.

ONE

Evolution

1

Introduction to Regional Integration

The state has dominated modern studies of world politics. It has long been the major actor in the global system, and for decades students of international relations have devoted their time and energy to the study of alliances, spheres of influence, changing patterns of cooperation and conflict, and fluctuations in the balance of power between and among states. But the state is not the only or even necessarily the best possible kind of political community. Many political scientists in fact argue that the modern state system is declining, undermined by challenges to its value and questions about its utility.

The most serious such challenges came during the first half of the twentieth century with two devastating world wars, each of which brought radical shifts in attitudes toward the relationship among states, and each of which led to renewed debate about the dangers of nationalism and the constant threat of war that seemed to hang over the state system. The pressures and desires to build peace through cooperation rather than competition reached a new level of intensity immediately after World War II, but plans to build a new world order dominated by Europe and North America were disrupted first by the cold war and then by the emergence of an increasingly demanding and influential bloc of Asian, Latin American, and African states.

For many, the cold war exemplified all of the doubts expressed about the value of the modern state, which was forged out of conflict and seemed unable to guarantee the safety of its citizens except through a balance of terror with other states. To work, a system of government must keep most of its people happy most of the time. Many theorists asked whether the modern state could ever do this, given its promotion of narrow nationalism and its potential for misunderstanding, conflict, and violence (prompted in part by the fact that states so rarely coincide with nations). These doubts encouraged widening support for the idea of peace and prosperity through international cooperation, collective security, and globalism. The search for

9

these goals took many different forms, the most obvious of which was an explosion in the number of international organizations, spearheaded by the creation of the United Nations in 1945.

The search for peace has been expressed most dramatically in experiments in regional integration. The European Union is only one of those experiments, but it has evolved the furthest and brought the greatest changes for its citizens and governments. Regional integration has also been tried in Latin America, the Caribbean, Southeast Asia, west, east, and southern Africa, and—since 1989—in North America but on a more modest scale (see Appendix II). The European Union could provide a model that might eventually lead to the breakdown of the state system as we know it and to its replacement with a new community of political and economic units and networks. Even so, we are still far from understanding the dynamics of the EU. In an attempt to provide some answers, this chapter surveys the major theories of integration and describes and assesses competing ideas about how the EU has evolved and what it has become.

International Organizations

The European Union is an international organization in the sense that its constituent members are nation-states, but it has moved well beyond conventional ideas about international cooperation. Most of the standard definitions of an international organization (IO) describe a body that promotes voluntary cooperation and coordination between or among its members but has neither autonomous powers nor the authority to impose its rulings on its members. The creation of IOs followed the emergence of the modern state system and was given a boost by both world wars. In 1914, the world had just 220 IOs; today there are well over 20,000.[1] Different kinds of IOs have developed for different reasons, and they have different structures, methods, and goals. Most fit broadly into one of two main categories:

Intergovernmental organizations (IGOs) consist of representatives of national governments and promote voluntary cooperation among those governments. IGOs have little or no autonomy in decisionmaking and little or no coercive power over their members. Examples include the United Nations, the Organization of American States, and NATO.

International nongovernmental organizations (INGOs) are made up of individuals or representatives of national nongovernmental organizations. They include multinational corporations such as Ford and General Motors, but most are interest groups that cooperate to pursue the collective goals of their members or to bring pressure on governments for policy change. Examples include the International Red Cross and Amnesty International. (Some INGOs, such as the Swiss-based

International Union for Conservation of Nature, are hybrids composed of both governmental and nongovernmental members.)

IOs can be regional, universal, specialized, or multipurpose. In structural terms, they can involve **cooperation** (working together on policy without making major commitments or structural changes), **association** (reaching a formal agreement that might bring structural changes), or **harmonization** (making adjustments to policies to bring them into alignment).

International cooperation rarely involves the surrender of significant **sovereignty** or independence by the participants (although no state has ever been truly independent because none has ever been wholly self-sufficient). But if cooperation does lead to the surrender of sovereignty, we begin to move into the realm of **supranationalism,** a process of cooperation that results in a shift of authority (and perhaps of sovereignty) to a new level of organization that is autonomous, that is above the state, and that has powers of coercion that are independent of the state. Structurally, supranationalism can take at least three different forms:

1. **Confederalism** is a structure in which the participants give up few powers to the "governing" body. Most INGOs, for example, work on a confederal basis, using the governing body to help them coordinate their activities and perhaps paying annual dues to the governing body but keeping a large measure of control over their own affairs. From 1776 to 1788 the United States was a confederal system, as was Switzerland until 1798 and Germany from 1815 to 1866. The European Union has many confederalist features, because the governments of the member states have worked hard to make sure they keep control over the key decisionmaking processes.

2. **Consociationalism** is a system sometimes used in (or proposed for) societies with deep social, cultural, religious, racial, or linguistic divisions. It involves government by a coalition representing the different groups in that society. As much decisionmaking as possible is delegated to the groups, power and resources are divided in proportion to the size of each group, and minorities may be deliberately overrepresented and protected by the power of veto. Smaller European states such as Belgium, Switzerland, Austria, the Netherlands, and Luxembourg have used elements of consociationalism at some time during the twentieth century.

3. **Federalism** is a structure in which the participants give up overall sovereignty to a governing body but retain many independent powers. The United States, for example, is a federal republic, but it only became such in 1789 when the original thirteen colonies agreed to move from a confederal relationship to a federal union, voluntarily

giving up power over areas such as common security but retaining their own sets of laws and a large measure of autonomy over local government (raising their own taxes, for example, and keeping powers over education, the police, and roads).

The most enthusiastic European integrationists would like to see a federal United States of Europe in which the current national governments would become little more than local governments, with the same kinds of powers as state governments in the United States. Before this could happen, the EU institutions would at least have to be able to act on behalf of all the member states in foreign relations, and a single European currency would have to exist.

Theories of Integration

Standard theories of political integration argue that people or states create alliances or common political units for one of three reasons: They may be forced together by a Napoleon or a Hitler, they may share common values and goals and may reach agreement on how to govern themselves as a whole, or they may come together out of a need for security in the face of a common external threat. A fourth possible reason is convenience or efficiency: The people or states may decide that they can promote peace and improve their quality of life more quickly and effectively by working together rather than separately.

Politics in Western Europe was long influenced and driven by the first three motives, but a shift to the fourth since 1945 has encouraged Europeans to develop the largest experiment in voluntary integration the world has ever seen. At least until the late 1970s, the focus was on integration in the interest of economic development: Barriers to trade were pulled down, national monetary and fiscal policies were harmonized, and the free movement of people, goods, money, and services was promoted—all in the hope of contributing to new levels of prosperity. The supporters of economic integration never saw such integration as an end in itself, however; as the EU member states built closer economic ties, some of their leaders flirted increasingly with ideas about political cooperation. Which came first is debatable; as Ernst Haas has argued, economic integration "may be based on political motives and frequently begets political consequences."[2]

In *The Uniting of Europe,* his groundbreaking 1958 study of the European Coal and Steel Community (ECSC), Haas defined **political integration** as "the process whereby political actors in several distinct national settings are persuaded to shift their loyalties, expectations and political activities toward a new center, whose institutions possess or demand jurisdiction over the pre-existing national states."[3] In his 1963 study of the

European Economic Community (EEC), Leon Lindberg defined political integration as the process by which (1) nations forego the desire and ability to conduct foreign and key domestic policies independently of each other, instead making joint decisions or delegating the decisionmaking process to new central organs, and (2) political actors such as policymakers, bureaucrats, legislators, and interest groups shift their political activities to a new center.[4]

The evolution of the European Union has been characterized by at least two major sets of conflicting views about the nature of integration.

1. Realism Versus Functionalism. Attempts to explain the mechanics of European integration usually fall into one of two major schools of thought (see Table 1.1). Realists argue that states are the most important actors in international relations, that domestic policy can be clearly separated from foreign policy, and that rational self-interest and conflicting national objectives lead states to protect their interests relative to other states. Realists talk about an anarchic global system in which states use both conflict and cooperation to ensure their security through a balance of power among states. They see the EU as a gathering of sovereign states, and they believe those states retain authority over their own affairs, give power to new cooperative bodies only when it suits them, and retain the right to take back that power at any time. In short, the EU exists only because the member states have decided it serves their best interests. Realism—associated with names such as Hans Morgenthau and Henry Kissinger—dominated the study of international relations from the 1940s to the 1960s and was taken a stage further in the 1970s and 1980s by neorealists who argued that the structure of institutions mattered more than their intentions. For example, neorealists have studied the changing power of states and the effect of such change on international relations.

A contrasting approach is offered by functionalists. While realists talk about competition and conflict, functionalists move from self-interest toward the common interests of states in cooperation. They argue that integration is a process that has its own internal dynamic and that if states cooperate in certain limited areas and create new bodies to oversee that cooperation, they will cooperate in other areas through a kind of "invisible hand" of integration. In short, functionalism argues that European integration has its own logic, which the EU member states find hard to resist; although membership involves contracts that could theoretically be broken, in reality they have an almost irresistible authority, and integration has become so much a part of the fabric of Western European society that secession would cost a state far more than continued integration.

2. Intergovernmentalism Versus Supranationalism. Debates have long raged about whether the EU is an organization controlled by governments

TABLE 1.1   Realism and Functionalism Compared

	Realism	*Functionalism*
Dominant goals of actors	Military security	Peace and prosperity
Instruments of state policy	Military force and economic instruments	Economic instruments and political acts of will
Forces behind agenda formation	Potential shifts in the balance of power and security threats	Mutual convenience and the expansive logic of sector integration
Policy issues	Emphasis on high politics, such as security and defense	Initial emphasis on low politics, such as economic and social issues
Role of international organizations	Minor; limited by state power and the importance of military force	Substantial; new, functional IOs will formulate policy and become increasingly responsible for implementation

Source: Adapted and expanded from a similar table in Robert O. Keohane and Joseph S. Nye, *Power and Interdependence: World Politics in Transition,* 2d ed. (Boston: Little, Brown, 1989).

working with each other as partners or whether it has developed its own authority and autonomy. At the heart of this debate has been the issue of how much power and sovereignty can or should be given up by national governments to bodies such as the European Commission and the European Parliament. Britons and Danes (and even the French at times) have balked at federalist or supranationalist tendencies, whereas Belgians and Luxembourgers have been more willing to give up sovereignty.

Some political scientists have questioned the assumption that intergovernmentalism and supranationalism are the two extremes on a continuum,[5] that they are a zero-sum game (one balances or cancels out the other), that supranationalism involves the loss of sovereignty, or that the EU and its member states act autonomously of each other. David Mitrany, for example, argues that governments cooperate out of need and that this is "not a matter of surrendering sovereignty, but merely of pooling as much of it as may be needed for the joint performance of the particular task."[6] Keohane and Hoffmann agree, arguing that the EU is "an experiment in pooling sovereignty, not in transferring it from states to supranational institutions."[7]

Leon Lindberg and Stuart Scheingold argue that it is wrong to assume that "each gain in capability at the European level necessarily implies a loss of capability at the national level"; they believe the relationship between the EU and its member states is more symbiotic than competitive.[8] Ernst Haas argues that supranationalism does not mean EU institutions exercise authority over national governments but feels it is a process or a style of decisionmaking in which "the participants refrain from unconditionally veto-ing proposals and instead seek to attain agreement by means of compro-mises upgrading common interests."[9]

Explaining European Integration

Functionalism has dominated the theoretical debates about how the EU has evolved since the 1950s. Jean Monnet and Robert Schuman (the two peo-ple most often described as the founders of the European Union) were func-tionalist in the sense that they opted for integrating a specific area—the coal and steel industry—with the hope that this would encourage integration in other areas. As Schuman put it, "Europe will not be made all at once or ac-cording to a single plan. It will be built through concrete achievements which first create a de facto solidarity."[10] Although some federalists have argued that "the worst way to cross a chasm is by little steps,"[11] function-alism is based on the idea of bridging the gaps between states incrementally by building functionally specific organizations. So instead of trying to co-ordinate major issues such as economic or defense policy, for example, functionalists believed they could "sneak up on peace"[12] by promoting in-tegration in relatively non-controversial areas such as postal services or a particular sector of industry or by harmonizing technical issues such as weights and measures.

Among the best-known exponents of this idea was the Romanian-born British social scientist David Mitrany, who defined the functional approach as an attempt to link "authority to a specific activity, to break away from the traditional link between authority and a definite territory."[13] Mitrany felt peace could not be achieved by regional unification (which would re-place international tensions with interregional tensions) or world govern-ment (which would threaten human freedom). Writing in wartime London in 1943, he argued instead that separate international bodies should be or-ganized, with authority in functionally specific fields, such as security, trans-port, and communication. They should be executive bodies with au-tonomous tasks and powers and should perform some of the same jobs as national governments, only at a different level. This focus on particular functions, he argued, would encourage international cooperation more quickly and effectively than grand gestures.[14] The dimensions and struc-tures of these international organizations would not have to be predeter-mined but instead would be self-determined.[15]

Once these functional organizations were created, Mitrany argued, they would find themselves having to work with each other. Rail, road, and air agencies would need technical coordination (on timetables, for example) and functional coordination (to deal with differences in densities of passen-ger and freight traffic, for example). Different groups of functional agencies might then have to work together, which would lead to coordinated international planning. This would result less in the creation of a new system than in the rationalization of existing systems through a process of natural selection and evolution. States could join or leave, drop out of some functions and stay in others, or try their own political and social experiments; in short, they would be allowed to share power only if they also shared responsibility. This could lead eventually to "a rounded political system . . . the functional arrangements might indeed be regarded as organic elements of federalism by installments."[16]

Haas's study of the ECSC in 1958 and Lindberg's of the EEC in 1963 led to an amendment and a revival of Mitrany's theories as **neofunctionalism.** This argues that certain prerequisites are needed before integration can proceed, including changes in mass attitudes that pull people away from nationalism and toward cooperation, a desire by elites to promote integration for pragmatic rather than altruistic reasons, and the delegation of real power to a new supranational authority. Once these changes have occurred, there will be an expansion of integration caused by **spillover,** described by Joseph Nye as a phenomenon in which "imbalances created by the functional interdependence or inherent linkages of tasks can press political actors to redefine their common tasks."[17] In other words, joint action in one area will create new needs, tensions, and problems that will increase the pressure to take joint action in another; for example, the integration of agriculture will only truly work if other sectors (say, transport and agricultural support services) are integrated as well.

Neofunctionalist ideas include the notion of an "expansive logic of sector integration" that Haas saw as being inherent in the ECSC.[18] The ECSC was created partly to achieve short-term goals (such as a desire to encourage Franco-German cooperation), but Monnet and Schuman also saw it as the first step in a process that would lead to political integration.[19] Haas argued that the process of spillover was not automatic and found that initially very few people strongly supported the ECSC idea. Once it had been working for a few years, however, labor unions and political parties became more enthusiastic because they began to see its benefits, and the pressure grew for integration in other sectors. Urwin noted that the sectoral approach of the ECSC was handicapped because it "was still trying to integrate only one part of complex industrial economies, and could not possibly pursue its aims in isolation from other economic segments."[20] This was part of the reason that only six years after the creation of the ECSC, agreement was reached among its members to achieve broader economic integration with the European Economic Community.

Spillover is such an ambiguous term that it needs to be broken down into more specific subcategories, of which there are at least three:

Functional spillover implies that if states integrate one sector of their economies (for example), the impossibility of isolating one economic sector from another will lead to the integration of other sectors.[21] The logical conclusion is that so many functional IGOs would have to be created to oversee this process, and so many bridges would have to be built across the chasm between states, that the relative power of national government institutions would decline, and the chasm would no longer exist. Eventually, complete economic and political union would be achieved (see Box 1.1).

Technical spillover implies that disparities in standards will lead different states to rise (or sink) to the level of the state with the tightest (or loosest) regulations. For example, although the poorer EU states (such as Greece and Portugal) may argue that environmental controls amount to a handicap, making it more difficult for them to catch up to their wealthier partners, the EU decisionmaking process still encourages the states with the strongest environmental laws (such as Germany and Sweden) to accelerate the adoption of tighter controls by the poorer states.

Political spillover is based on the argument that once different functional sectors become integrated, interest groups (such as corporate lobbies and labor unions) will increasingly switch from trying to influence national governments to trying to influence the new regional executive (which would encourage them in an attempt to win new powers for itself). Those groups would appreciate the benefits of integration and would act as a barrier to a retreat from integration, and politics would increasingly be played out at the regional rather than the national level.[22]

Neofunctionalist ideas dominated studies of European integration in the 1950s and 1960s but briefly fell out of favor in the 1970s, which Haas explained by arguing that they lacked strong predictive capacities.[23] But the ideas likely lost favor for other reasons. First, the process of integrating Europe seemed to have ground to a halt in the mid-1970s. The prevailing sense of despondency comes through clearly in a 1975 European Commission report on economic and monetary union, which complained that experience had done nothing to support the validity of the functional approach (that is, that unity would "come about in an almost imperceptible way") and that what was needed was "a radical and almost instantaneous transformation."[24]

The second problem was that the Commission was not providing the kind of leadership that was vital to the idea of neofunctionalism. Finally, the theory of spillover needed more elaboration. The most common criticisms of neofunctionalism were that it was too linear, that it needed to be expanded or modified to accommodate different pressures for integration, and that it needed to be seen in conjunction with other influences. Ten years after the original publication of *The Uniting of Europe*, for example, in a new edition of the book Ernst Haas was arguing that functional theory had

BOX 1.1
Stages in the Process of Regional Integration

Economic integration can take several forms, representing varying degres of integration,[1] but if a logical progression could be outlined along functionalist lines, it might look something like this:

1. Two or more states could create a **free trade area** by eliminating internal barriers to trade (such as tariffs and border restrictions) while keeping their own external tariffs against non-member states.

2. The growth of internal free trade might then increase the pressure on the member states to agree to a common external tariff; otherwise all of the goods coming in to the free-trade area from abroad would come through the country with the lowest tariffs. Agreement on a common external tariff would create a **customs union.**

3. The removal of internal trading barriers would expand the size of the market available to agriculture, industry, and services; thus, these sectors would want to expand their operations to other members of the customs union. This would increase investment in those countries and would also increase the demand for the reduction or removal of barriers to the movement of capital and labor, creating a **common market** (or a **single market**).

4. With citizens moving more freely among the member states of the common market, the pressure might then grow for coordinated policies on education, retraining schemes, unemployment benefits, pensions, health care, and other services. This in turn would increase the demand for coordinated interest rates, stable exchange rates, common policies on inflation, and ultimately a single currency, thereby creating an **economic union.**

5. The demands of economic integration might lead to growing political integration as the governments of the member states worked together more closely. The pressure would grow for common policies in almost every other sector, including foreign and defense policy, possibly leading to a **political union.**

Notes

1. Bela Balassa, *The Theory of Economic Integration* (Homewood, Ill.: Irwin, 1961), 2.

---

paid too little attention to (1) changes in attitude following the creation of a body like the ECSC, (2) the impact of nationalism on integration, (3) the influence of external events (including changes in economic and military threats from outside), and (4) social and political changes taking place separately from the process of integration.[25] He later wrote about "fragmented issue linkage," which he felt took place "when older objectives are questioned, when new objectives clamor for satisfaction, and when the rationality accepted as adequate in the past ceases to be a legitimate guide to future action."[26]

New variations on the theme of spillover were described in 1971 by Philippe Schmitter:

Spillaround is an increase in the scope of the functions carried out by an IO without a corresponding increase in authority or power. For example, governments of the EU member states have allowed the European Commission to become involved in new policy areas but have tried to prevent it from winning new powers over policy implementation. Spillaround involves an increase in the breadth but not the depth of authority.

Buildup is an increase in the authority or power of an IO (depth) without a corresponding increase in the number of areas in which the IO is involved (breadth). Joseph Nye wrote about "rising transactions" (or a growing workload), which "need not lead to a significant widening of the scope (range of tasks) of integration, but to intensifying of the central institutional capacity to handle a particular task."[27] This, for example, would explain why the growing workload of the European Court of Justice led to the creation of a subsidiary Court of First Instance to deal with less important cases (see Chapter 9).

Retrenchment is an increase in the level of joint arbitration between or among member states at the expense of the power and authority of the IO. This has happened at times of crisis in the EU, such as when member states have pulled out of attempts to build exchange rate stability as a prelude to establishing a single currency (see Chapter 4).

Spillback is a reduction in both the breadth and depth of the authority of an IO.[28] This has yet to happen in the case of the EU as a whole, although the powers of the European Commission over policy initiation have declined in relative terms as those of the European Parliament and the European Council have grown.

Joseph Nye gave new impetus to neofunctionalist ideas by taking them out of the European context and looking at non-Western experiences as well. He concluded that experiments in regional integration involved an **integrative potential** that depended on several different conditions:

- The economic equality or compatibility of the states involved (which is partly why questions have long been raised about the wisdom of allowing poorer southern and eastern European states to join the EU). At the same time, differences in the size or wealth of the member states may be less important than the presence of a central motive force that helps bring them together. For the EU, that force was once the tension between France and Germany (see Chapter 3) and is now the economic dominance of Germany.

- The extent to which elite groups that control economic policy in the member states think alike and hold the same values.

- The extent of interest group activity, or pluralism. Such groups play a key role in promoting integration if they see it as being in their interests.

- The capacity of the member states to adapt and respond to public demands (which depends in turn on the levels of domestic stability and the capacity—or desire—of decisionmakers to respond).[29]

On almost all of these counts, the EU has a relatively high integrative potential, in contrast to another key experiment in regional cooperation, the North American Free Trade Agreement (NAFTA) (see Box 1.2). The United States may be a strong motive force for integration, but it is much wealthier than Mexico in both per capita and absolute terms. Elite groups in Mexico are more strongly in favor of state intervention in the marketplace than are those in the United States and Canada, labor unions in the United States have been strongly critical of NAFTA, and public opinion in Mexico is heavily controlled and manipulated compared with that in the United States and Canada. NAFTA may help close some of the gaps, thereby leading to an improvement in integrative potential and removing some of the obstacles to a North American single market, but many obstacles remain.

New Developments in Integration Theory

Many theorists—notably Leon Lindberg—have emphasized that integration must be understood as a multidimensional phenomenon. They argue that it is impossible to separate economic and social pressures for integration from political pressures; that EU governments have given up powers over technical, social, and economic tasks but have been unwilling to give up political powers (although neofunctionalists would argue that this will happen as the pressures for integration increase); and that the EU experience has shown that integration often evolves because of political "acts of will" rather than because of functional or technical pressures.[30] In the end, the debate comes down to three basic questions: To what extent is integration brought about by coercion, altruism, or pragmatic considerations; to

BOX 1.2
NAFTA and the European Union Compared

Although the European Union has moved into the realms of economic and political union, one of the fundamental building blocks of economic integration is free trade. The reduction of barriers to trade has taken on a new significance for Americans, Canadians, and Mexicans, who are currently working on their own experiment in integration, the North American Free Trade Agreement (NAFTA).

NAFTA was born January 1, 1989, when a bilateral agreement between the United States and Canada came into force, aimed at reducing mutual barriers to trade. It did not promote the removal of all of those barriers, so—as economist Milton Friedman remarked in 1993—it was more a *managed* trade agreement than a free-trade agreement. Controversially, Mexico was admitted to NAFTA with the signing of a treaty in 1992 that came into force on January 1, 1994. Negotiations began in 1995 to extend NAFTA to Chile.

The goals of NAFTA are to phase out all tariffs on textiles, apparel, cars, trucks, vehicle parts, and telecommunications equipment over a period of ten years; to phase out all barriers to agricultural trade over a period of fifteen years; to allow banks, securities firms, and insurance companies total access to all three markets by the year 2000; to open up the North American advertising market; to allow truck drivers to cross borders freely by the year 1999; and to loosen rules on the movement of corporate executives and some professionals. Energy and transportation industries are still heavily protected under NAFTA, there is nothing approaching the free movement of people, and the three member states can apply their own environmental standards. No institutions have been created beyond two commissions that can arbitrate in disagreements over environmental standards and working conditions; special judges can also be impaneled to resolve disagreements on issues such as fishing rights and trade laws.

For some, NAFTA's true significance lies less in the content of the agreement than in the symbolism of its passage, representing as it does a shift in U.S. economic policy and in the structure of a U.S. economy gearing up for unparalleled levels of competition from abroad. Certainly it is a much looser arrangement than the European Union or even the European Economic Community in its early years. It is strictly intergovernmental, and although it will result in the reduction of trade restrictions, it involves the surrender of negligible levels of authority or sovereignty.

Whether NAFTA will become anything like the EU remains to be seen. Neofunctional logic suggests it might, but many obstacles will need to be removed: These include limited democracy and centralist-corporatist ideas of government in Mexico that run counter to traditions north of the Rio Grande; huge disparities in wealth, education, and per capita production; Canadian concerns about the cultural dominance of the United States; significant gaps in mutual knowledge and understanding among the citizens of the three countries; and myths, misconceptions, and sheer ignorance about free trade (at the height of the NAFTA debate in mid-1993, for example, a *New York Times*/CBS poll found that 49 percent of Americans had never heard of NAFTA).[1]

Notes

1. *New York Times*, July 12, 1993.

what extent is it voluntary; and to what extent does it have its own internal motive pressures?

Robert Keohane and Stanley Hoffmann argue that spillover is an important concept but that it cannot be seen in isolation from other broader influences and pressures. They make at least three key arguments about the nature of integration.

First, they argue that spillover is not automatic but that its success depends on prior intergovernmental bargaining. Once a bargain has been made, the work of the EU can expand in the way predicted by functionalist theory. They quote the 1986 Single European Act as an example, arguing that national governments took the final steps that led to its agreement.[31]

Second, Keohane and Hoffmann argue that institutional change in the EU must be seen as a form of adaptation to pressures from the global economy, such as growing economic competition from Japan and the United States or Europe's response to the turbulence in global currency markets in the 1970s (see Chapter 4).[32] They argue that the Single European Act was driven more strongly by events in the global economy outside Europe than by the internal logic of spillover.[33] The underlying thrust of this "political economy hypothesis" is that the EU has had to change to keep its businesses and economies competitive in the world economy. But the idea could also be applied to other policy areas; for example, greater EU foreign policy cooperation was encouraged by crises such as the Iraqi invasion of Kuwait in 1990 and the Bosnian civil war in the early 1990s.

Finally, Keohane and Hoffmann describe a "preference-convergence hypothesis," based on the argument that large-scale social change often comes as a result of the conjunction of unrelated events and that changes in EU policy and policymaking structures can come out of a convergence of national government preferences rather than from internal or external pressure.[34] It could be argued that the Single European Act and the Maastricht treaty both resulted from that kind of convergence (see Chapter 4), but it would be difficult to isolate the different pressures that brought them about.

The European Union is still far from the kind of entity federalists such as Monnet and Schuman had hoped for, but it has come a long way in only two generations. The member states have not yet transferred as many powers as the federalists would have liked, EU institutions do not yet have the kind of autonomy federalists had hoped for, the EU has faced many crises and has many critics, and no theories have yet fully explained the timetable of integration. As Ernst Haas argued in 1958, the causes of integration cannot be pinned down unless we can be clear about whether the rise in the number of common tasks (or transactions) precedes, reinforces, results from, or causes integration.[35]

None of these problems needs detract from the value of neofunctionalist theory, which has yet to be replaced by theories that better explain why and how the EU has evolved. Through a combination of political will on the part of elites, encouragement from the United States (at least in the early years), the need Europeans felt to protect themselves from each other, pressures for protection from external threats, and the need to rebuild the European economy to respond to competition from the United States and Japan, Europeans have built a complex web of economic, political, and social ties among themselves. How and why this has happened is examined in more detail in Chapters 2, 3, and 4.

Summary and Conclusions

Theories of economic and political integration have a lineage that dates back at least to the early work of David Mitrany in the 1930s and probably before.[36] Yet our understanding of the process—and of its motives and results—is still patchy at best. The European Union is an entirely new kind of organization for which most of the standard theories of international relations provide only a partial explanation.

The motives behind the creation of the EU are relatively clear (peace through cooperation being at the core—see Chapters 2 and 3), but the driving forces behind the development of the EU since the 1950s are still widely debated. Shared values have played a part, as have external threats, convenience, and the self-interest of elites, but whether the process of European integration has had its own internal logic or has been forced is still open to debate. Most explanations hover somewhere between the internal logic arguments of the neofunctionalists and the emphasis realists place on EU member states as rational actors.

Wherever the truth lies, the European Union has emerged as a new species of international organization that does not easily fit most of the conventional explanations about why states cooperate. Terms such as federal, confederal, intergovernmental, and supranational have only limited value in describing and understanding the EU. Attempts to define its nature are complicated by the fact that its dimensions and identity have changed over time. To grasp what the EU is today, we have to understand where it has come from.

Notes

1. Michael D. Wallace and J. David Singer, "Intergovernmental Organization in the Global System, 1815–1964: A Quantitative Description," *International Organization* 24:2 (Spring 1970), 239–287; Union of International Associations, *Yearbook of International Organizations* (Brussels: Union of International Associations, various years).

2. Ernst B. Haas, *The Uniting of Europe: Political, Social, and Economic Forces, 1950–1957* (Stanford: Stanford University Press, 1958), 12.

3. Ibid., 16.

4. Leon N. Lindberg, *The Political Dynamics of European Economic Integration* (Stanford: Stanford University Press, 1963), 6–7.

5. Robert O. Keohane and Stanley Hoffmann, "Conclusions: Community Politics and Institutional Change," in William Wallace (Ed.), *The Dynamics of European Integration* (London: Royal Institute of International Affairs, 1990).

6. David Mitrany, "The Functional Approach to World Organisation," in Carol A. Cosgrove and Kenneth J. Twitchett (Eds.), *The New International Actors: The UN and the EEC* (London: Macmillan, 1970).

7. Keohane and Hoffmann, "Conclusions," 277.

8. Leon N. Lindberg and Stuart A. Scheingold, *Europe's Would-Be Polity: Patterns of Change in the European Community* (Englewood Cliffs, N.J.: Prentice-Hall, 1970), 94–95.

9. Ernst B. Haas, "Technocracy, Pluralism and the New Europe," in Stephen R. Graubard (Ed.), *A New Europe?* (Boston: Houghton Mifflin, 1964), 66.

10. Robert Schuman, "Declaration of 9 May 1950," in David Weigall and Peter Stirk (Eds.), *The Origins and Development of the European Community* (London: Pinter, 1992), 58–59.

11. Clarence Streit, *Freedom's Frontier—Atlantic Union Now* (Washington, D.C.: Freedom and Union Press, 1961), 23.

12. Leon N. Lindberg and Stuart A. Scheingold, *Regional Integration: Theory and Research* (Cambridge: Harvard University Press, 1971), 6.

13. David Mitrany, *A Working Peace System* (Chicago: Quadrangle, 1966), 27.

14. Ibid., 27–31.

15. Ibid., 72.

16. Ibid., 73–84.

17. Joseph S. Nye, "Comparing Common Markets: A Revised Neofunctionalist Model," in Lindberg and Scheingold, *Regional Integration*, 200.

18. Haas, *The Uniting of Europe*, 283ff.

19. Cited in Derek Urwin, *The Community of Europe*, 2d ed. (London: Longman, 1995), 44–46.

20. Ibid., 76.

21. Stephen George, *Politics and Policy in the European Community*, 2d ed. (Oxford: Clarendon Press, 1990), 21.

22. Ibid., 22–23.

23. Ernst B. Haas, *The Obsolescence of Regional Integration Theory* (Berkeley: Institute of International Studies, University of California, 1975).

24. Commission of the European Communities, Economic and Monetary Union 1980 (the Marjolin Report) (Brussels: Commission of the European Communities, 1975), 5.

25. Haas, *The Uniting of Europe* (1968 edition), xiv–xv.

26. Ernst B. Haas, "Turbulent Fields and the Theory of Regional Integration," *International Organization* 30:2 (Spring 1976), 173–212.

27. Joseph S. Nye, *Peace in Parts: Integration and Conflict in Regional Organization* (Boston: Little, Brown, 1971), 67.

28. Philippe C. Schmitter, "A Revised Theory of Regional Integration," in Lindberg and Scheingold, *Regional Integration*, 242.

29. Nye, "Comparing Common Markets," 208–214.

30. James E. Dougherty and Robert L. Pfaltzgraff, *Contending Theories of International Relations*, 3rd ed. (New York: Harper and Row, 1990), 459.

31. Keohane and Hoffmann, "Conclusions."

32. Robert O. Keohane and Stanley Hoffmann, "Institutional Change in Europe in the 1980s," in Keohane and Hoffmann (Eds.), *The New European Community: Decisionmaking and Institutional Change* (Boulder: Westview Press, 1991), 22–23.

33. Ibid., 18–25.

34. Ibid., 24–25.

35. Ernst B. Haas, "The Challenge of Regionalism," in *International Organization* 12 (Autumn 1958), 445.

36. See, for example, Simeon E. Baldwin, "The International Congresses and Conferences of the Last Century as Forces Working Towards the Solidarity of the World," *American Journal of International Law* 1, Part 2 (July–October 1907), 565–578.

Further Reading

David Mitrany. *A Working Peace System* (Chicago: Quadrangle, 1966).

Arguably the grandparent of them all; one of the first modern expositions of the idea of building peace through cooperation.

Ernst B. Haas. *The Uniting of Europe: Political, Social, and Economic Forces, 1950–1957* (Stanford: Stanford University Press, 1968).

Still widely seen as the starting point for modern ideas about the mechanisms and motives of integration; essential reading for anyone trying to understand the roots of the EU.

James E. Dougherty and Robert L. Pfaltzgraff. *Contending Theories of International Relations*, 3rd ed. (New York: Harper and Row, 1990).

An introductory text that provides a comprehensive overview of theories of international relations, including chapters on realism, conflict, functionalism, and neofunctionalism.

John Eastby. *Functionalism and Interdependence* (Lanham, Md.: University Press of America, 1985).

A commentary on and guide to the work of functionalist theorists and the basic ideas underlying regional integration theory.

Brent F. Nelsen and Alexander C-G. Stubb (Eds.). *The European Union: Readings on the Theory and Practice of European Integration* (Boulder: Lynne Rienner, 1994).

A series of readings on European integration in theory and practice, bringing together selections from the speeches and writings of Mitrany, Churchill, Schuman, Monnet, Delors, Thatcher, and others.

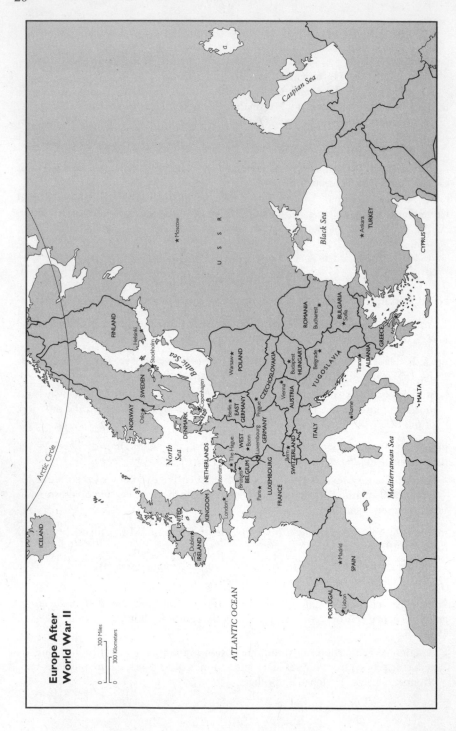

Europe After World War II

ATLANTIC OCEAN

ICELAND

IRELAND
Dublin ★

UNITED KINGDOM
London ★

NORWAY
Oslo ★

SWEDEN
Stockholm ★

FINLAND
Helsinki ★

Arctic Circle

North Sea

Baltic Sea

DENMARK
Copenhagen ★

NETHERLANDS
Amsterdam ★
The Hague ★

BELGIUM
Brussels ★

LUXEMBOURG
Luxembourg ★

WEST GERMANY
Bonn ★

EAST GERMANY
Berlin ★

POLAND
Warsaw ★

U S S R

Moscow ★

Caspian Sea

Black Sea

CZECHOSLOVAKIA
Prague ★

AUSTRIA
Vienna ★

HUNGARY
Budapest ★

ROMANIA
Bucharest ★

BULGARIA
Sofia ★

YUGOSLAVIA
Belgrade ★

ALBANIA
Tirana ★

GREECE
Athens ★

TURKEY
Ankara ★

CYPRUS

FRANCE
Paris ★

SWITZERLAND
Bern ★

ITALY
Rome ★

MALTA

Mediterranean Sea

SPAIN
Madrid ★

PORTUGAL
Lisbon ★

300 Miles

300 Kilometers

0

0

26

2

Context:
The Postwar World

World War II brought dramatic changes to the global balance of power. Prior to the war, Europe had dominated global trade, banking, and finance; its empires stretched around the world; and its military superiority was unquestioned. By 1945, the reality was very different. The war dealt a severe blow to European power and influence, clearing the way for the emergence of the United States and the Soviet Union as superpowers and creating a nervous new balance in the distribution of political influence in the world.

Before the war, the United States had been both pacifist and isolationist and preferred to limit its foreign influence largely to the Americas. So limited were its interests in fact that its defense forces ranked twentieth in the world in size, behind those of the Netherlands.[1] Although Neutrality Acts were passed in the period 1935–1939, the Roosevelt administration was clearly alarmed about the rise of fascist power in the 1930s and argued that isolationism was not the answer. When war had broken out in 1939, Roosevelt issued a proclamation of neutrality, but he also announced that he could not ask every American to "remain neutral in thought." A belief that Britain and France could defend themselves was shattered with the fall of France in 1940; only Britain now stood between the Germans and the Atlantic sea-lanes. Roosevelt did what he could to help Britain without overtly compromising U.S. neutrality, but three new factors transformed U.S. policy: the close personal friendship between Roosevelt and Winston Churchill, the success of the Royal Air Force in the Battle of Britain in 1940, and the Japanese attack on Pearl Harbor in December 1941.

Once the United States had become involved in the European theater, Roosevelt took the view that the postwar settlement would have to ensure the removal of the potential causes of future war and that the United States should be actively involved in creating this condition. Britain was initially the senior partner in the Atlantic Alliance because it had more troops in the

27

BOX 2.1
Two Crises That Changed Europe

Two major events in the mid-1950s exemplified the changes in the balance of power among Western Europe, the United States, and the USSR: the French defeat in Indochina and the Suez crisis.

Indochina 1954. Vietnam had been under French colonial control since the late nineteenth century. It was occupied by Japan during World War II and was taken back by the French in 1945, by which time a nationalist movement had emerged that demanded independence. Communist groups under the leadership of Ho Chi Minh launched an uprising in 1946 in the north of the country, enmeshing the French in an increasingly bitter war. The end of the war came in April 1954 with the surrender of twelve thousand French troops surrounded by Vietminh guerrillas in the village of Dien Bien Phu. Vietnam was given its independence but was partitioned with a view to being reunited in 1956. The loss of Indochina was a severe blow to French national pride. It marked the beginning of the end of unilateral French influence outside Europe and Africa and the replacement of the French military presence in Southeast Asia by the United States.

Suez 1956. If Dien Bien Phu had been the first critical blow to French aspirations to maintain global influence, the fatal blow was struck at Suez,[1] which also marked the beginning of the end of Britain's role as a major world power.

The Suez Canal had been built in the period 1856–1869 by the British and the French (using Egyptian labor) and had become a key conduit for British contacts and trade with India and the Pacific. Egypt became increasingly resentful over continued British control of the canal after World War II, especially after the 1952 coup that brought Gamal Abdel Nasser to power. Seeking a source of funds for his planned dam on the Nile at Aswan, Nasser nationalized the canal in July 1956. An outraged British government responded with sanctions and then—with French and Israeli collusion—launched an attack on the canal zone in October 1956.

The United States led the opposition to the attack, underlining the fundamental differences that had emerged between it and Britain regarding the new world order. The United States was hostile to the idea of colonialism and was eager to see Britain tie itself more closely to its European neighbors. The British, by contrast, refused to see themselves as European and saw their main interests as lying outside Europe, notably in the white dominions: Canada, Australia, and New Zealand. Suez changed those perceptions, and the focus of British interests shifted from the empire to Europe;[2] within five years, Britain had applied to join the EEC.

Notes

1. Maurice Vaisse, "Post-Suez France," in William Roger Louis and Roger Owen (Eds.), *Suez 1956: The Crisis and Its Consequences* (Oxford: Clarendon Press, 1989).

2. Lord Beloff, "The Crisis and Its Consequences for the British Conservative Party," in ibid.

field, but as the war went on, a gradual shift took place in the balance between the two countries. By the time of the D-Day landings in June 1944, U.S. troops outnumbered British troops, and the United States had assumed the dominant role in the planning of the Allied war effort. When the Soviet Union joined the Alliance, Roosevelt was clearly the senior partner in discussions with Stalin.

The change was symbolized by Allied research on the atom bomb. In 1940–1941, the British and the Americans were cooperating, but as U.S. research pulled ahead, the flow of information to Britain dried up, ending in 1946 with the McMahon Act forbidding the exchange of nuclear secrets: The United States did not want to give up the secrets of a technology that would determine its role in the postwar world. It was now a military superpower, and the wartime devastation of Europe had paved the way for the United States to become an economic superpower as well. Its strategic interests after the war encouraged it to play a central role in European reconstruction. The first phase in that process was dominated by U.S. interests in integration, by French interests in containing Germany, and by British resistance to any proposals that went beyond simple cooperation.

Political Reconstruction and Foreign Policy

World War II had left Western European states in varying conditions of political turmoil. For most, the immediate priority was to rebuild government institutions and political processes.

France emerged from the war in a state of confusion if not crisis, which persisted for more than a decade. Wartime collaboration had caused national trauma, and the only group that emerged with its credibility intact was the resistance, whose spirit was most powerfully embodied by Charles de Gaulle, leader of the Free French wartime government in exile. In 1946, the new constitution of the Fourth Republic went into force, but its prospects were compromised by the weakness of the executive and by the fact that it encouraged the existence of many different political parties.[2] The new government launched a plan for economic modernization and an extended welfare system and oversaw French participation in the earliest steps toward European integration, but its plans were undermined by a lack of strong leadership and by three external crises: Indochina in 1954, Suez in 1956 (see Box 2.1), and the mounting problems in Algeria, where the military refused to accept the idea of independence from France.

In 1958, de Gaulle was invited out of retirement to create the Fifth Republic, a new political system based around a strong executive and a relatively weak legislature, over which he presided until 1969. De Gaulle's appeal came from his credibility, the strength of his leadership, and his nationalism, which expressed itself most notably in his plans for a new Europe dominated by France and Germany and his opposition to U.S. influence in Europe. De Gaulle promoted economic modernization, withdrew France from most of its colonies in 1960–1962, redefined France's place in the world, and brought political stability.

Britain, it is often said, won the war but lost the peace. Britain's sense of national identity had been strengthened by its successful resistance to Nazi invasion. It was politically stable, its economy grew rapidly after the war, and it was wealthier and more powerful than France or Germany, but its role in the world was changing. The change began when Churchill was turned out of office in 1945 by voters looking for a new start. The new socialist Labour government embarked on a massive and popular program of nationalization and welfare provision and signaled the beginning of the end of Britain's imperial status by granting independence to India and Pakistan in 1947.

Many Britons still believed their country was a major world power and agreed with Churchill's analysis that Britain's three spheres of interest were its special relationship with the United States, the empire and the Commonwealth, and—last and definitely least—the rest of Europe. The British position was that the security of Western Europe had to be based on the unchallenged leadership of the United States;[3] cooperation with the rest of Europe was far from British minds, and few Britons even thought of themselves as European. Although Labour and Conservative governments alike were skeptical about European integration, the Suez Crisis forced a reappraisal because it revealed the fault lines in the transatlantic alliance and showed that Britain was no longer a great power. It also marked the beginning of a new (if halting) interest among Britons in forming alliances with the rest of Europe.[4]

Ireland, meanwhile, had remained neutral during the war but was economically tied to Britain, so its economic development and attitudes toward European cooperation were heavily subject to the British lead. The two countries signed a free trade agreement in 1966, and Irish citizens living in Britain had equal rights and privileges with British citizens.

Germany, for its part, had become introverted, not only because of the scale of the destruction it had suffered in the war and the immediate challenges Germans now faced simply to survive from day-to-day but also because of shame over both its part in starting the war and the actions it had taken during the war. It was faced with rebuilding its entire political and economic system. The four postwar occupying powers were divided on their plans for the new Germany, with the result that by 1948 the country had effectively been split into four sections: a socialist eastern sector and three capitalist western sectors. Few Germans were happy with this arrangement, but few felt they had much say in the decision.

The policy goals of the Western Allies were denazification (all vestiges of the Nazi system were removed), demilitarization (any West German capability to wage war was removed, and limits were placed on German military activities), democratization (a new constitution was drawn up and imposed on West Germany in 1949), and decentralization (a new federal administrative system was created that deliberately fragmented political power).[5] The conservative Christian Democrats won the 1949 elections, and the popular chancellor Konrad Adenauer set about siding West Germany firmly with the Western Alliance and rebuilding West German respectability; economic integration with its neighbors (especially France) fit well with these goals.

Austria had been made a province of Germany with the 1938 *Anschluss* and was divided into separate zones of occupation after the war, but the country was relatively undamaged by the war and was able to return to its 1920 constitution and to quickly hold democratic elections. The European Community accounted for about half of Austria's trade, and although it declared itself neutral in 1955, its economic interests pulled it increasingly toward integration with its Western European neighbors.[6]

Italy, like Germany, emerged from the war both introverted and devastated. Its main hope lay in rebuilding some of its lost respectability, a process that had begun when the government of the aging King Victor Emmanuel sided with the Allies against Hitler in 1943. The resistance came to be associated with the political left, but Christian Democrats consistently won the biggest share of the vote following the creation of the Italian republic in 1946. Italy's membership in the European Coal and Steel Community was negotiated by the administration of pro-European Prime Minister Alcide de Gasperi, who saw European integration as a way of fostering peace and of helping Italy deal with its internal economic problems, notably unemployment and the underdevelopment of the south.[7]

Italy was less successful than Germany in creating political stability, although its regular changes of government gave the impression of greater instability than actually existed. The country developed an extensive public sector and a multitude of political parties, suffered the consequences of political corruption and organized crime, and endured the persistence of major economic differences between the industrial north and the agrarian south. Membership in the EEC nonetheless contributed centrally to Italy's "economic miracle" of the 1960s and 1970s by providing new markets for Italian industry.[8]

Belgium, the Netherlands, and Luxembourg had all been occupied by the Germans. Agreement was reached in 1944 among the three governments in exile to promote trilateral economic cooperation after the war. This plan was made easier by the fact that Belgium and Luxembourg had agreed to an economic union as early as 1921, and all three states had a tradition of trade liberalism. Political cooperation was a significant departure for the

Netherlands, which had followed a policy of strict neutrality until 1940. The **Benelux** customs union was created in 1948 with the abolition of internal customs duties among the three countries and agreement on a joint external tariff. A treaty creating the Benelux Economic Union (BEU) was signed in the Hague in February 1958; although it came into force in November 1960, all three countries retained many protectionist measures and were still building the customs union well into the 1960s. The BEU was intergovernmental rather than supranational, leaving all true power in a trilateral Committee of Ministers. Even so, the BEU represented the first significant postwar experiment in European regional integration.

The Nordic states (Denmark, Finland, Iceland, Norway, and Sweden) had varied experiences during World War II. Denmark had tried to ensure its neutrality in 1939 by signing a pact with Hitler, but the Nazis invaded in 1940, and Denmark was occupied until 1945; so, too, was Norway. Iceland declared its independence from Denmark in 1944 and emerged from the war newly confident as a state and doubtful about international cooperation.[9] Finland briefly went to war with the USSR in 1939; it lost and had to cede territory. Hoping to regain that territory, it joined Germany in attacking Russia in 1941 but signed a separate peace in 1944. Finland followed a policy of neutrality after the war, but its decision in 1948 to sign a peace treaty with the USSR helped encourage Norway, Denmark, and Iceland to join NATO in 1949. Sweden alone had successfully retained its neutrality and did not join NATO.

These five countries enjoyed political stability after the war and had firmly established their independence, so intra-Nordic economic cooperation had its own logic. A Committee on Legislative Cooperation was set up in 1946 to bring new national laws into line with one another and to encourage a common Nordic position at international conferences. The five countries also developed joint ventures, such as the airline SAS, founded in August 1946. In 1948, Denmark, Iceland, Norway, and Sweden began to explore possibilities for a Nordic customs union but opted instead for more modest sectoral cooperation. They formed the Nordic Council in 1952 as a consultative body to promote the abolition of passport controls, the free movement of workers, and the development of more joint ventures. The Council had its own governing institutions, and its development was helped by the facts that its members all had small populations, were relatively wealthy and homogeneous, had few major internal social problems, and were governed by socialist or social democratic governments. Finland joined the Council in 1956.

Spain, Portugal, and Greece were exceptions to the prevailing rule of democratic stability in Western Europe after the war. All of these countries were poor and politically marginalized. Spain languished from 1939 under the rule of Francisco Franco, who declared Spain neutral in 1943. Between

1910 and 1928 Portugal experienced twenty-five revolutions and military coups, the last of which launched Antonio Salazar on a term in office that lasted until 1968. Greece was occupied in 1941–1944, and a conservative government was elected in 1946. With U.S. financial and military assistance driven by the Truman Doctrine, Greece experienced economic growth, but political tensions ultimately led to a military dictatorship in the period 1967–1973.

Economic Reconstruction and Cooperation

As Western Europeans worried about domestic reconstruction, changes were taking place at the global level that demanded new thinking. Economists on both sides of the Atlantic had given much thought during the war to the best means of achieving a stable and prosperous postwar world. In July 1944, representatives from the United States, Britain, and forty-two other countries met at **Bretton Woods,** New Hampshire, to plan for the postwar global economy. They agreed among them to an Anglo-American proposal to promote free trade, nondiscrimination, and stable rates of exchange—goals that were underpinned by the creation of GATT, the International Monetary Fund (IMF) and the World Bank (see Box 2.2).[10] First, though, Europe's economies had to be rebuilt and placed on a more stable footing. World War I had been fought mainly in Belgium and northern France, so the worst of the physical damage was geographically contained. By contrast, World War II had covered most of Europe, resulting in as many as 40 million deaths and leaving behind numerous pockets of devastation. Major cities lay in ruins, agricultural production was halved, food was rationed, and communications were disrupted because bridges, railroads, and harbors had been prime targets. Every country involved in the war had sustained heavy casualties and widespread physical damage. France, Denmark, and the Benelux countries had suffered heavily under the occupation. Many of Britain's major cities had been bombed, its exports had been cut by two-thirds, and its national wealth was cut by 75 percent. Before the war, Britain had been the world's second-largest creditor nation; by 1945 it was the world's biggest debtor nation. The USSR had sustained the heaviest losses on the Allied side, with severe fighting in the west (especially around Stalingrad) and an estimated 24 million deaths. Germany and Italy were left without governments, with their economies in ruins, and under Allied occupation. In all of Europe, only Spain, Portugal, Ireland, Switzerland, Sweden, and Finland were relatively undamaged or unchanged.

Because the wartime resistance had been allied with left-wing political ideas, and because its leaders were among the few whose credibility was still intact, there was a political shift to the left after the war, with socialist and social democratic parties winning power in several countries (West

BOX 2.2
The Bretton Woods System

The global economic system born out of Bretton Woods was underpinned by three new international organizations.

An International Trade Organization was designed to help bring down barriers to trade, such as tariffs and quotas. In the event, it was superseded by a looser arrangement, the **General Agreement on Tariffs and Trade** (GATT), signed by twenty-three states in Geneva in October 1947. GATT subsequently oversaw eight rounds of negotiations, during which barriers to trade were steadily removed through reciprocity (mutual agreement). Between 1948 and 1980 the average industrial tariff fell from 40 percent to just 4 percent,[1] the volume of world trade grew by 600 percent, its value in real terms grew by about 2,000 percent, and global production grew from $1.1 trillion in 1955 to $10.8 trillion in 1980.[2] (Despite some concerns about a trend toward "world government," GATT was replaced in January 1995 by the World Trade Organization.)

The **International Monetary Fund** (IMF) was developed to work out a fixed pattern of exchange rates that would allow international trade to grow. It was hoped this would prevent the kind of turmoil in international currency markets that had caused so many problems in the 1930s, when the global economy had broken down into four blocs based around the pound, the dollar, the franc, and the mark. The IMF would make short-term loans, mainly to richer countries and primarily to help those countries deal with balance-of-payments problems (which are created when a country imports more than it exports or sends more money abroad—as investments, loans, or grants, for example—than it receives).

The **World Bank** (the International Bank for Reconstruction and Development) was instituted to lend money to European countries affected by the war. When this role was taken over by the Marshall Plan, the Bank turned its attention to the rest of the world, lending money at commercial rates of interest, mainly for the building of economic infrastructure.

The IMF and the World Bank together functioned as something like a global central bank with a distinctly U.S. tilt. Both were headquartered in Washington, D.C., and the United States provided most of their capital and invested heavily in the rebuilding and the military security of Western Europe and Japan. Under U.S. economic leadership, the Bretton Woods system promoted stable monetary relations, expanded trade and economic growth, and saw the emergence of the dollar as the new international reserve currency. This was made possible, Joan Spero has argued, by the concentration of power in North America and Western Europe, a shared interest among Americans and Europeans in capitalism and economic liberalism, and U.S. willingness to assume leadership of the new system.[3]

Notes

1. Peter Calvocoressi, *World Politics Since 1945* (London: Longman, 1991), 153.

2. Gordon C. Schloming, *Power and Principle in International Affairs* (Orlando: Harcourt Brace Jovano-vich, 1991), 25.

3. Joan Edelman Spero, *The Politics of International Economic Relations* (New York: St. Martin's Press, 1985), 25.

Germany and Italy were notable exceptions). Many of the new governments launched programs of social welfare and nationalization, emphasizing central planning and government involvement in the economy. At the
heart of postwar economic policy were the theories of British economist
John Maynard Keynes, who argued in favor of some government control
over the economy in an attempt to control the cycle of booms and busts.
Keynesianism became the basis of postwar economic reconstruction as West
European governments expanded their control over their economies with
the goals of controlling inflation and rebuilding industry and agriculture.
But it soon became clear that substantial capital investment was badly
needed, and the readiest source of such investment was the United States.

U.S. policy on Europe after 1945 had initially been driven by President
Truman's desire to pull the military out of Europe as quickly as possible.
Within two years, the U.S. military presence had been cut by 95 percent, encouraged by public opinion at home, which favored leaving future peacekeeping efforts to the new United Nations. However, it was becoming increasingly obvious to European leaders that Stalin had plans to spread
Soviet influence and that the Nazi threat had simply been replaced by a
Soviet threat. Churchill helped spark a change in U.S. public opinion with
his March 1946 speech in Fulton, Missouri, in which he warned of the de-
scent of an iron curtain across Europe.

Truman's concerns about the future of Europe were growing. When an
economically exhausted Britain ended its financial aid to Greece and Turkey
in 1947, Truman argued that the United States needed to step into the vacuum to curb communist influence in the region. In an address to Congress
in March 1947, he outlined what became known as the **Truman Doctrine.**
Arguing that the world faced a choice between "freedom" and "totalitari-
anism," Truman held that it must be U.S. policy "to support free peoples
who are resisting attempted subjugation by armed minorities or by outside
pressures." This confirmed the end of U.S. isolationism and signaled a renewed interest in European reconstruction as a means of helping to contain
the Soviets.

By now the U.S. State Department had begun to realize that it had un-
derestimated the extent of the wartime economic destruction in Europe; despite an economic boom in the late 1940s, sustained growth was not forthcoming. Food rationing persisted (raising the specter of famine and
starvation), and there were fears of the possible threat of communist influence spreading across a destabilized Europe. The United States had emerged
from World War II in a strong economic position. Its industries were producing 40 percent of the world's armaments by 1944, there had been no direct attacks on its territory after Pearl Harbor, its exports had tripled during the war, and consumer spending was soaring. But it needed new
peacetime export markets.

Policymakers in the Truman administration believed European markets needed to be rebuilt and integrated into a multilateral system of world trade. Economic and political reconstruction would also help forestall Soviet aggression and the rise of domestic communist parties.[11] Some were thinking of the potential benefits of the kind of unified market the United States had built after 1787; as a senior British bureaucrat put it, "The Americans wanted an integrated Europe looking like the United States of America—'God's own country.'"[12]

Against this background, Secretary of State George Marshall argued that Europe should be given assistance. The United States had already provided more than $10 billion in loans and aid to Europe in 1945–1947,[13] but something bigger and more structured was needed. Although motivated by political considerations as much as anything, Marshall made his argument more palatable to Congress by couching it in humanitarian terms: "Our policy is directed not against any country or doctrine," he announced in a speech at Harvard in June 1947, "but against hunger, poverty, desperation and chaos." Although the United States had no intention of extending aid to the Soviet bloc, Marshall argued that the initiative should come from Europe and that "the program should be a joint one, agreed to by a number, if not all European nations."[14] The original April 1947 State Department proposal for the plan made clear that one of its ultimate goals was the creation of a Western European federation.[15] Many in the State Department and elsewhere felt long-term stability demanded coordinated regional economic management that would prevent the breakdown of Europe into rival economic and political blocs.[16]

The British and the French took up the offer and approached the Soviets with the idea of developing a recovery plan. The Soviets suspected the United States of ulterior motives and bowed out once they realized the plan would involve giving up industrial secrets.[17] In July 1947, sixteen European countries met in Paris and established the Committee on European Economic Cooperation. They listed their needs and asked the United States for $29 billion in aid, much more than the United States had envisaged. With congressional approval, the European Recovery Program (otherwise known as the **Marshall Plan**) ultimately provided just over $12.5 billion in aid to Europe between 1948 and 1951.[18] In April 1948, the same sixteen states created a new body—the Organization for European Economic Cooperation (OEEC)—to coordinate the program. The OEEC was based in Paris and was governed by a Council of Ministers made up of one representative from each member state; as its workload increased, it set up subsidiary agencies such as the European Productivity Agency and the European Payments Union, a clearinghouse for payments.

The treaty creating the OEEC listed goals that included the reduction of restrictions on trade and payments, the reduction of tariffs and other barriers to trade, and an examination of the possibilities for a free-trade area or customs union among its members.[19] The OEEC was created at U.S. insistence, Alan Milward noted, "as the first stage in the attempt to build a United States of Europe," but it ended up being "a clumsy, inadequate mixture of elements of forced international cooperation ... [and] supranationality."[20] Opposition from several European governments (notably Britain, France, and Norway) ensured that the OEEC remained a forum for intergovernmental consultation rather than becoming a supranational body with powers of its own.[21] Meanwhile, Marshall was awarded the 1953 Nobel Peace Prize for his efforts.

Although the effects of the Marshall Plan are still debated, there is little question that it helped underpin economic and political recovery in Europe and helped tie the economic and political interests of the United States and Western Europe more closely together. It was a profitable investment for the United States, but it also had an important influence on the idea of European integration; as Western Europe's first permanent organization for economic cooperation, it encouraged Europeans to work together and played a key role in showing Europeans how much mutual dependence existed among their economies.[22] It also helped liberalize inter-European trade and helped ensure that economic integration would be focused on Western Europe. It ended up being based less on integration than on cooperation, however, and fell far short of promoting federalism or political unity. (In December 1960, the OEEC was reorganized as the Organization for Economic Cooperation and Development [OECD].)

Security and the Cold War

The world entered World War II with three major powers, all European: Britain, Germany, and France. It emerged with two new superpowers, neither of them European: the United States and the USSR. In the process of encouraging a new postwar world order, the United States took over the role of global police, its main goal being to defend Western Europe (and ultimately itself) from the Soviet threat. Europeans found themselves caught in the middle of this new rivalry, with relatively little control over their own destiny.

Derek Urwin has argued that U.S. policy in Europe after World War II was based on two misconceptions: first, that Europe had the people, resources, and wealth to recover and second, that the Allies would continue to work together.[23] The United States wanted to share responsibility for security with the European powers and assumed that Britain would police the Mediterranean and the Middle East, that France would be dominant in continental Europe, and that the four Allies would share control of Germany. But a difference of opinion emerged almost immediately between the United States and its European Allies. Western Europeans wondered how much the United States could be relied on to defend Europe and doubted U.S. motives. These doubts created a split that pushed some Europeans (notably Britain) into the U.S. camp and pushed others toward thinking of greater European cooperation.

Although the United States had quickly pulled most of its troops out of Europe, many were as quickly sucked back in as the extent of the Soviet threat became more obvious. Between 1945 and 1948, the Allies were undecided about what to do with Germany, which was left in a state of limbo, divided four ways. The Americans and the British had begun to think Germany would have to be made self-sufficient, but the Soviets first wanted massive reparations and a guarantee of security from further German aggression.

In June 1948, as a first step toward rebuilding German self-sufficiency, the Western Allies agreed to create a new West German state and a new currency for their three zones. In response, the Soviets set up a blockade around West Berlin. For the next year, a massive Western airlift was maintained to supply West Berlin. Concerns about the West German threat had encouraged Britain, France, and the Benelux states to sign the Brussels Treaty in March 1948, pledging the countries to provide "all the military and other aid and assistance in their power" in the event of attack. The Berlin crisis now shifted the emphasis to the Soviet threat and led to the arrival in Britain in 1948 of the first U.S. bombers suspected of carrying nuclear weapons.

The U.S. Congress was wary about any direct commitments or entanglements in Europe but saw the need to counterbalance the Soviets and to ensure the peaceful cooperation of West Germany. In 1949, the North Atlantic Treaty was signed, through which the United States (entering its first peacetime alliance outside the Western Hemisphere) agreed to help its European allies "restore and maintain the security of the North Atlantic area." Canada also signed, as did Britain, France, Italy, the Benelux countries, Denmark, Iceland, Norway, and Portugal. The pact was later given more substance with the creation of the **North Atlantic Treaty Organization** (NATO), headquartered in Paris until it was moved to Brussels in 1966. The United States was now committed to the security of Western Europe.

Although NATO gave Europe more security and more space in which to focus on reconstruction, it soon became obvious that it was an unbalanced alliance; although only 10 percent of NATO forces were American, the United States exercised most of the political influence over NATO policy. (It was no accident that George Orwell described Britain as "Airstrip One" in his novel *1984*.) NATO members agreed that an attack on one would be considered an attack on them all but each agreed to respond only with "such actions as it deems necessary." This was an obviously loose arrangement designed to ensure that the United States would not immediately become involved in yet another European war. The Europeans attempted to take their own defense a step further in 1952 with proposals for the creation of a European Defence Community (EDC), but this faltered because of political opposition in Britain and France and the lack of a common European foreign policy (see Chapter 3).

Eager to encourage some kind of military cooperation, Britain invited its Brussels Treaty partners to join with West Germany and Italy to create the **Western European Union** (WEU).[24] The WEU was less supranationalist than the EDC, but it obliged each member to give all possible military and other aid to any member that was attacked. The WEU also went beyond purely defensive concerns, and agreements signed by the seven founding members in Paris in October 1954 included the aim "to promote the unity and to encourage the progressive integration of Europe." Within days of the launch of the WEU in May 1955, and the coincidental admission of West Germany into NATO, the Soviet bloc created the **Warsaw Pact.** The lines of the cold war were now defined, and its implications were illustrated only too clearly with events in Hungary in 1956.

In October 1956, the government of Imre Nagy announced the end of one-party rule, the evacuation of Russian troops from Hungary, and Hungary's withdrawal from the Warsaw Pact. As Britain and France were invading Egypt to retake the Suez Canal, the Soviets responded to the Hungarian decision by sending in tanks. The United States wanted to criticize the Soviet use of force and boast to the emerging Third World about the moral superiority of the West,[25] but it obviously could not do so while British and French paratroopers were storming the Suez Canal. Britain and France were ostracized in the UN Security Council, the British government fell, and the Suez invasion was quickly abandoned.

The consequences of the combination of France's problems in Indochina, the Suez crisis, and the Hungarian uprising were tumultuous:[26] Britain and France began steady military reductions, finally recognizing that they were no longer world powers capable of acting independently in the Middle East or perhaps anywhere; both countries embarked on a concerted program of decolonization; Britain began looking increasingly to Europe for its economic and security interests; and it became obvious to Europeans that the United States was the major partner in the North Atlantic Alliance, a fact that particularly upset the French. Still not fully convinced about the extent of the U.S. commitment to the defense of Europe, Britain and France clung to their one remaining symbol of independence: their own nuclear forces.

TABLE 2.1   The First Atom and Hydrogen Bomb Tests

	United States	*USSR*	*Britain*	*France*	*China*
Atom bomb	1945	1949	1952	1960	1964
Hydrogen bomb	1952	1953	1957	1968	1966

Europe Joins the Nuclear Club

During World War II, Britain and the United States had cooperated on the development of the atom bomb, but the United States had slowly marginalized the British contribution. Concerned that this was a sign of new U.S. isolationism, Britain developed its own atom bomb, carrying out its first test in 1952 (see Table 2.1). The French were initially undecided about whether to develop their own bomb, but their search for new respectability and their distrust of the United States convinced them to do so.

De Gaulle still harbored grudges because the Free French had not been sufficiently involved in wartime Allied planning, and he had been obsessed with the issue of French pride and independence since his return to power. He felt the world had been divided into two spheres—the Anglo-Saxon and the Soviet—and that France played an inferior role.[27] These feelings later led him to block British attempts to join the European Economic Community (see Chapter 3) as long as Britain maintained its special relationship with the United States. De Gaulle also felt that if it came to a showdown with the Soviets, the United States was unlikely to become involved in a European war unless France had an atom bomb that could act as a trigger. He ruled that no nuclear weapons would be based on French soil unless they were under the total control of France. The first French atomic test was carried out in 1960.

France later declared its independence in the military sphere as well. Since its creation, NATO had been commanded by a U.S. general with a British deputy, thus epitomizing—in de Gaulle's eyes—the power of the Anglo-Saxon bloc. He feared that U.S. domination of European defense policies had spread to politics and economics as well. France pulled out of the NATO joint command in 1966, although it still supported the Atlantic Alliance.

A certain amount of concern had always been present in Europe regarding U.S. influence in European defense and the reliance on nuclear weapons. Feelings ran particularly high in West Germany, which became increasingly alarmed during the 1950s at being used as a mock battlefield. Many West Germans preferred the development of conventional weapons and felt a strong West German army would reduce the need for a nuclear defense strategy. West German public opinion changed somewhat after events in Hungary in 1956 and the 1957 launch of the first Soviet satellite. After

1957, it became obvious that Europe could not rely on long-range U.S. nuclear bombers and needed nuclear weapons sited in Europe itself.

Beginning in the late 1950s, there was a massive buildup of U.S. nuclear warheads in Europe. Instead of guaranteeing European security, however, this buildup had the opposite effect of causing the Soviets to respond with their own buildup of nuclear weapons, thereby ushering in the era of Mutually Assured Destruction (MAD). The United States was concerned about the Soviets and also about Europeans having control over nuclear weapons and thereby having the power to start a war that could destroy the United States.

Rising concerns about the nuclear threat sparked a vocal antinuclear movement in Britain in the late 1950s, orchestrated by the Campaign for Nuclear Disarmament (CND). A series of symbolic marches was held from London to the nuclear weapons research establishment in the village of Aldermaston. The CND view was that nuclear weapons were wrong and that Britain was a very junior partner in an Atlantic Alliance based on nuclear weapons. Although British public opinion largely favored the Alliance and CND represented the views of only a small minority, its activities were symbolic of a growing rift within the Alliance.

Summary and Conclusions

World War II was a watershed in the evolution of the balance of global military, political, and economic power. In the 1920s and 1930s, Britain, France, and Germany were the major powers; their currencies were the most influential in the world; and their economic and military interests tended to be confined to their spheres of political interest: their colonies for Britain and France and Central Europe for Germany. At the end of World War II the United States was the dominant economic power in the world, and the new international order was based largely on U.S. enthusiasm for free trade, stable exchange rates, and an Atlantic Alliance to contain the Soviets.

The West Europeans found themselves junior partners in this new system, were faced with the urgency of rebuilding internal political and economic stability, and saw the historical threat of Germany and the rising threat of the Soviet Union hanging over them. An urgent response was needed to urgent problems, but there was little agreement on the best way to proceed. Each of the European states still had its own set of national interests, but the political fallout from the war and the changing balance of military power symbolized by Suez had already begun to show very clearly that these interests could not be maintained without some form of inter-European cooperation. Tired of war, of nationalism, and of expensive competition for economic and political influence, Western Europe experienced a groundswell of opinion in favor of cooperation. The first opportunity had been missed with the OEEC, which the United States had initially seen as the foundation for a new era of European integration but that ended up as little more than an exercise in intergovernmental cooperation. The way was now cleared for something less ambitious and more specific.

Notes

1. Christopher Thorne, *The Far Eastern War: States and Societies, 1941–45* (London: Unwin, 1986), 211–212.

2. William Safran, *The French Polity*, 4th ed. (New York: Longman, 1995), 8–9.

3. Stephen George, *An Awkward Partner: Britain in the European Community* (Oxford: Oxford University Press, 1990), 19.

4. David Dimbleby and David Reynolds, *An Ocean Apart* (New York: Vintage Books, 1988), 235.

5. David P. Conradt, *The German Polity*, 5th ed. (New York: Longman, 1993), 11.

6. D. Mark Schultz, "Austria in the International Arena: Neutrality, European Integration and Consociationalism," in Kurt Richard Luther and Wolfgang C. Muller (Eds.), *Politics in Austria: Still a Case of Consociationalism?* (London: Frank Cass, 1992).

7. Paul Ginsborg, *A History of Contemporary Italy: Society and Politics, 1943–1988* (London: Penguin, 1990), 16.

8. Ibid., 212–215.

9. Gunnar Helgi Kristinsson, "Iceland," in Helen Wallace (Ed.), *The Wider Western Europe: Reshaping the EC/EFTA Relationship* (London: Pinter, 1991).

10. Armand Van Dormael, *Bretton Woods: Birth of a Monetary System* (New York: Holmes and Meier, 1978).

11. Michael J. Hogan, *The Marshall Plan: America, Britain, and the Reconstruction of Western Europe, 1947–52* (New York: Cambridge University Press, 1987), 26–27.

12. Lawrence S. Kaplan, *The United States and NATO: The Formative Years* (Lexington: University of Kentucky Press, 1984), 131.

13. Alan S. Milward, *The Reconstruction of Western Europe 1945–51* (Berkeley: University of California Press, 1984), 46–48.

14. Office of the Historian, *Foreign Relations of the United States*, Vol. 3 (Washington, D.C.: U.S. Department of State, 1947), 230–232.

15. Quoted in John Gillingham, *Coal, Steel, and the Rebirth of Europe, 1945–1955* (Cambridge: Cambridge University Press, 1991), 118–119.

16. Hogan, *The Marshall Plan*, 36.

17. Dimbleby and Reynolds, *An Ocean Apart*, 188.

18. Milward, *Reconstruction of Western Europe*, 94.

19. Articles 4–6 of the Convention for European Economic Cooperation, quoted in Michael Palmer et al., *European Unity: A Survey of European Organizations* (London: George Allen & Unwin, 1968), 81.

20. Milward, *Reconstruction of Western Europe*, 208.

21. Immanual Wexler, *The Marshall Plan Revisited: The European Recovery Program in Economic Perspective* (Westport, Conn.: Greenwood Press, 1983), 209; Palmer et al., *European Unity*, 82; Milward, *Reconstruction of Western Europe*, 209–210.

22. Derek W. Urwin, *The Community of Europe* (London: Longman, 1995), 20–22.

23. Ibid., 13–14.

24. Clive Archer, *Organizing Western Europe* (London: Edward Arnold, 1990), 169.

25. Alan Sked and Chris Cook, *Post-War Britain: A Political History* (Harmondsworth: Penguin, 1984), 135–136.

26. See Albert Hourani, "Conclusions," in William Roger Louis and Roger Owen (Eds.), *Suez 1956: The Crisis and Its Consequences* (Oxford: Clarendon Press, 1989).

27. Don Cook, *Charles de Gaulle: A Biography* (New York: Putnam, 1983), 332–333.

Further Reading

Cyril E. Black et al., *Rebirth: A History of Europe Since World War II* (Boulder: Westview Press, 1992).

A history of postwar Europe that combines overview chapters with separate chapters on each of the major states and regions of Europe.

Alan S. Milward. *The Reconstruction of Western Europe 1945–51* (Berkeley: University of California Press, 1984).

A detailed study of the Marshall Plan and its contribution to the first moves toward European integration.

Michael J. Hogan. *The Marshall Plan: America, Britain, and the Reconstruction of Western Europe, 1947–52* (New York: Cambridge University Press, 1987).

Complements Alan Milward by describing and assessing U.S. motives and the consequences of the Marshall Plan.

David W.P. Lewis. *The Road to Europe* (New York: Peter Lang, 1993).

Combines a history of European integration with chapters on all of the major international organizations involved in Western European cooperation.

Clive Archer. *Organizing Western Europe* (London: Edward Arnold, 1990).

A guide to the history and structure of eight major European-dominated cooperative organizations, from the OEEC to the Western European Union.

3

Emergence: The Road from Paris

The history of Europe prior to World War II was one of almost constant conflict and tension, and hardly a decade went by without war breaking out between two or more European states. For many, World War I (or the Great War) had been the war to end all wars. In many ways it was a European civil war and brought to a head all of the tensions and political jealousies that plagued the European state system at the turn of the twentieth century. The League of Nations was created in 1919 to oversee the peace and prevent future conflict, but the peace treaty signed at Versailles contained the seeds of future conflict; it demanded drastic reparations from Germany, represented an attempt by Britain and France to stamp their authority on Europe, and was based on recriminations and inequality. As Jean Monnet noted, "A peace based on inequality could have no good results."[1]

The priorities after World War II were to avoid the mistakes of Versailles and to protect Europe both from itself and from external threats. The war had been physically and psychologically devastating, had discredited the old international order, had reminded Europeans that they were still capable of appalling cruelty and barbarism, and had raised urgent questions about how future European conflict could be avoided and how Europe could best go about rebuilding. Different states had different ideas about how this should be done, but most of the suggestions pointed toward greater inter-European cooperation, with the goal of building both political and economic security.

For many, the major internal threats were nationalism and the nation-state, both of which had been glorified, abused, and discredited by the fascists. The development of a new European identity would reduce the role of nationalism, thereby removing one of the recurring causes of European conflict. Because Germany had been at the root of three major conflicts in seventy years, many now argued that peace was impossible unless Germany could be contained and its power diverted to constructive rather than destructive ends. Germany had to be allowed to rebuild its economic base and its political system in ways that would not threaten European security; France was particularly eager to make sure this happened.[2]

The external threats to Europe came from the growing hostility between the two superpowers, leading to concerns that Europeans were becoming pawns in that hostility. There was a determination to protect Western Europe from the spread of Soviet influence, but there were also worries about the extent to which Western Europe and the United States could find common ground and to which Western Europe could rely on the U.S. protective shield. Perhaps Europe would have been better advised to take care of its own security. This, however, demanded a greater sense of unity and common purpose than Europe had ever been able to achieve before.

Political and Economic Security

The rising groundswell of opinion in favor of European cooperation after the war was reflected in the emergence (or reemergence) of several groups of pro-Europeanists. Some groups traced their roots back to the interwar years and to movements such as Pan-Europa, founded in 1923 by Austro-Hungarian aristocrat Count Richard Coudenhove-Kalergi. Others were born out of a concern to remove the causes of war and to respond to growing U.S. economic power. Among these were the United European Movement in Britain, the Europa-Bund in Germany, the Socialist Movement for the United States of Europe in France, and the European Union of Federalists.

The spotlight fell particularly on Britain, which had taken the lead during the war in the resistance to Nazism and was still the dominant European power. Winston Churchill had become the focus of Europeanist sentiment; his credentials were based on his charisma, his last-minute proposal for an Anglo-French Union in 1940, and suggestions he had made in 1942–1943 for "a United States of Europe" operating under "a Council of Europe" with reduced trade barriers, free movement of people, a common military, and a High Court to adjudicate disputes.[3] He made the same suggestions in a speech at the University of Zurich in 1946, but it was clear that Churchill felt this new entity should be based around France and Germany and would not necessarily include Britain; before the war he had argued that Britain was "with Europe but not of it. We are interested and associated, but not absorbed."[4]

The national pro-European groups decided to organize a conference aimed at publicizing the cause of European unity. The Congress of Europe was held in The Hague in May 1948, attended by delegates from sixteen

TABLE 3.1 Western European Membership of International Organizations

Year of foundation	1945	1948	1949	1949	1952	1955	1960
	UN	OEEC	Council of Europe	NATO	EU	WEU	EFTA[a]
Britain	*	*	*	*	1973	*	*
France	*	*	*	*	*	*	—
Germany	1973	1949	1951	1955	*	*	—
Italy	1955	*	*	*	*	*	—
Belgium	*	*	*	*	*	*	—
Netherlands	*	*	*	*	*	*	—
Luxembourg	*	*	*	*	*	*	—
Portugal	1955	*	1976	*	1986	1989	*
Spain	1955	1959	1977	1982	1986	1989	—
Greece	*	*	1949	1952	1981	—	—
Ireland	1955	*	*	—	1973	—	—
Finland	1955	—	1988	—	1995	—	1986
Sweden	1946	*	*	—	1995	—	*
Austria	1955	*	1956	—	1995	—	*
Denmark	*	*	*	*	1973	—	*
Iceland	1946	*	1950	*	—	—	1970
Norway	*	*	*	*	—	—	*
Turkey	*	*	1949	1952	—	—	—
Cyprus	1960	—	1961	—	—	—	—
Malta	1964	—	1965	—	—	—	—
Switzerland	—	*	1963	—	—	—	*

*Founder members; other dates refer to year of accession.
[a]By 1995, only Iceland, Norway, Switzerland, and Liechtenstein remained in EFTA.
UN = United Nations, OEEC = Organization for European Economic Cooperation,
NATO = North Atlantic Treaty Organization, EU = European Union, WEU = Western
European Union, EFTA = European Free Trade Association.

states and observers from the United States and Canada. Calls were made for a European assembly, a European court, and a charter of human rights, but the only tangible outcome was the creation of a European Movement with national groups in each country. The Movement took up the idea of a European assembly and urged influential Europeanists like Belgian Prime Minister Paul-Henri Spaak and Italian Prime Minister Alcide de Gasperi to promote the idea. After discussions among the governments of France, Britain, Italy, Belgium, the Netherlands, and Luxembourg, agreement was reached in January 1949 to create a ministerial council and a consultative assembly. The French and Italians wanted to use the name European Union, but the British insisted on the more ambiguous and noncommittal title Council of Europe.[5]

The **Council of Europe** was founded in London in May 1949 with the signing of a statute by ten European states. The statute noted the need for "a closer unity between all the like-minded countries of Europe" and described the Council's aims as including "common action in economic, social, cultural, scientific, legal and administrative matters"; defense was explicitly excluded from the list. The Council was headquartered in Strasbourg, France, and had a governing Committee of Ministers, on which each state had one vote, and a 147-member Consultative Assembly made up of representatives nominated from national legislatures. The Committee of Ministers met once or twice annually; although it initially consisted of the foreign ministers of member states, deputy ministers were soon sent instead. The Assembly had few powers over the Committee, which promoted national interests at the expense of European interests. Although membership in the Council of Europe had expanded to eighteen countries by 1965, the Council never became anything more than a loose intergovernmental organization. It made progress on human rights, cultural issues, and even limited economic cooperation, but it was not the kind of organization European federalists wanted.

Opening Moves: Coal and Steel (1950–1952)

The OEEC and the Council of Europe encouraged Europeans to think and work together, but the opposition of antifederalists (notably those in Britain and Scandinavia) ensured that neither organization would promote significant regional integration. Among those who felt something bolder was needed were French entrepreneur Jean Monnet (1888–1979) and Robert Schuman (1880–1963), French foreign minister from 1948 to 1953. Both were enthusiastic Europeanists, both felt something practical needed to be done that went beyond the noble statements of organizations such as the Council of Europe, and both felt the logical point of departure should be the perennial problem of Franco-German relations.

By 1950, it was clear to many that West Germany had to be allowed to rebuild if it was to play a useful role in the Western Alliance. The Western Allies had placed restrictions on its plans to rebuild heavy industry; one way of getting around these restrictions without allowing Germany to become a threat to its neighbors (particularly France) was to let it rebuild under the auspices of a supranational organization, thereby tying Germany (particularly the resources of the Ruhr) into the wider process of European reconstruction. It was important not to be too ambitious and to start with something small but meaningful. The Congresses of the European Movement in early 1949 had suggested that the coal and steel industries offered strong potential for common European organization for several reasons:[6]

1. Coal and steel were the fundamental building blocks of industry, and the steel industry had a tendency to create cartels; cooperation would eliminate waste and duplication, break down cartels, make coal and steel production more efficient and competitive, and boost industrial development.

2. The heavy industries of the Ruhr had been the traditional basis for Germany's power, and France and Germany had fought earlier over coal reserves in Alsace-Lorraine; creating a supranational coal and steel industry would contain German power. As Monnet put it, "Coal and steel were at once the key to economic power and the raw materials for forging weapons of war."[7]

3. Integrating coal and steel would ensure that Germany became reliant on trade with the rest of Europe, thereby underpinning its economic reconstruction and helping the French lose their fear of German industrial domination.[8]

Monnet felt that unless France acted immediately, the United States would become the focus of a new transatlantic alliance against the Soviet bloc, Britain would be pulled closer to the United States, Germany's economic and military growth would not be controlled, and France would be led to its "eclipse."[9] As head of the French national planning commission (the Commissariat du Plan), Monnet could see that effective economic planning was beyond the ability of individual states working alone. He also knew from personal experience that intergovernmental organizations tended to be hamstrung by the governments of their member states and to become bogged down in endless ministerial meetings. To avoid these problems, he proposed a new institution independent of national governments that would have a life of its own; in other words, it would be supranational rather than intergovernmental.

After discussions with Monnet and West German Chancellor Konrad Adenauer, Schuman took these ideas a step further at a press conference on May 9, 1950 (a date now widely seen as marking the birth of the idea of a united Europe). In what later became known as the Schuman Declaration, he argued that Europe would not be built at once or according to a single plan but only through concrete achievements:

> The coming together of the nations of Europe requires the elimination of the age-old opposition of France and Germany. ... With this aim in view, the French Government proposes that action be taken immediately on one limited but decisive point. It proposes that Franco-German production of coal and

steel as a whole be placed under a common High Authority, within the framework of an organization open to the participation of the other countries of Europe.[10]

This, Schuman went on, would be "a first step in the federation of Europe" and would make war between France and Germany "not merely unthinkable, but materially impossible."[11] The proposal was revolutionary in the sense that France was offering to sacrifice a measure of national sovereignty in the interest of building a new supranational authority that could end an old rivalry and help build a new European peace.[12] Only four other countries took up the invitation: Italy, which wanted respectability and economic and political stability, and the Benelux countries, which were in favor because they were small and vulnerable, had twice been invaded by Germany, and felt the only way they could have a voice in world affairs and ensure their security was to be part of a bigger unit. They were also heavily reliant on exports and had created their own customs union in 1948.

The other European states had different reasons for not taking part in the proposed Authority: Spain and Portugal were dictatorships and had little interest in international cooperation. For Denmark and Norway, the memories of the German occupation were still too fresh, while Austria, Sweden, and Finland wanted to remain neutral. Ireland was predominantly agricultural (and thus had little to gain from the proposal) and was tied economically to Britain. Britain still had too many interests outside Europe and exported little of its steel to Western Europe (4–6 percent annually[13]), and the new Labour government had only recently nationalized its coal and steel industries and did not like the supranational character of the Schuman proposal; as Prime Minister Clement Attlee told the House of Commons, his party was "not prepared to accept the principle that the most vital economic forces of this country should be handed over to an authority that is utterly undemocratic and is responsible to nobody."

The governments of the Six (the six member states) opened negotiations and on April 18, 1951, signed the Treaty of Paris creating the **European Coal and Steel Community** (ECSC). The new organization finally began work in August 1952 following ratification of the terms of the treaty in each of the member states (see Box 3.1). The ECSC was a small step in itself, but it represented the first time European governments had given significant powers to a supranational organization. The ECSC was allowed to pull down tariff barriers, abolish subsidies, fix prices, and raise money by imposing levies on steel and coal production. It faced national opposition, but its job was made easier by the fact that much of the groundwork had already been laid by the Benelux customs union.

John Gillingham has argued that the ECSC ensured that Germany did not become a threat to the new Europe but instead became its mainstay.[14] The ECSC showed that integration was feasible, and its very existence forced

BOX 3.1
The European Coal and Steel Community

The ECSC was governed by four institutions:

1. A High Authority of nine nominated members (at least one—and no more than two—from each member state). They served six-year terms and were expected to work toward removing all barriers to the free movement of coal and steel. They were given complete independence regarding decisions relating to the ECSC and had the power to issue binding decisions and recommendations, but they could not see themselves as representatives of their respective countries; they represented the joint interests of the ECSC. The Authority paved the way for the European Commission but had much greater power in its own constituency; for example, it could give orders to national coal and steel industries without the approval of national governments. Jean Monnet became the first president.

2. A Special Council of Ministers consisting of the relevant minister from each member state. The Council was created as a result of Benelux concerns about the power of the three larger countries and was designed to allow the smaller member states to balance the power of the High Authority, to prevent the French and the Germans from having too much power, and to represent the interests of member states.

3. A Common Assembly consisting of seventy-eight members chosen by national legislatures, with the numbers divided roughly on the basis of population (eighteen each from France, Germany, and Italy; ten each from Belgium and the Netherlands; and four from Luxembourg). The Assembly was the first international assembly in Europe with legally guaranteed powers. It became the forerunner of the European Parliament and helped Monnet circumvent the concerns of national governments about giving up powers; he argued that the High Authority would be responsible to the Assembly, which would eventually be directly elected. Although the Assembly was intended to provide democratic input into ECSC decisions, it had only advisory powers, and its members were not elected.

4. A Court of Justice consisting of seven judges (one from each country plus a seventh to create an odd number). The Court's tasks were to settle conflicts between states and rule on the legality of High Authority decisions on the basis of complaints from member states or national industries.

The Six were unable to agree on a single site for the ECSC, so the High Authority, the Council, and the Court were provisionally based in Luxembourg, and the Assembly was located in Strasbourg, France.

the Six to work together; even Britain was obliged to recognize its authority. Although the ECSC failed to achieve many of its goals (notably the creation of a single market for coal and steel),[15] it had ultimately been created to prove a point about the feasibility of integration, which it did. It continued to function independently until 1965 when the High Authority and the

Special Council of Ministers were merged with their counterparts in the EEC and Euratom, as discussed later in this chapter.

While the ECSC was at least a limited success, integrationists failed dismally with two much larger, more ambitious, and arguably premature experiments. The first of these was the **European Defence Community** (EDC), which was to promote Western European cooperation on defense while at the same time binding West Germany into a European defense system. Konrad Adenaeur had first broached the idea in 1949, but it was given a decisive push with the announcement of U.S. plans to rearm West Germany in the wake of the outbreak of the Korean war in June 1950.[16] In an attempt to defuse concerns about German rearmament, a draft plan was outlined by Jean Monnet and was made public in October 1950 by French Prime Minister René Pleven. Echoing ideas outlined by Churchill in a speech to the Council of Europe in August of that year,[17] the plan argued the need for a common defense and "a European Army tied to [the] political institutions of a united Europe [and a] European Minister for Defense."[18] The six members of the ECSC moved ahead with the plan, assuming that the EDC would have the same structure as the ECSC, and in May 1952 they signed a draft EDC treaty.

When it came to national ratification, however, problems arose, particularly in Italy and France. The French were still nervous about German rearmament so soon after the war and did not want to give up control over their military. Additionally, any talk of a European defense system that did not include Britain—still the strongest European military power—was pointless. Furthermore, observed Konrad Adenauer, Europe could not have a workable common defense force without a common foreign policy.[19] French national prestige, meanwhile, was struck a blow with the surrender at Dien Bien Phu in April 1954, further discouraging talk of giving up military sovereignty. Plans for the EDC were finally shelved in August 1954 when the French National Assembly voted it down on the basis that giving up the right to a national army was too much of a restriction on sovereignty. The EDC was replaced in 1955 by the Western European Union, a consultative organization that fell far short of being a common defense force (see Chapter 15).

The **European Political Community** (EPC), meanwhile, was intended to be the first step toward the creation of a European federation. A draft plan was completed in 1953, based around a European Executive Council, a Council of Ministers, a Court of Justice, and a popularly elected Parliament. With ultimate power resting with the Executive Council, which would represent national interests, the EPC was more confederal than federal in nature.[20] With the collapse of the EDC, however, all hopes for a European Political Community died, at least temporarily. The failure of these two initiatives was a sobering blow to the integrationists and sent shock waves through the ECSC; Monnet left the presidency of the High

Authority in 1955, disillusioned by the political resistance to its work and impatient to move on with the process of integration.[21]

From Paris to Rome (1955–1958)

Although the ECSC gained modest but solid achievements in its first four years, there were limits to its abilities, and Europeanists felt something more was needed to give integration new momentum. Schuman's original view was that political union would come about through economic integration, and although the six ECSC members agreed that coal and steel had been a useful testing ground, it was increasingly difficult to develop those two sectors in isolation. A meeting of the foreign ministers of the Six at Messina, Italy, in June 1955 resulted in a resolution that the time had come to "relaunch" the European idea. They agreed on a Benelux proposal "to work for the establishment of a united Europe by the development of common institutions, the progressive fusion of national economies, the creation of a common market, and the progressive harmonization of their social policies."[22]

A committee chaired by Belgian Foreign Minister Paul-Henri Spaak was set up to look into the options. Britain was briefly a member of the committee but withdrew when it became obvious that its hopes for a looser free trade agreement were at odds with the goals of the Six. As Spaak himself later admitted, the Treaty of Rome was motivated less by economic cooperation than by a desire to take another step toward political union.[23] The report of the Spaak committee led to a new round of negotiations, and the signing in March 1957 of the two Treaties of Rome, one creating the **European Economic Community** (EEC) and one the **European Atomic Energy Community** (Euratom). Following member state ratification, both came into force in January 1958 (see Box 3.2). The treaties of Paris and Rome have since been amended and to some extent supplanted by subsequent agreements, but they formed the foundations of the process of European integration and in many ways amounted almost to a constitution for Western Europe. The EEC Treaty committed the Six to the creation of a common market and to the harmonization of their economic policies. Action would be taken in areas where there was agreement, and disagreements could be set aside for future discussion. The common market was to be created within twelve years through the removal of all restrictions on internal trade; agreement on a common external tariff; the reduction of barriers to the free movement of people, services, and capital among the Six; the development of common agricultural and transport policies; and the creation of a European Social Fund and a European Investment Bank. The Euratom Treaty, meanwhile, was aimed at creating a common market for

BOX 3.2
The European Economic Community

Although the EEC and Euratom inherited the basic framework of the ECSC institutions, there were some changes. First, instead of a High Authority, the EEC had an appointed nine-member quasi-executive Commission, which had less power to impose decisions on member states and whose main job was to initiate policy and oversee implementation.

Second, the EEC Council of Ministers was given greater power over decisionmaking but still represented national interests. It had six members, but they shared seventeen votes (four each for France, Germany, and Italy; two each for Belgium and the Netherlands; and one for Luxembourg). Depending on their implications, some decisions had to be unanimous, whereas others could be taken by a simple majority or—more often—by a qualified majority of twelve votes from at least four states. This system made it impossible for the larger states to outvote the smaller ones. Although the qualified majority system was seen as a temporary measure, it remains in place today.

Third, a single Parliamentary Assembly was created to cover the EEC, ECSC, and Euratom; it had 142 members appointed by the member states. It could question or censure the Commission but had little legislative authority. The Assembly renamed itself the European Parliament in 1962.

Finally, a single Court of Justice was created with seven judges appointed for renewable six-year terms; it was responsible for interpreting the founding treaties and ensuring that the three institutions and the member states fulfilled their treaty obligations.

atomic energy. For de Gaulle, Euratom came too close to interfering in his domestic nuclear weapons policy, so he made sure it focused primarily on research. When West Germany and Italy began developing their own nuclear programs, Euratom funding was cut, and it rapidly became a very junior actor in the process of integration.[24]

Integration Takes Root

The integration of six Western European states under the ECSC, the EEC, and Euratom was a revolutionary development with enormous political and economic significance. Given the long history of inter-European hostilities and war, any integration at all was remarkable. It was by no means a trouble-free experience, however. Even Jean Monnet had warned that "Europe will be established through crises and ... the outcome will be the sum of the outcomes of those crises."[25]

The most serious of the early crises came in 1965, with French objections to the growth of European Commission powers. The roots of the problem went back to the collapse of de Gaulle's plans for political union (a collapse generated in part by French concerns about giving the Commission too much power), and the situation worsened because of the imperious manner in which de Gaulle rejected British membership in 1963 (discussed later in the chapter). At its heart were de Gaulle's attempts to discard the supranationalist elements of the Treaty of Rome and to build a Community dominated by France.[26] The final straw came with European Parliament demands for more power (especially over the budget), the fact that decisionmaking by majority vote on certain issues in the Council of Ministers was scheduled to come into force on January 1, 1966, and suggestions by the European Commission that it replace its reliance on national contributions of EEC members with an independent source of income and that more progress be made on a common agricultural policy.

This smacked of excessive supranationalism to the French, who insisted that EEC funding continue to come from national contributions, at least until 1970. The other five states disagreed, so in June 1965 France began boycotting meetings of the Council of Ministers, preventing any decisions from being taken on new laws and policies and setting off the "empty chair" crisis. The crisis was ended only with the **Luxembourg Compromise** (actually an agreement to disagree) of January 1966, through which the voting procedure in the Council of Ministers was changed. The goal—as before—was unanimity, but members would effectively be allowed to veto matters they felt adversely affected their own national interests. The effect was to curb the growth of Commission powers and put more power into the hands of the member states (in the form of the Council of Ministers). (The use of the veto had been virtually abandoned by the mid-1980s as the Council of Ministers shifted toward consensual decisionmaking.)

Along with the problems, though, there were many achievements. The Treaty of Rome had set a twelve-year deadline for the removal in stages of all of the barriers to the creation of a common market among the Six (Article 8). Although this did not happen until 1993, internal tariffs fell quickly enough to allow the Six to agree on a common external tariff in July 1968 and to declare that an industrial customs union existed.

Bureaucratic bloat and replication of effort were always possibilities when a new level of authority was created. Although critics of European integration regularly point accusatory fingers at the European Commission, its numbers remained low, and decisionmaking was streamlined in April 1965 with the Treaty Establishing a Single Council and a Single Commission of the European Communities (the **Merger Treaty**); the three Communities already had a common Parliament and Court of Justice. The decisionmaking process was given both authority and direction by the formalization in 1975 of regular summits of Community leaders coming together as the European Council (see Chapter 10). The EEC was also made more publicly accountable (and more democratic) with the introduction in 1979 of direct elections to the European Parliament.

Integration also brought the removal of quota restrictions, instituted by members to protect their home industries from competition and under which a country could limit or ban the import of products that competed directly with domestic products. One result was that between 1958 and 1965 intra-EEC trade grew three times faster than that with third countries.[27] An EEC report published in 1972 revealed an average annual growth of **gross national product** (GNP) in the Six of 5.7 percent, a 4.5 percent increase in per capita income and consumption, and a 50 percent reduction in the contribution of agriculture to GNP.[28]

The free movement of goods across borders would be restricted as long as EEC members had nontariff barriers such as different standards and regulations on health, safety, and consumer protection. Standards were harmonized during the 1960s and 1970s, but it was not until the 1986 Single European Act (see Chapter 4) that a concerted effort was made to finally bring all EEC members in line.

Another priority was to lift restrictions on the free movement of workers. Again, limits remained well into the 1990s, but steady progress was made toward easing them during the 1960s and 1970s.

One of the goals of the Treaty of Rome (Article 38) had been agreement on a Common Agricultural Policy (CAP), which was finally achieved in 1968 with the acceptance of a watered-down version of a plan drawn up by agriculture Commissioner Sicco Mansholt.[29] Its goals were to create a single market for agricultural products and to assure EEC farmers of guaranteed prices for their produce. CAP initially encouraged both production and productivity. It was also the largest single item in the EC budget and became enormously controversial (see Chapter 13).

The Six worked increasingly closer together on international trade negotiations and enjoyed a joint influence they would not have had negotiating individually. The EEC acted as one, for example, in the Kennedy Round of GATT negotiations in the mid-1960s and in reaching preferential trade agreements with eighteen former African colonies under the 1963 Yaoundé Convention (see Chapter 15).[30]

Enlargement I and II: Looking West and South

Winston Churchill had been an active proponent of European integration during both the war and his years in opposition (1945–1951), but neither the Labour government that ousted him in 1945 nor Churchill upon his return to office in 1951 took this philosophy any further. Britain was uncomfortable with the federalist tendencies of the ECSC and the EEC. It was not fond of the European Defence Community because it would have limited Britain's defense options at a time when the British military was strung out across the Middle East, East Africa, and Southeast Asia. It did not support Euratom because Britain was a nuclear power and did not want to give up its secrets to nonnuclear countries. Finally, the failure of the EDC had convinced many in the British government that the EEC had little potential; as Harold Macmillan recalled, the official view in the foreign policy establishment seemed to be "a confident expectation that nothing would come out of Messina."[31]

The Suez crisis finally put to rest Britain's nostalgic idea that it was still a great power and shook the foundations of the special relationship with the United States. It was also clear that global political and economic issues were being discussed and influenced bilaterally by the United States and the USSR. Britain decided to pursue the idea of a wider (but looser) free trade area based on the OEEC states, and in late 1957 the Maudling Committee (named after chief British negotiator Reginald Maudling) was formed by the OEEC Council to oversee discussions between Britain and the Six. Preparations for the EEC had gone too far, however, and de Gaulle—with his hostility toward Britain at a boil—had taken office; the Maudling negotiations collapsed, and in 1960 the OEEC was reorganized into the Organization for Economic Cooperation and Development (OECD).

Britain now went ahead with the creation of the **European Free Trade Association** (EFTA), a much looser intergovernmental body whose goal was free trade rather than economic and political integration. It was founded in January 1960 with the signing of the Stockholm Convention by Britain, Austria, Denmark, Norway, Portugal, Sweden, and Switzerland. Finland had taken part in the preparatory negotiations but decided not to become a founding member. Membership in EFTA was voluntary (unlike the contractual arrangements set up for the EEC by the Treaty of Rome). EFTA had no political goals and no institutions beyond a Council of Ministers that met two or three times a year and a group of permanent representatives serviced by a small secretariat in Geneva.

EFTA helped cut tariffs but achieved relatively little over the long term. Several of its members did more trade with the EEC than with their EFTA partners, and questions were raised early about Britain's motives in pursuing the EFTA concept. The Association was a marriage of convenience, created to prove a point about the relative merits of a looser free-trade arrangement with low tariffs. It soon became clear to Britain that political influence in Europe lay not with EFTA but with the EEC, that Britain risked political isolation if it stayed out of the EEC, and that the EEC was actually working; the continent had made impressive economic and political progress, and British industry wanted access to the rich European market.[32] In August 1961, barely fifteen months after the creation of EFTA, Britain applied for EEC membership, at the same time as Ireland and Denmark. They were joined by Norway in 1962.

Denmark's motives for wanting EEC membership were agricultural; it was producing three times as much food as it needed, and much of that was being exported to Britain. Furthermore, the EEC itself was a big new mar-

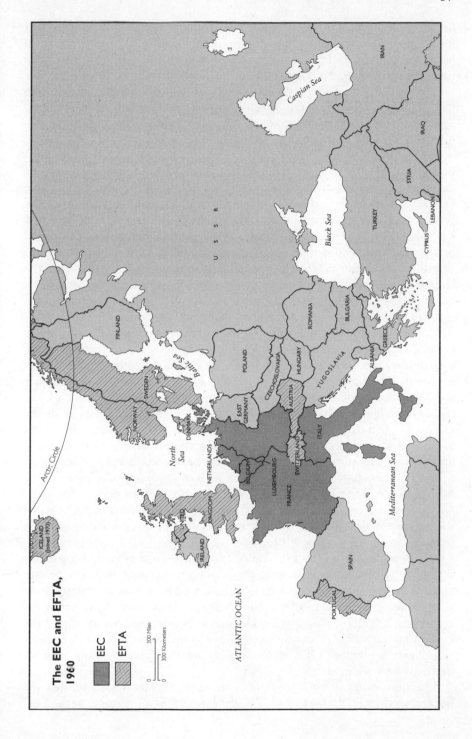

The EEC and EFTA, 1960

EEC

EFTA

ket for Danish agricultural surpluses and would provide a boost for Danish industrial development. Ireland, for its part, saw the EEC as a potential boost for its industrial plans and its desire to reduce its reliance on agriculture and on Britain. Norway followed the British lead because of the importance of EEC markets. With four of its members apparently trying to defect, EFTA ceased to have much purpose, so Sweden, Austria, and Switzerland applied for associate membership in the EEC; they were followed in 1962 by Portugal, Spain, and Malta.

Negotiations between Britain and the Six opened in early 1962 and appeared to be on the verge of a successful conclusion when they fell foul of de Gaulle's Franco-German policy and his animosity toward Britain. De Gaulle had plans for an EEC built around a Franco-German axis, saw Britain as a rival to French influence in the EEC, still resented the fact that he had not been given equal status at the wartime summits of the Allied powers, and resented Britain's lack of enthusiasm toward the early integrationist moves of the 1950s. He also felt British membership would give the United States too much influence in Europe, a concern that seemed to be confirmed at the end of 1962 when Britain accepted the U.S. offer of Polaris missiles as delivery vehicles for Britain's nuclear warheads.

Monnet, for his part, was eager for British membership and even tried to convince Adenauer of his point of view by suggesting that Adenauer refuse to sign the Franco-German treaty unless de Gaulle accepted the British application. But Adenauer shared de Gaulle's Anglophobia and agreed that the development of the Franco-German axis was key. In the space of just ten days in January 1963, de Gaulle signed a Friendship Treaty with the Germans and vetoed the British application. He further upset Britain and some of his own EEC partners by reaching the veto decision unilaterally and making the announcement at a press conference in Paris. Paul-Henri Spaak felt de Gaulle "had acted with a lack of consideration unexampled in the history of the EEC, showing utter contempt for his negotiating partners, allies and opponents alike."[33] Since Britain's application was part of the package with those of Denmark and Ireland, their applications were rejected as well.

Britain applied again in 1967, and its application was vetoed for a second time by de Gaulle. Following de Gaulle's resignation in 1969, Britain applied for a third time, and this time its application was accepted, along with those of Denmark, Ireland, and Norway. Following membership negotiations in 1970–1971, Britain, Denmark, and Ireland finally joined the EEC in January 1973; Norway would have joined as well, but a public referendum in September 1972 narrowly went against its membership. The Six had now become the Nine.

A second round of enlargements came in the 1980s, which pushed the borders of the EEC further south. Greece made its first overtures to the EEC

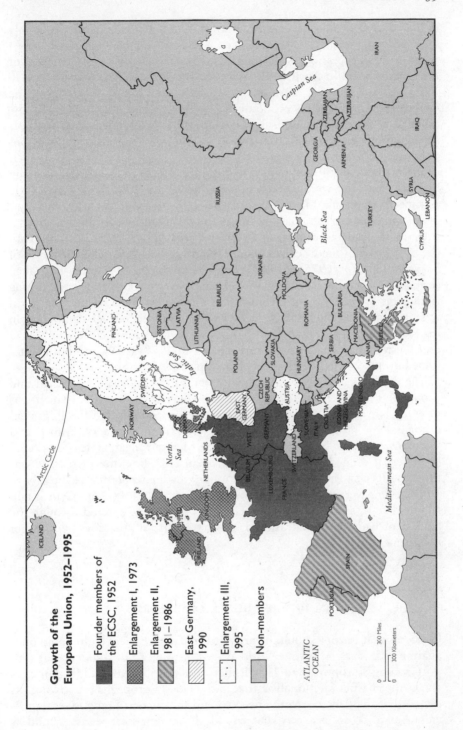

Growth of the European Union, 1952–1995

Founder members of the ECSC, 1952

Enlargement I, 1973

Enlargement II, 1981–1986

East Germany, 1990

Enlargement III, 1995

Non-members

in the late 1950s, but it was turned down on the grounds that its economy was too underdeveloped. It was given associate membership in 1961 as a prelude to full accession, which might have come sooner had it not been for the military coup in April 1967. With the return to civilian government in 1974, Greece applied almost immediately for full membership. The Commission felt Greece's economy was still too weak, but the Greek government responded that EEC membership would help underpin its attempts to rebuild democracy. The Council of Ministers agreed, negotiations opened in 1976, and Greece joined in 1981.

Spain and Portugal had requested negotiations for associate membership in 1962, but both were dictatorships; although the EEC Treaty says "any European State may apply to become a member of the Community," democracy has—in practice—been a basic precondition. Spain was given a preferential trade agreement in 1970 and Portugal in 1973, but only with the overthrow of the Caetano regime in Portugal in 1973 and the death of Franco in Spain in 1975 was EEC membership for the two states was taken seriously. Despite the two states' relative poverty, problems over fishing rights, and concerns about Spanish and Portuguese workers moving north in search of work, the EEC felt membership would encourage democracy in the Iberian peninsula and help link the two countries more closely to NATO and Western Europe. Negotiations opened in 1978–1979, and both states joined in 1986, bringing EEC membership to twelve.

The doubling of the membership of the EEC had several political and economic consequences: It increased the influence of the EEC (which was now the largest economic bloc in the world), it complicated the EEC's decisionmaking processes, it reduced the overall influence of France and Germany, and—by bringing in the poorer Mediterranean states—it altered the internal economic balance. Rather than enlarging any further, it was time to deepen the relationships among the existing twelve members. Applications were made by Turkey (1987), Austria (1989), and Cyprus and Malta (1990), and although East Germany in a sense entered through the back door with the reunification of Germany in 1990, there was no further enlargement until 1995.

Summary and Conclusions

Concerns that Europe should be protected from itself were highlighted once again in the years following World War II, leading to a confluence of support among European and U.S. leaders for the idea of building bridges across the chasm of nationalism that had divided Europeans for so long. At the core of the debate was the need to end the ancient Franco-German rivalry but to do so in a way that would allow both societies to rebuild as partners rather than competitors and that would prevent German military and industrial power from again becoming a threat to European peace.

Attempts to build supranationalist or federalist bodies were scuttled by Britain and were distrusted by some continental Europeans. The only alternative was to build smaller and less ambitious links among European states. The ECSC was a disappointing compromise for European federalists, but despite its modest aims and relatively colorless character, it survived when other, more ambitious attempts at integration failed, and it provided the seed that would produce the EEC and Euratom and pull Western Europe slowly—if reluctantly—into pooling its resources and its interests.

Only six states chose to take part in the experiment at first, but its successes, combined with the failures of other experiments that were either too modest (EFTA) or too ambitious (EDC), encouraged other European states to consider EEC membership. The Six became the Nine in 1973 and had reached twelve by 1986. There were problems along the way, though, bringing increased pressure to once again "relaunch" Europe by focusing on achieving the fundamental goals of the Treaty of Rome.

Notes

1. Jean Monnet, *Memoirs* (Garden City, N.Y.: Doubleday, 1978), 97.

2. John Gillingham, "Jean Monnet and the European Coal and Steel Community: A Preliminary Appraisal," in Douglas Brinkley and Clifford Hackett (Eds.), *Jean Monnet: The Path to European Unity* (New York: St Martin's Press, 1991), 131–137.

3. Quoted in Michael Palmer et al., *European Unity: A Survey of European Organizations* (London: George Allen and Unwin, 1968), 111.

4. Arnold J. Zurcher, *The Struggle to Unite Europe 1940–58* (New York: New York University Press, 1958), 6.

5. Derek W. Urwin, *The Community of Europe*, 2d ed. (Harlow, Essex: Longman, 1995), 34.

6. Alan S. Milward, *The Reconstruction of Western Europe 1945–51* (Berkeley: University of California Press, 1984), 394.

7. Monnet, *Memoirs*, 293.

8. Ibid., 292.

9. Ibid., 294.

10. Robert Schuman, "Declaration of 9 May 1950," in David Weigall and Peter Stirk (Eds.), *The Origins and Development of the European Community* (Leicester: Leicester University Press, 1992), 58–59.

11. Ibid., 58–59.

12. John Gillingham, *Coal, Steel, and the Rebirth of Europe, 1945–55* (New York: Cambridge University Press, 1991), 231.

13. Milward, *Reconstruction of Western Europe*, 402.

14. Gillingham, *Coal, Steel, and the Rebirth of Europe*, xi.

15. Ibid., 319.

16. Ibid., 262–263.

17. Sir Anthony Eden, *Memoirs: Full Circle* (London: Cassell, 1960), 32.

18. Pleven Plan, reproduced in Weigall and Stirk, *Origins and Development of the European Community,* 75–77.

19. Urwin, *Community of Europe,* 63.

20. Ibid., 64–65.

21. Monnet, *Memoirs,* 398–404.

22. Messina Resolution, reproduced in Weigall and Stirk, *Origins and Development of the European Community,* 94.

23. Urwin, *Community of Europe,* 76.

24. Ibid., 76–77.

25. Monnet, *Memoirs,* 518.

26. Don Cook, *Charles de Gaulle: A Biography* (New York: Putnam, 1983), 370–371.

27. Urwin, *Community of Europe,* 130.

28. Quoted in Ghita Ionescu, *Centripetal Politics: Government and the New Centres of Power* (London: Hart-Davis, McGibbon, 1975), 150–154.

29. See John Pinder, *European Community: The Building of a Union* (Oxford: Oxford University Press, 1991), 78–86; Urwin, *Community of Europe,* 132–135.

30. Urwin, ibid., 131.

31. Harold Macmillan, *Riding the Storm 1956–59* (New York: Harper and Row, 1971), 73.

32. Pinder, *European Community,* 46–47.

33. Paul-Henri Spaak, *The Continuing Battle: Memoirs of a European 1933–66* (Boston: Little, Brown, 1971), 375.

Further Reading

John Gillingham. *Coal, Steel, and the Rebirth of Europe, 1945–55* (New York: Cambridge University Press, 1991).

A detailed study of the background of the ECSC, its formation, and its early years of operation.

Francois Duchene. *Jean Monnet: The First Statesman of Interdependence* (New York: W. W. Norton, 1995).

A combined biography of Jean Monnet and history of European integration, written by Monnet's former speechwriter and press liaison officer.

Derek W. Urwin. *The Community of Europe,* 2d ed. (London: Longman, 1995).

A broad-ranging and detailed history of European integration, tracing events from World War II to Maastricht.

David Weigall and Peter Stirk (Eds.). *The Origins and Development of the European Community* (Leicester: Leicester University Press, 1992).

A complement to Urwin: a history of European integration from 1918 to 1991 told through documents, speeches, treaties, white papers, and excerpts from key texts.

John Pinder. *European Community: The Building of a Union* (Oxford: Oxford University Press, 1991).

A short and succinct survey of the origins and development of the European Union, assessing the underlying political and economic motives and describing the key steps in the construction of the EU.

4

Consolidation:
The Road to Maastricht

By 1986, EEC membership had grown to twelve, and the EEC had become known simply as the European Community (EC). Its member states had a combined population of 322 million and accounted for just over one-fifth of all world trade. The Community had its own administrative structure (the Commission and the Council of Ministers) and an independent body of law, and its citizens had direct (but limited) representation through the European Parliament, which also gave them a more direct psychological and political stake in the evolution of the Community.

But progress on integration remained uneven. The creation of a common market had been one of the fundamental goals of the Treaty of Rome, and yet in the early 1980s the EC still had far to go; the customs union was in place, but nontariff barriers remained to the free movement of people and capital—including different national technical, health, and quality standards and varying levels of indirect taxation (such as the **value-added tax** [VAT], a form of sales tax). Europe was also facing growing competition from Japan and the United States.

The term **Eurosclerosis** began to gain common currency in the early 1970s to describe the economic stagnation, double-digit inflation, and high unemployment that afflicted Europe, as well as the relative backwardness of European industry. European businesses were not competing strongly on the global market, scientists and industrialists were failing to collaborate, and the remaining barriers to internal trade denied European businesses full access to a true single market. The period from the 1950s to the early 1970s has been described as one in which the EEC focused on "low policy" issues such as agriculture and building the common market. Changes in the balance of global power combined with the relative U.S. decline, global exchange rate instability, and disparities in the economic performance of EU member states to lead to a shift to "high policy" issues such as foreign policy and economic union[1] and a return to the first principles of the EEC Treaty.

There could be no true single market without monetary union (uniform interest and inflation rates and complete financial integration[2]). In turn, it was a relatively short hop (in neofunctionalist terms) from monetary union to the creation of a single currency, which was a controversial idea because of its implications for national sovereignty; a state that gave up control over its currency would effectively give up control over its national economy. But monetary union was also fundamental to the idea of true economic union and in turn would be a significant step on the road to political union. These issues now began to concern EC leaders, who agreed on the three most important steps in the process of integration since the treaties of Paris and Rome: the launching of the European Monetary System and the signing of the Single European Act and the Treaty on European Union.

Toward Economic and Monetary Union

The EEC Treaty had mentioned the need to "coordinate" economic policies but had given the Community no specific powers to ensure this, and in practice coordination meant little more than "polite ritualistic consultation."[3] Monnet, Spaak, and others had long felt monetary union was essential, but the earliest proposals to move in that direction constantly met with concerns about loss of national sovereignty, especially from Charles de Gaulle.

New momentum came in 1969 with a change of leadership in both France and West Germany; Georges Pompidou was less averse than de Gaulle to strengthening EC ties, and Willy Brandt favored monetary union.[4] A prerequisite for a single currency was a system of fixed exchange rates, but this goal proved elusive. Turbulence in the international monetary system in the late 1960s gave the idea of monetary union new urgency and significance, but EEC leaders disagreed about whether economic union or monetary union should come first.[5] France thought monetary cooperation would lead to economic union, while West Germany thought economic union should come first. There was little question, though, that exchange rate stability was an essential foundation for both the common market and the Common Agricultural Policy.

The principle of **economic and monetary union** (EMU) was agreed on at a 1969 summit of EEC leaders at The Hague, and an ad hoc committee met in 1970 under the leadership of Luxembourg Prime Minister Pierre Werner to look into ways of resolving the differences between the "monetarists" and the "economists." The committee recommended movement on both fronts at the same time and the achievement of fixed exchange rates in stages by 1980.[6] The Six accordingly agreed to control fluctuations in the value of their currencies by holding their exchange rates steady relative to each other while holding their value within ± 1.125 percent of the U.S. dollar in a structure known as the **"snake in the tunnel."** They would meanwhile make more effort to coordinate national economic policies, with their finance ministers meeting at least three times annually. Membership in the snake was also open to states outside the EEC.

The Community could not have chosen a worse time to launch this initiative. The snake was born in February 1971, just six months before the Nixon administration took the United States off the gold standard. The growing U.S. defense budget had combined with weakening productivity, falling exports, rising inflation, and a growing balance-of-payments deficit to worsen U.S. domestic economic problems. In August, Richard Nixon signaled the end of the Bretton Woods system by imposing domestic wage and price controls and placing a 10 percent surcharge on imports. The suddenness of this decision, as Clifford Hackett noted, is still used by Europeans "as a measure of the episodic American failure to discuss solutions to common ailments."[7]

The move led to international monetary turbulence, which was deepened in 1973 with the Yom Kippur war between Egypt and Israel and the oil crisis sparked by the Organization of Petroleum Exporting Countries (OPEC). EC member states gave priority to controlling inflation and encouraging economic growth, and many left the snake: Britain left within eight weeks of joining; France at first refused to join, then joined, then left in 1974, then rejoined in 1975, then left again. Only West Germany, the Benelux countries, and Denmark were able to keep their currencies reasonably stable, and the snake soon became little more than a deutsche mark zone.[8] The goal of achieving EMU by 1980 was quietly abandoned.

A new initiative was launched in 1977, spearheaded by Commission President Roy Jenkins, that led to a proposal in 1978 by West German Chancellor Helmut Kohl and French President Valéry Giscard d'Estaing for a **European Monetary System** (EMS). The EMS was less ambitious and more flexible than the snake but again was based on stabilizing exchange rates. It came into force in March 1979, replacing the snake with an **Exchange Rate Mechanism** (ERM) (operating on a similar basis) founded on a **European Currency Unit** (ECU). The EMS used a system of fixed but adjustable exchange rates, setting the margins of fluctuation at ± 2.25 percent and at ± 6 percent for Italy (and later for Britain and Spain as well).

The goal of the EMS was to create a zone of monetary stability, with governments taking action to keep their currencies as stable as possible relative to the ECU, whose value was calculated on the basis of a basket of national currencies, weighted according to their relative strengths (see Chapter 12). Governments also deposited 20 percent of their gold and foreign currency reserves into a European Monetary Cooperation Fund, to which they could apply for short-term loans if they were having difficulty keeping the value of their currencies steady. The hope was that the ECU would slowly become the normal means of settling international debts between EC members, psychologically preparing them for the idea of a single European currency.

The EMS helped stabilize exchange rates and complemented the tendency among Western economies at the time to focus on controlling inflation.[9] Later, the Single European Act (discussed later in this chapter) helped free up the movement of capital and integrate the markets for financial services.[10] EMU was taken a step further in 1989 with the elaboration by Commission President Jacques Delors of a three-stage plan:

1. Stage one involved strengthening economic and monetary policy coordination with the goal of bringing all twelve currencies into the ERM by July 1990. Eight had joined by 1989; the exceptions were Britain, Greece, Portugal, and Spain. (Even non-EC states—such as Norway and Sweden—joined the ERM.)

2. Stage two originally involved the creation of a European System of Central Banks (or Eurofed) that would coexist with national central banks, working with them in a federal relationship and gradually taking over key monetary responsibilities. Eurofed was to have been in place by January 1994, but it was postponed to run from 1994 until 1997. Instead of a central bank, the European Monetary Institute (EMI) was created in 1994 to pave the way for stage three.

3. Stage three will involve fixed exchange rates and the creation of a single currency. The precondition is that member states will have to comply with economic convergence plans outlined in the Maastricht treaty (discussed later in this chapter), will have to be members of the ERM, and will have to have met the terms of ERM for at least two years without having had to devalue their currencies. If at least seven EU states meet these criteria, the European Council will set a date for stage three and will create a European Central Bank, which will subsequently have sole authority for setting monetary policy and will pave the way for the development of a single currency.

The Commission argued that the benefits of full EMU included a more efficient European economy; a more effective platform from which to deal with inflation, unemployment, and regional economic disparities; and a way of enabling the EC to take a stronger role in the international economy and cushion the effects of external problems and crises. Some of the member states demurred, however, finding that the effort involved in controlling exchange rates caused their economies to overheat. Britain initially stayed out of the ERM because of Margaret Thatcher's refusal to give up control over domestic fiscal policy, while Spain, Portugal, and Greece were concerned about the weaknesses of their currencies. Several exchange rate realignments were made during the 1980s to help member states build monetary stability, but this became more difficult because of the turbulence in world money markets in the early 1990s.

By 1992–1993, the ERM appeared to have collapsed. There was massive speculation on the world's money markets, which central bank intervention and increased interest rates failed to assuage, sending shock waves through the ERM. Britain and Italy pulled out, and Spain, Portugal, and Ireland devalued their currencies. EU finance ministers reached an emergency agreement to allow currencies to fluctuate by ± 15 percent (or to stay within the narrower band if they could).[11] Ironically, the crisis deterred speculation and reinforced currency stability, and EMU was back on track by 1994, although there was doubt about how soon stage three of the Delors Plan could be reached. Despite its problems, the EMS has emerged as a prime example of joint EU decisionmaking.[12]

Completing the Single Market

Economic integration was boosted by the early success of the EMS (or at least its survival against all the odds and its achievement of exchange rate "constraint"[13]) and by a landmark 1978 decision by the European Court of Justice that goods that met the standards of one EC member state could not be barred from sale in another member state (the Cassis de Dijon case; see Chapter 9). But there were concerns that progress on economic integration was being handicapped by inflation and unemployment and by the temptation of member states to protect their home industries and to fragment the internal market with nontariff barriers such as subsidies.[14] Competition from the United States and Japan was also growing, and reports from the Commission and Parliament showed the EC losing ground, especially in high-tech industries.

The 1981 European Council in London decided to ask the Commission and the Council of Ministers to investigate. In response, a decision was reached at the 1983 European Council in Stuttgart to revive the original goal outlined in the Treaty of Rome to create a common (or single) market. The Commission was asked to draw up a concrete list of suggestions, which took the form of a White Paper developed under the direction of internal market commissioner Lord Cockfield. Published in June 1985, the document listed nearly three hundred separate and specific pieces of legislation that would have to be agreed on and implemented to remove all remaining

TABLE 4.1   Exports of EU Member States to Other EU Members, 1970–1992
(as a percentage of all exports; ranked by percentage in 1992)

	1970	1980	1992
Portugal	41.9	54.9	75.2
Ireland	77.6	74.8	75.0
Belgium-Luxembourg	73.4	72.1	74.8
Netherlands	70.7	72.2	71.4
Spain	32.8	49.5	71.1
Austria	47.9	55.1	66.1
Greece	53.1	47.5	63.5
France	54.0	52.0	62.7
Italy	47.8	49.0	57.9
Britain	28.4	42.7	56.0
Sweden	50.3	49.3	55.7
Germany	46.3	49.2	54.4
Finland	45.5	39.2	51.5
Denmark	42.1	49.9	51.2
Average	47.5	50.5	59.1

Source: Calculated from figures in United Nations, *International Trade Statistics Yearbook* (New York: United Nations, 1974, 1986, 1993).

nontariff barriers and create a true single market.[15] This proposal promised to move the process of European integration onto a new plane and to have major political and economic consequences, including a shift in the balance of power away from the member states and toward the EC institutions.

David Cameron has argued that several different economic and political factors came together to make the Single European Act (SEA) possible. The member states had become increasingly dependent on intra-EC trade (see Table 4.1), they were experiencing declining growth and worsening unemployment, the EMS was off the ground, and European business strongly favored the single market. At the same time, the Commission—especially under its new president, Jacques Delors—was building a strong case for the single market. The Court of Justice had helped clear the way with the Cassis decision, and both Parliament and the Council of Ministers were pushing for the kinds of institutional reforms in the EC that would coincidentally fit with the goals of the single market.[16] Even lukewarm Europeans could accept the idea of a single market.

The **Single European Act** was signed in Luxembourg in February 1986 and, after ratification by national legislatures, came into force in July 1987. It had several goals (see Box 4.1), the most important of which was to complete the single market by midnight December 31, 1992. This would be achieved by removing all remaining physical barriers (such as customs and passport controls at internal borders), fiscal barriers (mainly in the form of

BOX 4.1
The Single European Act

The Single European Act not only removed most of the remaining physical, fiscal, and technical barriers to the creation of a true common market, but it also had important political consequences:

- It gave the EC responsibility over new policy areas that had not been mentioned in the Treaty of Rome, such as the environment, research and development, and regional policy.

- It gave new powers to the Court of Justice and eased its workload by creating a Court of First Instance to hear certain kinds of cases.

- It gave legal status to meetings of heads of government under the European Council and gave new powers to the Council of Ministers and the European Parliament (see Chapters 7 and 8).

    Under the new assent procedure, no new members could join the EC or be given associate membership without the approval of an absolute majority in Parliament.

    Under the cooperation procedure, decisionmaking was streamlined, and Parliament was given more power over the Council of Ministers. The use of qualified majority voting in the Council was expanded; unanimity would be needed only for decisions on new members and on the general principles of new policies. For all other decisions, a qualified majority would be sufficient. At the same time, when the Council had made a decision on the basis of a qualified majority, Parliament had the right to amend or reject the proposal, and it could be overruled only by unanimity in the Council. This was a major step toward giving Parliament true legislative powers.

- It gave legal status to European Political Co-operation (EPC) (foreign policy coordination) and said that member states should work toward a European foreign policy and work more closely together on defense and security issues.

- It made economic and monetary union an objective of the EC and promoted **cohesion** (reductions in the gap between rich and poor regions in the EC, thus avoiding a "two-speed Europe").

different levels of indirect taxation), and technical barriers (such as conflicting standards, laws, and qualifications), thereby creating "an area without internal frontiers in which the free movement of goods, persons, services and capital is assured" (SEA, Article 13). Even Margaret Thatcher was pleased: "At last, I felt, we were going to get the Community back on course, concentrating on its role as a huge market, with all the opportunities that would bring to our industries."[17]

The Single European Act was a remarkable achievement, widely acclaimed as the single most important and successful step in the process of European integration since the Treaty of Rome. In practical terms, it meant that the Commission and the Council of Ministers had to agree on 282 new pieces of legislation, which then had to be applied at the national level. To give the member states at least two years to implement those laws, they all had to be agreed on by the end of 1990. In the event, the deadline came and went with only 92 percent of the proposals adopted by the Council of Ministers and only 79 percent adopted and transposed into national law.[18] (Ironically, Denmark and Britain had the best implementation rates.) Regardless, the single market went into force in January 1993 with the understanding that the backlog of legislation would be cleared as soon as possible.

The SEA created the single biggest market and trading unit in the world. Its effects included the following: Many internal passport and customs controls were eased or lifted; banks could do business throughout the Community; companies could do business and sell their products throughout the Community, there was little to prevent EC residents from living, working, opening bank accounts, and drawing pensions anywhere in the EC; protectionism became illegal; and monopolies on everything from the supply of electricity to telecommunications were broken down. In legal terms, it was now almost as easy for Europeans to move among the twelve member states as it was for Americans to move throughout the United States. In short, the dream of British Foreign Secretary Ernest Bevin in 1951—"to be able to take a ticket at Victoria Station [in London] and go anywhere I damn well please"—had finally (almost) come true.

Social and Regional Integration

Social policy was long a poor relation of economic and political integration. Although the EEC Treaty made provision for the development of an EEC social policy, the issue was left in the hands of the member states and was very narrowly defined. It emphasized improved working conditions and standards of living for workers, equal pay for equal work among men and women, social security for migrant workers, and more geographical and occupational mobility for workers. The result was that social issues received little attention until the mid-1970s, when pressure began to grow to mitigate negative changes in the workplace brought on by increased competition and the opening of markets.

As it has since evolved, social policy covers such issues as unemployment, poverty, and consumer protection, with the overall goal of promoting economic and social cohesion. Even in the mid-1960s (before the poorer Mediterranean states and Ireland had joined), per capita GDP in the EEC's ten richest regions was nearly four times greater than that in its ten poorest regions. The gap closed in the early 1970s but grew again with the accession of Britain and Ireland. With the accession of Greece in 1981, the gap grew to the point at which the richest regions were five times richer than the poorest.[19] Social and regional policy has focused on trying to close the gap by helping poorer regions, revitalizing those affected by serious industrial decline, working to combat long-term unemployment, providing youth job training, and helping to develop rural areas. Economic assistance is given by the Commission in the form of grants from three separate funds known collectively as **structural funds**: the European Social Fund, the European Regional Development Fund, and part of the European Agricultural Guidance and Guarantee Fund (see Chapter 13).

The first real attempts to improve the quality of life and social security came only with the creation of the European Social Fund (ESF) in 1974. Its initial focus was employment and retraining, but in 1983 the Council of Ministers decided it should focus on youth unemployment and job creation in the poorest parts of the EC. The Single European Act made cohesion a central part of economic integration, under the assumption that the single market would create new jobs but that this would be insufficient. A boost for social policy came in 1989 with the Charter of Fundamental Social Rights for Workers (the Social Charter), which promoted free movement of workers, fair pay, better living and working conditions, freedom of association, and protection of children and adolescents. The Social Charter was adopted by eleven EC states at the December 1989 European Council, with Britain's Conservative government opting out because it did not want to give up control over employment law and policies.

The second major element in social policy was the European Regional Development Fund (ERDF). The Commission had given relatively little attention to regional disparities until Britain and Ireland joined the EEC in 1973, changing the economic balance of the Community because of their relatively low levels of prosperity. The Commission sponsored the 1973 Thomson Report on the regional implications of enlargement, which concluded that these disparities were an obstacle to a "balanced expansion" in economic activity and to EMU.[20] Although some development funds had been channeled through the European Investment Bank during the 1960s, it was clear that something much more was needed.

France and West Germany became interested in regional policy as a means of helping Britain integrate with its new partners, and the government of Prime Minister Edward Heath promoted the creation of a regional fund as a way of making EEC membership more palatable to Britons concerned about the potential costs of membership.[21] Agreement was reached among the Six to launch the ERDF in 1973, but plans were disrupted by the fiscal and economic crises of 1973. The Fund was finally launched in 1975. It was made clear that ERDF funds would not replace national spending on the development of poorer regions but instead would complement them (the concept of "additionality"). At most, ERDF funds would match existing spending, and they could be used only for projects that would create new jobs in industry or services or improve infrastructure. The identification of priority regions was left up to the member states.

Structural funds accounted for 18 percent of EC expenditures in 1984 and had risen to 32 percent (nearly $27 billion) by 1993. Despite increases in the funds made available under ERDF, regional disparities in the EU remain; the gap between the highest and lowest income levels in the EU is twice that in the United States, and neither the EU nor the member states have been able to deal effectively with unemployment, which ranged from 7 to 14 percent in most EU states in early 1995 compared with 5.4 percent in the United States and 3.0 percent in Japan.

Toward Political Union

The highly controversial idea of political integration long received less attention because of a prevailing feeling that there was little hope of building political union without first achieving economic union. False starts had been made with the European Political Community and with an attempt in 1961 to draw up a political charter that would spell out the terms of political union (the Fouchet Plan, named for Christian Fouchet, French ambassador to Denmark[22]). In the 1960s the foreign ministers of the Six looked at ways of promoting political union and concluded that it would best be done outside the EC framework rather than by giving the EC itself more power.

A report drawn up by Belgian diplomat Etienne Davignon and published in 1970 argued that a first step should be taken by encouraging cooperation in an area in which an obvious common set of interests already existed; he felt that foreign policy coordination was the answer, especially given the growing divergence between U.S. and Western European policies. The Davignon Report recommended quarterly meetings of the six foreign ministers, liaison among EC ambassadors in foreign capitals, and common EC instructions on certain matters for those ambassadors.

At Community summits in 1972 and 1974, proposals were tabled for reaching political union by 1980—a target that was wildly unrealistic, given prevailing ideas about the EC and about the work that needed to be done to achieve economic integration. Work developed instead on the coordination of foreign policies, or **European Political Cooperation** (EPC). EPC achieved some early successes, such as the 1970 joint EC policy declaration on the Middle East and the signing of the Yaoundé Conventions on aid to poorer countries. In 1975, the Final Act of the Conference on Security and Cooperation in Europe (held in Helsinki) was signed by Italian Prime Minister Aldo Moro "in the name of the European Community." By 1976, EC ambassadors to the UN were meeting weekly to coordinate their actions.

EPC was finally given legal status with the Single European Act. It worked well in some areas but was more reactive than proactive. This became clear during the 1990–1991 Gulf crisis when the EC issued common demands to the Iraqi regime and imposed an embargo on Iraqi oil imports, but the member states contributed at very different levels to the 1991 counterinvasion. Differences also became clear in December 1991 when Germany unilaterally recognized Croatia and Slovenia without conferring with its EC partners (see Chapter 15).

Political union remained on the agenda of European Councils during the 1970s and 1980s, with the focus for discussion coming from reports written by Belgian Prime Minister Leo Tindemans in 1976, the West German and Italian Foreign Ministers Hans-Dietrich Genscher and Emilio Colombo in 1981, and a group of Members of the European Parliament (MEPs) under the leadership of Italian Altiero Spinelli in 1984. Tindemans recommended continuing cooperation on foreign and economic policies, but he also suggested more powers for the European Council and a new and more powerful bicameral Parliament; the Spinelli report, motivated in part by a concern among MEPs to prove the worth of the now directly elected Parliament,[23] also suggested more powers for the European Council and the European Parliament (EP), and proposed a draft treaty on European Union. The reports set off a discussion about reforming EC institutions in a way that would allow the Community to respond more quickly and effectively to emergencies and to take real steps toward economic and political integration.

Determined to reassert French leadership in the EC, President François Mitterrand focused on the political union theme at the Fontainebleau European Council summit in 1984, with the result that a decision was taken at Milan in June 1985 to open an intergovernmental conference (IGC) on political union. The IGC finally opened in December 1990, alongside an IGC on economic and monetary union. The outcome was the **Treaty on European Union,** agreed at the Maastricht European Council summit in December 1991 and signed by the EC foreign and economics ministers in February 1992 (see Box 4.2). The original wording of the draft treaty mentioned the goal of federal union, but Britain balked at this, so it was changed to "an ever closer union among the peoples of Europe, in which decisions are taken as closely as possible to the citizen."

BOX 4.2
The Treaty on European Union

The Maastricht treaty has several elements:

- The creation of the European Union, a new label meant to symbolize the next stage in the process of European integration and based on three "pillars": a reformed and strengthened European Community and two areas in which there was to be more regularized intergovernmental cooperation—a Common Foreign and Security Policy (CFSP) and home affairs and justice. Responsibility for the CFSP would remain with the individual governments rather than being given to the EU.

- A timetable for the creation of a single European currency by January 1999 at the latest. For this to happen, a majority of member states would have to achieve inflation rates that were no more than 1.5 percent higher than the three lowest national rates in the EU, set long-term interest rates that were no more than 3 percent higher than the three lowest EU rates, reduce their budget deficits to less than 3 percent of GDP, and avoid having to devalue their currencies against any of those in the ERM for at least two years.

  If these terms were not met by the end of 1996, the EU leaders would decide in mid-1998 which EC states were ready for EMU, and they could launch a limited currency union among those states in January 1999. The European Central Bank would need to have been operating for at least six months before exchange rates could be fixed. Britain and Denmark were given the right to "opt out" of the final stage of EMU (or to "opt in," as British Prime Minister John Major preferred to put it).

- Extension of EU responsibility to new areas such as consumer protection, public health policy, transportation, education, and (except in Britain) social policy. All but Britain adopted the Social Charter on workers' rights.

- More intergovernmental cooperation on immigration and asylum, the creation of a European police intelligence agency (Europol) to combat organized crime and drug trafficking, the creation of a new Committee of the Regions (see Chapter 10), and more regional funds for poorer EC states.

- New rights for European citizens and the creation of an ambiguous European Union "citizenship," meaning, for example, the rights of citizens to live wherever they like in the EU and to stand for and vote in local and European elections.

- More powers for the European Parliament, including the codecision procedure under which certain kinds of legislation are subject to a third reading in Parliament before they can be adopted by the Council of Ministers (see Chapter 8).

The Maastricht treaty had to be ratified by the twelve member states before it came into force. A major setback came with its rejection in a Danish referendum in June 1992. Following agreement that Denmark could opt out of the single currency, common defense arrangements, European citizenship, and cooperation on justice and home affairs, a second referendum was held in May 1993, and the treaty was accepted. Following ratification in the other eleven states, the Maastricht treaty came into force in November 1993, eleven months late. With its passage, the European Community became one of the three "pillars" that made up the European Union. Although Maastricht proved a disappointment for European federalists, is often criticized as being "a treaty too far," and is often described as untidy, both Helmut Kohl and Dutch Prime Minister Ruud Lubbers declared that it had taken the EU beyond the point of no return.

Enlargement III: Looking North and East

Although any European state can apply to join the EU, in practice there are at least five basic requirements: In addition to being European and democratic, an applicant must follow free-market economic policies, accept the terms of Maastricht, and accept the **acquis communitaire** (the body of laws and regulations already adopted by the EU). Deciding which countries meet these criteria has been difficult, not least because of the problem of defining "Europe." There was little question about rejecting an application from Morocco in 1987, but the eastern borders of Europe are more debatable. Because these borders are usually demarked by the Ural Mountains, twenty-seven countries theoretically qualified for membership in 1992: six in Western Europe, seven in Eastern Europe, the three Baltic states, three former Soviet republics, the five former Yugoslavian states, and three Mediterranean states.

The issue of future expansion was divided in the 1980s and early 1990s by a debate over **deepening versus widening**. Deepeners wanted the EU to develop closer ties before it took on new members, while wideners argued that membership should be opened to other states immediately. John Major favored widening mainly because he wanted the process of integration to slow down, while Helmut Kohl wanted to bring in new Eastern European members to prevent them from breaking down into ethnic rivalries, as had occurred in Yugoslavia.

There were few questions about the attraction of EU membership for other Western European countries, and changes in Eastern Europe during 1989–1991 further broadened the possibilities (most notably by allowing East Germany into the EU through the back door in 1990). In 1991 Commission President Jacques Delors told the existing members to prepare

TABLE 4.2 Enlargement of the European Union

	Membership Application Lodged	Associate Membership	Full Membership
Britain	1961, 1967, 1969	—	1973
Ireland	1961, 1967, 1969	—	1973
Denmark	1961, 1967, 1969	—	1973
Norway	1962, 1967, 1969, 1992	—	—
Greece	1975	1961	1981
Spain	1977	—	1986
Portugal	1977	—	1986
Finland	1992	—	1995
Austria	1989	—	1995
Sweden	1991	—	1995
Turkey	1987	1963	—
Cyprus	1990	1972	—
Malta	1990	1970	—
Morocco	1987	—	—
Hungary	1994	1994[a]	—
Poland	1994	1994[a]	—

[a]Europe Agreements.

for an EU of twenty-four or even thirty members. Other Western European states were long the most obvious candidates for membership, if only because they would have to make the fewest adjustments. As a first step, the Luxembourg Declaration of 1984 had opened the door to cooperation between the EC and EFTA in areas of mutual interest. In 1989, Delors invited the seven EFTA members to open negotiations with the EU with the goal of creating a European Economic Space. This would link the nineteen members of the Community and EFTA, allowing EFTA some input into designing EC policies while its members began adopting EC regulations on trade.

In 1990, negotiations began on the creation of the **European Economic Area** (EEA), under which the terms of the SEA would be extended to the seven EFTA members, in return for which they would accept the rules of the single market. In a sense, the EEA would place EFTA states in a holding pattern prior to full EC membership, making them nonvoting associate members of the EC. The proposal made economic sense, given that 55 percent of EFTA exports went to the EC and 26 percent of EC exports went to EFTA.[24] The EFTA states were also stable and wealthy and would have to make relatively few adjustments to integrate themselves into the single market. Problems did arise, though. Norway and Sweden had tighter environmental regulations than those of the EC states and did not want to be obliged to import road vehicles with less stringent emission controls; Finland was concerned about its neutrality (as were Austria and Sweden) and about possible foreign ownership of its timber industry; Switzerland did not want to allow EC citizens to have residency rights. The collapse of the Soviet Union largely removed the problem of neutrality;[25] further, Ireland had already proved that it was possible to be a member of the EC and remain neutral.

Negotiations on the EEA were completed in February 1992, but the Swiss turned down membership in a December 1992 referendum; thus, only six EFTA states joined when the EEA finally came into force on January 1, 1994. Almost before it was born, however, the EEA had begun to lose its relevance because Austria, Sweden, Norway, and Finland had already applied for EC membership. Negotiations were completed in early 1994, referenda were held in each country, and all but Norway (where once again the vote went against membership) joined the EU in January 1995. This left just Norway, Switzerland, Iceland, and tiny Liechtenstein in EFTA.

The Swiss had considered applying for EC membership in 1992, but they rejected the EEA and are now completely surrounded by the EU. Demands on Switzerland to open its highways to EU trucks and intra-EU trade will undoubtedly increase the pressures for EU membership, although its neutrality and unique system of government remain major obstacles.[26] Iceland, for its part, has a population of just 300,000, relies largely on exports of fish, and does more than half its trade with the EU; it too will find the logic of joining the EU increasingly difficult to resist. With a population of just 30,000, Liechtenstein is little more than an enclave of Switzerland and will likely follow the Swiss lead.

Looking further east—and further into the future—moves us deeper into the realm of speculation. Turkey, Cyprus, and Malta have long had associate membership of the EU and have applied for full membership, but each has problems:

- The EC agreed in 1963 that Turkish membership was possible, but Turkey is big, poor, and predominantly Islamic (which raises economic and social questions); its application is opposed by Greece; and there is a debate about whether it is really European (Europe ends at the Bosphorus, so only a small part of Turkey is actually in Europe). On the other hand, it could provide a valuable bridge between the EU and the Middle East, a role given new significance by problems in the former USSR and the Balkans.[27] It has been an associate member since 1963, and applied for full membership in 1987.

- Cyprus has political problems, not the least of which is the division between Greek and Turkish sectors that has been in place since 1974. It has had associate membership since 1972 and applied for full membership in 1990.

- Malta has roughly the same population as Luxembourg and Iceland (about 350,000), but it is much poorer. There are also doubts about its links with Libya and about whether it should be granted the influence membership would give it over economic giants such as Germany. It has had associate membership since 1970 and applied for full membership in 1990.

The collapse of the USSR and the spread of democracy and free-market policies to Eastern Europe have raised the possibility of the EU looking east. There are strong political and economic arguments in favor. EU membership would likely underpin the transition for these states[28] in the same way it did for Greece, Portugal, and Spain; it would open up new investment opportunities; and it would pull Eastern Europe into a strategic relationship with the West that could be useful if problems in (or with) Russia worsen. In a sense, German reunification has been a test case; the sooner its problems can be ironed out, the stronger the case for admitting other Eastern European states. **Europe Agreements** were signed in the early 1990s with Poland, Hungary, the Czech Republic, Slovakia, Romania, and Bulgaria; those with Poland and Hungary came into effect in February 1994, paving the way for them to become the first East European states to join the EU.

Looking still further east, membership for the three Baltic states (Latvia, Lithuania, and Estonia) and the three former Soviet republics (Ukraine, Belarus, and Moldova) is not impossible, but this will depend on the resolution of questions over their relationship with Russia and on how quickly they are able to make the transition to free market policies. For the five former Yugoslavian states, membership will depend on a resolution of the social and political tensions in the region.

Summary and Conclusions

The ink had barely dried on the 1951 Treaty of Paris before the process of European integration was being dismissed by skeptics, and its demise has been predicted regularly ever since. But in the face of the doubters and despite many problems, much has been achieved. From a time in the 1970s when the experiment seemed to have become stuck in the doldrums, in the last decade the EU has picked up new speed and vitality.

- The single market was virtually completed by the early 1990s, opening up vast new opportunities for European business.

- Monetary union may occasionally have been put on life support, but its problems have yet to be declared terminal. The ERM broke down

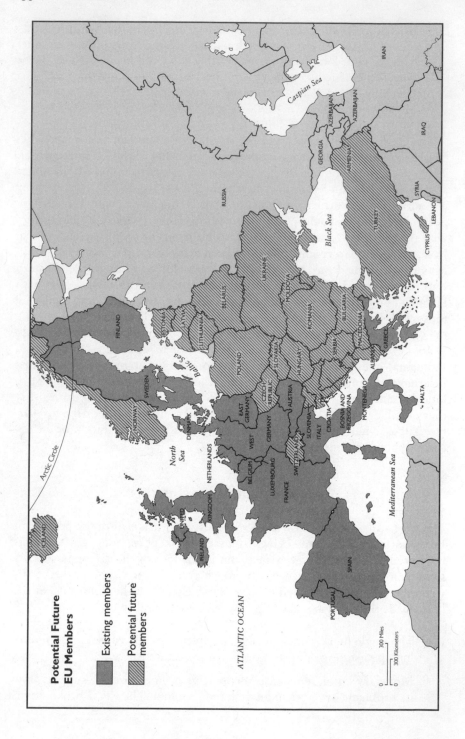

**Potential Future
EU Members**

Existing members

Potential future
members

briefly in 1993 and was in trouble again as this book went to press, but each crisis has given Europe's economists more insight into the problems of building a single currency.

- For all its problems, the Maastricht treaty was a substantial step toward political union.

- The member states have developed common positions in a wide range of policy areas—including social issues, internal security, and foreign policy—and have built a large body of common laws and regulations.

- Much of what the EU does is still shrouded in secrecy, and few of its officials are publicly accountable, but the EU has reformed its institutions to afford greater public input.

- EU membership has grown to fifteen; it now reaches from the Arctic Circle to the Aegean, from Berlin to the Straits of Gibraltar, and from Sicily to the North Atlantic coast of Ireland. It has a total population of nearly 370 million and a GDP of $6.8 trillion, and it accounts for 42 percent of all world trade. Meanwhile, several neighboring states hope to join the EU in the next few years.

Notes

1. Peter Ludlow, *Beyond 1992: Europe and Its World Partners* (Brussels: Center for European Policy Studies, 1989), 1–4.

2. George Zis, "European Monetary Union: The Case for Complete Monetary Integration," in Frank McDonald and Stephen Dearden (Eds.), *European Economic Integration* (London: Longman, 1992).

3. Tommaso Paddoa-Schioppa, *Financial and Monetary Integration in Europe: 1990, 1992 and Beyond* (New York: Group of Thirty, 1990), 18.

4. John Pinder, *European Community: The Building of a Union* (Oxford: Oxford University Press, 1991), 120–121.

5. Derek W. Urwin, *The Community of Europe*, 2d ed. (Harlow, Essex: Longman, 1995), 155.

6. Commission of the European Communities, "Economic and Monetary Union in the Community" (the Werner Report), *Bulletin of the European Communities*, Supplement 11 (1970).

7. Clifford Hackett, *Cautious Revolution: The European Community Arrives* (Westport, Conn.: Greenwood Press, 1990), 131.

8. Loukas Tsoukalis, *The New European Economy: The Politics and Economics of Integration* (Oxford: Oxford University Press, 1993), 181.

9. Hugo M. Kaufmann and Stephen Overturf, "Progress Within the European Monetary System," in Leon Hurwitz and Christian Lequesne (Eds.), *The State of the European Community, Vol. 1: Policies, Institutions and Debates in the Transition Years* (Boulder: Lynne Rienner, 1991), 186.

10. Pinder, *European Community,* 130–135.

11. Urwin, *Community of Europe,* 260.

12. Tommaso Paddoa-Schioppa, *Efficiency, Stability, and Equity: A Strategy for the Evolution of the Economic System of the European Community: A Report* (Oxford: Oxford University Press, 1987), 371.

13. Commission of the European Communities, *Report on Economic and Monetary Union in the European Community* (the Delors Report) (Luxembourg: Office for Official Publications of the European Communities, 1989).

14. Pinder, *European Community,* 65.

15. Commission of the European Communities, *Completing the Internal Market: The White Paper* (Luxembourg: Office for Official Publications of the European Communities, 1985).

16. David R. Cameron, "The 1992 Initiative: Causes and Consequences," in Alberta Sbragia (Ed.), *Euro-Politics: Institutions and Policymaking in the "New" European Community* (Washington, D.C.: Brookings Institution, 1992), 36–56.

17. Margaret Thatcher, *The Downing Street Years* (New York: HarperCollins, 1993), 556.

18. *Eurecom* 4:11 (December 1992).

19. Stephen George, *Politics and Policy in the European Community,* 2d ed. (Oxford: Oxford University Press, 1991), 190–191.

20. Commission of the European Communities, *Report on the Regional Problems of the Enlarged Community* (the Thomson Report), COM(73)550 (Brussels: Commission of the European Communities, 1973).

21. George, *Politics and Policy,* 193.

22. See Urwin, *Community of Europe,* 104–107.

23. Hackett, *Cautious Revolution,* 67; Rosa Maria Alonso Terme, "From the Draft Treaty of 1984 to the Intergovernmental Conferences of 1991," in Reinhardt Rummel (Ed.), *Toward Political Union: Planning a Common Foreign and Security Policy in the European Community* (Boulder: Westview Press, 1992), 269–270.

24. Rene Schwok, "EC-EFTA Relations," in Hurwitz and Lequesne, *The State of the European Community, Vol. 1.*

25. Ibid.

26. François Saint-Ouen, "Facing European Integration: The Case of Switzerland," *Journal of Common Market Studies* 26:3 (March 1988), 273–285.

27. Anna Michalski and Helen Wallace, *The European Community: The Challenge of Enlargement* (London: Royal Institute of International Affairs, 1992), 122.

28. Richard E. Baldwin, *Towards an Integrated Europe* (London: Centre for Economic Policy Research, 1994), 158.

Further Reading

Daniel Gros and Niels Thygesen. *European Monetary Integration: From the European Monetary System to European Monetary Union* (London: Longman, 1992).

A history of European monetary integration that discusses the evolution of the European Monetary System and prospects for EMU.

Gregory Treverton (Ed.). *The Shape of the New Europe* (New York: Council on Foreign Relations Press, 1992).

An edited collection of chapters written by scholars of European integration on Europe's prospects in the wake of the completion of the single market.

Peter Luff. *The Simple Guide to Maastricht* (London: European Movement, 1992).

A short (sixty-page) and accessible guide to the intricacies of the Treaty on European Union.

Andrew Duff, John Pinder, and Roy Pryce (Eds.). *Maastricht and Beyond: Building the European Union* (New York: Routledge, 1994).

A multiauthor collection that looks in detail at the content of Maastricht and assesses its likely effects on the policies and institutions of the EU.

Anna Michalski and Helen Wallace. *The European Community: The Challenge of Enlargement* (London: Royal Institute of International Affairs, 1992).

A short and succinct discussion of the potential members of the EU and the implications of enlargement.

5

Elaboration: The European Union Today

The emergence of the European Union has complicated discussions about the motives behind international cooperation and the nature of international relations, mainly because the EU only partly fits with conventional ideas about the ways societies organize and govern themselves.

Most political scientists agree that the EU is not a "state" because it lacks many of the conventional features of a state, including a strong and separate legal identity, political unity and sovereignty, powers of coercion, and significant financial independence. There may be a European bureaucracy and a growing body of European law—a proto-government—but there is no European police force, and the EU cannot yet raise direct and universal taxes. At the same time, although it has some of the features of an international organization, it has developed unprecedented levels of power and influence over its members. This has led some scholars to argue that the EU is not really an institution but is better approached as an ideal, a process, a regime, or even a network that has involved not so much a transfer of powers as a pooling of sovereignty.[1]

Jean Monnet argued in 1975 that he saw no point in trying to imagine what political form the United States of Europe would take and that "the words about which people argue—federation or confederation—are inadequate and imprecise."[2] He and his contemporaries might have been able to avoid the issue, but it is less easily avoided today. The idea of Europe has taken on new substance, making it essential to understand its political form and the direction in which the process of European integration is headed. That process has effectively gone beyond the point of no return; the ties Europeans have built since 1945 are too tightly knotted to be easily undone and have committed them to sinking or swimming together. Despite the doubts of the skeptics, political union is spoken of today less in terms of "if" than in terms of "when" and "how."

As discussed in the Preface, part of the reason so many Europeans and Americans are still confused and unclear about the European Union is because it has changed its form so often. Chapter 1 looked at the different theories that have been proposed to explain how and why integration occurs, and Chapters 2–4 looked at the stages in the process of European integration. This chapter attempts to pin down the identity of the European Union today—to describe the features of the EU as a **polity** (a politically organized system or regime) and to understand what the EU has become by looking at what it means to its citizens and to those outside Europe. The way it looks today is not the way it will look in five or ten years, so this chapter can be nothing more than a portrait in time of an entity that is growing and evolving. Like a snapshot of a child, we can use it to make some educated guesses about what the EU will probably become, but there is still some growing to be done, and the adult will be unlike any other political entity we have seen before.

The European Polity

The key to understanding the EU may be to see it as being caught in a complex network of competing tensions. Imagine someone trying to cross a patch of ground but being attached by ropes to several people standing on the periphery trying to pull that person in their direction. The people doing the pulling are of varying sizes and strengths, and their levels of energy and enthusiasm wax and wane, so the person being pulled moves according to the relative forces being applied. Eventually, that person will be pulled to a point where all those forces are in equilibrium.

At least five different sets of forces have been at work in Europe, pulling the EU in several directions:

1. Intergovernmental versus supranational. One of the fundamental tensions in the process of European integration has been that between the governments of the member states, which are trying to preserve their sovereignty by relating to each other as equals, and the different forces and impulses that compel or encourage them to give up that sovereignty to a new supranational authority.

2. Independence versus dependence. No person or state is truly independent. Europe after World War II consisted of several legally independent polities, but they were linked more closely than some of them cared to admit by history, culture, and shared political and economic interests. The process of integration has caused those ties to be strengthened and to have a clearer definition, so that the EU member states are moving from a high degree of independence to a high degree of mutual dependence.

3. Competition versus cooperation. The history of Europe until 1945 was one of competition, conflict, and constantly changing alliances and balances of power. Some of those conflicts persist, and the balance of power continues to change, but it does so inclusively rather than exclusively and out of a sense of both cooperation and competition. The conflicting goals of separate states have been replaced by the common goal of promoting mutual interests.

4. Autonomy versus unity. The process of integration has reduced the freedom of action of individual European states and has steadily forced them to work together by pulling down the structural, political, technical, physical, fiscal, and attitudinal barriers that have divided them. As the autonomy of the states declines, so does their individual sovereignty, and the possibility of European political union becomes more real.

5. Elitism versus democracy. The citizens of Western Europe have had relatively little input into the development of the EU, because most of the initiatives have come from political, economic, and social elites. Only the European Parliament is directly elected, but it has less power over decisionmaking than other appointed or indirectly elected bodies. The balance is changing, though, as citizens become more interested and involved in influencing EU policy.

Where the European Union sits on these five different continua is debatable, but it is probably somewhere in the shaded area of the diagram in Figure 5.1. Wherever the EU now sits and wherever it is headed, its political form has always had some combination of objective features and characteristics at a given point in time. What are those features in the mid-1990s?

First, the European Union has gone well beyond the powers of any international organization that has ever existed, and it has developed an unprecedented level of authority over its constituent members. It is not yet a federation nor even a confederation, and although it has several different "governing" institutions, it is not yet a government in itself; it is more like a network of institutions and national governments, all of which are still jostling to define their powers relative to the other institutions and member states. Although *supranationalism* may describe the political process of the EU, it has been argued that the EU has always rested ultimately on a set of intergovernmental bargains.[3] Opinion is divided about the extent to which it has moved beyond those kinds of bargains; realists argue that the member states are still the key actors and that integration moves according to the decisions they take, whereas neofunctionalists argue that integration has its own expansive logic and has taken on an irresistible life and momentum of its own.

FIGURE 5.1 Competing Tensions in the Process of European Integration

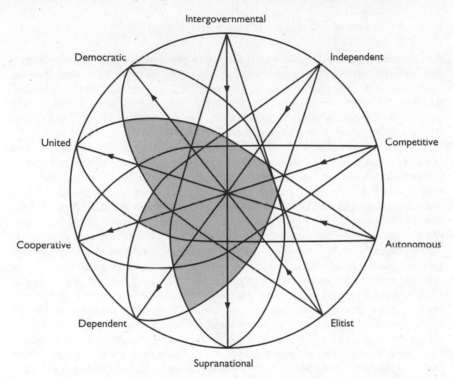

Second, although it has its own body of treaties and laws that amount to something like a constitution (see Box 5.1) and has a court that can adjudicate disputes between its member states, the EU has limited institutional independence and limited powers of coercion. It lacks the powers to raise taxes and to implement laws, it relies almost entirely on the voluntary compliance of the member states, and none of its institutions has either the power or the personnel to directly enforce the law. It has no police force (yet), no equivalent of the IRS or the FBI, and no common defense force.

Third, the EU has its own executive (the European Commission) and a directly elected proto-legislature (the European Parliament), but so much power has been kept in the hands of the intergovernmental Council of Ministers (where the key decisions are taken) that the Commission remains largely a servant of the national governments, and the Parliament has yet to win the kinds of powers to introduce, discuss, amend, reject, or accept laws that would make it a true legislature. Each of these institutions looks very different today from the way it looked in 1960, and the number of institutions has grown as the EU decisionmaking process has become more stable

BOX 5.1
A Constitution for Europe

A constitution, by definition, is a contract between a government and its citizens that outlines their relative powers, obligations, and responsibilities. Almost every modern state has a constitution, but the constitutions vary in terms of the extent to which they are followed and respected and the extent to which they actually make sense; human society contains so many ambiguities and contradictions that constitutions (like old trucks) need constant tinkering and refining to keep them roadworthy.

The European Union does not yet have a constitution in the sense of a single written document, but it does have a set of treaties, a rapidly expanding body of laws, and a growing body of traditions and legal precedents that together amount to something like a constitution. There have been so many amendments to the founding treaties that the powers and responsibilities of the EU are still ambiguous in many places and are still open to different interpretations. The same is true of the U.S. Constitution, which would be unintelligible in places were it not for more than two hundred years' worth of amendments and judicial interpretation and that in parts is anachronistic. For example, the "right" to bear arms and the ban on quartering troops in private homes grew out of particular historical circumstances, and the former idea is only kept alive today by opponents of gun control.

To have any meaning, a constitution must be respected, must have stability and permanence, must be capable of being enforced, and must be grounded in the reality of the prevailing political and social character of the state or body to which it applies; the greater the gap between constitutional principles and political reality, the weaker the constitution. The extent to which the treaties and laws of the EU meet these conditions is debatable. Each new treaty that is agreed on and each new law that is passed makes the European "constitution" increasingly messy. Its major guardian remains the European Court of Justice, which has helped to "constitutionalize" the founding treaties by trying to remove the differences between the Treaty of Rome and a conventional constitution, notably the lack of safeguards for individual rights and the absence of a constitutional right to European citizenship.[1]

Constitutions generally grow out of a crisis (such as a war or a revolution) or some watershed event (such as the independence of a former colony). No such crises or events have occurred in the European case; the EU has taken several decades to get to where it is today and has much more evolving to do. If present trends continue, a point will come when the EU has gained enough momentum and internal stability to make the need for a written constitution irresistible. The document that results will be evolutionary rather than revolutionary. The IGCs on economic and political union in 1990–1991 were important steps in that process, and the 1996 IGC on political union will almost certainly prove to be another.

Notes

1. G. Federico Mancini, "The Making of a Constitution for Europe," in Robert O. Keohane and Stanley Hoffmann (Eds.), *The New European Community: Decisionmaking and Institutional Change* (Boulder: Westview Press, 1991).

and predictable and its powers and responsibilities have grown. We should expect many more changes before the powers of these institutions are carved in stone.

Fourth, the EU is not very democratic. Most scholars agree that while democracy is noble in theory, most states have been built out of the self-interest of elites. The European Coal and Steel Community was the brainchild of a few members of the elites of the six founding states, and almost every subsequent expansion of European institutions and every key policy decision has been taken by political and economic elites. The balance is changing, though, and public opinion has played an increasingly important role since the institution of direct elections to the European Parliament in 1979. The Danish rejection of Maastricht in June 1992 also emphasized how dangerous it would be for the elites to overlook (and make assumptions about) the opinions of the people.

Finally, although the EU does not yet have exclusive responsibility for any single policy area, it has effectively taken over most or all responsibility for making and implementing policy on external and internal trade, agriculture, and foreign affairs. In other areas (such as the environment) the trend is in favor of the EU, while issues such as education, policing, and criminal law still rest largely with the member states (a situation that is little different from the federal government in the United States). The EU has also gone well beyond focusing on economic integration and has moved into the realms of social and political integration as well. The Single European Act and the Maastricht treaty represented quantum leaps in the process of the transfer (or pooling) of policy responsibility, and the agreement on a single currency will provide the final step in the integration of economic policy. Economic union will in turn provide effectively irresistible pressures to complete the integration of other internal policy issues.

All of this still begs the question of what kind of polity the European Union has become. Most people use labels to help them understand their environment, but there are no easy labels for the EU, or at least none on which most scholars can agree. Europeans know the dangers of the divisions they are leaving behind but are much less clear about the features of the unity toward which they are moving. As Benjamin Franklin argued after trying to find a model on which the new U.S. republic could be based, history consists only of beacon lights "which give warning of the course to be shunned, without pointing out that which ought to be pursued."[4] The EU today has some of the elements of a state but lacks others; it has some of the elements of a federation but lacks others; it is intergovernmental in some ways but supranationalist in others. To help pin down its character, we need to look in more detail at three core sets of ideas outlined briefly in Chapter 1, which together may hold the key to understanding what the European Union has become.

Confederalism

Confederalism is a system of government or administration in which two or more distinct political units keep their separate identity but hand specified powers to a higher authority for reasons of convenience, mutual security, or efficiency. The local units are sovereign, and the higher authority is relatively weak; it exists solely at the discretion of the local units and can do only what they allow it to do. Federalism is different in the sense that it involves the local units surrendering some of their sovereignty and giving up power over joint interests to a new and permanent national level of government. Both, in turn, are distinct from the unitary system of government used in countries such as Britain, France, Japan, and Italy, in which sovereignty rests almost entirely with the national government, which can abolish or amend local units at will.

Among the few examples of confederalism in practice at the state level are the United States in 1776–1788 and—to some extent—Switzerland today. In the case of the United States, the founders were concerned in equal measure about chaos (too little government) and tyranny (too much government), and until 1788 the original colonies related to each other as a loose confederation. The assumption was that they might cooperate sufficiently to eventually form a common system of government, but they did not do so; the 1781 Articles of Confederation created little more than a "league of friendship" that could not levy taxes or regulate commerce, and the army depended on state militias for its support. Only in 1787 did work begin on developing an entirely new federal system of government, redefining the idea of federalism in the process.

For its part, Switzerland was more purely confederal until 1798, and although it is now technically a federation, it has given up far fewer powers to the national government than has been the case in the United States. The Swiss encourage direct democracy by holding national referenda, have a Federal Assembly elected by proportional representation, and are governed by a Federal Council elected by the Assembly. One of the members of the Council is appointed to a one-year term as head of state and head of government.

The European Union is confederal in several ways. First, decisions taken by the leaders of the member states have resulted in a transfer of some authority from the parts to the whole, but the member states still have the upper hand, and the EU is governed as a whole through a process of negotiation and bargaining among national governments. Second, the member states are still distinct units with separate identities, have their own national currencies, can sign bilateral treaties with other states, and can still (tenuously) argue that the EU institutions exist at their discretion. A member state could theoretically leave the EU if it wished, and its action would not legally be defined as secession. Attempts to leave federations, by contrast, have almost always been defined as secession and have usually led to civil war (cf. the attempted secession of the Confederacy from the United States in 1861, of Biafra from Nigeria in 1967, and of Chechnya from Russia in 1994–1995). Third, there is no European government in the sense that the EU has recognizable leaders, such as a president, a foreign minister, or a cabinet. Finally, the EU may have its own flag and anthem, but most citizens still hold a much higher sense of allegiance toward national flags, anthems, and other symbols; progress toward building a sense of European citizenship has been mixed (as discussed later in this chapter). The waters have been further muddied by the fact that some EU institutions are more federal in nature and by the fact that the EU has been building a body of law that is obliging the member states to fall into line with each other by changing their national laws.

Consociationalism

This concept is unfamiliar to most Americans, and despite its value to helping us understand the EU, it is rarely mentioned in any discussions of European integration. The idea of consociationalism grew out of attempts in the 1960s to shed light on how deeply divided societies went about governing themselves. It was developed by political scientist Arend Lijphart in his 1968 study of politics in the Netherlands[5] and was later adopted by scholars in the field of comparative government as another means of understanding the different ways in which people can be governed. The term is usually applied to the structures and processes of parties and governments in small Western European states such as Austria and Belgium or is offered as a potential solution to the difficulty of governing divided communities such as Northern Ireland, Israel, and South Africa. But it can also shed light on how regional integration has evolved and what it can become.[6]

Lijphart described four preconditions for consociationalism,[7] all of which are found in the EU. First, there must be several groups of people who are insulated from each other in the sense that their interests and associations are inwardly directed, but although they have a high degree of self-determination, they also come under a joint system of government. Second, the political elites of the different groups must decide to work and share power with each other in this joint system as something like a grand coalition or a cartel, reaching decisions on matters of common interest as a result of agreements and coalitions among themselves; it helps if they are encouraged to do this by external threats. Third, all the groups have the power of mutual veto, but government is based on the consensus of the elites of each group. Finally, the different groups are represented proportionally in all the major institutions of their common government, but at the same time the rights and interests of minorities are protected from a dictatorship of the majority, and decisionmaking authority is delegated as much as possible to the different groups.

As Paul Taylor has put it, the leaders in a consociational system "are faced continually with the dilemma of acting to preserve the general system whilst at the same time seeking to protect and further the interests of the groups which they represent."[8] An element of selfishness is also involved, because the leaders tend to pursue their own definitions of the common interest at the expense of (or at least overlooking) the views of citizens. Ian Lustick argued that the leaders must be able to rise above the divisions among the groups, work with the elites of the other groups in a common effort, and be able to accommodate the different interests involved. Those interests tend to be defined by the elites, which usually express them vaguely in terms of the common welfare of those groups. The elites work with each other in a system of political or material exchanges, bargains and compromises; bureaucracies and legal agencies act as umpires in helping interpret the bargains that have been reached. A consociational system is like a set of delicately but securely balanced scales, but the stability of the entire system may occasionally oblige the leaders to use undemocratic methods to discipline the various segments.[9]

Federalism

A federal system is one in which national and local governments coexist with independent powers, but neither has supreme authority over the other. Unlike confederalism, federalism usually involves an elected national government that has sole power over foreign and security policy. There is usually a single currency and a common defense force, a national system of law that supersedes local law when the two conflict, a written constitution and a court that can arbitrate disputes among the different units of government, and at least two major levels of government, law, bureaucracy, and taxation. The national government has independent powers that can be expanded according to the interpretation of the federal constitution. The cumulative interests of the local units tend to define the joint interests of the whole, and the national government constantly couches its mission in terms of the importance of the citizens and describes itself as the servant of the people, functioning only for their convenience.

According to the Bill of Rights, the U.S. model of federalism prohibits the states from making treaties with foreign nations, from having their own currencies, or—without the consent of Congress—from levying taxes on imports or exports, maintaining a military in peacetime, or making agreements with other states or foreign nations. The federal government, for its part, cannot unilaterally redraw the borders of a state, impose different levels of tax by state, give states different levels of representation in the Senate, or amend the Constitution without the support of two-thirds of the states. The states, meanwhile, reserve all of the powers not expressly delegated to the national government or prohibited to them by the national government. Another key feature of the U.S. model is the common sense of identity of its citizens, most of whom place their loyalty to the United States above their loyalty to the states in which they live.

The EU member states can do almost everything the states in the U.S. model *cannot* do: They can make treaties, operate their own currencies, maintain an independent military, and the like. The EU institutions, meanwhile, have very few of the powers of the federal government in the U.S. model: They cannot levy taxes, they have no single currency or common military, they have no written constitution, they do not yet enjoy the undivided loyalties of most Europeans, and they do not have the sole power to negotiate with the rest of the world on behalf of the member states. The EU is not yet the kind of federal institution Jean Monnet and his colleagues foresaw, but it *has* moved closer to a federal structure than any other international organization,[10] and it has some of the features of a federal polity:[11]

- A system of treaties and laws protected by the European Court of Justice;

- The directly elected European Parliament, whose powers are counterbalanced by a Council of Ministers representing the interests of the individual member states;

- The EU budget, which is the germ of a fiscally independent supranational level of government; and

- An executive body (the European Commission) in which each member state is represented and that has the authority to oversee external trade negotiations on behalf of the fifteen EU member states.

One way of looking at the practice of federalism in the EU is to see the EU as a network in which individual member states are increasingly defined not by themselves but in relation to their EU partners and in which they prefer to interact with one another (rather than with third parties) because those interactions create incentives for self-interested cooperation.[12] Related to the neofunctionalist idea of the expansive logic of integration is the argument that the EU has become "co-optive," meaning that its participants have more to gain by being co-opted into the system than by going it alone.[13] Once the states are involved, they must take some of the responsibility for actions taken by the EU, and the governments of the member states find it increasingly difficult to get away with blaming Brussels.[14]

We should try not to think of federalism solely according to the way it is practiced in the United States. It is not an absolute or a static concept, and it has taken on different forms in different situations according to the relative strength and nature of local political, economic, social, historical, and cultural pressures. In the United States, federalism was in place long before this country began its westward expansion, it explicitly includes a system of checks and balances and a separation of powers, and it was adopted more to avoid the dangers of chaos and tyranny than to account for social divisions. In India, by contrast, federalism was seen as a possible solution to the difficulty of governing a state that was already in place and that had deep ethnic and cultural divisions; the national government has a fused executive and legislature.

European federalism could eventually look very different from U.S., Indian, or even German federalism. For example, it already includes the peculiarly European idea of **subsidiarity**, in which decisions are taken as close to the people as possible. In the U.S. federal model power has shifted almost imperceptibly toward the center. The presidency was much weaker than Congress, for example, until the administration of Franklin D. Roosevelt, when a combination of national emergencies and an entrepreneurial president caused the scales of power to tip in favor of the center. A European federation could become one in which the European level of government does as little as possible[15] (the dream of many Republicans in the United States).

The Idea of Europe

The European Union consists not only of the political and economic elites who have made most of the key decisions to date or of the institutions and laws they have created; it also involves nearly 370 million men, women, and children whose ideas about each other and about their place in the world are the lifeblood of the idea of Europe. The concept of the West is synonymous with Europe, and the "world culture" political scientist Lucien Pye described in 1966[16] is ultimately European culture (even if much of that culture has been exported and promoted by the United States, which is itself a product of European culture). Not only was nearly every part of the world colonized at some point by one European power or another (Japan and China are among the notable exceptions), but the spread of European ideas has meant that Western culture today is defined mainly in European terms. In short, we live in a European world.

This dominance has encouraged many Americans to think of Europe as the Old World: a relatively stable and unchanging region with a strong identity and many venerable institutions and traditions. Nothing could be further from the truth. Not only have Europeans constantly squabbled with each other and gone to war with tragic regularity and frequency, but the balance of power within Europe has often shifted, forcing mapmakers to constantly redraw the borders between different European tribes, nations, and states.

The changes continue, coming so fast that it is often difficult to keep up. In many ways, it is more accurate to think of Europe as new and dynamic rather than old and stable and to realize that many of its political institutions are relatively new. For example, no European country has a written constitution as old as that of the United States, a political party as old as the Democrats, or a judiciary as old as the U.S. Supreme Court. When the United States became independent in 1776, very few European countries existed in their modern form. England, France, Portugal, Spain, Sweden, and Switzerland were essentially in place, but almost all other European states are much younger—for example, Belgium (1830), Luxembourg (1848), Italy (1861), Poland and Hungary (1918), Yugoslavia (1918–1992), and Germany (1990). Other communities had a separate identity but (like Iceland, Ireland, Finland, and Norway) were provinces of bigger powers.

The prevailing situation in 1776 was only the latest chapter in the story of constant change that characterizes European politics. There were many more changes after 1776, culminating in two devastating world wars that began as little more than European civil wars and that ended in 1945 with a final realization that Europeans needed to work more closely together to save themselves from the nationalism that had brought so much havoc, death, and destruction. This was by no means the first time the idea of integration or unity had surfaced. The Roman Empire (200 B.C.–A.D. 400), the Frankish Empire (which peaked in the ninth century under the Emperor Charlemagne), the Holy Roman Empire (962–1250), the Napoleonic Empire (1804–1815), and Hitler's Third Reich (1933–1945) all stamped their own brands of unity on Europe, with different motives, ends, and consequences.

The European Union has been the most successful of all of the attempts to bring peace to Europe, but the "idea" of Europe remains ambiguous (see Box 5.2). Europe lacks most of the conventional features of a sovereign nation-state, including fixed boundaries, a dominant common culture, a dominant common language, a common history, and shared values and ideals.

First, the physical and cultural boundaries of Europe are unclear. They are usually defined as the Mediterranean, the Atlantic, the Arctic, and the Ural Mountains in the east and the Caucasus Mountains and the Bosphorus in the southeast. This means not only that Russians, Ukrainians, Georgians, and Turks could lay some claim to being European but also that more than 270 million "Europeans" (and nearly 150 million Russians) live in Europe outside the EU.

Second, few of the EU's fifteen member states are culturally homogeneous. Many have national minorities, and many have also experienced major influxes of immigrants since 1955—including Algerians to France, Turks to Germany, and Indians to Britain. Not only is there no dominant culture, but most Europeans shudder (not without reason) at the thought of their separate cultures being subordinated in any way to some kind of sterile, homogeneous Euroculture. As the French say, *vive la différence.*

BOX 5.2
The Development of a European Identity

One of the identifying features of a state is a sense among its residents of a common identity or citizenship. Although the European Council agreed in 1984 to promote the idea of "a people's Europe" and Maastricht contained a chapter on European citizenship, the development of a European identity cannot be forced or built by law—it ultimately lies with Europeans themselves, with how they perceive the European Union, and with how quickly they can overcome the myths, biases, and misunderstandings that are the heritage of hundreds of years of war.

There are signs that the change of attitude is slowly taking hold. Eurobarometer polls since 1982 have found that about half of all EU citizens "sometimes" or "often" feel a sense of European identity.[1] Europeans still see themselves primarily as citizens of particular member states, but increased mobility is changing their perceptions. As the barriers to movement within the EU are taken down, Europeans have fewer reminders of the differences that divide them and will tend to see other Europeans less as "foreigners" and more as partners in a joint venture. The gradual removal of border checks has been an important psychological step in that direction. Another step will come as Europeans see living in other parts of the EU less as emigration and more as a free choice based on factors such as employment, opportunity, and personal preference. By the late 1980s nearly 5 million Europeans lived in EU states other than their own; the biggest groups were Italians living in France and Germany, Spaniards and Portuguese living in France, and Irish living in Britain (see Table 14.1).

Other symbolic and functional changes are also important in this process. Europeans are still citizens of specific member states rather than of the EU, but the EU flag is increasingly visible throughout the Union, the "Ode to Joy" from Beethoven's Ninth Symphony has been adopted as the EU anthem, since 1985 national passports have been switched to a common burgundy-colored EU passport (still bearing the name of the member state of which the holder is a citizen), Europeans can live and work wherever they like in the EU, and they can vote and even stand for certain offices in the member states in which they live. There are still nonlegal barriers to the free movement of people (such as language, customs, job opportunities, and personal preferences), but the walls are coming down throughout the EU and are slowly being replaced by attitudes less burdened with narrow nationalism.

One of the great ironies and unanticipated consequences of European integration has been its role in giving national minorities a greater sense of their separate identity. Long unable to wrest powers of self-determination from member state governments, Basques, Catalans, Corsicans, Scots, and Walloons are reviving their separate identities as subgroups within the larger European Union. Where this will take them remains to be seen, but it injects an interesting new twist into discussions about the nature of citizenship in Europe.[2]

Notes

1. See Eurobarometer polls Nos. 26 (December 1986), 27 (June 1987), and 36 (December 1991) for comparative figures. They show the following numbers of people admitting to "sometimes" or "often" feeling a sense of European identity: in 1982 53 percent; in 1983 50 percent; in 1985 55 percent; in 1986 56 percent; in 1987 48 percent; and in 1991 48 percent.

2. See Chapter 1 in Elizabeth Meehan, *Citizenship and the European Community* (Newbury Park, CA: Sage, 1993).

Third, citizens of the EU speak at least thirty-six different languages,[17] and vigorously defend them as the symbol of their separate identities. The spread of English as the language of global commerce and diplomacy concerns the French in particular and other Europeans to some extent (see Chapter 14), but it is probably irresistible and will at least provide a way for Europeans to talk to each other. Nothing reminds them of their differences quite as strongly as traveling to a neighboring state and being unable to speak to many of the natives.

Finally, the histories of European states have overlapped for centuries as they have colonized, gone to war, or formed alliances with each other. But those overlaps have served mainly to emphasize differences rather than to give the states a sense of a shared past, and European integration grew in part out of the essentially reactive idea of wanting to put an end to conflict. The differences have been further emphasized by the records of some European states as colonial powers, which made them emphasize external links at the expense of internal links.

The development of a European identity has been helped in some ways by the relative introversion of Western Europe since 1945. Helen Wallace has argued that in trying to improve the way they manage their own affairs, taking more responsibility for each other, and dealing with the uncertainties posed by change in the Soviet Union and then in Russia, Europeans have become more introverted, and their internal preoccupations have heavily shaped their attitudes toward the rest of the world.[18] These preoccupations have also influenced the way outsiders look at the EU. Many Americans and Japanese see the EU as both a threat and an opportunity, while most Eastern Europeans view it as a new force for positive economic and political change and as a club many of them would very much like to join.

Wherever these trends lead, whatever Europeans can do to remind themselves of their similarities rather than their differences, and whatever political form the European Union finally takes, the process of European integration has ensured that Europeans will never see each other—or be seen by outsiders—in quite the same way again.

Summary and Conclusions

Coming to grips with the European Union is complicated by the facts that its character is constantly changing and that it fits none of the conventional ideas about the way modern societies govern themselves. It is distinctive and unique, but it cannot be neatly slotted into any of the usual ideas about government. "Boundaries are difficult to draw in a world of complex interdependence," argued Robert Keohane and Stanley Hoffmann; "because relationships cross boundaries and coalitional patterns vary from issue to issue, it is never possible to classify all actors neatly into mutually exclusive categories."[19]

The European Union in the mid-1990s has many intergovernmental characteristics, but these have given way over time to a growing emphasis on supranationalism. The member states are steadily answering to a new level of higher authority with some of the features of confederalism and some of federalism. Both of these concepts take many different forms, and for Euroskeptics to talk about federalism as some kind of hell toward which Europe should not travel is too simplistic. The European brand of federalism already has several unique features, and once it achieves some kind of regularity, those features will look very different from most of the characteristics we usually associate with federalism. Commonly overlooked in the debates about European integration is the idea of consociationalism. This theory as it now stands is too elitist and undemocratic; revived in a new form, it may be one of the most illuminating ways of trying to understand the political form of the European Union.

Notes

1. Robert O. Keohane and Stanley Hoffmann, *The New European Community: Decisionmaking and Institutional Change* (Boulder: Westview Press, 1991), 10.

2. Jean Monnet, *Memoirs* (Garden City, N.Y.: Doubleday, 1978), 523.

3. Keohane and Hoffmann, *The New European Community,* 10.

4. Benjamin Franklin, *Federalist,* no. 37.

5. Arend Lijphart, *The Politics of Accommodation: Pluralism and Democracy in the Netherlands* (Berkeley: University of California Press, 1968).

6. Paul Taylor, "Consociationalism and Federalism as Approaches to International Integration," in A.J.R. Groom and Paul Taylor (Eds.), *Frameworks for International Cooperation* (New York: St. Martin's Press, 1990).

7. Arend Lijphart, "Consociation and Federation: Conceptual and Empirical Links," *Canadian Journal of Political Science* 22:3 (1979), 499–515.

8. Taylor, "Consociationalism and Federalism," 174.

9. Ian Lustick, "Stability in Deeply Divided Societies: Consociationalism Versus Control," *World Politics* 31:3 (April 1979), 325–344.

10. Ernst B. Haas, *The Uniting of Europe: Political, Social, and Economic Forces, 1950–57* (Stanford: Stanford University Press, 1968), 59.

11. See William Wallace, *Regional Integration: The West European Experience* (Washington, D.C.: Brookings Institution, 1994), 38–40.

12. Keohane and Hoffmann, *The New European Community,* 13–14.

13. Martin O. Heisler, with Robert B. Kvavik, "Patterns of European Politics: The 'European Polity' Model," in Martin O. Heisler (Ed.), *Politics in Europe: Structures and Processes in Some Postindustrial Democracies* (New York: David McKay, 1973).

14. B. Guy Peters, "Bureaucratic Politics and the Institutions of the European Community," in Alberta Sbragia (Ed.), *Euro-Politics: Institutions and Policymaking*

in the "New" European Community (Washington, D.C.: Brookings Institution, 1992), 114–115.

15. Ibid., 110–111.

16. Lucien Pye, *Aspects of Political Development* (Boston: Little, Brown, 1966).

17. Victor Keegan and Martin Kettle, *The New Europe* (London: Fourth Estate, 1993), 92.

18. Helen Wallace, "What Europe for Which Europeans?" in Gregory F. Treverton (Ed.), *The Shape of the New Europe* (New York: Council on Foreign Relations Press, 1992), 16.

19. Keohane and Hoffmann, *The New European Community,* 12.

Further Reading

William Wallace. *Regional Integration: The West European Experience* (Washington, D.C.: Brookings Institution, 1994).

A study of the mechanics of European integration that draws conclusions about some of the lessons to be learned from the experience of the EU.

Simon Sefarty. *The Identity and Definition of Europe* (London: Pinter, 1992).

Examines the emerging idea of "Europe" and discusses its position in post–cold war global politics.

Elizabeth Meehan. *Citizenship and the European Community* (Newbury Park, Calif.: Sage, 1993).

An analysis of the meaning of European "citizenship," comparing it to national citizenship and looking at the possible emergence of a new European identity.

Most of the ideas about consociationalism have been published in journal articles or in chapters in books rather than as book-length studies. Among the key sources are the following:

Arend Lijphart. "Consociational Denmocracy." In Kenneth McRae (Ed.), *Consociational Democracy: Political Accommodation in Segmented Societies* (Toronto: McClelland and Stewart, 1974).

Arend Lijphart. "Consociation and Federation: Conceptual and Empirical Links." In *Canadian Journal of Political Science* 12:3 (September 1979), 499–515.

Paul Taylor. "Consociationalism and Federalism as Approaches to International Integration." In A.J.R. Groom and Paul Taylor (Eds.), *Frameworks for International Cooperation* (New York: St. Martin's Press, 1990).

TWO

———

Institutions

———

6

The European Commission

The European Commission is both the executive arm of the European Union and its bureaucracy; it is responsible for initiating and overseeing the implementation of EU law and for promoting the interests of the EU as a whole. It is the most supranational of the EU institutions and has long been at the heart of the process of European integration. Although it has no direct equivalent in the United States, it has elements of the powers of the executive branch, the federal bureaucracy, and the Supreme Court.

First, it is like the cabinet in the sense that it is headed by a group of twenty commissioners, each responsible for particular policy areas and for overseeing one or more directorates-general, the functional equivalent of federal government departments. But while the U.S. cabinet is appointed by the president with Senate approval, European commissioners are appointed by the member states and are subject to collective (but not individual) approval by the European Parliament.

Second, like the U.S. presidency, the Commission proposes new policy ideas and is responsible for drawing up the EU budget. Unlike the U.S. president, it can also draft new legislation.

Finally, once the new policies and laws have been discussed and amended by the Parliament and have been accepted or rejected by the Council of Ministers, the Commission (like the executive branch in the United States) oversees implementation by the member states. It can investigate suspected infringements or lack of compliance and if necessary can take a member state to the Court of Justice. Like the U.S. Supreme Court, the Commission can also mediate in disputes between member states over EU law.

The Commission is regularly the target of disdain and criticism, but its role is widely misunderstood. Euroskeptics grumble about waste and meddling by **Eurocrats** and complain that the leaders of the Commission are not elected and that its staff has little public accountability. For some, "Brussels" has become a codeword for some vague and threatening notion of government by bureaucracy, or "creeping federalism." But this is unfair. The Commission has much less power than its detractors often suggest, and

103

its powers are being reduced as those of other EU institutions grow. It is also very small given the size of its task; it had just 16,500 staff in 1993 (a ratio of 1:21,000 EU citizens), compared with the more than 3 million civilian federal bureaucrats in the United States (1:90 U.S. citizens).

At the same time, the Commission deserves credit for the critical role it has played in the process of European integration. It has not only encouraged member states to harmonize their laws, regulations, and standards in the interest of bringing down the barriers to trade but has also been the source of some of the defining policy initiatives in the process of that integration, including the single market and efforts to create a single currency. As John Fitzmaurice has put it, the Commission's role is that of "animator, impresario, and manager," faced with the challenges of making the EU system work and of turning political principles into real and effective policies.[1] Yet it appears to many Europeans to be remote and intrusive,[2] and they have little direct input into its work. There is a strong case for administrative reform, one that becomes more difficult to oppose as the powers of the European Union grow and as more states line up to join.

Evolution

The European Commission grew out of the separate administrative arms of the ECSC, the EEC, and Euratom. The ECSC had a nine-member High Authority based in Luxembourg, whose members were nominated for six-year terms by the six national governments. Its job was to oversee the removal of barriers to the free movement of coal and steel, and its powers were checked by a Special Council of Ministers and a Common Assembly (the forerunners, respectively, of the Council of Ministers and the European Parliament).

The Treaties of Rome created separate nine-member Commissions for the EEC and Euratom, whose members were nominated by national governments for four-year terms. Under the terms of the 1965 Merger Treaty, the three separate Commissions were merged in 1967 into a new Commission of the European Communities, known for short as the European Commission. As the Community expanded, the number of commissioners grew. At first there were nine (two each from France, West Germany, and Italy and one each from the Benelux states). The number increased to thirteen in 1973 with the accession of Britain, Denmark, and Ireland; to fourteen in 1981 with the accession of Greece; to seventeen in 1986 with the accession of Spain and Portugal; and then to 20 in 1995 with the accession of Austria, Sweden, and Finland.

The Commission has always been at the heart of the continuing debate over the balance of power between the EU and the member states. Concerns regularly surface about its supranationalist tendencies, and it has fought a constant tug-of-war with the intergovernmental Council of Ministers. European federalism was championed by the Commission's first president—Walter Hallstein of Germany—in the face of Charles de Gaulle's preference for limiting the powers of the EEC. The 1965 crisis broke when de Gaulle challenged the right of the Commission to initiate the policy process, and the Commission attempted to collect receipts from the EC's common external tariff.[3] This would have provided the Commission with an independent source of funds, thus loosening the grip of the member states. Although the Luxembourg compromise obliged the Commission to consult more closely with the Council of Ministers and de Gaulle was able to veto the reappointment of Hallstein in 1967, the crisis ironically confirmed the right of the Commission to initiate policies.

The Commission became less ambitious and aggressive and lost powers with the creation in 1965 of the Committee of Permanent Representatives (see Chapter 7), the creation in 1974 of the European Council (see Chapter 10), and the introduction in 1979 of direct elections to the European Parliament. Some argue that the Commission's powers and influence have continued to decline,[4] but it went through a newly assertive phase during the Delors presidency in the late 1980s and early 1990s[5] and generated some of the EU's most important policy initiatives.

Structure

The European Commission is based in Brussels. Until 1992 it was headquartered in the Berlaymont building near the city center, but it was then discovered (with delicious irony) that the Berlaymont did not meet one of the EC's own regulations on asbestos, so the building was emptied and renovated, and the Commission staff was relocated to various new and existing buildings around the city. The label "Commission" is used interchangeably (and confusingly) to describe two entities: the college of twenty commissioners that heads the institution and the 16,500 bureaucrats who make up its body. It has five main elements: the College of Commissioners, the president of the Commission, the directorates-general, the Secretariat General, and the advisory committees.

The College of Commissioners

The European Commission is led by a group of twenty commissioners, who function as something like the cabinet of the EU system, taking collective responsibility for their decisions. Each has a portfolio for which he or she

TABLE 6.1   The European Commissioners, January 1995

Name	Country	Key Portfolios
Martin Bangemann[a]	Germany	Industrial affairs, information, telecommunications
Monika Wulf-Mathies	Germany	Regional policy, relations with the Committee of the Regions, Cohesion Fund
Sir Leon Brittan[a]	Britain	Trade policy, external relations (North America, Southeast Asia, OECD, World Trade Organization)
Neil Kinnock	Britain	Transport
Mario Monti	Italy	Internal market, financial services, taxes
Emma Bonino	Italy	Consumer policy, fisheries
Yves-Thibault de Silguy	France	Economic and financial affairs
Édith Cresson	France	Science, education, research and development, human resources
Manuel Marín[a]	Spain	External relations (southern Mediterranean, Mideast, Latin America)
Marcelino Oreja	Spain	Relations with the European Parliament, culture, official publications, preparations for the 1996 IGC
Hans van den Broek[a]	Netherlands	External relations (Eastern Europe and former USSR), Common Foreign and Security Policy
Christos Papoutsis	Greece	Energy
Karel van Miert[a]	Belgium	Competition
João de deus Pinheiro[a]	Portugal	External relations (African, Caribbean, and Pacific [ACP] states)
Anita Gradin	Sweden	Justice, home affairs, immigration, financial control
Franz Fischler	Austria	Agriculture
Ritt Bjerregaard	Denmark	Environment, nuclear safety
Erkki Liikanen	Finland	Budget, personnel, administration
Pádraig Flynn[a]	Ireland	Employment, social affairs
Jacques Santer	Luxembourg	President

[a]Returning commissioners.

is responsible (see Table 6.1). One commissioner is appointed president. The twenty posts are distributed among the EU member states, with the five largest countries (Germany, Britain, France, Italy, and Spain) each having two posts and the rest having one each. Commissioners served four-year renewable terms until the end of 1994; under Maastricht, the terms were lengthened to five years effective January 1995, to coincide more closely with elections to the European Parliament.

Commissioners are appointed by their national governments, which—in practice—usually means the prime minister or the president in France. The appointments are made in consultation with the president of the Commission, and appointees also usually must be acceptable to the other commissioners, other governments, the major political parties at home, and the European Parliament. Parliament does not have the right to hold confirmation hearings on individual commissioners, but it has the powers to vet the College as a whole at the beginning of its term and also to fire the College, although this has never happened.

Despite the way they are appointed, commissioners are not supposed to be national representatives, and they must swear an oath of office before the European Court of Justice in Luxembourg saying they will renounce any defense of national interests. They agree to perform their duties "in complete independence, in the general interest of the [EU] . . . [and] neither to seek nor to take instructions from any Government or body." Their independence from their home governments is underwritten by the inability of national leaders to remove commissioners in midterm. Many are reappointed, and some resign, but others are recalled at the end of their terms because of a change of political leadership at home or political disagreements with their national leaders.

The most famous example of a fallout between a commissioner and a home government was that between Lord Cockfield and his sponsor, Margaret Thatcher. Cockfield was appointed in 1985 and was given responsibility to prepare for the single market. He began to pursue his job too enthusiastically for Thatcher's tastes, however, and she concluded that he had become "the prisoner as well as the master of his subject. It was all too easy for him, therefore, to go native and to move from deregulating the market to reregulating it under the rubric of harmonization."[6] She accordingly refused to reappoint him in 1989.

There are no formal rules on appointments, but commissioners tend to already have national political reputations at home, albeit sometimes modest ones. They may be well-respected members of an opposition party or someone the governing party would like to remove from the national political scene for some reason. At one time, many were political lightweights whose usefulness at home had ended, so they were "kicked upstairs" to the Commission. As the powers of the Commission have increased and the EU has become a more significant force in European politics, postings to the Commission have become more desirable and important, and commissioners are becoming both younger and more technocratic.[7] One indication of the change in emphasis came in 1994 when the former French Prime Minister Édith Cresson was appointed to one of the French posts and a former leader of the British Labour Party, Neil Kinnock, to one of the British posts.

At the beginning of each term, all twenty commissioners are given portfolios, which are distributed at the prerogative of the president. This has great political significance and is seen as an acid test of the president's abilities to lead.[8] The process is subject to lobbying by commissioners and national governments, and portfolios are reshuffled to reward efficiency, ability, and loyalty and to penalize incompetence. Despite regular claims of collegiality among commissioners, the College has its own internal hierarchy of positions. While the senior positions in most national cabinets are those dealing with foreign affairs, the economy, and either internal affairs or defense, the key posts in the Commission are those concerned with the budget, agriculture, and external relations. The hierarchy is also based in part on the different abilities and political skills of individual commissioners; some are respected and able, while others are not.

The reshuffling is usually done on the basis of seniority and political acceptability, with the longest-serving commissioners receiving the best portfolios as a form of recognition or promotion. Commissioners with a strong reputation in a particular area will normally keep the same portfolio (industrial affairs Commissioner Martin Bangemann, for example, has held that portfolio since 1989). Member state governments are obviously keen to see "their" commissioner win a good portfolio or one of particular interest to their country, so political influence is often brought to bear on the process. The Commission term that began in January 1989 was particularly important, given the imminent creation of the single market. Spain was eager to be given the budget portfolio, and Prime Minister Felipe Gonzalez tried to use his influence to obtain the job for one of the two Spanish commissioners. In the event, the budget portfolio went to German Commissioner Peter Schmidhuber, but the senior Spanish Commissioner Manual Marín was given two portfolios as consolation.

Little political direction is given to the College, mainly because commissioners must not seem to be promoting national interests or to be answering to their home governments. This gives them a high level of freedom of movement, although their decisions are collegiate. Every commissioner has his or her personal staff of about half a dozen assistants and advisers, called a *cabinet,* which is headed by a *chef* and provides advice and the basic information and services that help commissioners do their jobs; the quality of the *cabinet* staff can have a major bearing on the performance of a commissioner. The respective *chefs de cabinet* meet every Monday to prepare the weekly meeting of the College on Wednesday. *Cabinet* members usually come from the same country as the commissioner, although at least one commonly comes from another member state. Advisers are usually recruited from the same national political party as that of the commissioner or from the national bureaucracy.

There are already concerns that the College has become too big, making more urgent the need to decide what to do when more states join the EU. At the time of the Maastricht negotiations, a suggestion was made that each member state be limited to one commissioner, and Germany proposed that membership be capped at ten. The issue of size—and of how the Commission is appointed—is certain to be on the agenda of the 1996 IGC.[9] One option may be to create a two-tier Commission, with senior commissioners from the larger states and deputies from newer and/or smaller states.[10]

The President

The dominating figure in the Commission hierarchy is undoubtedly the president, the person who comes closest to being able to claim to be the leader of the EU (although this is a debatable proposition, given the way power is divided and dissipated within the system). The president is technically no more than a first among equals and can be outvoted by other commissioners, but—as with prime ministers in parliamentary systems—the president's trump card is the power of appointment: The ability to distribute portfolios is a potent tool for patronage and political manipulation.

The new assertiveness of Jacques Delors in the period 1985–1994 may also have heralded the emergence of a more presidential system of government (see Box 6.1).[11] Delors personalized his position to an unprecedented degree, often issuing reports and papers with little or no prior consultation with his peers and taking responsibility for economic policy issues that were really the job of the relevant commissioner.[12] He also came to the job with firm ideas about a strong, federal Europe asserting itself internationally,[13] and he used this vision to push the EU in many new directions. He was succeeded in January 1995 by Jacques Santer, former prime minister of Luxembourg, who entered office faced not only with having to follow a very tough act but also with having to guide the EU toward achieving economic and monetary union, preparing for further enlargement, developing a common foreign and security policy, and setting up the 1996 IGC.

The president of the Commission is comparable in some ways to the president of the United States. He or she oversees meetings of the College, decides on the distribution of portfolios, represents the Commission in dealings with other EU institutions, represents the EU at meetings with national

BOX 6.1
Jacques Delors at the Helm

Arguably the most assertive, productive, and controversial of all Commission presidents, Jacques Delors of France served five consecutive terms at the head of the Commission between 1985 and 1994. Born in Paris in 1925, Delors was a banker and a labor leader before serving briefly as an MEP and becoming economics and finance minister under President François Mitterrand during 1981–1984. He was single-minded, hardworking, demanding, and sometimes short-tempered; a fellow commissioner once described his management method as a form of "intellectual terrorism," and a British minister once described the Delors Commission as "practitioners of Rottweiler politics."[1] Despite this, he had a strong sense of mission and direction and possessed canny political abilities.

Delors will be remembered for at least three key achievements: the completion of the single market, his plan for economic and monetary union, and his promotion of the Social Charter. (Maastricht, too, was negotiated during his administration, but it remains too controversial to be described as a success.) Although he usually had the strong support of François Mitterrand and Helmut Kohl, he did not fare as well with Margaret Thatcher. Both were strong-willed and stubborn, and while Delors was a moderate socialist and a federalist, Thatcher was a conservative and was lukewarm on Europe. War broke out between the two at the 1986 European Council in London. After telling Thatcher in private about the troubled financial state of the EC (and leading her to conclude that he represented "a new breed of unaccountable politicians" in the Commission), Delors had little to say at the press conference on the outcome of the Council, prompting Thatcher to quip: "I had no idea you were the strong, silent type."[2]

When Delors declared in July 1988 that within ten years 80 percent of Europe's economic and social laws would be decided in Brussels, it was a red flag to the conservative Thatcher bull. In a speech in November of that year in Bruges, Belgium, Thatcher argued against the federalist tendencies of the EC: "We have not successfully rolled back the frontiers of the state in Britain only to see them reimposed at a European level, with a European super-state exercising a new dominance from Brussels."[3]

Delors left the Commission at the end of 1994 at age sixty-eight. He surprised everyone (including François Mitterrand) by turning down the chance to run for president of France, an office many felt he could have won.

Notes

1. George Ross, *Jacques Delors and European Integration* (New York: Oxford University Press, 1995), 51.

2. Margaret Thatcher, *The Downing Street Years* (New York: HarperCollins, 1993), 558.

3. Ibid., 744–745.

governments and their leaders, and is generally responsible for ensuring that the Commission gives impetus to the process of European integration.

In other respects, the two presidencies are very different. Not only are Commission presidents appointed rather than elected, but they are not accountable to Parliament in the way U.S. presidents are accountable to Congress, and they are clearly subservient to the leaders of the member states—to the point where they sometimes seem to be little more than glorified functionaries. In many ways the Commission president has the same status as early-nineteenth-century U.S. presidents, who had less of a role in government than either Congress or the states and were seen more as executives than as leaders. However, just as Franklin Delano Roosevelt gave the job a newly powerful and assertive role in government in the 1930s, so the presidency of the Commission took on a new and more forceful character under Delors.

There are no formal rules regarding how the president is appointed. It has become normal for the leaders of the member states to decide on the appointment at the European Council held during the June before the term of the incumbent Commission ends, settling on someone acceptable to all of them and to the Commission itself. Maastricht made the appointment subject to confirmation by Parliament. The struggle to find a successor for Jacques Delors in 1994 gives some insight into the nature of the process. A successor was to have been appointed at the European Council meeting in Corfu in June. The favorite was Jean-Luc Dehaene, the incumbent prime minister of Belgium, who would have been the first conservative in many years to head the Commission and who had a reputation for engineering political compromises. His candidacy was strongly supported by Germany and France, but the Dutch were upset because outgoing Prime Minister Ruud Lubbers was not at the top of the list; and Italy, Spain, and Portugal all questioned the Franco-German assumption that Dehaene's candidacy was assured.[14]

Eight of the twelve leaders initially supported Dehaene, while Spain, Italy, and the Netherlands opted for Lubbers, and Britain favored Sir Leon Brittan, one of its commissioners. In the event, every leader ultimately fell in behind Dehaene except John Major, who vetoed Dehaene's appointment. Major argued that Dehaene was an interventionist who favored big government, but in truth he was probably trying to appease right-wing Euroskeptics in his own party at home. Although Major was painted as the sole voice of dissent, the tussle also revealed the resentment among smaller EU states about the assumptions by Germany and France that their favored candidate would win.[15] Having failed to reach agreement, the twelve leaders met at an emergency European Council in Brussels on July 15 and opted for Jacques Santer as a compromise. Santer was narrowly confirmed by the

TABLE 6.2 Presidents of the European Commission

1958–1967	**Walter Hallstein** (West Germany) Christian Democrat; foreign minister 1951–1958. Federalist who provided dynamic and aggressive leadership, establishing the central role of the Commission in EU affairs. His attempts to expand the powers of the Commission and the European Parliament led to the crisis of 1965. Reappointment vetoed by de Gaulle in 1967.
1968–1969	**Jean Rey** (Belgium) Centrist; economics minister in postwar governments. Appointed commissioner for external relations in 1958 and became first president of the newly merged European Commission. Subsequently served as an MEP and chaired the committee that produced the 1980 Rey Report on EC institutional reform.
1970–1972	**Franco Maria Malfatti** (Italy) Christian Democrat; minister for state industries. Reflecting the trough into which the EC had sunk, he resigned unexpectedly from his post as Commission president and returned to Italian politics.
1972	**Sicco Mansholt** (Netherlands) Centrist; agriculture minister. Appointed agriculture commissioner in 1958 and became principal architect of the Common Agricultural Policy (for which he is now mainly remembered). Author of 1968 Mansholt Plan on reform of agricultural policy. Served an interim term of nine months as president.
1973–1976	**François-Xavier Ortoli** (France) Gaullist; bureaucrat who headed the National Planning Commission before being elected to the French National Assembly in 1968. Became minister of economic affairs and finance. Following his term as president, served as commissioner for economic affairs.
1977–1980	**Roy Jenkins** (Britain) Socialist; home secretary and chancellor of the exchequer in Wilson governments. His term as president saw the creation of the EMS and establishment of the right of the Commission president to represent the EC at world economic summits, but the Commission lost power to the European Council and Parliament.
1981–1984	**Gaston Thorn** (Luxembourg) Socialist; elected to Luxembourg Parliament in 1959 and appointed to European Parliament, where he later became vice president of the Liberal Group. Minister of foreign affairs and foreign trade 1969–1980 and prime minister 1974–1979. Not regarded as a strong president.
1985–1994	**Jacques Delors** (France) Socialist; economics and finance minister in first Mitterrand government (1981–1983). Longest-serving and most productive Commission president. His term saw the passage of the Single European Act, revival of economic and monetary union, the Maastricht treaty, and the creation of the European Economic Area.
1995–	**Jacques Santer** (Luxembourg) Christian Democrat; prime minister from 1984 until his appointment. Chosen as a compromise after Britain vetoed the first choice of the other eleven, Jean-Luc Dehaene, prime minister of Belgium. Santer chaired the negotiations leading to the SEA in 1986.

European Parliament a week later and began making his decisions on portfolios in October.

The president is usually someone with a strong political reputation, a
strong character, and proven leadership abilities, but to date the incumbents
have proved very different in their styles and abilities; Walter Hallstein, Roy
Jenkins, and Jacques Delors are remembered as the most active and the re-
mainder as relatively passive (see Table 6.2). There is an unwritten understanding that the job will alternate between large and small countries.
Presidents served two-year renewable terms until 1994, when the term was
increased to two and a half years. Two commissioners are also appointed as
vice presidents, but they do little more than make themselves available to
stand in for an incapacitated or otherwise unavailable president.

Directorates-General

Below the College, the European Commission is divided into twenty-three
directorates-general (DGs). Every DG is responsible for a specific area and
ideally should be tied to a particular commissioner, but there are more DGs
than commissioners, so some commissioners have more than one DG, some
(more rarely) have none, and some DGs report to more than one commissioner. The DGs are usually known by their numbers rather than their
areas, so the directorate-general dealing with external economic relations is
DGI, the DG concerned with economic and financial affairs is DGII, and so
on (see Table 6.3). Each DG has its own director-general who reports to the
relevant commissioner.

The size of DGs varies roughly according to the size of their jobs; DGIX
(personnel and administration) employs about 2,800 people and DGVI
(agriculture) about 900, while the smallest DGs may employ fewer than
150 people. The Commission is required to ensure balanced representation
by nationality at every level, but nearly one in four Eurocrats is Belgian,[16]
mainly because of locally recruited secretarial and support staff. Although
the people who eventually become directors-general theoretically work
their way up through the ranks of the Commission, appointments at the
higher levels are based less on merit than on nationality and political affili-
ation.

Member states exert pressure to ensure that they receive what they regard
as a fair balance of senior positions and that they control departments close
to their hearts; it is widely recognized, for example, that Germany will dominate the upper reaches of DGIV (competition), that France will dominate
DGVI (agriculture), and that there will be a British lilt to the DGs dealing
with external relations (DGI and DGIA). In a practice known as *para-
chutage*, a government that lacks a suitable candidate on the Commission

TABLE 6.3   Directorates-General of the European Commission

DGI	External Economic Relations
DGIA	External Political Relations
DGII	Economic and Financial Affairs
DGIII	Internal Market and Industrial Affairs
DGIV	Competition
DGV	Employment, Industrial Relations, and Social Affairs
DGVI	Agriculture
DGVII	Transport
DGVIII	Development
DGIX	Personnel and Administration
DGX	Information, Communication, and Culture
DGXI	Environment, Nuclear Safety, and Civil Protection
DGXII	Science, Research, and Development
DGXIII	Telecommunications, Information Technologies, and Industries
DGXIV	Fisheries
DGXV	Financial Institutions and Company Law
DGXVI	Regional Policy
DGXVII	Energy
DGXVIII	Credit and Investments
DGXIX	Budgets
DGXX	Financial Control
DGXXI	Customs Union and Indirect Taxation
DGXXII	Disbanded; formerly Co-ordination of Structural Policies
DGXXIII	Enterprise Policy, Distributive Trades, Tourism, and Cooperatives

staff for a post under its control will often recruit a bureaucrat from home rather than let the job go to a candidate from another state, regardless of their relative qualifications.[17]

About two-thirds of Commission staff members work on drawing up new laws and policies or on overseeing implementation, about 20 percent are involved in research, and the rest (about 2,500) are involved in translation and interpretation; although the Commission mainly uses English and French, each document must be translated into the eleven official EU languages. The vast majority of Commission staff members work in offices in and around Brussels, but some work in Luxembourg, in other parts of the EU, or in the Commission's overseas offices.

Recruitment is both complex and competitive. About five hundred new positions become vacant each year, for which there are literally thousands of applicants. A university degree and fluency in at least two EU languages are minimum requirements, and specialist professional training (in law, business, finance, or science, for example) is increasingly required. Entrance exams are held in fifteen countries in eleven languages, and the process is so convoluted and detailed that applicants may have to wait as long as three years to learn whether they have been accepted. Once appointed, Commission staff members are well paid, and redundancies are rare. An affirmative action policy has ensured that women are well represented at the lower levels of the Commission and increasingly at the higher levels as well, although the College has been dominated by men. The first two women commissioners were Vasso Papandreou of Greece and Christiane Scrivener of France, appointed in 1989; the 1995 College had a record five women among its twenty members.

The Secretariat General

Administration is overseen by a secretary general supported by a staff of about 350. The secretary general chairs the weekly meetings of the *chefs de cabinet,* sits in on the weekly meetings of the commissioners, directs Commission relations with Parliament, and generally makes sure the work of the Commission runs smoothly. The job of secretary general was held for nearly thirty years by Emile Noël of France and since 1987 has been held by David Williamson of Britain.

Advisory Committees

Most of the work of discussing and sorting out the details of proposed laws and policies is left to a series of expert and consultative committees. The expert committees consist of national officials and specialists appointed by national governments. Most are basically permanent and have fixed numbers of members, while others meet on an ad hoc basis to discuss Commission proposals. The consultative committees consist of people with sectional interests and are set up and funded directly by the Commission. Members are nominated by EU-wide organizations such as the European Trade Union Confederation and the Committee of Professional Agricultural Organizations. Committees are a good point of contact for lobbyists; any interest group or lobbyist who wants to influence EU policy would be well advised to lobby or to give testimony before one of these committees.

How the Commission Works

The foundations of the Commission's power lie in the treaties of Paris and Rome, the Single European Act, and the Maastricht treaty. The Commission is neither a full-blown "government" nor a "bureaucracy" in the literal sense of the term, but it has elements of both because its key task is to ensure that EU policies are advanced in the light of the treaties. It does this in five ways.

BOX 6.2
European Union Law

The Commission adopts six hundred to seven hundred new legal instruments every year, far more than most EU citizens probably realize, and the volume has risen steadily as the power and reach of the EU have expanded. EU laws take one of five different forms.

Regulations are the most powerful EU laws and play a central role in developing a uniform body of EU law. Usually fairly narrow in their intent, they are often designed to amend or adjust an existing law. A regulation is binding in its entirety on all member states and is directly applicable in the sense that it does not need to be turned into national law. Regulations usually go into immediate force on a specified date, usually upon—or soon after—publication in the *Official Journal of the European Communities*. The EU adopts between three hundred and four hundred new regulations each year.

Directives are binding on member states in terms of goals and objectives, but the states decide how best to achieve those goals. They can be directed at all or some member states; most focus on outlining general policy goals, while some are aimed at harmonization and set a date by which they must be implemented. The governments of the member states must tell the Commission what they plan to do to achieve the goals of a directive. The EU adopts sixty to eighty directives each year.

Decisions are also binding and can be aimed at one or more member states, at institutions, or even at individuals. They are usually fairly specific in their intent and have administrative rather than legislative goals. Some are aimed at making changes in the powers of the EU, some are directed toward purely internal administrative issues (for example, staff appointments and promotions), and others are issued when the Commission has to ajudicate disputes between member states or corporations. The EU adopts about 160 to 190 decisions each year.

Recommendations and Opinions have no binding force, so it is debatable whether they are actually sources of EU law.[1]

Notes

1. D. Lasok and J. W. Bridge, *Laws and Institutions of the European Communities*, 4th ed. (London: Butterworths, 1987), 130.

Powers of Initiation

The Commission is legally obliged to ensure that the principles of the treaties are turned into practical laws and policies (Article 155 of the EEC Treaty); in this respect it is sometimes described as the "guardian" of the treaties. It has the sole power to initiate new legislation and can also draw up proposals for entire new policy areas (as it did with the Single European Act and the Delors package for Economic and Monetary Union) and pass them on to Parliament and the Council of Ministers for discussion and adoption.

Although neither Parliament nor the Council can initiate the law-making process and must wait for the Commission to generate proposals, pressure and influence are brought to bear on the Commission from many different quarters. Under Article 152 of the EEC Treaty, the Council of Ministers can ask the Commission to "undertake any studies that Council considers desirable for the attainment of the common objectives, and to submit to it any appropriate proposals"; Maastricht gave the same powers to Parliament, adding to a trend in which policy ideas come from outside the Commission. A proposal may also come from a commissioner or a staff member of one of the DGs, may come as a result of a ruling by the Court of Justice, or may flow out of one of the treaties. Member-state governments, interest groups, and even private corporations can exert direct or indirect pressure on the Commission. Since the mid-1970s, increasing numbers of policy suggestions have come from the European Council.

The issue of competence and authority has been at the heart of the Commission's relations with other EU institutions and with the member states. Consider, for example, Article 3b of the Maastricht treaty: "In areas that do not fall within its exclusive competence, the Community shall take action, in accordance with the principle of subsidiarity, only if and in so far as the objectives of the proposed action cannot be sufficiently achieved by the member states and can therefore, by reason of the scale or effects of the proposed action, be better achieved by the Community." Which policy areas fall under this definition—and which do not—is often a matter of opinion, and both the Commission and the member states can use differences of opinion to press their cases against each other.

Typically, a piece of EU legislation will begin as a draft written by middle-ranking Eurocrats in one of the directorates-general. It will then be passed up through the ranks of the DG, probably being amended or revised along the way. The draft will finally reach the College of Commissioners, which meets every Wednesday to go through the different draft laws. Meetings take place in Brussels or in Strasbourg if Parliament is in plenary session. By a majority vote (a quorum is eleven), the College can accept a law, reject it, send it back for redrafting, or defer making a decision. Once passed by the College, it will be sent to the European Parliament for an opinion and then to the Council of Ministers for a decision. This process can take from months to years, and Commission staff members will be involved at every stage—consulting widely with national bureaucrats and interest groups, working with and making presentations to the Council of Ministers and the European Parliament, and carrying out their own research into the implications of the new law.

Powers of Implementation

Once a law or policy has been accepted, the Commission is responsible for ensuring that it is implemented by the member states (Article 155). It has no power to do this directly but instead relies heavily on national bureaucracies.[18] The Commission has the powers to collect information from member states so it can monitor implementation; to take to the Court of Justice any member state, corporation, or individual that does not conform to the spirit of the treaties or follow subsequent EU law; and (if necessary) to impose sanctions or fines if a law is not being implemented. This can be difficult, especially because governments have sometimes worked with their industries to hide the fact that they are breaking the law or not implementing an EU law. The Commission has its own monitoring teams, but they lack the personnel to police every member state, so the Commission usually has to rely on two other methods:

1. Member-state reports. Every member state is legally obliged to report back to the Commission on the progress it is making in meeting deadlines and incorporating EU law into national law.

2. Whistle-blowing. The Commission relies to some extent on member states reporting on each other and on individuals, corporations, and interest groups drawing attention to laws being broken and failures to implement EU law. One example of this came in 1986, when Britain set out to privatize its water industry, which had been notorious among environmentalists for its secrecy. Interest groups noted that it was illegal under EU law for a private company to regulate itself, and the internal workings of the water supply industry were finally made public; the extent to which Britain was breaking EU laws on water quality was also revealed.[19]

The Commission adds to the pressure by publicizing progress on implementation, hoping to embarrass the laggards into action. Under the terms of the Single European Act, for example, 282 separate pieces of legislation had to be agreed on and implemented within a period of five years. In September 1989, halfway through that period, the Commission published a table of the leaders and the laggards, which showed that the wealthier countries had generally made the most progress and the poorer countries the least. Of the laws agreed on by that time, France, the Netherlands, Denmark, and Britain had implemented 50 percent or more, while Spain, Italy, and Portugal had implemented less than half.

If a member state falls behind schedule, the Commission can issue a warning (a Letter of Formal Notice) giving it time to comply (usually about two months). If the member still fails to comply, the Commission can issue a Reasoned Opinion explaining why it feels there may be a violation. If there is still noncompliance, the state can be taken to the European Court of Justice, although this only happens in about 5–8 percent of cases (see Table 6.4). Until 1993, compliance was based on goodwill and an agreement to "play the game"; Maastricht gave the Commission new powers to take a state back to the Court, which can then impose a fine. The Commission decides which cases should go to the Court, and thus uses the Court to make rules on its behalf.[20]

Italy, Greece, Spain, and Portugal have been the worst offenders; Italy has had the most proceedings started against it (more than one hundred each year in the period 1990–1992), and it has also been taken to Court more often than almost any other member state. Portugal has had many proceedings started against it; this has reflected problems in reporting, and most problems have been resolved in time to prevent Court action. Ironically, Britain and Denmark—two of the most lukewarm members of the EU—have some of the best records of compliance, a reflection of the seriousness with which both countries have traditionally taken their interna-

TABLE 6.4   Infringements of EU Law, 1990–1992

	1990		1991		1992	
	Procedures Begun[a]	Taken to Court of Justice	Procedures Begun[a]	Taken to Court of Justice	Procedures Begun[a]	Taken to Court of Justice
Italy	111	25	115	24	137	11
Spain	114	3	79	2	127	5
Portugal	178	2	86	2	116	1
Greece	120	10	88	9	112	4
France	76	6	54	4	111	1
Belgium	68	13	71	8	110	6
Luxembourg	43	4	64	4	97	14
Germany	61	5	60	1	97	5
United Kingdom	44	2	63	0	97	3
Ireland	52	3	59	3	88	9
Netherlands	61	2	62	7	73	5
Denmark	36	3	52	1	45	0
Total	964	78	853	65	1,210	64

[a]On noncompliance or nonreporting of directives, treaty obligations, regulations, and decisions.

Source: Commission of the European Communities, "Tenth Annual Report to the European Parliament on Commission Monitoring of the Application of Community Law—1992," *Official Journal of the European Communities* 36, C233 (August 30, 1993), 14.

tional treaty obligations. Most cases of noncompliance come less from a deliberate avoidance by a member state than from differences over interpretation or differences in the levels of efficiency of national bureaucracies; the latter accounts, for example, for many of Italy's infringements because its national bureaucracy is notorious for delay, inefficiency, and corruption.

Acting as the Conscience of the EU

The Commission is expected to rise above competing national interests and to represent and promote the general interest of the EU (however that is defined). It is also expected to help smooth the flow of decisionmaking by mediating disagreements within or between member states and other EU institutions. It represents EU interests at meetings of the Council of Ministers and the European Council and reminds other segments of the EU system about the basic goals of European integration.

Managing EU Finances

The Commission ensures that all EU revenues are collected, plays a key role in drafting and guiding the budget through the Council of Ministers and Parliament, and administers EU expenditures, especially under the Common Agricultural Policy and the structural funds (Article 228). (See Chapter 11 for more details.)

External Relations

The Commission acts as the EU's main external representative in dealings with international organizations such as the United Nations, the World Trade Organization (WTO), and the OECD (Articles 228–231). Negotiations under the auspices of GATT were overseen by the Commission acting on behalf of EU member states; thus the Commission has increasingly become the most common point of contact for U.S. and Japanese trade negotiators.

The Commission is also a key point of contact between the EU and the rest of the world. As the power and significance of the EU have grown, more than 140 governments have opened diplomatic missions in Brussels accredited to the EU. The EU has also opened more than 110 offices in other parts of the world, staffed by Commission employees. The growing significance of the EU and the Commission can be seen in the numbers of foreign leaders who visit Brussels (which is also the headquarters of NATO). Maastricht included the proviso that the Commission would be centrally involved in developing the EU's common foreign and security policy; its role in this area has already been helped by the fact that it is relatively permanent, whereas the presidency of the Council of Ministers (which technically runs EU foreign policy) is not.[21]

The Commission also oversees the process by which applications for full or associate membership are considered. Although the applications initially go to the Council of Ministers, the Commission looks into all of the implications and reports back to the Council. If the Council decides to open negotiations with an applicant, the Commission oversees the process.

Summary and Conclusions

The European Commission is the main executive and bureaucratic arm of the EU; it is responsible for ensuring that the underlying goals and principles of the treaties are turned into practical law and policies. As the power and reach of the EU have grown, so have the size and workload of the Commission, but it has much less power than most EU citizens probably think. The status of the Commission has been exaggerated in part because of traditional concerns and doubts about bureaucracies and in part because of the secrecy that surrounds the work of the much more powerful Council of Ministers.

The Commission has been behind much of the legal output of the EU as well as some of the most critical EU policy initiatives of the last 10–20 years. Its powers have depended largely on a combination of its leadership—particularly the incumbent president—and the changing attitudes of the leaders of member states toward the work of the Commission. As time goes on, pressure is likely to grow for the Commission to become more accountable and for EU citizens to have more say through the European Parliament in the appointment of commissioners and the president. For example, pressure is growing for each commissioner to be subject to confirmation by the Parliament. Political union—whatever form it takes—will almost inevitably lead to pressure for a directly elected president, whose position and powers would be tied more closely to the balance of political party groups in the European Parliament. Although the true nexus of EU powers lies in the relationship between the Commission and the Council of Ministers, this is slowly changing as the Parliament becomes more powerful and assertive.

Notes

1. John Fitzmaurice, "The European Commission," in Andrew Duff et al. (Eds.), *Maastricht and Beyond: Building the European Union* (London: Routledge, 1994), 181.

2. B. Guy Peters, "Bureaucratic Politics and the Institutions of the European Community," in Alberta Sbragia (Ed.), *Euro-Politics: Institutions and Policymaking*

in the "New" European Community (Washington, D.C.: Brookings Institution, 1992), 89.

3. See Derek W. Urwin, *The Community of Europe*, 2d ed. (London: Longman, 1995), 107–113.

4. For example, see Stephen George, *Politics and Policy in the European Community*, 2d ed. (Oxford: Oxford University Press, 1991), 12–14.

5. Peter Ludlow, "The European Commission," in Robert O. Keohane and Stanley Hoffmann (Eds.), *The New European Community: Decisionmaking and Institutional Change* (Boulder: Westview Press, 1991), 116–121.

6. Margaret Thatcher, *The Downing Street Years* (New York: HarperCollins, 1993), 547.

7. Richard O'Toole, "The Decisionmaking Process Within the Commission of the European Communities in Light of the Single European Act," *Irish Studies in International Affairs* 2:1 (1986), 65–76.

8. Guy de Bassompierre, *Changing the Guard in Brussels: An Insider's View of the EC Presidency* (New York: Praeger, 1988), 8.

9. For more discussion, see Fitzmaurice, "The European Commission."

10. Juliet Lodge, "EC Policymaking: Institutional Dynamics," in Juliet Lodge (Ed.), *The European Community and the Challenge of the Future* (New York: St. Martin's Press, 1993).

11. Helen Wallace, "The Council and the Commission After the Single European Act," in Leon Hurwitz and Christian Lequesne (Eds.), *The State of the European Community: Policies, Institutions, and Debates in the Transition Years* (Boulder: Lynne Rienner, 1991).

12. Peters, "Bureaucratic Politics," 116–117.

13. Desmond Dinan, *Ever Closer Union? An Introduction to the European Community* (Boulder: Lynne Rienner, 1994), 203.

14. Lionel Barber, "Looking for the New Mr. Europe," *Europe* 338 (July–August 1994), 34–35.

15. *The Economist,* July 2, 1994, 45–46.

16. Peter Ludlow et al. (Eds.), *The Annual Review of European Community Affairs 1991* (London: Brassey's, 1991), 455.

17. *The Economist,* March 20, 1993, 60.

18. Heinrich Siedentopf and Jacques Ziller, *Making European Policies Work: The Implementation of Community Legislation in the Member States* (London: Sage Publications, 1988).

19. John McCormick, *British Politics and the Environment* (London: Earthscan, 1991), 97–98.

20. Peters, "Bureaucratic Politics," 103.

21. Peter Ludlow, "Europe's Institutions: Europe's Politics," in Gregory F. Treverton (Ed.), *The Shape of the New Europe* (New York: Council on Foreign Relations Press, 1992).

Further Reading

David Spence and Geoffrey Edwards. *The European Commission* (New York: Stockton, 1994).

A detailed study of the structure and workings of the Commission; the only full-length published study of the Commission to date.

Roy Jenkins. *European Diary 1977–1981* (London: Collins, 1981).

An illuminating study of the inside workings of the Commission, written by one of its former presidents.

David Grant. *The House That Jacques Built* (London: Nicholas Brealey, 1994).

One of the first English-language biographies of Jacques Delors.

George Ross. *Jacques Delors and European Integration* (New York: Oxford University Press, 1995).

A fascinating study of the internal workings of the Commission under Delors, written by a scholar who was given unparalleled access to its meetings and documents.

Most of the remaining sources of information on the Commission are journal articles and book chapters, one of the best of which is Peter Ludlow, "The European Commission," in Robert O. Keohane and Stanley Hoffmann (Eds.), The New European Community: Decisionmaking and Institutional Change (Boulder: Westview Press, 1991). For an assessment of post-Maastricht prospects for the Commission, see John Fitzmaurice's chapter in Andrew Duff et al. (Eds.), Maastricht and Beyond: Building the European Union (London: Routledge, 1994).

7

The Council of Ministers

The Council of Ministers is the major decisionmaking branch of the EU, the primary champion of national interests, and arguably the most powerful of the EU institutions. Once the Commission has proposed a new law or policy and Parliament has given its opinion and proposed amendments, the Council of Ministers is responsible for accepting, amending, or rejecting the new law or policy. Although it must work closely with the other institutions, it has the final say on what will and what will not become EU law.

Despite its powers, the Council is less well-known and more poorly understood than either the Commission or the Parliament. Its deliberations are secretive, there has been surprisingly little scholarly study of its structure and processes, and most EU citizens tend to associate EU law with the Commission, forgetting that the Council of Ministers makes the final decisions. In many ways, its law-making powers make the Council more like the legislature of the EU than the European Parliament, although new powers for Parliament in recent years have made the two bodies into "colegislatures." Growing pressure for institutional reform could mean that the Council of Ministers will eventually be replaced with a new upper legislative chamber, directly accountable to EU voters and representing the member states in the same way the U.S. Senate represents the fifty states.

The Council of Ministers is a forum in which incumbent national government ministers meet to discuss, build consensus, and take decisions on EU law and policy. The term *Council of Ministers* is misleading, because the Council actually consists of several different councils, depending on the topic under discussion. For example, foreign ministers will meet to deal with foreign affairs, transport ministers to discuss new proposals for transport policy and law, and so on. To ensure that the Council does not become too parochial and nationalistic, the appropriate European commissioner sits in on Council meetings. Overall direction is provided by the presidency of the Council, which is held in rotation for six-month terms by each EU member state. (To confuse the issue further, the term *Council* is often used to describe both the Council of Ministers and the European Council.)

Opinion is divided on whether the Council is intergovernmental or supranational, with debate complicated by the Council's changing role, powers, and methods. Although it is usually seen as the main forum for the representation of national interests, Peter Ludlow argues that it is "part of the supranational reality" of the EU.[1] Wolfgang Wessels argues that it is "the major control mechanism through which states give up autonomy [in return] for well-guaranteed access and influence" and feels the transfer of powers to the EU and their use by the Council have pushed the Council closer to having the same features of "cooperative federalism" as those found in the governments of the United States and Germany.[2] Changes in its voting procedures (discussed later in this chapter) have altered the Council's priorities over time, tending to push it more toward supranationalism.

Evolution

The Council of Ministers grew out of the Special Council of Ministers of the ECSC, which was created at the insistence of the Benelux countries to defend their national interests in the face of the dominance of France, Germany, and Italy. Because its members consisted of national government ministers, the ECSC Council provided an intergovernmental balance to the supranationalist inclinations of the High Authority.

A separate Council of Ministers was created for the EEC in 1958, where the idea of defending national interests was taken a step further with a weighted system of voting designed to prevent large countries from overwhelming small ones. The Council had only six members, but among them they had seventeen votes: four each for the three largest countries, two each for the Netherlands and Belgium, and one for Luxembourg. In the case of simple majority voting, the big three could outvote the small three, but some votes required a qualified majority, meaning a measure needed twelve votes from at least four states to pass. This protected small states and large states from each other, but it also encouraged them to work together. The Merger Treaty created a single Council of Ministers in 1967.

It was assumed that once Europe began to integrate and the member states learned to trust each other, the Council would become less important and the Commission would be able to initiate, decide, *and* implement policy. In the event, the power and influence of the Council grew because member states were disinclined to give up powers to the Commission. The result was an emphasis on and perpetuation of the idea of the EEC as an intergovernmental rather than a supranational body, which displeased those who supported a federal Europe. The Luxembourg Compromise introduced the power of veto, but it was rarely used, and decisionmaking in the Council became increasingly consensual over time. It has recently shifted more toward majority voting, thus forcing member states to put EU interests above national interests. Several developments have added to the power and influence of the Council:[3]

1. It has increasingly reached its own nonbinding agreements, reducing the need to agree on formal laws and thus bypassing both the Commission and Parliament.

2. As the interests and reach of the EU have spread, the Council has become involved in new policy areas not covered by the founding treaties.

3. The presidency of the Council of Ministers has become an increasingly important part of the EU decisionmaking system and the source of many key initiatives taken on issues such as EMU and foreign policy.

At the same time, both the European Council and the European Parliament have made inroads into the power of the Council of Ministers. The former has more power over deciding the broad goals of the EU, and the latter—particularly since direct elections began in 1979—has demanded and won a greater say in decisionmaking. Under the terms of the Single European Act and the Maastricht treaty, Parliament has had more power to comment on Council decisions and to force amendments (see Chapter 8).

Structure

The Council of Ministers (officially the Council of the European Union) is based in the Charlemagne Building in downtown Brussels, across from the Berlaymont, the former headquarters of the European Commission. It has four main elements: the councils of ministers themselves, the Committee of Permanent Representatives, the presidency, and the Secretariat General.

The Councils

Nearly two dozen different technical councils come under the general heading of the Council of Ministers. Although supposedly equal in terms of their status and powers, some are—in Orwellian terms—more equal than others and have more well-defined identities.[4] The most important and focused of these councils is the General Affairs Council (GAC), which brings the EU

TABLE 7.1   The Council of Ministers: Frequency of Meetings, 1967–1993

Council	1967	1970	1975	1980	1985	1990	1993
General and foreign	7	12	16	13	14	13	19
Agriculture	8	15	15	15	14	14	11
Economy and finance	1	1	8	9	7	10	11
Internal market	—	—	—	—	—	7	6
Technology and industry	1	1	—	—	1	4	5
Environment	—	—	3	2	3	4	5
Fisheries	—	—	—	7	3	3	5
Research	—	—	2	—	2	4	5
Labor and social affairs	1	3	2	2	2	3	4
Transport	1	3	2	2	3	4	4
Development cooperation	—	—	2	1	2	3	2
Budget	—	—	3	5	5	2	2
Education	—	—	1	1	1	2	2
Energy	—	1	—	2	3	1	2
Consumer protection	—	—	—	—	1	2	2
Health	—	—	—	—	—	2	2
Euratom	1	2	—	—	—	—	—
Miscellaneous	—	3	2	4	8	8	9
Total	20	41	56	63	69	86	96

Source: Annual Reports of the General Secretariat of the Council of the European Union (various years).

foreign ministers together at least once every month except for August (when much of Europe goes on vacation) to deal broadly with internal *and* external relations and to discuss politically sensitive policies and proposals for new laws. Below the GAC, the two most powerful councils are Ecofin (consisting of economics and finance ministers and responsible for the EMS) and the Agriculture Council. Below them are councils dealing with issues such as the internal market and the environment; these meet less often and are relatively junior members of the Council hierarchy.

Each council normally consists of the relevant government minister from the national governments and the relevant member of the European Commission, whose presence ensures that the councils do not lose sight of broader EU interests. Frequency of meetings depends on the importance of the council's area. The GAC, Ecofin, and the Agriculture Council tend to meet monthly because of the sheer volume of work with which they have to deal, but the councils on issues such as education, transport, or energy meet perhaps only two to four times each year. Altogether, the technical councils now meet about eighty to one hundred times each year (see Table 7.1). Most meetings are held in Brussels, but councils also occasionally convene in Luxembourg. Most meetings last no more than one or two days, depending on the agenda. Some are informal, but most are full negotiating and legislative sessions.[5]

In an ideal world, each of the councils would consist of the relevant and equivalent ministers from each member state, but this does not always happen. First, not all member states send their ministers but instead send deputy ministers or senior diplomats. The relevant minister may want to avoid political embarrassment on some issue; may have other, more urgent problems to deal with at home; or may not think the meeting is important enough to attend. For a time in the late 1980s, for example, British Environment Minister Nicholas Ridley (who was notoriously unsympathetic to environmental issues) refused to attend meetings of the Environment Council. Unless councils are attended by all of the relevant ministers, it is difficult to take major decisions.

Second, not every member state has an identical set of ministers, and each divides policy portfolios in ways that are often different. For example, some member states have ministers of women's affairs, while others do not. France has a minister of culture, making it almost unique in the EU. The result is that council meetings are often attended by a mixed set of ministers with different responsibilities.

Permanent Representatives

Between meetings of ministers, national interests in the Council are protected and promoted by national delegations of thirty to forty professional diplomats, each headed by a permanent representative. The representatives meet every week in the powerful and secretive Committee of Permanent Representatives (known by its French acronym COREPER), a body about which most EU citizens know very little. No mention of COREPER was made in the Treaty of Paris, but a Coordinating Committee helped to prepare ministerial meetings in the ECSC, and member states began to appoint permanent representatives to the EEC in 1958.[6] COREPER was finally recognized in the 1965 Merger Treaty, by which time the growing workload of the Council had led to a decision to create two committees: Permanent representatives meet in COREPER II and their deputies in COREPER I. COREPER II deals with broad issues coming before the GAC and Ecofin, while COREPER I concentrates on the work of most of the other councils.

The permanent representatives act as a valuable link between Brussels and the member states, ensuring that the views of the member states (or at least their governments) are represented and that the capitals are kept informed on what is happening in Brussels. Because they work with each other so much and come to know each other well, the representatives are occasionally torn between defending national positions and trying to ensure that their meetings lead to successful conclusions.[7]

As a body, COREPER acts as a clearinghouse for proposals and a melting pot of ideas, where national positions are outlined and debated and compromises are often reached that reduce the workload for the ministers themselves. COREPER sets up specialist working groups to study the law or policy under discussion and to try to reach common positions. It plays a key role in organizing Council meetings by preparing Council agendas, deciding which proposals go to which council, deciding which of the proposals can be automatically approved by the Council (A points) and which need discussion (B points), and overseeing the committees and working parties set up to sift through the proposals. Meetings of COREPER II are prepared by senior members of the national delegations, known as the **Antici Group** (after the Italian diplomat who chaired its first meeting in 1975).

Much like a national legislature, the Council of Ministers also has a complex network of committees and working groups that do most of the preparatory work and try to reach agreement on proposed legislation before it goes to the Council. There are eight standing committees (including those on energy, education, and agriculture), each made up mainly of national government officials but occasionally including representatives from interest groups (for example, the Committee on Employment includes representatives from industry). The working groups analyze Commission proposals and try to identify points of agreement and disagreement. They come and go according to the Council's workload, but as many as 180 may be functioning at any one time.

The Presidency

The presidency of the Council of Ministers (and of the European Council) is held not by a person but by a country (in effect, the prime minister—or president in the case of France—and the foreign minister of that country). Every EU member state takes turns holding the presidency for spells of six months—beginning in January and July each year—in alphabetical order by the name of each state in its own language (see Table 7.2). Six months is usually a long enough time to make an impression on the direction of the EU, but it is also a short enough period to ensure that every member state is periodically at the helm and to guarantee a balance between small and large countries. But the workload of the presidency is not spread evenly, because negotiations on farm prices take place in the spring, and most of the work on the EU budget is concentrated in the second half of the year. To make sure every member state has a turn at being responsible for the budget, the cycle of presidencies beginning in January 1993 inverted each pair of states, so instead of beginning with Belgium and moving on to Denmark, Denmark was first and Belgium followed.

BOX 7.1
The Democratic Deficit

The lack of institutional openness and accountability has been a recurring problem throughout the short history of the EU. The European Parliament is the only directly elected body in the EU system, but most of the power resides with the Commission and the Council of Ministers—neither of which is directly elected, and neither of which has much public accountability. As one MEP put it in 1991, if the EC were a state and applied for Community membership, it would be turned down on the grounds that it was not a democracy.[1] Descriptions of the way EU institutions work commonly include words such as "remote," "secretive," and "elitist."

The **democratic deficit** is usually defined as the lack of accountability of the EU institutions,[2] or the gap between the powers transferred to the EU and the ability of the European Parliament to oversee and control those powers.[3] Several other problems add to the deficit:

- Meetings of the Council of Ministers and the College of Commissioners are closed to the public.

- Key decisions are taken by the European Council or the Council of Ministers with little reference to the people, either directly or through the European Parliament.

- The Commission is an unelected executive with considerable powers. Both the College and COREPER meet in closed sessions, the groundwork for many important decisions is laid (and decisions are effectively taken) by nonelected bureaucrats, and many in COREPER are national bureaucrats rather than employees of the Council of Ministers.

- The input of national legislatures into the work of the Commission is severely limited.

- Few European citizens feel they can directly influence the EU policy process or even know how to go about exerting such influence.

As the breadth and depth of European integration have grown, so have the value, influence, and power of the presidency. The state holding the presidency today has several responsibilities.

First, it sets the agenda for Council meetings and also effectively for the EU as a whole. The presidency looks out for the broader goals of the EU but also gives the incumbent member state the chance to push issues of special interest further up the EU agenda, although it must balance this with the task of brokering agreements among the member states as a whole.

Second, the presidency arranges and chairs meetings of the Council of Ministers and COREPER and oversees Council relations with other EU institutions. An active presidency will lean heavily on COREPER to push its favorite proposals and to ensure that agreement is reached.[8]

• Many bureaucratic hurdles are placed in the path of public access to EU institutions and documents, as anyone who has tried to gain access to EU institutional libraries in Brussels (including myself) well knows. Ironically, the Brussels libraries contain few documents that are not freely available in EU depository libraries in the United States.

The European Parliament has exploited the sympathy of some member states and the guilt of others to encourage more accountability[4] but it still comes up against concerns about loss of sovereignty. The most serious effect of the democratic deficit is that the EU seems distant and inaccessible to the citizens of the EU, a fact that does little to promote public enthusiasm for European integration. As integration proceeds and the number of member states grows, the pressure for fundamental reform increases.

Notes

1. David Martin, quoted in Vernon Bogdanor and Geoffrey Woodcock, "The European Community and Sovereignty," *Parliamentary Affairs* 44:4 (October 1991), 481–492.

2. Ibid.

3. Brigitte Boyce, "The Democratic Deficit of the European Community," *Parliamentary Affairs* 46:4 (October 1993), 458–477; Shirley Williams, "Sovereignty and Accountability in the European Community," in Robert O. Keohane and Stanley Hoffmann (Eds.), *The New European Community: Decisionmaking and Institutional Change* (Boulder: Westview Press, 1991), 162.

4. Desmond Dinan, *Ever Closer Union? An Introduction to the European Community* (Boulder: Lynne Rienner, 1994), 257.

TABLE 7.2   Schedule of Presidencies of the Council of Ministers

1983 first half	West Germany	1993 first half	Denmark
1983 second half	Greece	1993 second half	Belgium
1984 first half	France	1994 first half	Greece
1984 second half	Ireland	1994 second half	Germany
1985 first half	Italy	1995 first half	France
1985 second half	Luxembourg	1995 second half	Spain
1986 first half	Netherlands	1996 first half	Italy
1986 second half	United Kingdom	1996 second half	Ireland
1987 first half	Belgium	1997 first half	Netherlands
1987 second half	Denmark	1997 second half	Luxembourg
1988 first half	West Germany	1998 first half	United Kingdom
1988 second half	Greece	1998 second half	Austria
1989 first half	Spain	1999 first half	Germany
1989 second half	France	1999 second half	Finland
1990 first half	Ireland	2000 first half	Portugal
1990 second half	Italy	2000 second half	France
1991 first half	Luxembourg	2001 first half	Sweden
1991 second half	Netherlands	2001 second half	Belgium
1992 first half	Portugal	2002 first half	Spain
1992 second half	United Kingdom	2002 second half	Denmark

Third, it mediates and bargains and is responsible for promoting cooperation among member states. The success of a presidency is measured according to the extent to which it is able to encourage compromise and agreement among the EU members. At the same time, it is evaluated as much by what it delays or opposes as by what it promotes.[9]

The presidency oversees EU foreign policy for six months, acts as the main voice of the EU on the global stage, coordinates member-state positions at international conferences and negotiations in which the EU is involved, and (along with the president of the Commission) represents the EU at meetings with the president of the United States and at the annual meetings of the Group of Seven (G7) industrialized countries. Finally, it hosts the biannual summit of the European Council (see Chapter 10).

To ensure continuity from one presidency to the next, the Council uses a troika system in which ministers from the incumbent presidency work closely with their predecessors and their successors. When France took over the presidency in the first half of 1995, for example, French ministers worked particularly closely with their German predecessors and their Spanish successors.

Holding the presidency allows a member state to convene meetings and launch strategic initiatives on issues of particular national interest, to try to bring those issues and initiatives to the top of the EU agenda, and to earn prestige and credibility (assuming it does a good job). The presidency allows the leaders of smaller states to negotiate directly with other world leaders—which they might otherwise rarely be able to do—and also helps the process of European integration by making the EU more real to the citizens of that country; it helps them to feel more involved and to see that they have a stake in the development of the EU.

The main disadvantage of the job is the huge amount of work involved, a burden that is especially onerous to member states with limited resources. A member state can pass up its turn as president, as Portugal did immediately after it joined the EC in 1986 on the grounds that it was not yet in a position to do a good job. A member state can also ask another state to help bear some of the workload. Ireland, for example, won widespread respect for its presidency in the first half of 1990 but had difficulty meeting its foreign policy obligations. Officially neutral, Ireland has full-time embassies in barely thirty countries, which means it lacks an intelligence-gathering system and a pool of foreign policy experts; the Irish Parliament does not even have a foreign affairs committee. Ireland's low-key approach led to the old joke that its most useful role in international relations lies in occupying the seat between Iraq and Israel at international gatherings. Ireland dealt with its resource problem by asking Italy (which was next in line for the presidency) to help with information gathering.

The record of some recent presidencies illustrates the often very different styles and priorities different member states bring to the job.

Italy. The Italian presidency during the second half of 1990 was overseen by Prime Minister Giulio Andreotti and Foreign Minister Gianni de Michelis. Sidetracked by domestic political problems, Andreotti was less visible than de Michelis, a colorful socialist with long black curly hair and a passion for disco dancing. The IGCs on political and monetary union were held during this presidency, and de Michelis made his mark by outlining his concept of a new European "architecture" of cooperation and security stretching from San Francisco to Vladivostok. He emphasized the dangers of allowing Germany and France to dominate Europe, argued in favor of enlargement, and spoke of the benefits of a new "pentagon" of southeastern European states based on the old Austro-Hungarian empire (Italy, Austria, Hungary, Yugoslavia, and Czechoslovakia) that could act as a counterweight to Germany. Italy also promoted the idea of a Citizen's Europe, the completion of the single market, and road transit arrangements across Austria and Switzerland.[10] Despite all of these ideas, Italy's presidency is remembered less for its bold statements than for its generally poor organization.

Luxembourg. Luxembourg had last had the presidency when the Single European Act was under discussion, and it returned to the presidency in the first half of 1991 as several key international issues were emerging—notably the Gulf crisis, discussions under the auspices of GATT, relations with the dying Soviet Union, and proposals on the integration of EFTA into the Community. In short, a state with a population under 400,000 had the helm when the EC was wrestling with major issues in international relations. Prime Minister Jacques Santer and Foreign Minister Jacques Poos were helped by the fact that Luxembourg was seen as an honest broker and was unencumbered by a history of involvement in big-power competition. In many ways, Luxembourg was ideally placed to help work out compromises that kept the larger member states happy. Santer also helped to lay much of the groundwork for Maastricht and developed a reputation that contributed to his appointment as Commission president in 1994.

Portugal. Portugal had turned down its first opportunity to hold the presidency in 1986, so the first half of 1992 was its first turn at the helm. Prime Minister Anibal Cavaco Silva and Foreign Minister João de Deus Pinheiro took a notably low-key approach, concentrating on guiding Maastricht through the national ratification process rather than launching any new initiatives. Portugal had a strong interest in seeing Maastricht succeed because of the new emphasis it would place on regional development. Portugal won praise for doing a competent job but found itself stretched by two crises: the outbreak of fighting in Bosnia in the spring and the Danish rejection of Maastricht in June.

Belgium. In the second half of 1993, Belgium inherited the residual doubts about Maastricht, even though Danish voters had said yes in a second referendum in May 1993. It also had to deal with the continuing problem of unemployment in the EU and with concerns over the EU's apparent inability to respond to the Balkan crisis. Under the circumstances, the main job facing Prime Minister Jean-Luc Dehaene and Foreign Minister Willy Claes was restoring confidence. They began by helping to steer budgetary reforms through the Commission and Parliament, and they helped build an EU consensus on negotiations under the Uruguay Round of GATT. Belgian bureaucrat Youri Devuyst has argued that Belgium's strength stems from the fact that it sees European integration as being in its national interest, thereby helping it create a positive climate for interaction among the member states.[11]

Greece. Greece took over the presidency in the first half of 1994, just three months after national elections had returned the ailing Andreas Papandreou to power. Given all of the crises brewing in the EU at the time, the changes among Greek officials in Brussels, major economic problems at home, and the fact that Greece's track record in handling the presidency was not strong, little was expected of the new team of Papandreou and his European minister, Theodoros Pangalos. Greece did better than expected, overseeing the completion of membership negotiations with four new applicant states, several initiatives in foreign policy, and early preparations for the 1996 IGC on the future of the European Union.[12] But it failed to give the EU the leadership it needed on the Balkan crisis, and the Corfu European Council was unable to agree on a new president for the Commission.

Germany. Helmut Kohl had high hopes for the German presidency in the second half of 1994, but he was preoccupied by the October national elections, which he won with a reduced majority. Since Foreign Minister Klaus Kinkel was from a small party that was in coalition with Kohl's Christian Democrats, there were questions as well about changes in that office. Kohl's priorities were to strengthen ties with Eastern Europe, to build the Franco-German axis, to address the EU's continuing economic problems, and—as he announced after his election victory—to assure a place for himself in history as the person who presided over the reunification of Germany *and* the unification of Europe.

As the EU membership expands, the pressure to rethink the presidency and the structure of the Council of Ministers will grow. As the EU becomes bigger and more powerful, the smaller states will be less likely to be able to take on the responsibilities of the presidency; as the number of member states grows, each will have to wait longer for its turn (enlargement to fifteen members in 1995 put the presidency on a seven-and-a-half-year cycle). Past suggestions include that made in 1975 by the Tindemans committee to lengthen the term to twelve months and one by Jacques Delors to allow only the larger states to hold the presidency; neither won much support. One more realistic solution may lie in regionalizing the presidency; for example, the Benelux countries might have a joint presidency, as might the Iberian states (Portugal and Spain) and the Scandinavian states. Regional groupings such as these could alternate with the bigger states holding the presidency alone.

The Secretariat General

This is the bureaucracy of the Council, consisting of about 2,200 staff members based in Brussels, most of whom are translators and service staff. The office is headed by a secretary general appointed for a five-year term. The Secretariat supports the presidency and the Council by preparing draft agendas, keeping records, and generally giving the work of the Council some continuity by working closely with the permanent representatives and briefing every Council meeting on the status of each of the agenda items. Noting that the Secretariat is still poorly understood and largely ignored, Peter Ludlow has described it as "the powerbroker, an instrument of political management that no presidency can dispense with and most presidencies end up following."[13]

How the Council Works

The European Commission has a virtual monopoly on proposing new laws and policies. Theoretically, if the Commission did not feed proposals to the Council, the Council would have nothing to do. In practice, the Council and Parliament can instruct the Commission to investigate an issue and to outline proposals for new policies or laws. Over the years, the Council has exploited loopholes in the treaties to expand this power. The struggle between the Council and the Commission for power and influence has become one of the most important internal dynamics of EU decisionmaking.

What happens to a Commission proposal when it reaches the Council depends on its complexity and urgency and the extent to which problems have already been ironed out in discussions between Council and Commission staff. The more complex proposals usually go first to one or more specialist working parties, which look over the proposal in detail and identify points of agreement and disagreement.[14]

The proposal then goes to COREPER, which considers the political implications and tries to clear up as many of the remaining problems as it can, ensuring that the meeting of ministers is as quick and as painless as possible. The proposal then moves on to the relevant Council; if agreement has been reached by working parties or by COREPER, the proposal is listed as an A point, and the Council will approve it without debate. If agreement has not been reached, or if the item was left over from a previous meeting, it is listed as a B point. The Council has to discuss B points and try to reach a decision. A tendency toward trying to govern on the basis of consensus has meant that issues rarely come to a vote, but if they do, the founding treaties give the Council three options.

First, a **simple majority** was once needed mainly if the Council was dealing with a procedural issue or working under treaty articles, with each minister having one vote. But the SEA and Maastricht broadened the number of issues and areas in which a majority vote could be used (notably including matters related to the single market). Exemplifying the secrecy with which the Council works, no reliable statistics are publicly available on the frequency of majority voting, although rumors suggest that such votes are relatively rare and painless.[15]

In practice, the "vote" rarely (if ever) comes down to a show of hands but is often deduced by the chair simply by silence, the absence of opposition, or both.[16] Negotiations are occasionally allowed to run on until the opposition has been worn down and a consensus has emerged, which is part of the reason Council meetings often drag on until the small hours of the morning. Even so, the increased use of the majority vote has helped speed up the decisionmaking process.[17]

If a single member state refuses to adopt the consensus, the presidency will occasionally resort to setting up a package deal in which several proposals are carefully tied together, and the dissenting state is encouraged to give in on the proposals it opposes in return for having its favored proposals go through.[18]

Second, **unanimity** was once needed if the Council was looking at a new law that would set off an entirely new policy area or substantially change an existing policy. Since the SEA and Maastricht, the need for unanimity has been restricted mainly to votes on issues dealing with foreign policy, justice, and certain financial areas or to instances in which the Council wants to change a Commission proposal against the wishes of the Commission. Each minister again has one vote and may abstain.

Third, a **qualified majority** is needed for almost every other kind of decision on which ministers have failed to reach a consensus. Rather than each minister having one vote, each is given several votes very roughly in proportion to the population of his or her member state (see Table 7.3). Through December 1994, the Council had a total of seventy-six votes, with the Big Four states having ten each, Spain eight, and so on down the line to

TABLE 7.3   Qualified Majority Voting in the Council of Ministers

Member State	Number of Votes Through December 1994	Number of Votes Since January 1995	Number of Citizens per Vote (millions)
Germany	10	10	8.09
Britain	10	10	5.82
France	10	10	5.77
Italy	10	10	5.71
Spain	8	8	4.89
Netherlands	5	5	3.04
Greece	5	5	2.06
Belgium	5	5	2.02
Portugal	5	5	1.97
Sweden	—	4	2.18
Austria	—	4	1.98
Denmark	3	3	1.73
Finland	—	3	1.68
Ireland	3	3	1.17
Luxembourg	2	2	0.12
Total	76	87	4.24 (average)
Qualified majority	54	62	—
Blocking minority	23	26	—

Luxembourg with two votes. To be successful, a proposal had to win fifty-four of the seventy-six votes (just over 71 percent of the total). To help the smaller states further, there was also a **blocking minority** by which twenty-three votes *against* a proposal would be enough to defeat it. This allowed three or more states to form a blocking minority, and it also prevented two big states from defeating a proposal. The system forces states to form coalitions, encourages cooperation, and reduces the tendency toward nationalism inherent in the way the Council of Ministers is structured.

With the accession of three new members in January 1995, the total number of votes was increased to eighty-seven, the qualified majority to sixty-two (or 71 percent of the total), and the blocking minority to twenty-six. Concerned that the power of the bigger states would be reduced, Britain and Spain had tried to keep the blocking minority at twenty-three but agreed to twenty-six on the condition that a delay would be built in to allow the Council to do "all within its power" to reach a compromise that would make such a minority unnecessary.

Since the Luxembourg Compromise, each member state has had the implied power to veto issues it believes affect its vital national interests. Although it is rarely used, the very existence of the veto can be employed as a threat, and governments can use it to convince their citizens that national sovereignty has not been compromised by EU membership.

BOX 7.2
Meetings of the Council of Ministers

Meetings of the Council of Ministers can often seem chaotic and unwieldy, with national delegations of perhaps half a dozen members, delegations from the Commission and the Secretariat, and a phalanx of interpreters. There may be as many as 120–130 people in the meeting room at any one time (although that number can rise to 250–300 at key meetings of the General Affairs Council). If the meeting threatens to get out of hand, the president can call for a restricted session and clear the room of everyone but "ministers plus two," "ministers plus one," or ministers and the commissioner.

The delegations are seated at a table in alphabetical order according to the names of their states in their national languages, with the Commission delegation at one end and the delegations from the presidency and the Secretariat at the other. (Each pair of states was inverted in 1993; see p. 129.) The member state holding the presidency not only chairs the meeting but also has separate national representation. National delegations are normally headed by the relevant minister, backed up by national officials and experts. The performance of individual ministers is influenced by several factors, including national interests, their ideological leanings, public opinion at home (especially if an election is in the offing), and their own personalities and relationships with other ministers.

In addition to general discussions, there are regular postponements and adjournments, huddles of delegates during breaks, regular communication with national capitals, and a constant flow of ministers and officials coming and going. When negotiations are becoming bogged down, the president might use a device known as a *tour de table,* during which the heads of delegations are asked in turn to give a brief summary of their positions on an issue. This procedure gives every delegation the chance to take part in discussions and raises possible new points of agreement and compromise, but it can also be time-consuming.

Council meetings are not the only forum in which discussions take place and decisions are made. In addition to the preparatory committee and working party meetings, Council meetings also break for lunches attended only by ministers and translators, and agreements are often reached over a meal.

The seating plan for Council meetings in the second half of 1995 was as follows:

President   Secretariat
(España)

España		France
Italia		Deutschland
Ireland		Ellás (Greece)
Nederland		België/Belgique
Luxembourg		Denmark
Portugal		United Kingdom
Osterreich (Austria)		Suomi (Finland)
		Sverige (Sweden)

Commission

TABLE 7.4 Workload of the Council of Ministers

	Meetings Held	Permanent Staff	Regulations Adopted	Directives Adopted	Decisions Adopted	Total New Laws Adopted
1988	77	1,990	434	63	131	628
1989	87	2,164	394	79	161	634
1990	86	2,183	380	65	169	614
1991	83	2,097	335	72	174	581
1992	89	2,147	383	166	189	738[a]
1993	96	2,170	319	63	164	546

[a]Increased workload caused by completion of single market and reforms to agriculture, fisheries, and transport policies.

Source: Commission of the European Communities, General Report of the Activities of the European Communities (various years).

Before the Council can adopt a proposal, it must ask Parliament for an opinion, which is nonbinding. This consultation procedure applies to specific areas, including fiscal harmonization, industry, economic and social cohesion, foreign policy, and the amendment of key treaties. Changes under the Single European Act and Maastricht gave Parliament the right to a second reading (the cooperation procedure) and a third reading (the codecision procedure) for specified kinds of legislation (see Chapter 8). When everyone has had their say, a final decision is reached by the Council of Ministers, and the proposal is either rejected or becomes law.

The volume of the Council's work has grown rapidly. In 1970 the Council met just forty-one times; in 1993 it met ninety-six times. In 1970 the Council adopted 345 new pieces of legislation; by the early 1990s it was adopting 550–650 new laws each year (see Table 7.4). These figures reflect the growth of the EU and the movement of the Council into new areas of policy not covered by the founding treaties. The frequency of particular council meetings also reflects the changing priorities of the European Union; the councils that meet most frequently are those dealing with foreign affairs, agriculture, and economic issues, while those that meet least often deal with issues such as education and health. Before 1987 there were no meetings on the internal market, but after 1987 the Internal Market Council became one of the busiest of all the councils.

When the membership of the European Community was small, the workload was lighter, and it was also easier to reach decisions. As both membership and the workload increased, the number of technical councils grew, and more of the preparatory work was delegated to support staff. Much of this work is accomplished in meetings of Council and Commission staff, by Council working parties, and by COREPER. The informal meetings outside the technical councils are designed to clear up as many points of disagreement as possible so the final meeting of the councils can be short and straightforward.

Because the Council of Ministers is a meeting place for national interests, the keys to understanding how it works are found in terms such as compromise, bargaining, and diplomacy. The ministers are leading political figures at home, so they are motivated by national political interests.[19] They are also ideologically driven; thus Council decisions will be influenced by the relative weight of left-wingers, right-wingers, and centrists. The authority of different ministers will also depend to some extent on the stability of the governing party or coalition in their home states. All of these factors combine to pull ministers in many different directions and to deny the Council the kind of permanence and regularity enjoyed by the Commission.

Summary and Conclusions

Speaking at the first session of the ECSC Council of Ministers in September 1952, West German Chancellor Konrad Adenauer argued that the Council stood "at the crossroads of two kinds of sovereignty, national and supranational. . . . While it must safeguard the national interests of the member states, it must not regard this as its paramount task . . . [which] is to promote the interests of the Community."[20]

The Council has been torn ever since between these two goals, which some see as compatible and others as contradictory. The Council is made up of national government ministers with their own parochial concerns, so its work is ultimately the sum of those concerns. The search for compromise can encourage ministers to reach decisions that promote the broader EU interest, but the Council continues to tend toward being intergovernmental. It is the most powerful of the EU institutions (except for the European Council, which is more a process than an institution), but its role will almost inevitably change as public demands for accountability and closure of the democratic deficit grow. The Council must at least become more open and less secretive, and it will likely be transformed at some point into a directly elected body, but one that still represents the national interests of EU member states.

Notes

1. Peter Ludlow, "Europe's Institutions: Europe's Politics," in Gregory F. Treverton (Ed.), *The Shape of the New Europe* (New York: Council on Foreign Relations Press, 1992), 64.

2. Wolfgang Wessels, "The EC Council: The Community's Decisionmaking Center," in Robert O. Keohane and Stanley Hoffmann (Eds.), *The New European*

Community: Decisionmaking and Institutional Change (Boulder: Westview Press, 1991), 137.

3. Neill Nugent, *The Government and Politics of the European Union* (Durham, N.C.: Duke University Press, 1994), 124–125.

4. Helen Wallace, "The Council and the Commission After the Single European Act," in Leon Hurwitz and Christian Lequesne (Eds.), *The State of the European Community: Policies, Institutions, and Debates in the Transition Years* (Boulder: Lynne Rienner, 1991), 26.

5. Ibid., 24.

6. Fiona Hayes-Renshaw, Christian Lequesne, and Pedro Mayor Lopez, "The Permanent Representations of the Member States of the European Communities," *Journal of Common Market Studies* 28:2 (December 1989), 119–137.

7. Ibid.

8. Guy de Bassompierre, *Changing the Guard in Brussels: An Insider's View of the EC Presidency* (New York: Praeger, 1988), 48.

9. Christopher Brewin and Richard McAllister, "Annual Review of the Activities of the European Community in 1990," *Journal of Common Market Studies* 29:4 (June 1991), 385–430.

10. Ibid.

11. Youri Devuyst, "The Belgian Presidency of the Council: A Turning Point Toward a Revitalized European Union?" *Newsletter* of the European Community Studies Association 7:1 (Winter 1994), 12–15.

12. Peter Ludlow, "The Greek Presidency," *Newsletter* of the European Community Studies Association 7:3 (Fall 1994), 9–11.

13. Ludlow, "Europe's Institutions," 63.

14. For a more detailed explanation of the process, see Hayes-Renshaw, Lequesne, and Lopez, "Permanent Representations."

15. Wallace, "The Council and the Commission," 25.

16. Wessels, "The EC Council," 147.

17. Ludlow, "Europe's Institutions," 62.

18. De Bassompierre, *Changing the Guard in Brussels,* 35.

19. B. Guy Peters, "Bureaucratic Politics and the Institutions of the European Community," in Alberta Sbragia (Ed.), *Euro-Politics: Institutions and Policymaking in the "New" European Community* (Washington, D.C.: Brookings Institution, 1992), 79.

20. Cited in Jean Monnet, *Memoirs* (Garden City, N.Y.: Doubleday, 1978).

Further Reading

Given its powers and significance, the Council of Ministers is surprisingly poorly served in terms of book-length studies. Among the more useful sources of information:

Guy de Bassompierre. *Changing the Guard in Brussels: An Insider's View of the EC Presidency* (New York: Praeger, 1988).

A look at the inside workings of the Council of Ministers and the European Council by a Belgian diplomat with extensive experience in the meeting rooms of Brussels.

Emil Joseph Kirchner. *Decision-making in the European Community: The Council Presidency and European Integration* (Manchester: Manchester University Press, 1992).

An assessment of the role of the presidency of the Council of Ministers in the process of European integration.

In addition, several journal articles and book chapters provide useful details, including Wolfgang Wessels, "The EC Council: The Community's Decisionmaking Center," in Robert O. Keohane and Stanley Hoffmann (Eds.), *The New European Community: Decisionmaking and Institutional Change* (Boulder: Westview Press, 1991); and Fiona Hayes-Renshaw, Christian Lequesne, and Pedro Mayor Lopez, "The Permanent Representations of the Member States of the European Communities," *Journal of Common Market Studies* 28:2 (December 1989), 119–137.

8

The European Parliament

At first glance, the European Parliament (EP) looks and sounds much like the legislature of the EU: It is the only directly elected institution in the EU system, and it has many of the trappings of a legislature, including party groupings and committees. But it lacks three of the defining powers of a legislature: It cannot introduce laws, enact laws, or raise revenues. It can ask the Commission to propose a new law or policy, can amend some laws as they go through the Commission and the Council of Ministers, has equal powers with the Council over the EU budget, must approve and can fire the Commission, and can veto applications from aspirant EU members. But the Commission still holds the power of initiation, and the Council has most of the real power of decisionmaking. In short, Parliament either shares powers with or negates the powers of other EU institutions.

Most of the EP's handicaps can be traced to the unwillingness of the governments of EU member states to give up their powers over decisionmaking in the Council of Ministers and to the emphasis the Treaty of Rome places on Parliament's "advisory" and "supervisory" powers.[1] Parliament also has a credibility problem: Few EU citizens know (or care) what it does or have the kinds of psychological ties to the EP that they have to their national legislatures. Further, European political parties have yet to develop consistency or a widespread following. In some ways, the EP suffers a double bind: Few voters are interested in it because of its limited powers, but its powers are limited largely because so few voters care. To make matters worse, media coverage of Parliament tends to focus on the trivial at the expense of the significant; the intricacies of the budgetary process make less interesting headlines than easy charges that European legislators are overpaid, underworked, occasionally corrupt, or fascinated by the search for aliens (some EP members recently suggested that a European observatory for UFOs be created).

In fairness, Parliament is a much more substantial body than most Europeans realize. With increasing confidence, it has used arguments about democratic accountability to win more responsibilities and to be taken more seriously. (In a sense, the way the EP has had to wring concessions from the other EU institutions is little different from the way budding legislatures took powers away from the aristocracy in medieval Europe.) The EP has become less a body that reacts to Commission proposals and Council votes and has increasingly launched its own initiatives and forced the other institutions to pay more attention to its opinions. Parliament has had a say over the budget since the 1970s, it has slowly won more rights to amend legislation and to check the activities of the other institutions, it has been a valuable source of ideas and new policy proposals, and it has acted as both the conscience of the EU and the guardian of its democratic ideals.[2] With the introduction of direct elections in 1979, Parliament could claim to be the only democratically elected and accountable institution in an EU system that is undemocratic and secretive. This gives it a critical role in building bridges across the chasm that still separates EU citizens from EU institutions.

Evolution

The European Parliament began in 1952 as the Common Assembly of the ECSC. The Assembly met in Strasbourg and consisted of seventy-eight members appointed by the national legislatures of the six ECSC members, although Article 12 of the Treaty of Paris held out the possibility that members could eventually be directly elected. The Assembly had the power to force the High Authority of the ECSC to resign through a vote of censure, but it never used this power and ended up as little more than an advisory forum for the discussion of High Authority proposals.[3] The treaties of Rome did not create separate assemblies for the EEC and Euratom but instead transformed the ECSC Common Assembly into a joint European Parliamentary Assembly. Its powers were expanded to give it coresponsibility with the Council of Ministers over the budget, but its suggestions for amendments to EEC law and policy were nonbinding. In 1962, the Assembly was renamed the European Parliament.

The new Parliament still consisted of members appointed by national legislatures from among their own numbers. This system had two important effects. First, only pro-European legislators put their names forward for appointment to the European Parliament. Second, since Members of the European Parliament (MEPs) were also members of national legislatures, they placed national interests above European interests, mainly because their jobs at home depended on the support of voters. As a result, the European Parliament was seen as a junior member of the EC system, and it has since had to work to change its image and to win more power and credibility.

Article 138 of the EEC Treaty also mentioned the possibility of direct elections, and although Parliament pursued that goal, the Council of

TABLE 8.1   Growth of the European Parliament

Year	Membership	
1952	78	Common Assembly of the ECSC
1958	142	Parliamentary Assembly of the European Communities
1973	198	Fifty-six seats added for Britain, Ireland, and Denmark
1976	410	Membership increased in anticipation of first direct elections
1981	434	Twenty-four seats added for Greece
1987	518	Eighty-four seats added for Spain and Portugal
1994	567	Adjustments made to account for the reunification of Germany
1995	624	Fifty-seven seats added for Austria, Finland, and Sweden

Ministers blocked its proposals throughout the 1960s and early 1970s.[4] At stake were concerns about the tendency toward supranationalism and the determination of the Council (and of national leaders such as Charles de Gaulle) to keep a firm grip on decisionmaking powers. The 1976 European Council finally agreed on the need for direct elections, which were held for the first time in 1979. This was a watershed; now that its members were directly elected and met in open session, Parliament had a moral advantage over the Council of Ministers (which is not directly elected and whose meetings are still closed to direct public access). MEPs could now claim they were the elected representatives of the citizens of the EU and that they should be allowed to represent the interests of the voters.

EP membership had expanded to 410 members by the 1979 elections (see Table 8.1) and has since expanded further to account for new members. More seats were added for Greece in 1981 and for Spain and Portugal in 1987. A major reconfiguration was made for the 1994 elections to take account of the reunification of Germany; every member state except Denmark, Ireland, and Luxembourg was given more seats, bringing the total to 567. The most recent enlargement in January 1995 pushed the number of seats to 624.

Structure

The European Parliament is the only directly elected international assembly in the world and is slowly accumulating the law-making powers usually associated with national legislatures. It consists of a single chamber, and its 624 members are directly elected by universal suffrage for fixed, renewable five-year terms.

One of Parliament's major handicaps is that it must divide its time among three different cities. The parliamentary chamber is situated in the Palace of

TABLE 8.2   Presidents of the European Parliament

Beginning of Term	Name	Member State	Party Group
Common Assembly of the ECSC			
Sept. 1952	Paul-Henri Spaak	Belgium	Socialist
May 1954	Alcide de Gasperi[a]	Italy	Christian Democrat
Nov. 1954	Giuseppe Pella	Italy	Christian Democrat
Nov. 1956	Hans Furler	Germany	Christian Democrat
European Parliament			
Mar. 1958	Robert Schuman	France	Christian Democrat
Mar. 1960	Hans Furler	Germany	Christian Democrat
Mar. 1962	Gaetano Martino	Italy	Liberal Democrat
Mar. 1964	Jean Duvieusart	Belgium	Christian Democrat
Sept. 1965	Victor Leemans	Belgium	Christian Democrat
Mar. 1966	Alain Poher	France	Christian Democrat
Mar. 1969	Mario Scelba	Italy	Christian Democrat
Mar. 1971	Walter Behrendt	Germany	Socialist
Mar. 1973	Cornelis Berkhouwer	Netherlands	Liberal Democrat
Mar. 1975	Georges Spenale	France	Socialist
Mar. 1977	Emilio Colombo	Italy	European People's Party
July 1979	Simone Veil	France	Liberal Democrat
Jan. 1982	Pieter Dankert	Netherlands	Socialist
July 1984	Pierre Pflimlin	France	European People's Party
Jan. 1987	Sir Henry Plumb	Britain	Conservative
July 1989	Enrique Baron Crespo	Spain	Socialist
Jan. 1992	Egon Klepsch	Germany	EPP
July 1994	Klaus Hänsch	Germany	Socialist

[a]Died in office August 1954.

Europe in Strasbourg, France. This is where members have most of their plenary sessions, but they meet here for just three or four days each month (except in August). Plenaries can become bogged down in procedure, there is too little time to achieve much, and most of the real work is done in committees; attendance is usually low, and the chamber is often less than half full. Plenaries can also last until late in the day and may be followed by evening meetings of the party groups or EP committees. The many empty seats and the occasional dozing legislator do little to help the credibility of Parliament.

The administrative Secretariat is in Luxembourg. This is where most of the Parliament's 3,250 support staff work, more than one-third on translation and interpretation. Few MEPs need to visit or spend time here, so the Secretariat is relatively isolated.

Parliamentary committees meet in Brussels for two to three weeks every month (except in August). This is where most of the real bargaining and revising take place, and since "additional" plenaries can be held in Brussels, committee meetings are relatively well attended, and MEPs tend to spend most of their time in Brussels.

The President

Much like the speaker of the U.S. House of Representatives, the president of the EP presides over debates during plenary sessions, passes proposals to committees, and represents Parliament in its relations with other institutions. The president must be an MEP and is elected by other MEPs for two-and-a-half-year renewable terms (half the span of a parliamentary term) (see Table 8.2). The president would probably be from the majority party bloc if there was one, but because no one party has ever had a majority, the president is chosen as a result of interparty bargaining. In 1989, the two largest party groups—the socialists and the conservative European People's Party (EPP)—struck a five-year bargain whereby a Spanish socialist, Enrique Baron Crespo, was appointed president for one term on the understanding that he would be replaced by someone from the EPP. In 1992, Crespo duly stepped aside for Egon Klepsch, a German Christian Democrat famous for an incident in 1982 when he was seen pressing the voting button of an absent colleague during a parliamentary vote. His name has since entered the parliamentary lexicon: "To Klepsch" means to cast more than one vote. Klepsch was succeeded in 1994 by Klaus Hänsch, a Social Democrat.

To help deal with the many different party groups in Parliament, the president has fourteen vice presidents. The president and the vice presidents make up the Bureau of the EP, which functions much like a governing council. The Bureau, in turn, meets with the heads of all of the political groups in Parliament in the Enlarged Bureau, which decides the agenda for plenary sessions and manages the committee system.

Committees

Much like the U.S. Congress, the European Parliament has a series of nineteen standing committees (and a changing number of ad hoc committees) that meet in Brussels to consider legislation relevant to their areas. The number of committees, and the importance of their work, has grown as the powers of the EP have grown. As is the case in the U.S. Congress, the committees have their own hierarchy, which reflects the differing levels of parliamentary influence over different policy areas. Among the most powerful are those that deal with the environment and the budget. Seats on committees are divided on the basis of a balance of party groups, the seniority of MEPs, and national interests. For example, member states such as Ireland and Denmark have a particular interest in agriculture and less interest in foreign and defense issues.

BOX 8.1
Parliament's Multisite Dilemma

The European Parliament's low credibility is not helped by its division among three different sites, which not only forces a tiring and time-consuming travel schedule on MEPs but also encourages many to skip the Strasbourg plenary sessions because they are the least important. The division also inflates the parliamentary budget; about $60 million (10 percent of the total budget) is spent moving MEPs, staff, and files back and forth. The absurdity of this arrangement reflects poorly on Parliament and on MEPs, despite the fact that many favor holding plenaries in Brussels.

The ECSC Treaty includes the stipulation (Article 77) that the seat of the institutions would have to be worked out by common accord of the member state governments. Luxembourg was tailor-made to be a European District of Columbia, but France has stubbornly refused to give up the parliamentary chamber. Both countries may find themselves fighting an increasingly lonely battle. Brussels may be shabbier and more expensive than either Strasbourg or Luxembourg, but it is steadily emerging as the true administrative center of the EU. It is already home to the Commission and the Council of Ministers, and plans have been launched to make Brussels a major European hub for air travel.

With national governments bickering over the issue of a site, the Court of Justice took matters into its own hands with a December 1991 ruling that Parliament could move its administrative staff from Luxembourg to Brussels. Belgium went a step further in January 1992, when work was begun on a smart new complex of office buildings in central Brussels—which contains a 750-seat chamber ideally suited to hold parliamentary plenaries. At 4 million square feet, the International Congress Center (opened in 1993) is one of the largest official buildings in Europe. The move outraged the governments of France and Luxembourg, and the French government refuses to even discuss the issue of a site until it is guaranteed that the parliamentary chamber will remain in Strasbourg.

The European Council decided in December 1992 that the EP Secretariat would remain in Luxembourg permanently and that plenaries would be held in Strasbourg but that "additional" plenaries could meet in Brussels. The EP signed a lease on the new Brussels complex, and additional plenaries have been held there since September 1993. New buildings have also been finished for the Commission and the Council of Ministers. As the powers and workload of Parliament increase and the commute becomes more onerous, fewer MEPs are likely to attend Strasbourg plenaries, and the focus of their activities will inevitably shift to Brussels.

European Elections

The European Parliament is elected for fixed five-year terms, and all of its members stand for reelection at the same time. The number of seats is divided very roughly on the basis of population, with Germany having ninety-nine seats and Luxembourg only six. Given the math used in the calculations, the larger countries are underrepresented, and the smaller countries are overrepresented (see Table 8.3).

TABLE 8.3   Distribution of European Parliamentary Seats by Population

	Population (million) 1993	Population per Seat	Number of Seats	Number of Seats if Distributed by Population
Germany	80.90	817,000	99	137
United Kingdom	58.20	669,000	87	98
France	57.70	663,000	87	97
Italy	57.10	656,000	87	96
Spain	39.10	611,000	64	66
EU average		592,000		
Netherlands	15.20	490,000	31	26
Greece	10.30	412,000	25	17
Belgium	10.10	404,000	25	17
Portugal	9.84	394,000	25	17
Sweden	8.72	415,000	21	15
Austria	7.92	396,000	20	13
Denmark	5.18	324,000	16	9
Finland	5.04	315,000	16	9
Ireland	3.50	233,000	15	6
Luxembourg	0.39	65,000	6	1
Total	369.19		624	624

Source: Calculated on the basis of population figures from Economist Intelligence Unit Country Reports, Third Quarter, 1994.

Every country except Britain uses multimember districts and variations on the theme of proportional representation (PR). Most member states treat their entire territory as a single electoral district, while Belgium, Ireland, and Italy have three to five "Euro-constituencies." All of these countries divide up their seats among parties according to the share of party vote. France, for example, has eighty-seven seats, so if French Party A wins 50 percent of the vote, it will be given 50 percent of the French seats (forty-four), and if Party B wins 40 percent of the vote, it will be given 40 percent of the seats (thirty-five), and so on. Unlike any of its EU partners, the United Kingdom (except for Northern Ireland) uses the same winner-take-all, single-member district system it uses at home (the same system used by the U.S. House of Representatives).

The single-member system has the advantage of tying individual MEPs to a particular district and making them responsible to a distinct group of voters. Under PR, by contrast, voters are represented by a group of MEPs from different parties, and constituents may never get to know or develop ties with a particular MEP. PR has the advantage, however, of more accurately reflecting the proportion of the vote given to different parties. The unfairness of winner-take-all was reflected in the 1989 election in Britain when the Green Party won 15 percent of the vote; this would have given it twelve seats under PR, but it ended up with no seats at all. The main disadvantage of PR is that it spreads the distribution of seats so thinly that no one party has enough seats to form a majority. While that situation encourages legislators from different parties to work together and reach compromises, it also makes it more difficult to get anything done.

The logistics of European elections are impressive. There were about 270 million eligible voters in 1994, almost half again as many as the number in the United States. Voters must be eighteen years of age and must be citizens of one of the EU member states. Some member states restrict voting to their own citizens, but there is a slow trend toward abolishing the national distinctions—allowing EU citizens to vote in their country of residence and even to run for Parliament wherever they live, regardless of their citizenship. The Maastricht treaty included the goal of extending this policy to every member state by December 31, 1993, but it also contained an escape clause that allows member states to delay implementing this rule "where warranted." Member states also have different rules on the minimum age for candidates, which ranges from eighteen to twenty-five.

Turnout varies from one member state to another but is generally higher than voter turnout for elections in the United States; just over 56 percent of Europeans voted in 1994, compared to an average of 55 percent in presidential election years in the United States and 30 percent in midterm elections. Belgium and Luxembourg usually have the best turnout (90 percent or more), while in Britain, Portugal, and the Netherlands, barely one in three of those eligible voted in 1994. There has been a tendency for turnout to fall in some of the poorer EU states (Portugal, Ireland, and Spain), to hold steady or decline slightly in the original six founder states (Italy excepted), and—ironically—to grow slightly in the two most skeptical members, Britain and Denmark (see Table 8.4). Turnout at European elections is generally lower than that at national elections in the member states, and average turnout has fallen steadily from more than 67 percent in the 1979 elections to just under 59 percent in the 1994 elections. There are several possible reasons.

- There is the sheer novelty of European elections, which have been a feature of the electoral calendar only since 1979.

- Few European voters really know what Parliament does or what issues are at stake, and turnover among MEPs has been so high that none has developed the kind of transnational reputation that would encourage voters to turn out. As a result, EU voters have developed very few psychological ties to the European Parliament, which still seems anonymous and distant to most.

- No change of government is at stake, as there would be in a national election, so voters feel there is less to be lost or gained. The membership of the Commission bears no relation to that of Parliament.

- Party groups in the European Parliament are still learning how to coordinate their election campaigns across all of the member states, and campaigns are still national rather than European. The Greens were the only group to run an EU-wide campaign in 1989, campaigning on their opposition to the single market, disarmament, and more devolution of powers to the local level.

- The media and national governments still tend to downplay the significance of European elections.

- Some voters have little interest in the EU or may be skeptical or hostile to the entire concept, making them disinclined to take part in European elections.

Another factor influencing turnout is that most voters still feel European elections are a poll on their national governments rather than an opportu-

TABLE 8.4 Turnout at European Elections, 1979–1994
(ranked by turnout in 1994)

	1979	1984	1989	1994	Change 1979–1994
Belgium[a]	91.4	92.2	90.7	90.7	− 1.3
Luxembourg[a]	88.9	87.0	87.8[e]	90.0	+ 1.1
Greece[a]	78.6[b]	77.2	79.8[e]	79.9	+ 1.3
Italy	85.5	89.9	81.5	74.8	−10.7
Spain	—	68.9[c]	54.8	59.6	− 9.3
Germany	65.7	56.8	62.4	58.0	− 7.7
France	60.7	56.7	48.7	53.5	− 7.2
Denmark	47.8	52.3	46.1	52.5	+ 4.7
Ireland	63.6	47.6	68.3[e]	37.0	−26.6
United Kingdom	32.6	32.6	36.2	36.4	+ 3.8
Portugal	—	72.2[d]	51.3	35.7	−36.5
Netherlands	58.1	50.5	47.2	35.6	−22.5
EU Total	62.0	61.0	58.4	56.4	− 5.6
Average	67.3	64.8	62.9	58.6	− 8.7

[a]Voting compulsory.
[b]Elections of October 1981.
[c]Elections of June 1987.
[d]Elections of July 1987.
[e]General election held same day.

nity to influence EU policies, about which many voters are still confused and uncertain. In 1994, for example, disgruntled Spanish voters used the European election to take seats away from the governing Socialist party of Felipe Gonzalez, British voters used it to state their disenchantment with the governing Conservative Party of John Major (the opposition Labour Party ended up with more than three times as many seats), and Italian voters used the election to make a statement about their general disgust with the corrupt and discredited leadership of the now defunct Christian Democrats. As the influence of the European Union spreads, as more voters understand the stakes of European elections, and as the powers of the European Parliament grow, turnout may improve.

The Party System

MEPs do not sit in national blocs but come together in cross-national ideological groups with roughly similar goals and values. After the 1989 elections, for example, sixty-six parties were represented in Parliament. Many of them consisted of as few as one or two members; they could achieve nothing by themselves, so they worked to build alliances with other parties. Some groups are marriages of convenience, bringing together MEPs with different policies; over time, however, the groups have built more focus, and they cover a much wider spectrum of ideologies and policies than is the case with the U.S. Congress, which has never had a significant left-wing party. A minimum of twenty-six MEPs is needed to form a group if they all come from one member state, twenty-one if they come from two member states, sixteen if they come from three states, and thirteen if they come from four or more states.

No one party group has ever had enough seats to form a majority, so multipartisanship has been the order of business. The balance of power is also affected by changes in the number and makeup of party groups. Through all the changes, three groups have developed a particular consistency: the Socialists (on the left), the Liberals (on the center-right), and the European People's Party (on the right) (see Tables 8.5 and 8.6). Moving from left to right on the ideological spectrum, the party groups after the 1994 elections were as follows:

Group of the European United Left (EUL).   This group is all that remains from the game of musical chairs played on the left of the chamber since the mid-1980s. Eurocommunists formed a Communist Group in 1973, but the collapse of the Soviet Union in 1989 encouraged Italian and Spanish communists to form their own European United Left, while more hard-line communists from France, Greece, and Portugal formed Left Unity. By 1994, only the EUL remained, made up mainly of Spanish, French, and Italian communists.

Group of the Party of European Socialists (PES). The socialists have consistently been the largest group in Parliament, adding to the concerns of conservative Euroskeptics about the interventionist tendencies of the EU. PES has shades of opinion ranging from ex-communists on the left to more moderate social democrats toward the center. It has members from every EU country, with the British Labour Party forming the single biggest national bloc. PES has a potential ally in the *European Radical Alliance,* which consists mainly of French left-wingers.

Liberal, Democratic, and Reformist Group (LDR). The LDR contains members from every EU member state except Greece and Germany, but it is difficult to pinpoint in ideological terms. Most of its members fall in the center or on the moderate right, and the group has suffered over the years from defections to the EPP.

Group of the European Democratic Alliance (EDA). Consisting mainly of French and Irish conservatives, the EDA is a center-right group created when French Gaullists defected from the LDR in 1965. It has been reluctant to link up with its most natural ally, the European People's Party. In the 1994 elections, French center-right defectors created a new, anti-Maastricht *Europe of the Nations Group.*

Group of the European People's Party (EPP). This is the major group on the right and has consistently been the second-largest bloc in Parliament. The group was once dominated by German and Italian Christian Democrats, but it changed its name to the EPP in 1976 and finally allowed the European Democrats (British and Danish conservatives) to join in 1992 on the condition that they accept the principles of the EPP, including federalism and a social Europe. The group is right of center and contained representatives from every EU member state in 1994. It would have fared even better had not *Forza Europa* (consisting entirely of members of Italy's *Forza Italia* party) formed its own splinter group.

The Green Group. Usually associated with environmental issues, the Greens in fact pursue a much wider variety of interests related to social justice, and they refuse to be placed on the traditional ideological spectrum. Once part of the Rainbow Group, the Greens formed their own group after the 1989 elections increased their numbers. German Greens form the biggest single national bloc.

Two disbanded groups are also worth mentioning.

Technical Group of the European Right (ER). This group once included Italian neofascists, but they decided to sit as independents in 1989, leaving this far-right group dominated by members of the French National Front

TABLE 8.5 Results of European Elections, 1979–1994

	Bl	Dn	Gm	Gr	Sp	Fr	Ir	It	Lx	Nl	Pt	UK	EC
1979													
Socialist	7	4	35	—	—	22	4	13	1	9	—	18	113
EPP	10	—	42	—	—	8	4	30	3	10	—	—	107
EDA	—	3	—	—	—	—	—	—	—	—	—	61	64
Comm.	—	1	—	—	—	19	—	24	—	—	—	—	44
LDR	4	3	4	—	—	17	1	5	2	4	—	—	40
EPD	—	1	—	—	—	15	5	—	—	—	—	1	22
Ind.	1	4	—	—	—	—	—	1	5	—	—	—	11
Nonattached	2	—	—	—	—	—	—	4	—	2	—	1	9
Total	24	16	81	—	—	81	15	81	6	25	—	81	410
1984													
PES	7	4	33	10	—	20	—	12	2	9	—	33	130
EPP	6	1	41	9	—	9	6	27	3	8	—	—	110
ED	—	4	—	—	—	—	—	—	—	—	—	46	50
Comm.	—	1	—	4	—	10	—	26	—	—	—	—	41
LDR	5	2	—	—	—	12	1	5	1	5	—	—	31
EDA	—	—	—	—	—	20	8	—	—	—	—	1	29
ARC	4	4	7	—	—	—	—	3	—	2	—	—	20
ER	—	—	—	1	—	10	—	5	—	—	—	—	16
Ind.	2	—	—	—	—	—	—	3	—	1	—	1	7
Total	24	16	81	24	—	81	15	81	6	25	—	81	434
1989													
PES	8	4	31	9	27	22	1	14	2	8	8	46	180
EPP	7	2	32	10	16	6	4	27	3	10	3	1	121
LDR	4	3	4	—	6	13	2	3	1	4	9	—	49
ED	—	2	—	—	—	—	—	—	—	—	—	32	34
Green	3	—	8	—	1	8	—	7	—	2	1	—	30
EUL	—	1	—	1	4	—	—	22	—	—	—	—	28
EDA	—	—	—	1	—	13	6	—	—	—	—	—	20
ER	1	—	6	—	—	10	—	—	—	—	—	—	17
LU	—	—	—	3	—	7	1	—	—	—	3	—	14
ARC	1	4	—	—	2	1	1	3	—	—	—	1	13
Ind.	—	—	—	—	4	1	—	5	—	1	—	1	12
Total	24	16	81	24	60	81	15	81	6	25	24	81	518

(continues)

and the German Republican Party. The ER is the most nationalistic group in the European Parliament and is largely shunned by other party groups. Its mainly French and Belgian members declared themselves independent in 1994.

The Rainbow Group (Arc-en-Ciel, or ARC). Following the departure of the Greens in 1989, the Rainbow Group was left with just thirteen MEPs who represented a variety of regional and minority interests and lacked a particular ideological direction.

	Bl	Dn	Gm	Gr	Sp	Fr	Ir	It	Lx	Nl	Pt	UK	EC
1994													
PES	6	3	40	10	22	15	1	18	2	8	10	63	198
EPP	7	3	47	9	30	13	4	12	2	10	1	19	157
LDR	6	5	—	—	2	1	1	7	1	10	8	2	43
EUL	—	—	—	4	9	7	—	5	—	—	3	—	28
FE	—	—	—	—	—	—	—	27	—	—	—	—	27
EDA	—	—	—	2	—	14	7	—	—	—	3	—	26
Green	2	1	12	—	—	—	2	4	1	1	—	—	23
ERA	1	—	—	—	1	13	—	2	—	—	—	2	19
EN	—	4	—	—	—	13	—	—	—	2	—	—	19
Ind.	3	—	—	—	—	11	—	12	—	—	—	1	27
Total	25	16	99	25	64	87	15	87	6	31	25	87	567

ARC	Rainbow Group
Comm.	Communist
ED	European Democrats
EDA	Group of the European Democratic Alliance
EN	Europe of the Nations Group
EPD	European Progressive Democrats
EPP	Group of the European People's Party
ER	Technical Group of the European Right
ERA	European Radical Alliance
EUL	Group of the European United Left
FE	Forza Europa
Green	Green Group
Ind.	Independents
LDR	Liberal, Democratic, and Reformist Group
LU	Left Unity
PES	Group of the Party of European Socialists

In addition to the formal party groups, some MEPs sit as independents, describing themselves as nonattached. The number of nonattached legislators is usually high immediately after an election, but it begins to fall as they slowly join party groups. Cutting across the party groups are smaller *intergroups* tied to specific issues, such as joint stands on a foreign policy issue or a new initiative on European integration. One of the most famous of these intergroups was the Crocodile Club led by Italian Altiero Spinelli (a former European commissioner), which was behind a 1984 draft treaty on European Union that eventually provided one of the sparks that led to the 1991 Maastricht treaty.

Candidates for elections are chosen by their national parties, but they have an independent mandate and cannot be bound by those parties.[5] Parliament was once seen as a haven for also-rans, but the quality of candidates competing in European elections is improving, although many MEPs are still people who have failed to win office in national elections or who have been temporarily sidelined in (or have retired from) national politics. Among the MEPs in the early 1980s were former German Chancellor

TABLE 8.6   The European Parliament by Party Group

	After 1984 Elections	After 1989 Elections	After 1994 Elections
Communists	48	—	—
Left Unity	—	14	—
European United Left	—	28	28
Socialists	165	180	198
European Radical Alliance	—	—	19
Rainbow	20	14	—
Greens	—	29	23
Liberal, Democratic, and Reformist	44	49	43
European Democratic Alliance	29	22	26
Europe of the Nations	—	—	19
European People's Party	115	121	157
European Democrats	66	34	—
Forza Europa	—	—	27
European Right	16	17	—
Independent or nonattached	15	10	27
Totals	518	518	567

Willy Brandt, former French President Valéry Giscard d'Estaing, former Italian Prime Minister Emilio Colombo, and former Belgian Prime Minister Leo Tindemans. Parliament also contained several future members of the European Commission, including Jacques Delors, Ray MacSharry, Christiane Scrivener, Carlo Ripa de Meana, Karel van Miert, and Martin Bangemann.

Since the first direct elections in 1979, MEPs have taken their jobs more seriously and are kept much busier working on issues that have growing relevance and importance to the work of the EU. Until 1987, average attendance at plenaries was about 42 percent; since then it has grown to about 58 percent. It was once usual for MEPs to hold a dual mandate (sitting in both the EP and their home legislatures), but only 6 percent of MEPs in the 1989 Parliament sat in their home legislatures as well,[6] and some member states (such as Spain and Belgium) have outlawed the dual mandate. This trend has not only weakened the links between national legislatures and the EP but has also given the EP greater independence and helped improve the credibility of MEPs.

Relatively speaking, women are well represented in the EP; the percentage has grown steadily from 16 percent in 1979 to 19 percent in 1989, to 25 percent in 1994.[7] This is above the average for liberal democracies (16 percent) and well above the figures for the United States (11 percent) and most EU member states (several of which are in single digits).[8]

How Parliament Works

Although it cannot introduce new legislation, Parliament's powers to influence and amend EU legislation have grown steadily. In addition to the advisory and supervisory powers set out in the treaties, Parliament has a number of essentially negative powers as well. The Commission tries to anticipate the EP's position when drawing up a proposal,[9] Parliament can delay or kill a proposal simply by sitting on it, and Parliament has the power to dismiss the Commission (see the section Powers over Other Institutions). Unfortunately, the concern of member states with preserving their powers over decisionmaking in the Council of Ministers has created a legislative process of mind-numbing complexity (see Box 8.2).

Powers over Legislation

A tradition of nonmandatory consultation developed in the 1960s and 1970s under which Parliament was allowed to comment on proposed legislation, the Commission agreed to adopt suggested amendments whenever possible, and both the Council and the Commission agreed to explain themselves if they did not adopt those amendments. The EP can also produce "own initiative" reports on policy issues it wants to encourage the Commission to address. Maastricht gave Parliament the same power as the Council of Ministers to request proposals on new legislation from the Commission, as long as those proposals were related to Maastricht.

Article 149 of the EEC Treaty made provision for a **consultation procedure** that allowed Parliament to give a nonbinding opinion to the Council of Ministers before it adopted a new law in selected areas (such as aspects of transport policy, citizenship issues, the EC budget, and amendments to the treaties). The Council could then ask the Commission to amend the draft, but the Commission had no obligation to respond. Although this did not seem like much of a power, no limit was placed on how long Parliament could take to give an opinion, thus giving it the power of delay—a traditional attribute of opposition parties in many national legislatures.[10] This power was given new significance with a Court of Justice decision in 1980 (the isoglucose case) that annulled a law adopted by the Council on the grounds that Parliament had not yet given an opinion; Parliament has since been able to threaten delays as a means of having the Council take its opinion seriously.[11]

The Single European Act increased the powers of Parliament, amending Article 149 to introduce a **cooperation procedure** under which Parliament had the right to a second reading for certain laws adopted by the Council of Ministers—notably those relating to aspects of economic and monetary

BOX 8.2
Consultation, Cooperation, and Codecision Procedures

Consultation

Step 1   The Commission proposes new legislation.

Step 2   Parliament gives its opinion (no time limit).

Step 3   The Commission may amend the proposal.

Step 4   With unanimity or a qualified majority, the Council of Ministers may adopt the amended proposal, or with unanimity it may add its own amendments. The proposal then becomes law. However . . .

Cooperation

Step 5   On certain kinds of legislation, Parliament has the power to consider the Council decision (also known as its common position), and within three months it may:
- Accept the common position by an absolute majority of votes cast or fail to act; in either case, the proposal becomes law.
- Reject the common position by an absolute majority of MEPs, in which case Council has three months to overrule Parliament by unanimity.
- Propose amendments by an absolute majority of MEPS. If the Commission agrees with Parliament, Council has three months to overrule unanimously, to accept by a qualified majority, or to take no action (in which case the proposal lapses). If the Commission opposes Parliament, Council may adopt the proposal. However . . .

Codecision

Step 6   On certain kinds of legislation, Council has three months to consider Parliament's amendments and can accept them by qualified majority or by unanimity (depending on the position of the Commission). If Council cannot muster enough votes, a conciliation committee can be formed with Parliament.

Step 7   An equal number of Council members and MEPs meet to try to reach agreement on a joint text (much like a conference committee in the U.S. Congress). They have six weeks. If they agree, the text goes back to the full Council and Parliament.

Step 8   Council and Parliament each have six weeks to adopt the new text, by a qualified majority and an absolute majority, respectively. If either fails, the proposal dies.

Step 9   If the conciliation committee fails to agree, Council (after another six weeks) can go back to its original common position and adopt the proposal by a qualified majority.

Step 10 Parliament has six weeks to overturn the Council decision by an absolute majority of MEPs, in which case the proposal dies. If the vote fails, the proposal becomes law.

policy and the European Social Fund. This meant Parliament was now involved directly in the legislative process and no longer had a purely consultative role.[12] Once the Council has adopted a law, Parliament has three months either to accept the Council's decision (in which case it becomes law) or to reject the decision by an absolute majority of MEPs (in which case the Council has three months to overrule the rejection unanimously). If Parliament fails to act within three months, the law comes into force by default.

The delays and challenges to the Council that are built into this system forced the Council to take Parliament's opinions even more seriously. The change also encouraged party groups in Parliament to work more closely together and made the EP a new target for lobbyists trying to influence the shape of new legislation. Lobbyists increasingly see Parliament as an influential arena, and more and more interest groups, corporations, and foreign governments are opening offices in Brussels and Strasbourg or are hiring professional lobbying consultants.[13] The exact number of lobbyists is unknown, but in 1993 there were 525 EU-level interest groups recognized by the Commission, nearly half of which were industrial or commercial groups.[14]

Maastricht strengthened the powers of Parliament even further by again amending Article 149 to introduce a **codecision procedure**, under which Parliament was given the right to a *third* reading on certain kinds of legislation, notably laws relating to the single market, consumer protection, and the environment. Under the **assent procedure**, Parliament has equal power with the Council over decisions on allowing new members to join the EU and giving other countries associate status, as well as on the EU's international agreements; all of these decisions must win the support of a parliamentary majority, effectively giving Parliament the power of veto.

The issue of new members took on new significance in the early 1990s as the line of aspiring EU members grew. The power over international agreements has been used regularly as well, as in 1988 when Parliament refused to renew an EU trade agreement with Israel because of Israeli policy on the West Bank. It approved renewal only when the Israelis agreed to respect their obligations on exports from the West Bank. Maastricht extended Parliament's powers over foreign policy issues by obliging the presidency of the European Council to consult with the EP on the development of a common foreign and security policy.

Powers over the Budget

Parliament has joint powers with the Council of Ministers over fixing the EU budget, so that between them the two institutions constitute the "budgetary authority" of the EU. Parliament meets with the Council biannually to adopt a draft and then to discuss amendments. It can ask for changes to the budget, ask for new appropriations for areas not covered (but it cannot make decisions on how to raise money), and ultimately—with a two-thirds majority—completely reject the budget (see Chapter 11). Because the budget is so small, David Marquand argues that "its right to reject the budget looks suspiciously like a right to cut off its nose to spite its face."[15]

Powers over Other Institutions

Parliament has several direct powers over other EU institutions, including the right to debate the annual program of the Commission, a practice introduced by Jacques Delors in the mid-1980s and that has since been used by the Commission to emphasize its accountability to Parliament.[16] It can also take the Commission or the Council to the Court of Justice over alleged infringements of the treaties, and it must approve the appointment of the president and all of the commissioners, although it cannot vote on individual commissioners. In the future commissioners will likely be called before parliamentary committees for confirmation, in much the same way cabinet nominees in the United States must appear before Senate committees.[17]

The most potentially disruptive of Parliament's powers is its ability—with a two-thirds majority—to force the resignation of the entire College of Commissioners through a vote of censure. Much like a nuclear weapon, though, this power is mainly a deterrent. It has never been used, and it would only be needed if the operations of the EU had broken down so badly that the different institutions were failing to communicate. The Commission would also be unlikely to ignore Parliament to the point at which the EP would want to use this power. Even if Parliament were to fire the Commission, it does not have the power to appoint new commissioners, so the existing commissioners could (in theory) simply resume their seats.[18] Parliament is not tied to the Commission in the same way as national legislatures and executives are tied. Commissioners are not elected, and they are nonpartisan, so the rise and fall of party groups in Parliament has no direct effect on the EU executive. If it did, Parliament's role in the EU decisionmaking process would be much more important, and voters would probably be more inclined to turn out at European elections.

Parliament has also taken the initiative to win new powers for itself. For example, it introduced its own question time in 1973 and thus can question commissioners and the Council of Ministers, helping to make them more accountable. It initiated the 1992 reconfiguration of the number of seats in Parliament. It can generate public debate on EU policies and—in the words of former British MEP Barbara Castle—can "raise hell" if necessary.[19] And it has tried—without much success—to forge an alliance with national legislators and to develop a symbiotic relationship that it hopes could be used to their mutual benefit to hold national government ministers more accountable.[20] Little love is lost between the two sides, though: National legislators resent the posturing and lifestyles of MEPs, and MEPs resent not being taken more seriously by national legislators.[21]

Summary and Conclusions

The European Parliament is the only directly elected and accountable institution in the EU system, and it has steadily accumulated greater powers over legislation and over the other EU institutions. But it is only a proto-legislature. It has won new powers and has helped close the democratic deficit, but much still needs to be done before it can become a true law-making institution. First, the EP needs to win more powers to check and balance those of the Commission and the Council of Ministers. Second, turnout at European elections needs to improve so Parliament can strengthen its claims to represent European voters. Third, the party structure needs to be tightened for party groups to develop more consistency. Fourth, parties need to improve their coordination and to run campaigns that are more truly Europewide and that are based on common European issues. Finally, Parliament needs to settle on a single site for all its work. As time goes on, the pressure for institutional reform grows. Among the possible changes: an end to the Commission monopoly over the introduction of legislation, the conversion of the Council of Ministers into a directly elected body along the lines of the U.S. Senate (thereby creating a new bicameral legislature), and a much-needed simplification of the legislative process.

Notes

1. Clive Archer and Fiona Butler, *The European Community: Structure and Process* (New York: St. Martin's Press, 1992), 33.

2. Juliet Lodge, "EC Policymaking: Institutional Dynamics," in Juliet Lodge (Ed.), *The European Community and the Challenge of the Future*, 2d ed. (New York: St. Martin's Press, 1993).

3. John Gillingham, *Coal, Steel, and the Rebirth of Europe, 1945–55* (New York: Cambridge University Press, 1991), 282.

4. Michael Palmer, *The European Parliament: What It Is, What It Does, How It Works* (Oxford: Pergamon Press, 1981), 23.

5. Lodge, "EC Policymaking," 24.

6. Clifford Hackett, *Cautious Revolution* (Westport, Conn.: Greenwood Press, 1990), 53.

7. T. T. Mackie and F.W.S. Craig, *Europe Votes 2* (Chichester: Parliamentary Research Services, 1985), 242; T. T. Mackie (Ed.), *Europe Votes 3* (Brookfield, Vt.: Dartmouth, 1990), 5–16; Martin Westlake, *A Modern Guide to the European Parliament* (London and New York: Pinter and St. Martin's Press, 1994), 106.

8. Inter-Parliamentary Union (IPU), *Distribution of Seats Between Men and Women in National Parliaments* (Geneva: IPU, 1993).

9. John Fitzmaurice, "An Analysis of the European Community's Cooperation Procedure," *Journal of Common Market Studies* 26:4 (June 1988), 389–400.

10. Anne Daltrop, *Politics and the European Community* (London: Longman, 1990), 83.

11. Shirley Williams, "Sovereignty and Accountability in the European Community," in Robert O. Keohane and Stanley Hoffmann (Eds.), *The New European Community: Decisionmaking and Institutional Change* (Boulder: Westview Press, 1991), 165.

12. Fitzmaurice, "Analysis of the European Community's Cooperation Procedure."

13. Axel Krause, *Inside the New Europe* (New York: HarperCollins, 1991), 6–11.

14. Sonia Mazey and Jeremy Richardson, *Lobbying in the European Community* (Oxford: Oxford University Press, 1993).

15. David Marquand, *Parliament for Europe* (London: Jonathan Cape, 1979), 96.

16. Archer and Butler, *The European Community*, 33.

17. Neill Nugent, *The Government and Politics of the European Union* (Durham, N.C.: Duke University Press, 1994), 183.

18. Daltrop, *Politics and the European Community*, 81.

19. Cited in Ibid., 82.

20. Lodge, "EC Policymaking," 22.

21. Desmond Dinan, *Ever Closer Union? An Introduction to the European Community* (Boulder: Lynne Rienner, 1994), 290.

Further Reading

Francis Jacobs, Richard Corbett, and Michael Shackelton. *The European Parliament*, 3rd ed. (New York: Stockton, 1995).

The standard study of the EP, written by three staff members. Describes the powers and workings of Parliament and discusses potential future changes in those powers.

Martin Westlake. *A Modern Guide to the European Parliament* (London and New York: Pinter and St. Martin's Press, 1994).

A critical and analytical guide to the European Parliament that examines its structure, functions, and powers.

T. T. Mackie (Ed.). *Europe Votes 3* (Brookfield, Vt.: Dartmouth, 1990).

A country-by-country study of the 1989 EP elections, packed with statistics but with no analysis or commentary.

Juliet Lodge (Ed.). *Euro-Elections 1994* (London and New York: Pinter and St. Martin's Press, 1994).

An edited collection of studies of different aspects of the 1994 European Parliament elections, with a focus on the fallout from the SEA and Maastricht.

9

The Court of Justice

The European Court of Justice has been one of the most important champions of European integration but has pursued the cause largely out of the public eye. As media and political interest has focused on the Commission and the Council of Ministers, the Court has quietly and anonymously gone about the business of interpreting EU law, working far away from the political fray in its Luxembourg headquarters.

But its role has been crucial: Without a body of law that can be uniformly interpreted and applied throughout the EU, the Union would have no authority, and its decisions and policies would be arbitrary and largely meaningless. By working to build such a body of law, the Court of Justice—the most purely federal of the EU institutions—has been a key player in promoting integration. It made its most fundamental contribution in 1963 and 1964 (discussed later in this chapter) when it declared that the Treaty of Rome was not only a treaty but was a constitutional instrument that imposed direct and common obligations on member states and took precedence over national law.

The European Court of Justice is often confused with two other European-based international courts: the Strasbourg-based European Court of Human Rights (which comes under the jurisdiction of the Council of Europe and promotes human rights issues in Europe) and the International Court of Justice (which is part of the UN system, is based in The Hague, and arbitrates on issues relating to UN activities). Although EU member states have no obligation to accept the rulings of either of these courts, they cannot ignore the rulings of the European Court of Justice, which are final.

Unlike the U.S. Supreme Court, which bases its rulings on judicial review of the Constitution, the Court of Justice has no constitution beyond the accumulated treaties and laws agreed on by the member states, including Paris and Rome, the Single European Act, and Maastricht. Among them, these treaties amount to something like a "constitution" for the European Union, but they need the kind of clarification that only the Court can provide. Just as the U.S. Supreme Court has helped clarify its own powers with decisions such as *Marbury v. Madison, 1803* (establishing the power of judicial review) and helped push the federal government into new policy areas with decisions such as *Brown v. Board of Education, 1954* (desegregation), the Court of Justice has done much the same with decisions such as *Flaminio Costa v. ENEL, 1964* (establishing the primacy of EU law) and the Cassis de Dijon case of 1979 (which greatly simplifed completion of the single market).

The Court has the power to rule on the "constitutionality" of all EU law, to rule on conformity with the treaties of any international agreement considered by the EU, to give rulings to national courts in cases in which there are questions about EU law, and to rule in disputes involving EU institutions, member states, individuals, and corporations. Recent Court rulings have helped increase the powers of Parliament, strengthened the rights of EU citizens, promoted the free movement of workers, reduced gender discrimination, and helped the Commission break down barriers to competition.[1]

Evolution

The Court was born in 1952 as the Court of Justice of the ECSC, which was to be a watchdog for the Treaty of Paris and to rule on the legality of decisions made by the ECSC High Authority in response to complaints submitted by either the member states or the national coal and steel industries; the Treaty of Paris was its primary source of authority. It made 137 decisions during its brief existence, many of which are still relevant to EU law today.[2]

The Treaties of Rome created separate courts for the EEC and Euratom, but a subsidiary agreement signed the same day gave jurisdiction over the treaties to a common seven-member Court.[3] Members were appointed by the Council of Ministers on the recommendation of the member states. The new Court heard cases involving disputes between Community institutions and member states, and its verdicts were final. As the work of the Community expanded, as its membership grew in the 1970s and 1980s, and as the Court issued more and more judgments against Community institutions and member states, its power, reach, and significance grew.

Although decisionmaking in the EU essentially revolves around the axis of the Commission and the Council of Ministers, the Court has made decisions that have had far-reaching consequences for the process of European integration, and it is often argued that the Court has done more than the Commission or the Council for the cause of European integration.[4] Three of its most famous cases illustrate its contribution.

First, EU law is directly and uniformly applied in all of the member states as a consequence of the 1963 decision *Van Gend en Loos* (Case 26/62), one of the most important ever handed down by the Court. A Dutch transport company had brought an action against Dutch customs for increasing the duty it had to pay on a product imported from Germany. Its lawyers argued that this went against Article 12 of the EEC Treaty, which—in the interest of building the common market—prohibited new duties or increases in existing duties. The Dutch government argued that the Court had no power to decide whether the provisions of the EEC Treaty prevailed over Dutch law and that resolution fell exclusively within the jurisdiction of national courts. The Court disagreed, ruling that the treaties were more than international agreements and that EC law was "legally complete ... [and] produces direct effects and creates individual rights which national courts must protect."[5]

Second, the principle of the primacy of EU law was established with the 1964 decision *Flaminio Costa v. ENEL* (Case 6/64). Costa was an Italian who had owned shares in Edison Volta, an electricity supply company. When the company was nationalized in 1962 and made part of the new National Electricity Board (ENEL), Costa refused to pay his electric bill (which was about $1.50) because he claimed he had been hurt by nationalization, and he argued that nationalization was contrary to the spirit of the Treaty of Rome. The local court in Milan asked the European Court for a preliminary ruling, which elicited complaints from both the Italian government and from ENEL that there were no grounds for taking the case to the European Court. The government further argued that a national court could not take a dispute over domestic law to the European Court.

The Court of Justice disagreed, arguing that by creating "a Community of unlimited duration, having its own institutions, its own personality, its own legal capacity ... [and] real powers stemming from limitation of sovereignty or a transfer of powers from the States to the Community, the Member States have limited their sovereign rights, albeit within limited fields, and have thus created a body of law which binds both their nationals and themselves." It also argued that "the executive force of Community law cannot vary from one State to another in deference to subsequent domestic laws, without jeopardizing the attainment of the objectives of the Treaty [of Rome]."[6]

Third, the issue of the supremacy of EEC law was confirmed—and the jurisdiction of the Community extended—with a dispute that broke in 1967 over the issue of human rights. The EEC Treaty said nothing about human rights, a reflection once again of how little authority the member states were prepared to give up to the EEC and how focused they had been on economic integration. In October 1967, the German Constitutional Court argued that the EEC had no democratic basis because it lacked protection for human rights and that the Community could not deprive German citizens of the rights they had under German law.[7] The Court of Justice refuted this in *Nold v. Commission* (Case 4/73), in which it established that "fundamental rights form an integral part of the general principles of law."[8]

Structure

The Court of Justice is based in a squat, glass and rustproof steel building in the Centre Européen, a cluster of EU institutions situated on the Kirchberg Plateau above the city of Luxembourg. The land was bought by the Luxembourg government in 1961 as a site for the EC institutions, presumably in the hope that they would all eventually be moved there. The Palais de Justice was opened in 1973 and was extended in 1988 and 1992, and it now makes up part of a modest but not insubstantial complex that includes the Secretariat of the European Parliament, buildings for the Commission and the Council of Ministers, the seat of the Court of Auditors, and the headquarters of the European Investment Bank.

The Court has four main elements: the judges, the president of the Court, the advocates general, and the Court of First Instance.

The Judges

The Court of Justice has fifteen judges, each appointed for a six-year renewable term of office. About half come up for renewal every three years, so terms are staggered. Although most judges are renewed at least once, the Court has more turnover than the U.S. Supreme Court, in which appoint-

TABLE 9.1 Presidents of the European Court of Justice

Term	Name	Country of Origin
1958–1961	A. M. Donner	Netherlands
1961–1964	A. M. Donner	Netherlands
1964–1967	Charles Hammes	Luxembourg
1967–1970	Robert Lecourt	France
1970–1973	Robert Lecourt	France
1973–1976	Robert Lecourt	France
1976–1979	Hans Kutscher	Germany
1979–1980	Hans Kutscher	Germany
1980–1984	J. Mertens de Wilmars	Belgium
1985–1988	McKenzie Stuart	United Kingdom
1988–1991	Ole Due	Denmark
1991–1994	Ole Due	Denmark
1994–	G. C. Rodriguez Iglesias	Spain

TABLE 9.2 Judges of the European Court of Justice, September 1995
(by year of appointment)

	Member State of Origin	Year of Appointment
G. C. Rodriguez Iglesias (president)	Spain	1986
G. Federico Mancini	Italy	1982
C. N. Kakouris	Greece	1983
F. A. Schockweiler	Luxembourg	1985
J. C. Moitinho de Almeida	Portugal	1986
P.J.G. Kapteyn	Netherlands	1990
C. Gulmann	Denmark	1991
J. L. Murray	Ireland	1991
D.A.O. Edward	United Kingdom	1992
J. P. Puissochet	France	1994
G. Hirsch	Germany	1994
Peter Jann	Austria	1995
M. Watheiet	Belgium	1995
Leif Sevon	Finland	1995
Hans Ragnemalm	Sweden	1995

ments are for life. Life appointments have the benefit of encouraging independence and exploiting experience, but they also allow little turnover, cause appointments to become relatively highly charged political issues, allow two-term presidents to change the ideological balance of the Court, and reduce the influx of new thinking into the work of the Court. New appointments to the European Court, by contrast, are both relatively frequent and nonpolitical. The European Court has had more than fifty judges since it was created, almost three times the turnover of the U.S. Supreme Court.

Theoretically, the European judges are appointed by common accord of the member state governments, so there is no national quota and no "Spanish place" or "French place" on the Court. Judges do not even have to be EU citizens; as Court President Lord McKenzie Stuart quipped in 1988, it could be made up "entirely of Russians."[9] In practice, because every member state has the right to make one appointment, all fifteen judges are national appointees. Parliament has argued more than once that it should be involved in the appointment process—even proposing in the 1980s that half of the judges be appointed by Parliament and half by the Council of Ministers and that the de facto national quota be abandoned. The persistence of the quota emphasizes the fact that national interests are still a factor in EU decisionmaking. How long the quota will stay in effect remains to be seen.

Until 1994, there were only twelve member states, so a thirteenth judge was chosen from one of the Big Five states on a rotating basis by common accord (or, failing that, by drawing lots). This was done to ensure that there was an odd number of judges, because all votes are taken on the basis of a simple majority. (When the ECSC was founded with six member states, for example, there were seven judges.) In the event of a split vote, the vote of the most junior judge present was excluded.

In addition to being acceptable to all of the other member states, judges must be scrupulously independent and must avoid promoting the national interests of their home states. Upon their appointment, they must take a short oath: "I swear that I will perform my duties impartially and conscientiously; I swear that I will preserve the secrecy of the deliberations of the Court." They must also be legally competent, or as Article 32b of the Treaty of Paris so thoughtfully puts it, they must "possess the qualifications required for appointment to the highest judicial offices in their respective countries or . . . [be] jurisconsults of recognized competence." Appointees to the U.S. Supreme Court do not have to be lawyers, although in practice most are. Some European judges have come to the Court with experience as government ministers, some have held elective office, and others have had careers as lawyers or academics.

European judges enjoy immunity from having suits brought against them while they are on the Court, and even after they have left they cannot be sued for decisions they made. They are not allowed to hold administrative or political office while on the Court. They can resign, but they can only be removed by the other judges and the advocates general (not by member states or other EU institutions), and then only by unanimous agreement that they are no longer doing their job adequately.[10] So far, all of the judges have been men.

To speed up its work, the Court is divided into chambers of between three and six judges, which used to hear only cases that did not need to be brought before the full Court. Most staff cases, for example, used to go to chambers before the existence of the Court of First Instance. Because the workload of the Court has increased, though, any case can now be assigned to a chamber, including preliminary rulings and actions brought by or against member states (unless a member state or an institution specifically asks for a hearing before the full Court). To further help with the workload, each judge and advocate general has his or her own team of assistants and legal secretaries, known as a *cabinet* (English translation: chamber). These groups are roughly equivalent to the cabinets of European commissioners and are responsible for helping with research and keeping records. The secretaries are similar to law clerks in the United States (bright graduates invited to serve for a year or two on the staff of a judge), except they have usually had other legal experience and generally serve much longer terms.

Unlike all of the other EU institutions, in which English is slowly becoming the working language, the Court mainly uses French, although a case

BOX 9.1
Liqueur, Beer, and the Single Market

Of all the cases heard and rulings made by the Court regarding the single market, few were more fundamental to the market's completion than those establishing the principle of **mutual recognition,** under which a product made and sold legally in one member state cannot be barred from another member state.

The roots of the issue go back to a 1979 case arising out of a refusal by West Germany to allow imports of a French blackcurrant liqueur, Cassis de Dijon, on the grounds that its wine-spirit content (15–20 percent) was below the minimum set by the West German government for fruit liqueurs (25 percent).[1] The importer charged that this amounted to a "quantitative restriction on imports," which is prohibited under Article 30 of the Treaty of Rome. The Court of Justice agreed, ruling that alcoholic beverages lawfully produced and marketed in one member state could not be prohibited from sale in another on the grounds that they had a lower alcohol content. Although this established the principle of mutual recognition, it did not prevent challenges from occurring.

The issue came up again in the 1984 case *Commission v. Germany* over the question of beer imports into Germany.[2] The Germans have long taken pride in their beer, which, thanks to the Reinheitsgebot (a purity law passed in 1516 by the duke of Bavaria), is allowed to contain only malted barley, hops, yeast, and water. Germans drink more beer than anyone else in the world (an average of thirty-eight gallons per person per year, compared to twenty-four gallons per person per year in the United States), and they long refused to import foreign beer on the grounds that most such beer contained "additives" such as rice, maize, sorghum, flavoring, and coloring. The Commission took Germany to the Court on the grounds that a 1952 German law effectively prevented any beer from being imported or sold in Germany that did not meet the Reinheitsgebot, thereby infringing Article 30 of the Treaty of Rome.

Germany argued that since the average German male relies on beer for a quarter of his daily nutritional intake, allowing imports of "impure" foreign beer would pose a risk to public health. The Court disagreed and ruled in 1987 that Germany could not use the public-health argument to ban beer imports and had to accept foreign beer imports as long as brewers printed a list of ingredients on their labels. The sky did not fall on Germany; even though its market is now open, beer drinkers remain loyal to domestic brews, which still account for 98 percent of German beer sales.

The Court decision greatly simplified decisions on issues of trade between member states, and the precedent was used to open European domestic markets to all kinds of food and drink imports. Another Court ruling in 1988 overturned an Italian prohibition on the import of German pasta made from a combination of durum wheat and common wheat.[3] Based on a 1967 Italian law that said dry pasta could only be made from durum wheat, both the manufacturer and the importer had been fined. They took the case to the Court of Justice, which ruled in their favor, again upholding Article 30 of the Treaty of Rome.

Notes

1. *Rewe-Zentral AG v. Bundesmonopolverwaltung für Branntwein* (Case 120/78), in Court of Justice of the European Communities, *Reports of Cases Before the Court,* 1979.

2. *Commission of the European Communities v. Federal Republic of Germany* (Case 178/84), in Court of Justice of the European Communities, *Reports of Cases Before the Court,* 1987-3.

3. *3 Glocken GmbH and Gertraud Kritzinger v. USL Centro-Sud and Provincia Autonoma di Bolzano* (Case 407/85), in Court of Justice of the European Communities, *Reports of Cases Before the Court,* 1988-7.

can be heard in any of twelve languages (the eleven official languages plus Irish) at the request of the plaintiff or the defendant. The Court has about 780 staff members, most of whom are bureaucrats or translators.

The President

The judges elect one judge by majority vote to be president of the Court for a three-year renewable term. The president presides over meetings of the Court and is responsible for technical issues such as distributing cases among the judges and deciding the dates for hearings. Presidents also have considerable influence over the political direction of the Court, much like the chief justice of the U.S. Supreme Court. Just as the U.S. Supreme Court is sometimes activist (becoming involved in decisions that have important political implications) and sometimes more restrained, in recent years the European Court has become both busier and more cautious, in part because of complaints from some member states that the Court has been biased in favor of the Commission.

The Advocates General

In a system based on the French legal model, the Court's nine advocates general are advisers who look at each of the cases as they come in, study the arguments, and deliver preliminary opinions in court before the judges on what action should be taken and which EU law applies. The judges are not obliged to agree with the opinion or even to refer to it, but it gives them their main point of reference from which to reach a decision. Although in theory advocates general are also appointed by common accord, in practice one is appointed by each of the Big Five member states, and the rest are appointed by the smaller states. Most have been men; the first woman— Simone Rozès of France—was appointed in 1981. One of the advocates general is appointed first advocate general on a one-year rotation.

The Court of First Instance

The Court of Justice has become much busier over time. In the 1960s, it heard about 50 cases per year and made 15 to 20 judgments; today it hears 400 cases per year (about twice the volume of cases coming before the U.S Supreme Court) and makes well over 200 judgments (see Table 9.3). It was particularly busy after 1987, hearing cases and making preliminary rulings on issues relating to the single market in the lead-up to 1992.

As the volume of work grew during the 1970s and 1980s, there were more and more delays, with the Court taking up to two years to reach a decision. To help clear the logjam, agreement was reached under the Single European Act to create a subsidiary Court of First Instance. One judge is appointed to the court from each of the member states for a total of fifteen, and the court uses the same basic procedures as the Court of Justice (although it has no advocates general and does not have its own staff). The court began work in November 1989 and issued its first ruling in February 1990. It is the first point of decision on some of the less complicated cases involving aspects of competition, actions brought against the Commission under the ECSC Treaty, and disputes between EU institutions and their staff. If the cases are lost at this level, the parties involved have the right to appeal to the Court of Justice, in much the same way parties losing a case in a federal district court in the United States can appeal to the Supreme Court.

TABLE 9.3   Activities of the Court of Justice and the Court of First Instance

	Court of Justice			Court of First Instance	
	Preliminary Hearings	Total Cases Brought	Judgments	Total Cases Brought	Judgments
1985	139	433	255	—	—
1986	91	328	197	—	—
1987	144	395	317	—	—
1988	173	372	311	—	—
1989	138	385	253	169	—
1990	140	380	225	52	59
1991	182	340	227	92	52
1992	162	438	256	115	94
1993	203	486	272	189	76

Source: Commission of the European Communities, General Report on the Activities of the European Communities (Luxembourg: Commission of the European Communities, various years).

Sources of European Union Law

While the U.S. Supreme Court interprets law on the basis of the Constitution, the EU does not have a constitution, so the Court of Justice has to rely on several different sources for its authority. D. Lasok and J. W. Bridge distinguish between primary and secondary sources.[11] The **primary sources** are the "constitutional treaties" of the EU, including the treaties of Paris and Rome, the 1965 Merger Treaty, treaties of accession signed by new members, the Single European Act, the Maastricht Treaty on European Union, various other key EU agreements, and all related annexes and amendments. Some of these (such as the Paris and Rome treaties) were self-executing in the sense that they automatically became law in the member states once they were ratified, although the Court has often had to confirm just what self-execution actually means. Others (notably the Single European Act) required changes in national laws before they came into effect. The Court has played a particularly valuable role in promoting these changes.

The Court also bases its decisions on **secondary sources,** so described because they come out of the primary sources. These consist of all the individual binding laws adopted by the EU (regulations, directives, and decisions—see Chapter 6), relevant international law (most of which is weak and vague but which the Court still often uses to create precedent), and—when EU or international law is unclear—its own interpretation. Judgments by the Court have helped give EU law more focus and strength, thus making up for the weaknesses that have often arisen out of the compromises made to reach agreement on various laws. The Court not only gives technical interpretations but often goes a step further, filling in gaps and clarifying confusions—occasionally creating entirely new laws in the process.

As the European Union evolves, pressures will almost certainly grow for agreement on a constitution that brings together all of the principles established by the treaties and case law. Although this is unlikely to happen until consensus is reached on the balance of power between EU institutions and member states, Federico Mancini, a judge on the Court of Justice, believes the direction in which EU case law has moved since 1957 "coincides with the making of a constitution for Europe." He notes that the EU was created by a treaty (unlike the United States, which is founded on a constitution), that the EEC Treaty did not safeguard the fundamental rights of individuals or recognize a right to European citizenship, and that the main work of the Court has been to "constitutionalize" the Treaty and "to fashion a constitutional framework for a quasi-federal structure in Europe." In this it has been helped by the Commission, as the guardian of the treaties, and by national courts, which have been indirectly responsible for some of the Court's biggest decisions and have lent credibility by adhering to those decisions.[12]

BOX 9.2
The Court of Auditors

Although independent from the Court of Justice and—under the terms of Maastricht—given the status of a full Community institution, the Court of Auditors is an important part of the legal-administrative cluster of institutions headquartered in Luxembourg. Situated beside the Court of Justice building, it was founded in 1977 to replace the separate auditing bodies for the EEC and Euratom and the ECSC. It is the EU's financial watchdog, charged with auditing EU accounts.

The Court is headed by fifteen auditors, one appointed from each member state for a six-year renewable term. Nominations come from the national governments and must be approved unanimously by the Council of Ministers following nonbinding approval by Parliament (which the EP would like to have become binding approval). The auditors then elect one of their group to serve as president for three-year renewable terms. The members of the Court must be members of an external audit body in their own country or have other appropriate qualifications, but they are expected to act in the interests of the EU and to be completely independent. About four hundred staff members back up the work of the Court.

The Court's brief is to carry out annual audits of the accounts of all EU institutions to ensure that revenue has been raised and expenditure incurred in a lawful and regular manner and to monitor the Union's financial management. Its most important job relates to the EU budget, which it audits on the basis of both accounts supplied by the Commission by June each year and its own independent research. The Court reports back to the Commission, the Council of Ministers, and Parliament by the end of November. Parliament is supposed to approve the Court's report by the following April, but it can use the report to force changes in the Commission's spending and accounting habits.

The Court has issued often scathing criticisms of waste, mismanagement, and fraud in the EU's financial affairs. It has found everything from excessive expense claims by European commissioners to massive fraud in funds made available under the Common Agricultural Policy. It has been particularly critical in recent years of the inadequacy of steps taken by the Commission to keep an eye on how structural funds are used and managed. Although the nature of its work would seem to make it unpopular with the Commission, in fact the two bodies have a close working relationship. The Court also has a symbiotic relationship with Parliament; each has helped promote the powers and profile of the other.

How the Court Works

The European Commission is often described as the guardian of the treaties of Paris and Rome, but it is the European Court that is charged under each of the founding treaties with ensuring "that in the interpretation and application of this treaty the law is observed." The Court is the supreme legal body of the EU; its decisions are final, and it is the final court of appeal on all EU laws. As such, the Court has played a vital role in determining the character of the EU and in extending the reach of EU law. For example, when the Community slipped into a hiatus in the late 1970s and early 1980s, the Court kept alive the idea of the Community as something more than a customs union.[13] It has been particularly involved in cases relating to the internal market, and the Cassis de Dijon decision is credited by some with allowing the SEA initiative to restore the progress of the EU.[14]

The overall goal of the Court is to help build a body of common law for the EU that is equally, fairly, and consistently applied throughout the member states. It does this by interpreting EU treaties and laws and in some cases taking responsibility for directly applying those laws. EU law takes precedence over the national laws of member states when the two come into conflict, but only in areas in which the EU is active and the member states have given up powers to the EU. The Court, for example, does not have powers over criminal or family law; it has made most of its decisions on the kinds of economic issues in which the EU has been most actively involved and has had much less to do with policy areas in which the EU has been less active, such as education and health.

Court proceedings usually begin with a written application made to the Court, which is filed with the Court registrar and published in its *Official Journal*. This describes the dispute and explains the grounds on which the application is based. The president then assigns the case to a chamber and appoints a judge-rapporteur from among the judges to draw up a preliminary report on the case; the first advocate general appoints an advocate general to the case. The defendant is notified and has one month to lodge a statement of defense; the plaintiff then has a month to reply and the defendant a further month to reply to the plaintiff. The advocate general then examines the case in detail and delivers a submission at an administrative meeting of the Court. The parties involved can appear, expert reports can be commissioned, and witnesses can be called to give testimony.

The case is then argued by the parties involved at a public hearing before a chamber of three or six judges or before the full Court (a quorum is eight judges; all fifteen judges will usually be present only for the most important cases). The judges sit in order of seniority, wearing gowns of deep crimson; the lawyers appearing before them wear whatever garb is appropriate in their national courts. When the hearing is over, the judges retire to the Deliberation Room, with its sweeping—and presumably inspiring—views of the city of Luxembourg. Having reached a conclusion, they return to Court to deliver their judgment.

The entire process can take as long as a year for preliminary rulings, while most other cases may take as long as two years. Court decisions are technically supposed to be unanimous, but votes are usually taken on a simple majority, as in the U.S. Supreme Court. Unlike the U.S. Court, all the decisions of the European Court are secret, so it is never publicly known who—if anyone—dissented. Once a judgment has been made, details of the case are published in the *Report of Cases Before the Court* (also known as the *European Court Reports*).

The Court has no direct powers to enforce its judgments; implementation is left up mainly to national courts or the governments of the member states, with the Commission keeping a close watch. Maastricht gave the Court of Justice new powers by allowing it to impose fines, but the question of how the fines would be collected was left open. It will also take some time before the implications of this new power become clear.

The work of the Court falls under two main headings.

Preliminary Rulings

These rulings make up the most important part of the Court's work and account for 25 to 30 percent of the cases it considers. Under Article 177 of the EEC Treaty, a national court can ask the European Court for a ruling on the interpretation or validity of an EU law that arises in a national court case. The issue of validity is particularly critical, because chaos would reign if national courts could declare EU laws invalid.[15] Members of EU institutions can ask for preliminary rulings, but most are made on behalf of a national court and are binding on the court in the case concerned. (The word *preliminary* is misleading, because the rulings are usually requested and given *during* cases, not before they open.)

Van Gend en Loos and *Flaminio Costa v. ENEL* are the classic examples of preliminary rulings, but another ruling that had crucial implications for individual rights came in 1989. During a vacation in France, a British citizen named Ian Cowan was mugged outside a subway station in Paris. Under French law, he could have claimed state compensation for damages, but the French courts held that he was not entitled to damages because he was neither a French national nor a resident. Cowan argued that this amounted to discrimination, and the Court of Justice was asked for a ruling. In *Cowan v. Le Tresor Public* (Case 186/87), the Court argued that because Cowan was a tourist and was receiving a service, he could invoke Article 7 of the EEC Treaty, which prohibits discrimination between nationals of member states on the grounds of nationality.[16]

Direct Actions

These are cases in which an individual, corporation, member state, or EU institution brings proceedings directly before the Court of Justice (rather than a national court), usually with an EU institution or a member state as the defendant. They can take several forms.

Actions for Default. These are cases in which a member state has failed to meet its obligations under EU law; they can be brought either by the Commission or by a member state. The defending member state is given two months to make restitution, so most of these cases are settled before they go to the Court. If a state fails to comply once an action has been brought, the case goes to the Court, which investigates the problem and decides on the measures to be taken; these can involve the state's EU payments (under the Regional Development Fund, for example) being suspended or the member being fined.

The Commission has regularly taken member states to the Court, claiming they have not met their obligations under the Single European Act. Although individuals cannot bring such cases, interest groups have reported a member state to the Commission for failing to enforce an EU law, and the Commission then takes the member state to court. Private companies are also often involved, especially in issues involving competition and trade policy. Even U.S. and Japanese companies can take a case to the Court if they think a member state is discriminating against them or their products.

No member state has ever refused to accept a Court ruling on a major issue, although states often take their time implementing rulings. For example, in the famous Lamb War of 1978–1980, France was slow to accept a 1979 ruling that it must open its markets to imports of British lamb and mutton, under Articles 12 and 30 of the EEC Treaty. When France continued to refuse to comply, the Commission began a second action (*Commission v. France,* Case 24/80) under Article 171, which obliges a member state to comply with a judgment of the Court, and a third case under Article 169 regarding illegal charges on imports. Britain returned the compliment in 1983 by taking its time accepting imports of French long-life milk (milk that is specially treated and packed to extend its life).

Actions to Annul. These actions are aimed at ensuring that EU laws (even nonbinding opinions and recommendations) conform to the treaties, and they are brought in an attempt to cancel those that do not conform. The defendant is almost always the Commission or the Council, because proceedings are usually brought against an act one of them has adopted.[17] One exception was Luxembourg's inconclusive attempt in 1981 to challenge a European Parliament resolution that all future plenary sessions of Parliament should be held in Strasbourg (Case 230/81). It has become increasingly common since the mid-1980s for member states to use such actions as a means of annulling new laws on which they were outvoted in the Council of Ministers.[18]

The EEC Treaty gave the power to bring actions for annulment only to member states, the Council of Ministers, and the Commission. Parliament was excluded because at the time its opinions had no binding value. But as

Parliament's powers grew, so did the political significance of its inability to challenge the legality of EU law. The Court has helped redress the balance by slowly building the number of circumstances in which Parliament can challenge the law. In addition to being allowed to bring actions for failure to act (see the next section), since 1990 Parliament has been able to bring actions for annulment when the security of its interests are at stake.[19] Actions can be brought on grounds of lack of competence, a treaty infringement, or misuse of powers.

Actions for Inactivity. These actions relate to the failure of an EU institution to act in accordance with the terms of the treaties, and they can be instituted by other institutions, member states, or individuals who are directly and personally involved. For example, the European Parliament brought such an action against the Council of Ministers in 1983 (Case 13/83), charging that the Council had failed to agree to a Common Transport Policy as required under the EEC Treaty. The Court ruled in 1985 that although there was an obligation, no timetable had been agreed on, so it was up to the member states to decide how to proceed.[20]

Actions for Damages. These are cases in which damages are claimed by third parties against EU institutions or their employees. A claim could be made that the institution was acting illegally, or an individual could claim his or her business was being hurt by a piece of EU law. Most of these cases are heard by the Court of First Instance.

Actions by Staff. These cases involve litigation brought by staff members against EU institutions as their employers, and they are the only cases in which a private individual can go directly to the Court. For example, someone who works for the European Parliament might ask the Court for a ruling on the application of a staff regulation, an instance of gender discrimination, a biased staff report, or a decision to hold a civil service exam on a religious holiday in their home country. Staff actions account for about one-third of the Court's workload, but most are dealt with by the Court of First Instance.

The Court also has the power of opinion in cases in which a decision is needed on the compatibility of draft international agreements with the treaties. The Commission, the Council of Ministers, or member states can ask for a Court opinion, and if the Court gives an unfavorable ruling, the draft agreement must be changed accordingly before the EU can sign it. Finally, the Court can be called in to arbitrate both on contracts concluded by or on behalf of the EU (conditional proceedings) and in disputes between member states over issues relating to the treaties.

Of all the cases brought to the Court between 1952 and 1989 (more than 6,600), 55 percent were related to the EEC Treaty, 8 percent to the ECSC Treaty, and just 0.2 percent to the Euratom treaty; the remaining 36 percent were cases brought by the staff members of EU institutions.[21] In terms of who brought those cases, 46 percent were preliminary hearings requested by national courts, 31 percent were brought by private individuals, 15 percent by the Commission, and 4 percent by governments; 4 percent were miscellaneous.[22]

Summary and Conclusions

Although it is much smaller than the other EU institutions and is physically distant from the political battles fought in Brussels and Strasbourg, the European Court of Justice has played a crucial role in the process of European integration by helping to give the treaties both strength and stability. Its fifteen judges are charged with interpreting the treaties and adjudicating in disputes over their meaning, as well as in disputes involving EU institutions and member states.

The Court has made many significant rulings with important constitutional implications, defining the reach and the meaning of the founding treaties in particular. While struggles continue to be waged over the relative powers of the Commission, the Council of Ministers, and the European Council, the Court of Justice has steadily established its authority and acted as an anchor for the underlying principles of European integration. In this respect, there are many parallels with the U.S. Supreme Court and its role in clarifying the meaning of the U.S. Constitution and the relative powers of the presidency, Congress, and the individual states.

One critical element missing from the work of the European Court of Justice is a written constitution for the EU. As the reach of the EU spreads, the pressure to combine the treaties into a single constitution will almost inevitably grow, placing the Court of Justice at the heart of deliberations about the future course of the EU.

Notes

1. For examples, see Alain Van Hamme, "The European Court of Justice: Recent Developments," in Leon Hurwitz and Christian Lequesne (Eds.), *The State of the European Community, Vol. 1: Policies, Institutions, and Debates in the Transition Years* (Boulder: Lynne Rienner, 1991).

2. D. Lasok and J. W. Bridge, *Law and Institutions of the European Communities,* 4th ed. (London: Butterworths, 1987), 13.

3. K.P.E. Lasok, *The European Court of Justice: Practice and Procedure* (London: Butterworths, 1984), 2.

4. For example, see Jean Paul Jacqué and Joseph Weiler, *On the Road to European Union—A New Judicial Architecture* (Florence: European University Institute, 1990).

5. *Van Gend en Loos v. Nederlandse Administratie Belastingen* (Case 26/62), in Court of Justice of the European Communities, *Reports of Cases Before the Court,* 1963.

6. *Flaminio Costa v. ENEL* (Case 6/64), in Court of Justice of the European Communities, *Reports of Cases Before the Court,* 1964.

7. G. Federico Mancini, "The Making of a Constitution for Europe," in Robert O. Keohane and Stanley Hoffmann (Eds.), *The New European Community: Decisionmaking and Institutional Change* (Boulder: Westview Press, 1991), 187.

8. *Nold, Kohlen- und Baustoffgrosshandlung* (Case 4/73), in Court of Justice of the European Communities, *Reports of Cases Before the Court,* 1974.

9. L. Neville Brown and Tom Kennedy, *The Court of Justice of the European Communities,* 4th ed. (London: Sweet and Maxwell, 1994), 45.

10. Lasok, *European Court of Justice,* 7–8.

11. Lasok and Bridge, *Law and Institutions,* chapter 4.

12. Mancini, "The Making of a Constitution for Europe," 177–179.

13. Martin Shapiro, "The European Court of Justice," in Alberta Sbragia (Ed.), *Euro-Politics: Institutions and Policymaking in the 'New' European Community* (Washington, D.C.: Brookings Institution, 1992).

14. Nicholas Colchester and David Buchan, *Europower: The Essential Guide to Europe's Economic Transformation* (London: Economist Books, 1990).

15. Brown and Kennedy, *Court of Justice,* 173–176.

16. *Cowan v. Le Tresor Public* (Case 186/87), in Court of Justice of the European Communities, *Reports of Cases Before the Court,* 1989.

17. Lasok, *European Court of Justice,* 323.

18. Neill Nugent, *The Government and Politics of the European Union,* 3rd ed. (Durham, N.C.: Duke University Press, 1994), 182.

19. Van Hamme, "European Court of Justice," 50.

20. *European Parliament v. Council* (Case 13/83), in Court of Justice of the European Communities, *Reports of Cases Before the Court,* 1985.

21. Commission of the European Communities, *General Report of the Activities of the European Communities* (Luxembourg: Office for Official Publications of the European Communities, 1990).

22. Emile Noel, *Working Together: The Institutions of the European Community* (Luxembourg: Office for Official Publications of the European Communities, 1988), 38.

Further Reading

Much has been written about the Court of Justice, but a good deal of this work has been by lawyers, with their uniquely detailed, legalistic style, and it provides little political analysis. Among the more accessible general studies of the organization, jurisdiction, and procedure of the Court are the following:

D. Lasok and J. W. Bridge. Law and Institutions of the European Communities, 4th ed. (London: Butterworths, 1987).

L. Neville Brown and Tom Kennedy. The Court of Justice of the European Communities, 4th ed. (London: Sweet and Maxwell, 1994).

Trevor C. Hartley. The Foundations of European Community Law, 3rd ed. (Oxford: Clarendon Press, 1994).

For more detail on the nature of EU law, see Penelope Kent, *European Community Law* (London: Pitman, 1992); and for a discussion of a constitution for Europe by a judge on the Court of Justice, see G. Federico Mancini, "The Making of a Constitution for Europe," in Robert O. Keohane and Stanley Hoffmann (Eds.), *The New European Community: Decisionmaking and Institutional Change* (Boulder: Westview Press, 1991).

10

The European Council and Other Institutions

The European Council is the newest, the most ambiguous, and arguably the most powerful of the EU's five major institutions (although it is more a process or a forum than an institution).[1] Simply defined, European Council is a collective term for the heads of government of EU member states, their foreign ministers, and the president of the Commission. This small group convenes periodically at short summit meetings and provides strategic policy direction for the EU. The Council is something like a steering committee or a board of directors for the EU; it sketches the broad picture and leaves it to the other institutions (particularly the Commission and the Council of Ministers) to fill in the details.

The Council was created in 1974 in response to a growing feeling among EC leaders that the Community needed stronger leadership to clear blockages in decisionmaking and to give it a sense of direction. Nothing was said in the treaties of Paris or Rome about an institution like the European Council, and the Treaty of Rome has never been amended (as it technically should have been) to create the Council. Its existence was only finally given legal recognition with the Single European Act. Maastricht elaborated on its role but provided little clarity: Article D of the Common Provisions of Maastricht said the Council would "provide the Union with the necessary impetus for its development and shall define the general political guidelines thereof." Because the Common Provisions were not incorporated into the treaties, the European Council was left to interpret its own role, which cannot be challenged by the Court of Justice.[2]

The Council is almost purely intergovernmental in nature and has no direct equivalent in the United States; it would be as though the governors of the fifty states met every year to take broad decisions on federal government policies and the governance of the United States but made themselves subject neither to the Constitution nor to rulings of the Supreme Court. The fact that the European Council has this kind of power and communal leadership again reflects the unwillingness of the member states to give up power to the EU.

At the same time, though, the Council has been an important motor for integration and has launched major new initiatives (such as the European Monetary System in 1978, the SEA in 1985, and the Maastricht treaty in 1991), issued major declarations on international crises, reached key decisions on EC institutional changes (such as the 1974 decision to begin direct elections to the European Parliament), and given new momentum to EU foreign policy. It has been argued that without these regular summits, the EC would not have survived the Eurosclerosis of the 1970s, launched the single market program in the 1980s, or adjusted to radical changes in the international environment in the 1990s.[3] But the Council has also had its failures, including its inability to speed up agricultural and budgetary reform or to reach agreement on common EU responses to either the 1990–1991 Gulf War or the Bosnian conflict.

Evolution

The idea of formal high-level meetings among the leaders of the EC traces its roots back to Charles de Gaulle's ideas about political union. As early as 1959, his Prime Minister Michel Debré proposed regular meetings among EEC foreign ministers, and three such meetings were held during 1960. In July 1960, de Gaulle broached the idea of a European political union that would include periodic summit meetings of heads of state or government and foreign ministers.[4] Although his motives were distrusted by many of his EEC partners, the idea survived, and the first formal summits were held in Paris in February 1961 and in Bonn in July of that year. At the Paris meeting, a committee was created to look into European Political Cooperation. Headed by Christian Fouchet, the French ambassador to Denmark, the group produced a draft treaty for a "union of states," which included a specific recommendation for a council of heads of government or foreign ministers that would meet every four months and take decisions on the basis of unanimity. Because at heart the Fouchet plan was an attempt to build an EEC dominated by France, the proposal met with little support outside that country.[5]

No more summits were held until 1967 and 1969, by which time it was becoming increasingly obvious to many that the EC lacked a sense of direction. The abandonment of the Bretton Woods system in 1971 provided final proof of the lack of leadership in the EC and of its inability to respond quickly and effectively to major external crises. Georges Pompidou's anger over Nixon's unilateral decision was compounded in 1973 when the superpowers disregarded any European opinion in the resolution of the energy crisis that year.[6] The EC's halfhearted response to the crisis prompted French Foreign Minister Michel Jobert to declare that Europe was a "nonentity."[7] Decisionmaking had become blocked by struggles over national interests in the Council of Ministers; what was needed, Jean Monnet argued at the time, was "a supreme body to steer Europe through the difficult transition from national to collective sovereignty"; he even suggested calling it the "Provisional European Government."[8]

Despite doubts among small member states about both the value of summits and the effects they would have on the decisionmaking abilities of the Commission and the Council of Ministers, agreement was reached at a summit in Copenhagen in December 1973 to encourage more frequent meetings among heads of government. The EC was by now in the depths of Eurosclerosis, and the urgency of taking action was brought to a head by changes of leadership in Britain, Germany, and France. In Britain, pro-European Prime Minister Edward Heath lost the February 1974 election to Harold Wilson, who demanded a renegotiation of the terms of Britain's membership. In West Germany, Willy Brandt was replaced as chancellor in May by Helmut Schmidt, and German foreign policy switched from a focus on *Ostpolitik* (accommodation with the East) to a focus on the EC. Meanwhile, Pompidou had died, and in late May pro-European Valéry Giscard d'Estaing was elected president of France. Schmidt and Giscard were both economists who had worked together as finance ministers in the early 1970s, and both appreciated the complexity of the kinds of economic issues that were jostling for attention.

This combination of crises and changes in leadership formed the background to the December 1974 summit of heads of government in Paris, where it was decided to formalize the links among them. Giscard and Schmidt argued for the need to bring leaders together regularly to provide policy direction and clear logjams. A declaration was issued committing heads of government to meet at least three times annually and emphasizing the need for "an overall approach" to the challenges of integration and the need "to ensure progress and overall consistency in the activities of the Communities and in the work on political co-operation."

The wording of the declaration was kept deliberately vague; it said nothing about the precise powers of the new body or its relationship to the other institutions and gave it no legal standing. The new body even lacked a name until Giscard's announcement at a press conference at the close of the meeting that "the European summit is dead, long live the European Council."[9] Legal recognition was finally given by the Single European Act. Although this did little more than confirm the membership of the Council and reduce the number of annual meetings from three to two, by the second half of the 1980s the Conclusions of Council summits had acquired a quasilegal status in EC politics.[10]

Structure

The 1974 Paris Declaration was careful not to allow the creation of the European Council to disturb or complicate the existing EC decisionmaking system. For example, concerns among the Benelux states that the summits would weaken the supranationalist elements of the EC were offset in part by an agreement on direct elections to the European Parliament.[11] Suggestions that a new secretariat be created for the Council were outweighed by desires to not create yet another bureaucracy or weaken the work of existing institutions. The Council has been institutionalized to the extent that it exists and follows increasingly routine patterns of functioning, but it is the only branch of the EU without a secretariat or a large, salaried body of staff.

The Council has multiple personalities. It can be seen as the decisionmaker of last resort, as a collective presidency in which sovereignty is pooled, as a body that parallels other EU institutions by dealing with issues outside their competence, or as a true "council" that can engineer broad package deals.[12] There are three keys to understanding the way it works and fits into the EU system:

1. Flexibility. The lack of rules, regulations, and attendant bureaucrats gives the Council a level of freedom and independence enjoyed by very few governing bodies.

2. Informality. European Council summits are built on months of advance preparation, but there is no set agenda, summits try to keep away from formal votes, and meetings are kept as small and informal as possible.

3. Delegation. Any signs that the Council is becoming bogged down in the routine day-to-day business of the EU have regularly been resisted.[13] The Council focuses on the big picture, leaves the other institutions to work out the details, and acts something like a "court of appeal" if attempts to reach agreement at a lower level fail.[14]

The original plan announced at Paris in 1974 was that the Council would meet every four months—once in each of the countries holding the presidency of the Council of Ministers that year (April and December) and once in Brussels (July). This schedule was subject to change, though, and emergency meetings could be convened at any time. The first meeting of the European Council was held in Dublin in March 1975 under the lumbering title "the Heads of Government Meeting as the Council of the Community and in Political Cooperation." It met more or less triannually throughout the 1970s and 1980s, but a decision was taken at the December 1985 summit to hold just two regular summits each year, in June and December. Emergency summits are held either in Brussels or in the country holding the presidency (see Appendix IV).

Meetings are hosted by the country holding the presidency and take place either in the capital of that country or in a regional city or town, such as Milan, Edinburgh, Strasbourg, or—in December 1991—Maastricht in the Netherlands, where the Treaty on European Union was agreed on. The Greeks have used their summits to mix business and pleasure, convening them on the Aegean islands of Rhodes (1988) and Corfu (1994). The Council brings together the president and senior vice president of the Commission, the heads of government (and the French head of state), and small retinues of staff and advisers. Organization is left largely to the presidency, which in effect means the prime minister and the foreign minister of the country holding the presidency. Some heads of government take a hands-on approach to determining the agenda, while others are more low-key. The major goal of each summit meeting is to agree on a set of Conclusions of the Presidency. An advanced draft of this document usually awaits the leaders at the beginning of the summit, and it provides the focus for their discussions (see Box 10.1).

How the Council Works

Preparation is the key to the success of European summits.[15] Officially, the Council has no set agenda, but some direction is needed, so senior officials from the country holding the presidency usually work with the Council of Ministers to identify agenda items, which are channeled through the Antici Group to COREPER (see Chapter 7). Preparation begins as soon as a member state takes over the presidency in January or July. The monthly meetings of the foreign ministers under the General Affairs Council try to resolve potential disagreements, and as the date for the summit approaches, the prime minister and foreign minister of the state holding the presidency become increasingly involved. The more agreements they can broker in advance, the less likely it is that the summit will end in failure.[16]

About ten days before the summit, the foreign ministers meet to finalize the agenda and to iron out any remaining problems and disputes. The items on the agenda depend on circumstances: National delegations normally have issues they want to raise, there has to be some continuity from previous summits, and leaders often have to deal with a breaking problem or an emergency that requires a decision, such as aid to Russia or progress on world trade talks. Some issues (especially economic issues) are routinely discussed at every summit. The Commission may also promote issues it would like to see discussed, and an active presidency might use the summit to bring items of national or regional interest to the attention of the heads of gov-

BOX 10.1
European Summits

Summits usually run for a period of two days, although emergency summits will normally last no more than a day. They begin with informal discussions over breakfast and move into nuts and bolts at morning and afternoon plenary sessions. The first plenary includes an address by the president of the European Parliament. Formal dinners in the evening were once followed routinely by a "fireside chat" among the heads of government and the president of the Commission, but it has become more common to hold another plenary session. Overnight, officials from the presidency and the Secretariat of the Council of Ministers work on the draft set of Conclusions, which are discussed at a second plenary on the morning of the second day and—if necessary—at a third in the afternoon. The summit normally ends with the publication of the Conclusions.

During summit plenaries, the prime ministers of the member states (and the president of France) sit around a table with their respective foreign ministers and two officials from the Commission, including the president. To keep the meeting intimate and manageable, few other people are allowed into the meeting chamber: no more than one adviser per country, interpreters, and two officials from the country holding the presidency, one from the Council of Ministers Secretariat, and three from the Commission—about sixty people in all. Every delegation has a nearby suite it can use as a base, but national delegations are limited to seventeen members each. Contacts among national delegations are maintained by the Antici Group, whose members are allowed to come and go from the meeting chamber.

European Council decisions are usually taken on the basis of unanimity or at least consensus, but an occasional lack of unanimity may force a formal vote, and some member states may want to attach conditions or reservations to the Conclusions. In addition to the formal plenary sessions, summits usually break out into several subsidiary meetings, including those of foreign ministers and regular bilateral meetings of prime ministers over breakfast or coffee.

The summits are always major media events and are surrounded by extensive security. In addition to the substantive political discussions that take place, enormous symbolism is attached to the outcomes of the summits, which are assessed according to the extent to which they represent breakthroughs or show EU leaders to be bogged down in disagreement. Failure and success reflect not only on the presidency but on the entire process of European integration. The headline-making nature of the summits is sufficient to focus the minds of participants and to encourage them to agree. A "family picture" is also taken of the fifteen leaders and the president of the Commission, symbolizing the process of European integration. The smiles would look very shallow if major disagreements had not been resolved.

ernment. Calls are occasionally made for the launch of a major policy initiative, such as the decision taken at the 1989 Strasbourg summit to call an intergovernmental conference on economic and monetary union. Some summits are routine and result in general agreement among leaders; in others, deep differences in opinion arise, with some member states perhaps refusing to agree to a common set of conclusions.

The exact role of the European Council has been kept deliberately ambiguous by its members. An attempt to define that role was made at the Stuttgart European Council in 1983 and its agreement on the Solemn Declaration on European Union, drawn up to preempt the draft treaty on European Union being worked on by Parliament. "A good rule of thumb in European matters," mused Guy de Bassompierre, "is that the more solemn the declaration, the more empty it is of true content."[17] Combining the 1974 Paris Declaration and the 1983 Stuttgart Declaration produces a list of goals for Council summits that can be summed up as follows:

- To exchange views and reach a consensus;

- To give political impetus to the development of the EU;

- To begin cooperation in new policy areas;

- To provide general political guidelines for the EU and the development of a common foreign policy;

- To guarantee policy consistency; and

- To reach common positions on foreign policy issues.[18]

More specifically, the Council makes the key decisions on the overall direction of political integration and EMU, internal economic issues, foreign policy issues, budget disputes, treaty revisions, new member applications, and institutional reforms (such as enlargement of the European Parliament). The summits achieve all this through a combination of brainstorming, intensive bilateral and multilateral discussions, and bargaining. The mechanics of decisionmaking depend on a combination of the quality of organization and preparation, the leadership skills of the presidency, and the ideological and personal agendas of the individual leaders (see Table 10.1). The interpersonal dynamics of the participants are also important.

1. The political significance of the Franco-German axis has always been critical, and it has been given additional influence by the strong personal relations that have usually existed between the leaders of the two states (Brandt and Pompidou, Schmidt and Giscard, and Kohl and Mitterrand).

2. Leaders who have been in office for a long time (such as a Felipe Gonzalez or a Helmut Kohl) or who have a solid base of political support at home (such as a Franz Vranitsky) will be in a very different negotiating positions from those who have not. In late 1994, for example, John Major suffered from low popularity and a rebellion by anti-EU members of his party, Silvio Berlusconi faced corruption

TABLE 10.1 Leaders of EU Member States, June 1995

State	Leader	Beginning of Term in Office	Party	Ideology[a]
Spain	Felipe Gonzalez	1982	Socialist	L
Greece	Andreas Papandreou	1993	Socialist	L
Netherlands	Wim Kok	1994	Socialist	L
Portugal	Anibal Cavaco Silva	1985	Social Democrat	CL
Austria	Franz Vranitzky	1990	Social Democrat	CL
Denmark	Poul Nyrup Rasmussen	1994	Social Democrat	CL
Ireland	John Bruton	1994	Fine Gael	CL
Sweden	Ingvar Carlsson	1994	Social Democrat	CL
Luxembourg	Jean-Claude Juncker	1994	Christian Social	CL
Finland	Paavo Lipponen	1995	Social Democrat	CL
Germany	Helmut Kohl	1982	Christian Democrat	CR
Belgium	Jean-Luc Dehaene	1992	Christian Democrat	CR
United Kingdom	John Major	1990	Conservative	R
France	Jacques Chirac	1995	Gaullist	R
Italy	Lamberto Dini	1995	Caretaker	—

[a]L = left, CL = center left, CR = center right, R = right.

charges as his government in Italy teetered on the brink of collapse, and the socialist François Mitterrand had to cohabit with a legislature dominated by conservatives as his final term drew to a close with no obvious successor in sight. These political problems unavoidably affected the judgment and performance of the leaders.

3. Some leaders are respected and have strong credibility, while others do not. Despite the closeness of the 1994 German federal elections, Helmut Kohl has been a towering influence on the EU stage since 1982, and by late 1994 he had become something of an elder statesman of European integration (helped, of course, by the dominating economic power of Germany). Margaret Thatcher may have irritated and harangued her colleagues, but her political skills, grasp of detail, and leadership abilities were unquestioned. By contrast, the return to power of the ailing and aging Andreas Papandreou of Greece in 1993 was widely regretted.[19]

In addition to the regular biannual summits, occasional emergency meetings of the Council can also be convened to deal with a breaking issue or a persistent problem. Examples include the February 1988 summit in Brussels to agree on budget reforms, the November 1989 summit in Paris to discuss rapidly changing events in Eastern Europe, the October 1992 summit in

Birmingham to discuss the crisis in the ERM, and the July 1994 summit convened to choose a successor to Jacques Delors.

Because the European Council obviously has much more power over decisionmaking than any other EU institution, it has tended to take power away from the other institutions. It can, in effect, set the agenda for the Commission, override decisions reached by the Council of Ministers, and largely ignore Parliament. Any hopes the Commission might have held for developing an independent sphere of action and power have largely disappeared with the rise of the European Council. Certainty regarding the present and potential future role of the Council is clouded by its ambiguities, and opinion remains divided over whether it is an integrative or a disintegrative body.[20]

Other EU Institutions

As the reach of the EU has broadened and deepened, the work of its specialized agencies—and the pressure for the creation of new agencies—has grown. Some agencies have been there from the beginning, while others have been set up more recently in response to new needs. The European Council summit in Edinburgh in December 1992 agreed on the annual program for the meetings of Parliament, the Commission, the Council of Ministers, the Courts, and three existing specialized bodies: the Economic and Social Committee, the Committee of the Regions, and the European Investment Bank. This cleared the way for a decision at the October 1993 European Council in Brussels on the creation and/or siting of several new bodies.

Economic and Social Committee

Based in Brussels, the Economic and Social Committee (ESC) is one of the weaker and more obscure EU institutions, although it has some uses. A purely advisory body, it was set up under the Treaty of Rome to give employers, workers, and other sectional interests a forum in which they could meet, talk, and give advice to the Commission and the Council of Ministers. The idea flowed out of the Consultative Committee set up by the ECSC and copied the parallel bodies that existed in five of the six founder members of the EEC (West Germany was the exception). It was founded in part because few people thought the European Parliament would represent sectional interests, and it has since been described as a "functional complement" of the EP.[21]

The ESC has 220 members, drawn from the member states roughly in proportion to population size (see Table 10.2). They are proposed by national governments and confirmed by the Council of Ministers for renewable four-year terms. There are three groups of members: About one-third

TABLE 10.2 Membership of the ESC and the CoR

Germany	24	Portugal	12
United Kingdom	24	Austria	11
France	24	Sweden	11
Italy	24	Denmark	9
Spain	21	Finland	9
Belgium	12	Ireland	9
Greece	12	Luxembourg	6
Netherlands	12		
		Total	220

come from industry and services (such as banking and insurance), one-third from labor unions, and the rest from a variety of backgrounds—mainly agriculture, small businesses, and the professions. A president is elected by the ESC for a two-year term, and a Secretariat of just over 500 staff members supports the work of the Committee.

The ESC as a whole meets in Brussels nine or ten times each year for two-day summits (its members are unpaid but can claim expenses). The three groups hold separate meetings (a total of about ninety times per year) to discuss issues of common interest; they break down into smaller sections and study groups to deal with specific issues, such as agriculture, social issues, transport, energy, regional development, and the environment. The ESC publishes information reports, communicates with other international organizations, tries to promote understanding among its members, lobbies the Commission, and issues opinions on topics of interest. Although questions have long been raised about its value, the ESC was given new areas of interest under the SEA and Maastricht, and it can now consult with the Commission and the Council of Ministers on topics as varied as agriculture, the movement of workers, social policy, regional policy, and the environment.

The basic weakness of the ESC is that neither the Commission nor the Council of Ministers is obliged to act on its opinions or views, which are occasionally ignored. "Consultation" is an ambiguous and often meaningless concept, and although the Commission can "take note" of an ESC opinion and the Council of Ministers can recognize a "useful" opinion, this amounts to little. The influence of the ESC is further minimized by the fact that its members are unpaid part-time appointees and are not officially recognized as representatives of the bodies they belong to; further, EU proposals are often sent to the ESC only after they have reached an advanced stage of agreement by the Council of Ministers. The best that can be said of the ESC is that it is another forum for the representation of sectional interests, but as the European Parliament becomes stronger and the number of lobbyists in Brussels grows, the Committee in its present form becomes less significant.

Committee of the Regions

Disparities in wealth and income across Western Europe have always posed a handicap to the process of integration; there can never be balanced free trade, a true single market, or even meaningful economic and political union as long as some parts of the EU are richer or poorer than others. The setting up of the European Regional Development Fund in 1975 was one approach to the problem, as was the creation in 1985 of an ad hoc Assembly of European Regions and the creation by the Commission in 1988 of a Consultative Council of Regional and Local Authorities. The need for a stronger response led to the creation under the terms of Maastricht of a new Committee of the Regions (CoR).

Based in Brussels, the CoR has the same membership structure as the Economic and Social Council: 220 members appointed by the member states for four-year renewable terms and confirmed by the Council of Ministers (see Table 10.2). It provides a channel for local units of government to express their views. Although Maastricht does not specify what qualifications Committee members should have beyond saying they should be "representatives of regional and local bodies," most are elected local government officials. Because the CoR is so new, predictable working patterns have yet to emerge, but it meets in plenary session roughly as often as the ESC and has the same advisory role. It can give opinions on matters relating to regional and local issues, but—as with the ESC—its opinions can be ignored by the Commission and the Council of Ministers. The CoR suffers from the same structural problems as the ESC, and some doubt whether it is needed, given the role played by the European Parliament.

European Investment Bank

Based in Luxembourg, the European Investment Bank (EIB) is an autonomous institution that was set up in 1958 under the terms of the Treaty of Rome to encourage "balanced and steady development" within the EEC by granting loans and giving guarantees. It must give preference to projects that help the poorer regions of the EU, that support the modernization and improved competitiveness of EU industry, and that are of common interest to several member states or to the EU as a whole. The EIB's major focus in recent years has been on projects that help promote the single market through the development of trans-European road, rail, and communications networks;[22] its single biggest project was the Channel tunnel between Britain and France, which opened in 1994. It has also supported the Airbus project and France's high-speed train system (see Chapter 11).

The EIB has a staff of about 750 and is managed by a board of governors consisting of the finance ministers of the member states, a twenty-three-member board of directors appointed by the board of governors (three each from France, Germany, Italy, and Britain and one each from the remaining member states) who serve five-year renewable terms, and a six-person management committee appointed for six-year renewable terms by the board of governors. In 1994 the president was Sir Brian Unwin of Britain.

The EIB's funds come from borrowing on worldwide capital markets and from subscriptions by EU member states. Its loans have risen steadily in recent years, from 7 billion ECU ($8.4 billion) in 1991 to 15.3 billion ($18.4 billion) in 1992 and 19.6 billion ($23.5 billion) in 1993. Most of its loans go either to the EU's poorest regions (Italy and Spain have been the major beneficiaries) or to outside the EU. The bank deals only in large loans of more than 10 million ECUs ($12 million), it rarely lends more than half of the total investment cost of a project, and it often cofinances projects with other banks.

European Monetary Institute

Based in Frankfurt, the EMI was founded in 1994 as a result of the agreement reached at Maastricht to move ahead with the second stage of the Delors Plan on EMU. The EMI is not a central bank, and its precise job has been left deliberately ambiguous, but it is charged with helping to coordinate monetary policies and developing the ECU and is widely seen as the embryo for a future central bank. It is also an important vehicle for keeping the member states focused on developing a single currency. The EMI's task was complicated by the effective suspension of the ERM in August 1993, which raised questions about the ability of the EMI to encourage the coordination of monetary policies among EU member states. Jacques Delors favored a strong role and greater powers for the EMI in the interests of promoting phase two of his plan on EMU, but others (notably the famously independent German Bundesbank) opposed this view, arguing that the EMI should have a purely advisory role.[23]

Hungarian-born Belgian banker Alexandre Lamfalussy was appointed first president of the EMI, which is governed by a council consisting of the governors of the central banks of EU member states. It will eventually have a projected staff of about 250. The central bank (or Eurofed) will probably be governed by its own council, consisting of members serving five-year nonrenewable terms. This nonrenewability will allow the members to develop independence from national heads of government; they could only be removed for personal misconduct, and then only by the European Court of Justice, not by the member states.

BOX 10.2
Specialized Agencies of the European Union

Among the growing network of agencies dealing with specific aspects of the work of the EU are the following:

- *European Centre for the Development of Vocational Training (CEDEFOP).* Created in 1975, CEDEFOP is based in Thessaloniki, Greece. Its eighty staff members work with the Commission to promote vocational training within the EU. This training mainly involves information exchange and the organization of courses, seminars, and pilot projects.
- *Foundation for the Improvement of Living and Working Conditions.* Established in 1975, this agency is based in Dublin and employs about seventy people. Its brief is to develop ideas on medium- and long-term improvements of working conditions in the EU.
- *European Training Foundation.* Created in 1990, this agency is based in Turin, Italy. Its projected staff of about three hundred will promote vocational training in Eastern Europe and the former USSR, working closely with CEDEFOP and the Tempus program (see Chapter 13).
- *Agency for Health and Safety at Work.* Flowing out of the Social Charter, the agency is located in Bilbao, Spain.
- *Office for Harmonization in the Internal Market.* Bringing together the EC Design Office and the EC Trademark Office, this agency was set up in 1993 in Alicante, Spain, and is eventually expected to have a staff of about two hundred. Its job will be to maintain a register of designs and to implement trademark law.
- *European Science and Technology Assembly.* Based in Brussels, the Assembly was created in 1994 to bring together one hundred research scientists and corporate research directors to advise the Commission on priorities for current and future research programs.
- *European Monitoring Centre for Drugs and Drug Addiction.* Based in Lisbon, Portugal, the Centre is part of a new program to fight crime and drug addiction. Its projected staff of about thirty will provide member states and the EU with information on drugs and drug addiction that can be used in antidrug campaigns.
- *European Veterinary Inspection Agency.* Part of the Commission (rather than a decentralized agency), this agency is sited in Dublin and is responsible for overseeing the Commission's work in veterinary and plant health inspection.
- *Translation Centre.* Based in Luxembourg, this agency has been set up specifically to help all of the new specialized agencies (except the EMI) with their translation needs.
- *Common Appeal Court for Community Patents.* Not yet established as this book went to press, this agency is likely to be sited in Luxembourg along with all of the other EU courts.

European Bank for Reconstruction and Development

Based in London, the European Bank for Reconstruction and Development (EBRD) is not actually part of the EU, but it was founded in 1990 on EU initiative, derives 51 percent of its capital from the EU, deals in ECUs, and will inevitably have a growing influence on EU decisions. Much like the International Bank for Reconstruction and Development (the World Bank), the EBRD was founded to provide loans, encourage capital investment, and promote trade, but its specific focus is on helping East European countries make the transition to free-market economies. Suggested by François Mitterrand in October 1989 and endorsed by the European Council in December of that year, the EBRD began operations in March 1991. East and West European states are members, as are the United States and Russia. While the World Bank lends mainly to governments, the EBRD (at the insistence of the United States) makes 60 percent of its loans to the private sector. In its first full year of operations (1992), it approved projects worth $1.3 billion.

London was chosen as the site of the EBRD because it is one of the world's four biggest stock markets, is the world's largest market for insurance and foreign exchange, has a large financial sector, and operates in English—the language of international finance. London's hopes of becoming the financial capital of Europe were dashed in October 1993, however, with the decision to site the new European Monetary Institute in Frankfurt, which is now widely seen as the most likely home of a future European central bank.

The EBRD's first president was French economist Jacques Attali, a former adviser to François Mitterrand. The bank was created with an opening capital of $12 billion, which Attali saw as the seed of a new Marshall Plan that could invest ten times that amount in Eastern Europe. The varied levels of transition in eastern Europe complicated EBRD's task, as did its sluggish bureaucratic procedures. The Bank's credibility was further undermined by Attali's behavior, notably his decision to spend $66 million on sumptuous interior decorations for the London headquarters building. Against a background of growing criticism (or, according to the French media, a "British press campaign"[24]), he resigned in June 1993 and was replaced by Jacques de Larosière, former governor of the Bank of France and president of the IMF, who streamlined decisionmaking and speeded up the disbursement of funds.

European Environment Agency

The EC began developing environmental policies in 1972 (see Chapter 14) and instituted a series of five-year environmental action programs in 1973.

With new powers over environmental policy given to the Commission by both the SEA and Maastricht, the need for a new system of administration became more pressing, which led to a May 1990 decision to create the EEA. Further progress became bogged down over lack of agreement on a site for the EEA; the stalemate finally ended in 1993 with the decision to locate it in Copenhagen.

The EEA will have a staff of about fifty, and its main job will be to provide information; this makes it very different from the U.S. Environmental Protection Agency, which has a staff of fifteen thousand and is responsible for ensuring that states implement most of the major pieces of federal environmental law. EU member states opposed the idea of creating an inspectorate that could become involved in national environmental monitoring.[25] The EEA will set up a European Information and Observation Network to collect information from the member states and neighboring non-EU states. This information will then be used to help develop national environmental protection policies and to measure the results of these policies. The EEA will also publish reports on the state of the European environment every three years and will work with other international organizations, such as the OECD, the Council of Europe, and the UN Environment Program.

European Medicines Evaluation Agency

Roughly parallel to the U.S. Food and Drug Administration (FDA) (but without FDA-style centralization), the European Medicines Evaluation Agency (EMEA) was set up in 1995 with EU funding in an attempt to harmonize (but not replace) the work of existing national drug regulatory bodies. The hope is that this plan will not only reduce the $350 million annual cost drug companies incur by having to win separate approvals from each member state but that it will also eliminate the protectionist tendencies of states unwilling to approve new drugs that might compete with those already produced by domestic drug companies. The EU is currently the source of about one-third of the new drugs brought onto the world market each year.

Based in London, the EMEA was born after more than seven years of negotiations among EU governments and replaced the Committee for Proprietary Medicinal Products set up in 1977. It is focusing initially on new drugs (rather than trying to establish standards for existing drugs). It has a staff of two hundred, and decentralizes its decisionmaking structure by working through a computer-linked network of about three thousand experts throughout the EU. Its decisions must be ratified by the Commission, and member states are then given a maximum of ninety days to lodge objections. It hopes to reach its decisions within a maximum of three hundred days (which compares well with the average of five hundred days taken by the U.S. FDA). EMEA's first administrator was Fernand Sauer of France.[26]

European Police Office (Europol)

With the Maastricht treaty making justice and home affairs one of the three pillars of the European Union, some direction had to be given to the development of police cooperation. Based in The Hague, Europol is charged with setting up an EU-wide system of information exchange targeted at combating terrorism, drug trafficking, and other serious forms of international crime.

Summary and Conclusions

By bringing together the leaders of the fifteen EU member states on a regular basis, the European Council provides the kind of leadership and direction that was patently missing from the European Community in the 1960s and early 1970s. It deliberately keeps away from the details of European integration, instead providing the impetus for "high policy" issues, such as economic union, political union, and a common foreign policy.

Opinion is divided on whether the European Council contributes to—or detracts from—European integration. On the one hand, it has encouraged integration by helping to steer the EU through major crises, encouraging consensus among EU leaders that might never have been achieved otherwise, and agreeing on some of the biggest integrative initiatives since the mid-1970s. On the other hand, the Council has taken away from the powers of the Commission and the European Parliament, has helped promote intergovernmentalism by keeping decisionmaking powers in the hands of the member states, and has long failed to make much progress on critical issues such as budgetary reform.

At the opposite end of the scale, the growing workload of the EU has spurred the creation of a growing number of specialized agencies charged with encouraging cooperation on everything from monetary to environmental policy, with underpinning the single market, and with promoting vocational training, worker health and safety, and the fight against drugs and crime. All of these agencies have a deliberately decentralized focus, encouraging coordination rather than integration but opening the door to federalism a little wider. In their own ways, both the European Council and the specialized agencies are promoting the kind of cooperation neofunctionalists would portray as a process of bridge building across the chasm that divides states.

Notes

1. Strictly speaking, the European Council overlaps at almost every turn with the Council of Ministers, and many scholars feel the two should be studied as one. However, differences in the briefs, agendas, and powers of the two institutions make it more informative to approach them separately.

2. Neill Nugent, *The Government and Politics of the European Union* (Durham, N.C.: Duke University Press, 1994), 155.

3. Desmond Dinan, *Ever Closer Union? An Introduction to the European Community* (Boulder: Lynne Rienner, 1994), 230.

4. Annette Morgan, *From Summit to Council: Evolution in the EEC* (London: Chatham House, 1976), 9.

5. Mary Troy Johnston, *The European Council: Gatekeeper of the European Community* (Boulder: Westview Press, 1994), 2–4.

6. Morgan, *From Summit to Council,* 14–17.

7. Philippe Moreau Defarges, "Twelve Years of European Council History (1974–1986): The Crystallizing Forum," in Jean-Marc Hoscheit and Wolfgang Wessels (Eds.), *The European Council 1974–1986: Evaluation and Prospects* (Maastricht: European Institute of Public Administration, 1988), 38–39.

8. Jean Monnet, *Memoirs* (Garden City, N.Y.: Doubleday, 1978), 502–503.

9. Morgan, *From Summit to Council,* 5.

10. Peter Ludlow, "Europe's Institutions: Europe's Politics," in Gregory F. Treverton (Ed.), *The Shape of the New Europe* (New York: Council on Foreign Relations Press, 1992), 62.

11. Johnston, *The European Council,* 14.

12. Wolfgang Wessels, "The European Council: A Denaturing of the Community or Indispensable Decision-Making Body?" in Hoscheit and Wessels, *The European Council 1974–1986,* 9–11.

13. See, for example, Ad Hoc Committee for Institutional Affairs, *Report to the European Council* (the Dooge Report) (March 1985), Bull. EC 3-1985.

14. Guy de Bassompierre, *Changing the Guard in Brussels: An Insider's View of the EC Presidency* (Westport, Conn.: Praeger, 1988), 78.

15. See ibid., 80–87, for more detail on the organization and outcomes of the European Council.

16. See Johnston, *The European Council,* 27–31.

17. De Bassompierre, *Changing the Guard,* 78.

18. Paris Declaration 1974, in European Parliament, Committee on Institutional Affairs, *Selection of Texts Concerning Institutional Matters of the Community from 1950 to 1982* (Luxembourg: European Parliament, 1982); Statement of the European Council London 1977, in Commission of the EC, *Bulletin* 7 (1977); and Solemn Declaration of Stuttgart 1983, in Commission of the EC, *Bulletin* 6 (1983).

19. Dinan, *Ever Closer Union?* 245.

20. See Johnston, *The European Council,* 41–48.

21. Nugent, *Government and Politics of the European Union,* 241.

22. Peter Doyle, Interview with Sir Brian Unwin, president of the EIB, *Europe* 334 (March 1994), 12–14.

23. Bruce Barnard, "European Monetary Institute," *Europe* 334 (March 1994), 8.

24. *The Times* (London), June 26, 1993.

25. Ken Collins and David Earnshaw, "The Implementation and Enforcement of European Community Environment Legislation," in David Judge (Ed.), *A Green Dimension for the European Community* (London: Frank Cass, 1993), 238–239.

26. *The Economist*, May 7, 1994, 74.

Further Reading

Simon Bulmer and Wolfgang Wessels. *The European Council: Decisionmaking in European Politics* (London: Macmillan, 1987).

One of the earliest full-length studies of the Council and its work.

Jan Werts. *The European Council* (Amsterdam: North-Holland, 1992).

A look at the history and organization of the Council, with details on how it works and how it relates to other EU institutions. Ends with a survey of the results of Council meetings between 1975 and 1991.

Mary Troy Johnston. *The European Council: Gatekeeper of the European Community* (Boulder: Westview Press, 1994).

One of the most recent of several studies of the European Council, which focuses particularly on the extent to which the EC has become institutionalized and on its impact on integration.

Martin Westlake. *The European Council* (New York: Stockton, 1995).

A study of the structure and workings of the Council and of how it fits with the other EU institutions.

THREE

Policies

11

Policy Processes and the Budget

Public policy is whatever governments do or do not do. When parties or candidates run for office, they normally put forward a list of ideas and proposals for dealing with the needs and demands of their constituents. Once elected, ideally they govern on the basis of those ideas (or variants), which together constitute their policies. Discussions of policy often include words such as goals, programs, platforms, objectives, values, and needs. The options governments choose and the ones they ignore collectively define their policies, which are usually expressed as laws, orders, regulations, public statements, and actions. Put another way, if elections and public opinion are the inputs of politics in a democracy, public policies are the outputs.

Debates rage about how policy is made and implemented at the national level in democracies, even though most have relatively predictable, stable, and institutionalized systems of government. Defining political powers and policy processes in the European Union is much more difficult. Not only is its governing structure very different from the structures found in conventional states, but the EU is still evolving, and the balance of power among its institutions and member states is constantly changing, complicating the tasks of defining and identifying the key sources of power and of describing (or at least predicting) how that power is used.

Much of the problem stems from the EU's lack of a constitution and the many ambiguities built into its major treaties. Maastricht, for example, tried to define the powers of the EU by focusing on subsidiarity and saying that the EU should act only if "the objectives of the proposed action cannot be sufficiently achieved by the Member States and can therefore, by reason of the scale or effects of proposed action, be better achieved by the Community" (Article 3b). But how can the member states or the EU institutions be absolutely certain about what can and what cannot be better undertaken by one side or the other? Maastricht goes on to list specific and noble "tasks" of the EU, including working toward sustainable growth, high employment, and improvements in the standard of living in member states. These are very general goals, and little is said about who is responsible for achieving them or how they will be achieved. Under these circumstances, the relative powers of EU institutions and member states remain ambiguous and poorly defined.

If the sources and parameters of EU powers are ambiguous, there is little question that its authority has deepened and broadened. From a time when the EU dealt only with coal and steel policy, the member states have transferred so many powers that the EU now touches (to varying degrees) on most aspects of economic, foreign, social, agricultural, and environmental policy. But despite this "Europeanization" of the policy process, concerns about loss of sovereignty, and complaints about the mythical monolith of "Brussels," the EU still has relatively limited powers of enforcement and implementation and has a very small budget. Against that background, this chapter will look at how EU policy is made and implemented and will discuss one of the key influences on EU policy authority—the budget.

The European Union Policy Cycle

There are many different ways of approaching the study of public policy, but the most common method is to describe it in terms of a cycle. Reduced to its key elements, the EU policy cycle—and the key players in that cycle—can be expressed as follows.

Agenda Setting

Before a policy choice can be made (at any level), the existence of a problem must be recognized. In other words, something must have been identified and accepted as a legitimate concern of government and as meriting a government reponse. Different people see problems differently at different times and will argue over whether they are even problems at all. Their assessments and decisions are influenced by prevailing economic, social, and ideological values (problems routinely go in and out of fashion) and by the extent of government authority.

At the national government level, policy often goes through an "issue attention cycle," meaning issues move up and down the agenda according to changing levels of public and political interest.[1] The EU has witnessed less of an issue attention cycle than "issue attention growth"; as a new level of government in the making, its interests have expanded, and its authority has spread to new areas. Precisely how and why this has happened is debatable, and it raises questions about the extent to which agenda setting is a reactive or a proactive phenomenon. In some respects, it is reactive at the EU level in the sense that spillover and external events cause issues (particularly foreign policy issues) to be brought to the policy agenda. In other respects it is proactive because particular heads of government or Commission presidents (for example) have pushed issues onto the agenda through the political acts of will discussed in Chapter 1 or by other means.[2]

One important difference betwen agenda setting by national governments and that by the EU lies in the relative roles of public accountability (see Box 11.1). Elected leaders at the national level often push issues onto the policy agenda in response to public opinion, ostensibly because they want to represent the public will but also because they want to be reelected. In that sense, agenda setting is voter driven. In the EU, however, the only directly elected policymakers are Members of the European Parliament, and they have limited influence on the overall policy process. Most policymaking power currently rests with the Commission and the Council of Ministers, neither of which is directly elected or accountable to an EU-wide constituency and thus is less subject to voter influence.

Another important difference between national and EU agenda setting lies in the extent to which easily identified solutions exist. At the national or subnational level, it is easier (but by no means easy) to identify problems and their causes and so to push the issue onto the policy agenda and formulate a response. At the EU level, the sheer complexity and variety of the needs and priorities of the fifteen member states make it much more difficult to be certain about the existence or the causes of problems or the potential effects of policy alternatives. This makes it more difficult to make the case for putting an issue on the agenda.

The European Council outlines the broad policy goals of the EU and often sparks new policy initiatives, but the pressures and influences that lead to those initiatives can come from many different sources: public opinion, treaty obligations, judgments of the Court of Justice, personal initiatives of individual leaders, internal and external pressures (such as struggles over the EU budget, the need to respond to security problems such as the 1990–1991 Gulf crisis and the Balkan war, or the shock of the Danish rejection of Maastricht in 1992), and changes in the outside world (such as the collapse of the Soviet Union or changes in the global economy) (see Figure 11.1).

Agenda setting in the EU is based in part on the extent to which national governments are prepared to allow the EU to have authority in different fields; on the extent to which economic, political, or technical pressures demand an EU response, and on the compromises reached in the process of resolving the often conflicting demands and needs of the member states. The EU is guided through this by the three founding treaties and subsequent amendments, notably the Single European Act and the Maastricht treaty. These documents lay down the basic goals of the EU, and many policies are made on that basis. The treaties act as something like a constitution for the EU, but constitutions usually describe what governments *can* do rather than what they *should* do. Not only are the EU treaties often prescriptive, but

BOX 11.1
The Pressures for Agenda Setting

Most studies of public policy argue that agenda setting is determined in one of three ways.[1] The pluralist approach argues that policymaking in government is divided into separate arenas that are influenced by different groups and that government is ultimately the sum of all the competing interests in a society. The elitist approach argues that decision-making is dominated by a power elite consisting of individuals with the means to exert influence, be it money, status, charisma, or some other commodity. The state-centric approach argues that the major source of policies is the environment in which policymakers find themselves and that government itself, rather than external social interests, is the locus of agenda setting.

Agenda setting in the EU—as in every level of government—arguably reflects elements of all three of these approaches. First, it is **pluralist** to the extent that groups play a role in determining EU priorities. The most fundamental of those "groups" are the member states themselves, but pluralists usually think in terms of more specific interest groups. The ECSC was at heart a coalition of the coal and steel industries of its six member states; farmers have exerted enormous influence through their defense of the Common Agricultural Policy; the EU has paid more attention to environmental policy, in part because environmental interest groups have successfully lobbied the Commission and Parliament and have occasionally used the EU to bypass their own national governments.[2]

Second, EU agenda setting is **elitist** to the extent that priorities have long been set by the leaders of the member states, the Council of Ministers, and the unelected and largely unaccountable European commissioners. The democratic deficit is derived largely from the fact that so few individuals in the EU power structure are elected and that so many of their meetings take place out of public view. The rise of interest group lobbying and the growing powers of the European Parliament are helping to make the process more open and democratic.

Finally, EU agenda setting is **state-centric** (or rather superstate-centric) to the extent that the setting of the EU agenda has been determined in large part by the nature of integration. EU leaders made a conscious decision to sign the Single European Act, for example, which meant the EU had to become involved in a wide variety of new policy areas and deepened its authority in policy areas in which it was already involved. Despite the fact that EU institutions have been constrained by the limits placed on their powers and their briefs by national governments, the member states have found themselves (willingly or unwillingly) giving up more sovereignty, and thus they find their own national agendas set increasingly by the pressures and needs of European integration.

Notes

1. B. Guy Peters, *American Public Policy: Promise and Performance* (Chatham, N.J.: Chatham House, 1993), 45–47.

2. See John McCormick, *British Politics and the Environment* (London: Earthscan, 1991), chapter 7.

FIGURE 11.1   The European Union Policymaking Process

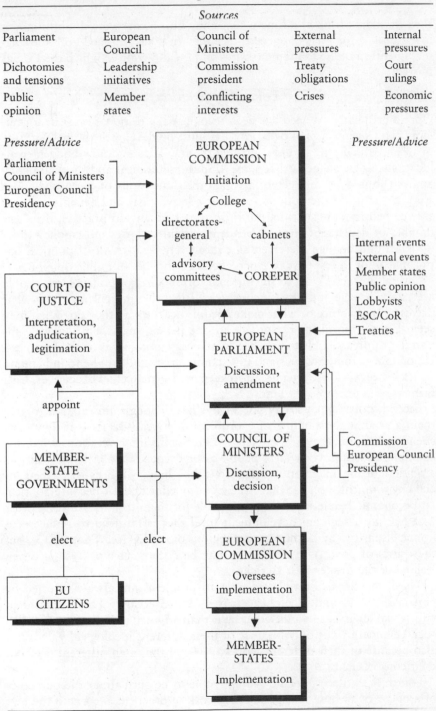

Sources

Parliament	European Council	Council of Ministers	External pressures	Internal pressures
Dichotomies and tensions	Leadership initiatives	Commission president	Treaty obligations	Court rulings
Public opinion	Member states	Conflicting interests	Crises	Economic pressures

Pressure/Advice

Parliament
Council of Ministers
European Council
Presidency

Pressure/Advice

EUROPEAN COMMISSION

Initiation

College

directorates-general   cabinets

advisory committees   COREPER

Internal events
External events
Member states
Public opinion
Lobbyists
ESC/CoR
Treaties

COURT OF JUSTICE

Interpretation, adjudication, legitimation

EUROPEAN PARLIAMENT

Discussion, amendment

appoint

MEMBER-STATE GOVERNMENTS

COUNCIL OF MINISTERS

Discussion, decision

Commission
European Council
Presidency

elect   elect

EU CITIZENS

EUROPEAN COMMISSION

Oversees implementation

MEMBER-STATES

Implementation

they were drawn up at a time when many Europeans were doubtful about integration. Much has happened since then that has changed both the original intention of the founding treaties and the direction in which the EU has moved.

Policy Formulation

Once a problem or a need has been recognized, a response must be formulated. This means a plan or a program must be developed to deal with the problem, which may include agreeing on new laws and new budgetary allocations. Logic suggests that some kind of methodical and rational policy analysis should be conducted in which the dimensions of the problem are studied and all of the options and their relative costs and benefits are considered before taking action, but this rarely happens. In practice, the sheer number of dependent and independent variables causes most policy to be designed and applied incrementally, intuitively, as a result of political opportunism, or in response to emergencies or changes in public opinion.

Several obstacles exist to the rational formulation of policy. First, people are unpredictable and often inconsistent. It is often difficult to know what drives human nature or what makes people act the way they do. What may seem logical, moral, or reasonable to one person may seem illogical, immoral, or unreasonable to another. In an entity as complex as the European Union, few common values and little common ground will be found among Greek office workers, Viennese storekeepers, German chief executives, Irish farmers, and unemployed Finns.

Second, policymakers may not always have enough information to give them a clear understanding of a problem or its causes. Even if they have such information, they are unlikely to agree on its interpretation. What, for example, causes poverty? Are people poor because they lack the will, the ambition, or the imagination to improve their lives; is it because of their social environment, because they are lazy or uneducated, or because political and economic barriers make it impossible for them to improve their lives? The EU has a regional development fund that is targeted to reduce economic disparities by helping poorer regions of the EU (see Chapter 13), but the causes of poverty in rural Italy may be different from those in urban Ireland or the former East Germany.

Third, the causes of and responses to problems are always affected by personal, social, and ideological biases. A conservative French president will see policy issues in a different light than a Dutch socialist or a Swedish social democrat, not only because of their different ideological values but also because of their different worldviews and the often different needs of their constituencies.

Fourth, it is often difficult or impossible to be sure about the outcomes of a policy or of how that policy will work in practice. Even with the best intentions and the finest research and planning, policies often have unintended or unanticipated results.

Finally, the distribution of power in any system of government is often ambiguous, in part because constitutions are subject to different interpretations but also because the process of government is determined largely by *implied* powers; by the personal values, biases, and abilities of officeholders and by the varied ways in which different officeholders use and manipulate the powers of the same office. For example, the role of the European Commission in the policy process has depended less on the terms of reference of its president than on the personality of the president. Jacques Delors pushed the influence of the office to new limits and launched major new policy initiatives, leading the EU to formulate policy in many new areas. He stood in stark contrast to relatively passive presidents such as Jean Rey or Gaston Thorn.

The major focus of policy formulation in the EU is the Commission, which has the sole power to initiate new legislation, is responsible for protecting the treaties and ensuring that their spirit is expressed in specific laws and policies, and is charged with overseeing the EU budget. However, its proposals are routinely and often extensively changed as they go through the directorates-general, as a result of lobbying by interest groups or national governments, as a response to internal and external emergencies and crises, and as they are discussed by the Council of Ministers and the European Parliament. The Commission has been described as an "adolescent bureaucracy" in the sense that its relationship with interest groups is still fluid, and it tends to be more open to their inputs than are national bureaucracies,[3] but the term could also be used to describe its limited policy-making resources and the changeability of its powers.

Legitimation

Policies cannot work unless, at a minimum, they are based on legal authority and win public recognition. Leon Lindberg has argued that "the essence of a political community . . . is the existence of a legitimate system for the resolution of conflict, for the making of authoritative decisions for the group as a whole."[4] The less legitimacy such a community enjoys, the less it will be able to achieve by democratic means. In political systems founded on the rule of law (government on the basis of a mutually agreed upon set of rules and laws), there are usually few questions about the authority of government to make and implement policies. With the EU, however, authority and legitimacy have long been major bones of contention. As discussed in Part 1, the history of the EU has been driven by debates over the authority of EU institutions and fears about the loss of national sovereignty. Among the EU's fundamental handicaps have been the democratic deficit and what might be called the "legitimacy gap": the gap between what EU institutions would like to be able to do and what EU citizens and governments allow them to do.

That gap is wide, but it has slowly been closed, helped in part by two key phenomena: direct elections to the European Parliament and the passage of time. In the first case, despite its weaknesses and low voter turnout, Parliament is still the only institution in the EU system that is directly accountable to the citizens. Voting in fair, regular, and competitive elections is one of the foundations of political legitimacy, and direct elections have given EU voters a direct psychological tie to the EU, which has helped promote its credibility and legitimacy. In the second case, the legitimacy of the EU can be said to be growing simply because EU citizens are learning to live with the effects of European integration, and the EU is becoming more real, more permanent, and more acceptable as time goes on (see the discussion on European citizenship in Chapter 5).

Implementation

Policy statements are only words until policies are implemented and enforced. This usually means agreeing on new laws and regulations, passing instructions on to bureaucrats, and informing the people affected by the new policy—arguably the most difficult step in the entire policy cycle. Implementation has been described as "a process of interaction between the setting of goals and the actions geared to achieving them."[5] To assume that once a government has made a decision it will automatically be enforced is delusory; policies can be reinterpreted and redefined even at the stage of implementation.[6] This can happen for any number of reasons: lack of political agreement; lack of funding; lack of workable or realistic goals; a failure to understand the causes of a problem; a redefinition of priorities as a result of changed circumstances or new data; lack of agreement on underlying goals and the best methods of implementation; conflicting interpretations; lack of public support; inefficiency or stagnation or conflicting interests within bureaucracies; and unanticipated structural problems or side effects.

Although the Council of Ministers has the final authority in making decisions, they are in fact made as the result of an interplay among the Council, the Commission, and Parliament, with the Court of Justice providing interpretation when necessary. Responsibility for implementation lies with the Commission, although implementation is carried out through the member states (actually, their bureaucracies). Limits on Commission resources and staff mean it must rely to some extent on reports from member states, individuals, and interest groups in helping to ensure implementation.

The Court of Justice plays a crucial role in ensuring that laws are uniformly interpreted and applied and that disputes are resolved.

Implementation is being made easier by the creation of new specialized agencies, such as Europol and the European Monetary Institute, but it still depends on many different factors over which the EU has varied levels of control. These include the efficiency of the institutions responsible for implementation, the cooperation of the subjects of policy (people, corporations, public agencies, and governments), and the authority of the EU (which is tenuous in the sense that the EU has few convincing powers of enforcement; European integration has been based from the beginning on the voluntary cooperation of the member states). The Commission is also subject to many of the problems and pitfalls commonly associated with bureaucracies, including limited accountability and an inclination toward self-justification; the tenure of bureaucrats ultimately depends on how much they have to do, and some are inclined to exaggerate their importance in the interests of guaranteeing continued power and budgetary allocations.

Evaluation

The final stage in the policy cycle is to determine whether a law or policy has worked. This is difficult unless specific goals were set and unless bureaucrats can be trusted to report accurately to the government on the results of policies. In many cases it is almost impossible to know which actions resulted in which consequences or whether the results are being accurately reported. Assuming that the outcomes of policies can be identified and measured (in whole or in part), adjustments can be made, or policies can be abandoned altogether. Evaluation in the EU is conducted by a combination of the Commission, the Council of Ministers, the European Council, the European Parliament, and reports from member states, interest groups, and individuals.

Policymaking in the EU

Writing about the policy process in the United States, Guy Peters argues that "American government has a number of structures but no real organization." He notes the lack of effective coordination and control, which he argues was intentional, given the concern of the framers of the Constitution about the potential for tyranny of a powerful central executive.[7] In many respects, the same can be said about policymaking in the EU. There is no true organization, in large part because of the ubiquitous concerns about loss of sovereignty. A simple description of the policy cycle in the EU would read as follows: The European Council sets the agenda, the Commission initiates and implements policy, the European Parliament discusses and amends, the Council of Ministers makes the final decisions, and the Court of Justice interprets and adjudicates. But the absence of central control has created a policy process that is driven largely by compromise, opportunism, and unpredictable political pressures.

Compromise and Bargaining

Except in dictatorships, all politics is a matter of compromise. The fewest compromises are necessary in unitary systems of government with majoritarian political parties (such as Britain or Spain), where the focus of political power rests with a national government made up of a single political party and local government has little independent political power. In federal systems that have constitutional balances between national and local government (such as Germany and the United States) or in countries governed by coalitions (such as Italy or Belgium), more compromises are needed. With a polity such as the European Union, where power is still unclearly defined and political relationships are still evolving, it could be argued that the entire policy process revolves around compromise. Nowhere is this more obvious than in the European Parliament, where more than sixty political parties are represented and no one party group has a majority.

Robert Keohane and Stanley Hoffmann have argued that the negotiations involved in EU policymaking take place between governments and that successful spillover requires prior intergovernmental bargains.[8] One bargaining mechanism often used by the EU is the package deal, which links a series of usually unrelated but often controversial policy issues together to make sure everyone benefits, providing a sugar coating for the pill. The creation of the Common Agricultural Policy was based around such a deal, with France winning concessions on agriculture in return for concessions given to German industry. The negotiations leading up to the Maastricht treaty were also riddled with compromises and package deals, especially over the timetable for the development of a common currency.

Turf Battles

Politics, by definition, is about struggles for power and influence, but such struggles are magnified in the EU by the extent to which member states and institutions compete with each other, unconstrained by the presence of a constitution. Guy Peters describes three sets of interconnected "games" being played out in the EU: a national game among member states, which are trying to extract as much as possible from the EU while giving up as little as possible; a game played out among EU institutions, which are trying to win more power relative to each other; and a bureaucratic game in which the DGs in the Commission are developing their own organizational cultures and competing for policy space.[9]

Peters goes on to argue that policymaking has become fragmented as institutional and policy goals have parted company and different policy communities have emerged.[10] Keohane and Hoffmann argue that the EU has become a network of institutions that out of self-interest prefer to interact with each other rather than with outsiders.[11] There is little doubt that the constant give-and-take has brought many changes in the balance of power, posing a stark contrast between the EU and national systems of government in democracies, which usually have stable constitutions and relatively stable rules of procedure and decisionmaking.

The Democratic Deficit

Despite all the weaknesses, limitations, and inconsistencies found in the practice of democracy, most liberal democracies have high levels of public accountability, and public opinion plays a vital role in policymaking. The same is not true of the EU, where secrecy abounds. Public opinion has played an increasingly important role, notably with the growth of lobbying, direct elections to Parliament, and the effects of the national referenda on Maastricht. But the links between the governors and the governed are still poorly developed, and EU institutions have little direct public accountability, so policymaking remains largely a top-down phenomenon.

Incrementalism

Because of concerns over the loss of national sovereignty, the absence of a consensus about the wisdom of European integration, and the need for constant compromise, EU policymaking is generally slow and cautious. The EU has occasionally made relatively radical changes (as occurred after the passage of the Single European Act and the Maastricht treaty, for example), but most EU policymaking is based on gradualism and incrementalism. Because there are so many counterweights and counterbalances in the policy process, member states and EU institutions can rarely take the initiative without conferring first with other member states or EU institutions.

The process sometimes slows to the point where critics of integration complain about Eurosclerosis, but this is probably unfair. The EC did hit the doldrums in the 1970s, and there have been many teething troubles (not surprisingly, given the sheer immensity of the task and the fact that the EU is sailing in largely uncharted waters), but it has made policy decisions that have accelerated the process of integration, such as plans for a single currency, convergence on foreign policy, and enlargement. None of these ini-

BOX 11.2
Spillover at Work: Completing the Single Market

Even though work on the common market evolved throughout the 1960s and 1970s, it had become obvious by the early 1980s that many barriers—visible and invisible—remained to the creation of a true common market. Concerns about EC competitiveness and the superiority of the new technologies being used by U.S. and Japanese corporations added to the pressure for change.

The role of spillover in generating the SEA is debatable,[1] but the 1985 Cockfield White Paper listed nearly three hundred new laws whose agreement led the EC to become more deeply involved in new policy areas, such as the environment, worker health and safety, and internal security. Member states were encouraged by the Commission to make changes in a wide variety of new areas, ranging from indirect taxation to capital movements. The pressure to remove frontier controls led to increased concerns about control of terrorism and drugs, pushing the EU further into the realms of justice and security and leading to the creation of Europol. In short, although the SEA was immediately focused on completion of the common market, it was also a step toward economic federalism because it gave the EU so much control over internal and external trade.[2]

Notes

1. See, for example, the discussion in Robert O. Keohane and Stanley Hoffmann, "Conclusions: Community Politics and Institutional Change," in William Wallace (Ed.), *The Dynamics of European Integration* (London: Royal Institute of International Affairs, 1990).

2. John Pinder, "The Single Market: A Step Towards Union," in Juliet Lodge (Ed.), *The European Community and the Challenge of the Future* (New York: St. Martin's Press, 1993), 61–62.

tiatives came out of the ether; all emerged incrementally from a combination of opportunity and need.

Spillover

Although this concept is usually identified with neofunctionalist theories of regional integration, it can be applied equally to policymaking at the national and subnational levels. The more a government feels it needs to be involved in the administration of society, the more policy spillover will occur. Privatization has cut the size of the public sector in most EU member states, but most still have large welfare systems and publicly owned and operated industries and services, which widen the set of government interests. Critics of the EU (like critics of the U.S. federal government) charge that it has tried to become involved in too many policy areas, but it has often had little choice; the creation of a new government program can reveal or create new problems, which in turn can lead to a demand for additional supporting programs. As Aaron Wildavsky put it, policy becomes its own cause.[12] (See Box 11.2.)

The EU Budget

The critical influence in policy cycles at any level of government is ultimately the budget. The amount of money a government has available—and how and where it decides to raise and spend that money—ultimately affects its policy choices and the true effectiveness of policy implementation. It is often less a question of how *much* is raised and spent than of *how* money is raised and spent. The budget is arguably at the heart of all politics in the sense that it shows where the true powers and priorities of governments lie.[13]

Budgets are always controversial because of concerns about who pays and who benefits and because of questions about whether finite resources are being used to the best possible effect. The EU budget is no exception, but the controversy it attracts is surprising considering how small it is: about $84.5 billion in 1993, or about 1.3 percent of the combined GDPs of the twelve member states, and smaller than the budget of many of the bigger U.S. states. Less than 5 percent of the budget (about $4 billion) is spent on administration. However, about half of the EU expenditure goes to agricultural price supports, which says much about the way the EU has evolved.

The budget has several other revealing features, as seen in Table 11.1. First, unlike almost any national budget, the EU budget must be balanced. Article 199 of the Treaty of Rome holds that revenue and expenditure must be the same. Because the budget cannot go into the red, there is no EU debt, so the EU is spared the problems that normally accompany debts (such as interest payments). At the same time, it also means the EU has to find new sources of revenue to keep its books balanced.[14]

Second, the sources and the quantity of EU revenues have been at the heart of the conflicts that have emerged during the evolution of the EU. John Pinder has argued that the budget has been an arena for struggles about the distribution of gains from integration and a focus for conflict over the powers of institutions.[15]

Battles have raged over the balance between national contributions (which give member states leverage over the EU) and the EU's own sources of revenue. The fact that the budget is so small emphasizes just how much power over policy remains with the member states, who hold responsibility for the most expensive elements of policy activity (such as defense, education, health, and welfare). Unlike almost any other international organization, however, the EU has guaranteed sources of income over which its member states have no legal control.

TABLE 11.1   The European Union Budget, 1993 (figures rounded)

	Billion ECU	Billion US$	% of Total
Revenues			
Value-added tax (VAT) own resources	35.6	42.7	52.0
GNP-based own resources	16.6	19.9	24.3
Customs duties on industrial imports	12.3	14.8	18.0
Own resources collection costs	1.4	1.7	2.0
Sugar and isoglucose levies	1.1	1.3	1.6
Agricultural levies	1.0	1.2	1.5
Budget balance from previous year	1.0	1.2	1.5
Balance of VAT own resources and GNP-based own resources from previous years	−1.1	−1.3	−1.6
Other revenue	0.5	0.6	0.8
Total	68.4	82.1	100.0
Expenditures			
Common Agricultural Policy	35.4	42.5	50.3
Regional Development Fund	8.0	9.6 ⎤	
Social Fund	5.8	7.0 ⎟	31.5
Cohesion Fund	1.6	1.9 ⎟	
Other structural funds	6.8	8.2 ⎦	
Research	2.7	3.2 ⎤	
Education	0.3	0.4 ⎬	5.8
Other internal policies	1.1	1.3 ⎦	
Cooperation (East and Central Europe)	1.6	1.9 ⎤	
Cooperation (Latin America)	0.6	0.7 ⎟	5.8
Cooperation (Mediterranean states)	0.4	0.5 ⎟	
Other external activities	1.5	1.8 ⎦	
Administration	3.4	4.1	4.8
Reserves	1.2	1.4	1.7
Total	70.4	84.5	100.0

Source: Commission of the European Communities, *XXVIIth General Report of the Activities of the European Communities 1993* (Luxembourg: Office for Official Publications of the European Communities, 1994).

Finally, decisionmaking on the budget is unusual in the sense that it follows a timetable that has specific deadlines, and the input and authority of the Council of Ministers and Parliament are more equally balanced than is the case with decisionmaking in almost any other part of the EU policy process. Both institutions consider the draft budget twice, and both have the power of amendment, which must be accepted by the other. In this area the

Council of Ministers begins to look more like the upper chamber of a legislature and Parliament like the lower. The Commission, meanwhile, plays
roughly the role of the White House in drawing up the U.S. federal budget.

Revenues

The EEC and Euratom—like most international organizations—were originally funded by national contributions, while the Coal and Steel
Community had its own income, which was raised by a levy on producers.
The contributions to the EEC were calculated very roughly on the basis of
size; thus France, Germany, and Italy each contributed 28 percent, Belgium
and the Netherlands 7.9 percent, and Luxembourg 0.2 percent. In an attempt to win more independence, in 1965 the Commission proposed that
the revenue from tariffs placed on imports from outside the EC should go
directly to the Community, thereby providing the EC with its *own resources*. At the same time, Parliament began pushing for more control over
the budget as a means of gaining more influence over policy. De Gaulle
thought the Commission already had too much power, and it was these
proposals (combined with France's opposition to reform of the Common
Agricultural Policy) that led to the 1965 empty chair crisis.

Pressure for budgetary reform persisted regardless, and changes between
1970 and 1975 led gradually to an increase in the proportion of revenues
derived from the EC's own resources: customs duties, levies on agricultural
imports, and a proportion (no more than 1 percent) of value-added tax
(VAT). Two problems with this formula emerged. First, it took no account
of the relative size of member-state economies. This became a particular
problem for Britain, which paid much more to the EU coffers than it received. Second, the amounts involved were insufficient to meet the needs of
the Community, which was not allowed to run a deficit or to borrow to
meet shortfalls. The EC's freedom of action was reduced further by the fact
that two-thirds of spending went to agricultural price supports, which grew
as European farmers produced more crops (see Chapter 13). At the same
time, revenue from customs duties fell because the Community's external
tariffs were reduced, revenue from agricultural levies fell as the EC's self-
sufficiency in food production grew, and income from VAT failed to grow
quickly enough because consumption was falling as a percentage of EC
GDP.[16] The problem was compounded by the unwillingness of some member states to raise the limit on the EC's own resources.

By the early 1980s the Community was on the brink of insolvency, and
it was obvious that either revenues had to be increased or expenditures had
to be restructured or cut. The issue of budget reform was brought to a head
by Margaret Thatcher's insistence on a recalculation of the British contribution. A complex deal was reached at the 1984 Fontainebleau European

TABLE 11.2   EU Revenues by Member State, 1992

	Total Contribution (in million ECUs)	Share of EU total (%)	Share of Total EU Population (%)	Share of Total EU GDP (1991) (%)
France	9,049.8	17.2	16.4	19.0
Italy	7,775.6	14.8	16.7	18.2
Spain	7,567.6	14.4	11.5	7.7
Germany	7,299.9	13.9	22.7	26.7
Greece	4,332.6	8.2	3.0	1.1
United Kingdom	4,314.6	8.2	16.8	15.5
Portugal	2,978.0	5.7	3.0	1.1
Netherlands	2,705.0	5.1	4.4	4.6
Ireland	2,602.4	4.9	1.1	0.7
Belgium	2,404.6	4.6	2.9	3.1
Denmark	1,311.4	2.5	1.5	2.1
Luxembourg	287.5	0.5	0.1	0.1
Total	52,629.0	100.0	100.0	100.0

Source: Court of Auditors, Annual Report Concerning the Financial Year 1992, *Official Journal of the European Communities,* C309, 36 (November 16, 1993).

Council in which Britain was given a rebate and its contribution was cut, and the Community's own resources were increased with the setting of a new ceiling of 1.4 percent from VAT. More reforms agreed on at an extraordinary meeting of the European Council in Brussels in February 1988 resulted in the current system of revenue raising:

- Revenues from VAT accounted for 52 percent of total revenues in 1993. Most of the revenues raised with VAT still go to the national governments, but a maximum of 1.4 percent goes to the EU (although a decision was made in 1992 to reduce it to 1 percent by 1999). One problem is that different member states have different rates of VAT and so end up making different levels of per capita contributions to the EU.

- About 24 percent of revenues in 1993 came from national contributions based on national GNP levels. Each member state pays a set amount in proportion to its GNP.

- About 18 percent of revenues in 1993 came from fixed customs duties levied on industrial imports from nonmember states. The balance came from sources that included levies and premiums on agricultural imports (aimed at bringing import prices up to EU levels) and levies and duties placed on internal trade in certain agricultural products in an attempt to limit surplus production.

TABLE 11.3   Changes in EU Expenditure, 1984–1993

Item	1973 (%)	1985 (%)	1991 (%)	1992 (%)	1993 (%)
Common Agricultural Policy	74.2	64.5	53.1	50.7	50.3
Structural funds	12.4	18.4	24.9	29.0	31.5
Internal[a]	1.4	3.4	7.5	6.1	5.8
External[b]	0.9	4.3	6.1	6.2	5.8
Administration	5.9	7.8	6.7	6.4	4.8
Reserves	5.2[c]	1.6	1.7	1.6	1.7
Total (billion ECUs)	5.1	30.9	59.4	63.9	70.4

[a]Research, education, and other internal policies.
[b]Aid to East and Central Europe, ACP, and other states.
[c]Refunds to member states.
Source: Court of Auditors, Annual Reports in *Official Journal of the European Communities* (several years).

This formula produces a system in which the largest and richest states pay the most, but—as Table 11.2 shows—there is a sliding scale of payments.

Expenditures

As in almost any budget, EU expenses consist of a combination of compulsory payments over which it has little or no control (such as agricultural price supports) and noncompulsory payments over which it has more control (such as spending on regional or energy policy). Just over 53 percent of the EU's spending is obligatory. Total spending is divided as follows.

- About half goes to agricultural subsidies and supports to fisheries. These guarantee minimum prices to farmers for their produce, regardless of volume. Over time, Europe's farmers have produced more, spending on agriculture has grown, and overproduction has reached embarrassing proportions. In 1993, the EU spent $42 billion on agricultural subsidies, a fact that particularly upset the United States, which felt European farmers were given an unfair advantage over their U.S. counterparts. (However, not only are many U.S. farmers heavily subsidized, but as a percentage of EU spending, agriculture receives less each year; from a time in the 1970s when it accounted for nearly three-fourths of EU spending, the proportion has been reduced to about 50 percent.)

- About one-third of spending goes to the structural funds: development spending on poorer regions of the EU, spending under the European Social Fund aimed at helping offset the effects of unemployment, and investments in agriculture. The proportion of EU expenditures in this area has almost tripled since the mid-1970s.

- About 6 percent goes as aid to Eastern and Central Europe and to the poorer countries of Africa, Latin America, and Asia.

- About 5 percent goes to administrative costs.

Under the current budgetary system, Germany, Britain, and France are net contributors; Italy and the Netherlands contribute about as much as they receive; and the remaining states are net recipients of EU funds.

Summary and Conclusions

The policy process of the European Union is complex, confusing, and constantly changing. The challenge of identifying the sources of, controllers of, and limits on power is heightened by the sheer novelty of the EU and by the lack of a constitution that could provide a guide through the maze. We can try to make analogies between policymaking units in the United States and those in the EU, but there are limits to how far that exercise can go. The Commission is like the federal Cabinet, but not exactly. Parliament is like the House of Representatives, but not exactly. The Council of Ministers is like the Senate, but not exactly. The difficulties go on.

As argued in Chapter 5, the key to grasping how the EU works is to appreciate that it is a work in progress. Trying to understand it is a bit like trying to understand the evolution of the human species. Anthropologists have filled in many (but not all) of the links between apes and humans, we have artists' impressions showing how we have changed, and we know what we look like now, but it is anyone's guess what we will look like in another million years or what factors (environmental or other) will be the major determinants of how we evolve.

In a 1992 edited book on the EU, the authors did not use words such as centralization, uniformity, coherence, and decisiveness to describe politics and policymaking in the EU; instead, they used words such as leadership, coalitions, decentralization, diversity, bargaining, convergence, policy differentiations, and national government discretion.[17] It will be some time before the process becomes more settled and predictable.

Notes

1. Anthony Downs, "Up and Down with Ecology—The 'Issue Attention Cycle,'" *Public Interest* 28 (1972), 28–50.

2. See Robert O. Keohane and Stanley Hoffmann, "Conclusions: Community Politics and Institutional Change," in William Wallace (Ed.), *The Dynamics of European Integration* (London: Royal Institute of International Affairs, 1990).

3. Sonia Mazey and Jeremy Richardson, "Pressure Groups and Lobbyists in the EC," in Juliet Lodge (Ed.), *The European Community and the Challenge of the Future* (New York: St. Martin's Press, 1993), 40–41.

4. Leon N. Lindberg, *The Political Dynamics of European Economic Integration* (Stanford: Stanford University Press, 1963), vii.

5. Jeffrey L. Pressman and Aaron Wildavsky, *Implementation,* 3rd ed. (Berkeley: University of California Press, 1984), xxiii.

6. B. Guy Peters, "Bureaucratic Politics and the Institutions of the European Community," in Alberta Sbragia (Ed.), *Euro-Politics: Institutions and Policymaking in the "New" European Community* (Washington, D.C.: Brookings Institution, 1992), 103.

7. B. Guy Peters, *American Public Policy: Promise and Performance* (Chatham, N.J.: Chatham House, 1993), 17.

8. Robert O. Keohane and Stanley Hoffmann, "Institutional Change in Europe in the 1980s," in Robert O. Keohane and Stanley Hoffmann, *The New European Community: Decisionmaking and Institutional Change* (Boulder: Westview Press, 1991), 17.

9. Peters, "Bureaucratic Politics," 106–107.

10. Ibid., 115–121.

11. Keohane and Hoffmann, "Institutional Change," 13–14.

12. Aaron Wildavsky (Ed.), *Speaking Truth to Power* (Boston: Little, Brown, 1979), 62–85.

13. Aaron Wildavsky, *The Politics of the Budgetary Process,* 4th ed. (Boston: Little, Brown, 1984).

14. Michael Shackleton, *Financing the European Community* (New York: Council on Foreign Relations Press, 1990), 2.

15. John Pinder, *European Community: The Building of a Union* (Oxford: Oxford University Press, 1991), 142.

16. Shackleton, *Financing the European Community,* 10–11.

17. Sbragia, *Euro-Politics,* 2–3.

Further Reading

Svein S. Andersen and Kjell A. Eliassen (Eds.). *Making Policy in Europe* (London: Sage, 1993).

An edited collection of studies of the EU policymaking process, including chapters on specific policy areas.

Robert Leonardi (Ed.). *European Community Policies and Politics: An Annual Review* (London: Pinter, 1992).

An edited collection of studies of political and policy developments in the EU and the member states, with separate chapters on most of the major policy areas.

Jill Preston (Ed.). *Spicers European Union Policy Briefings* (New York: Stockton, various years).

A series of detailed (but expensive) briefings on different EU policy areas, including guides to competition and trade, the environment, regional policy, the structural funds, and telecommunications.

Alberta Sbragia (Ed.). *Euro-Politics: Institutions and Policymaking in the "New" European Community* (Washington, D.C.: Brookings Institution, 1992).

A set of studies of selected EU institutions and policies and the links between the two. The chapter by Guy Peters is especially good.

Michael Shackleton. *Financing the European Community* (New York: Council on Foreign Relations Press, 1990).

A short assessment of the dimensions of the EU budget and the politics of recent budgetary reforms.

12

Economic Policy

For most of its short life, the European Union has been driven mainly by the goal of economic integration. It began life in the early 1950s as a limited experiment in economic cooperation, was broadened in the 1960s to become a customs union, wrestled during the 1970s with attempts to build common economic policies and exchange rate stability, focused in the late 1980s on completing the single market, and is now working on the uphill task of reaching agreement on a single currency. The EU made variable progress in other policy areas (such as agriculture, the environment, and development aid to poorer countries), but it has steadily begun to pay more attention to issues outside the economic sphere. The change in emphasis was symbolized by the way "Economic" was quietly dropped from the title "European Economic Community" during the 1980s and then, in 1993, by the way the Community became part of a "European Union" that also focused on foreign policy, security, and justice.

Elements of a common market were built during the first ten to fifteen years, the Common Agricultural Policy was in place by the late 1960s (in the sense that farmers were being paid guaranteed prices for their produce), and a customs union was completed with the agreement on a common external tariff in 1968. But nontariff barriers persisted, including varying technical standards and quality controls, different health and safety standards, and different levels of indirect taxation. The gap between dream and reality widened in the mid-1970s as recession encouraged member states to think more about protecting their national markets than about building a new European market.

The mood changed in the 1980s with the sense that something radical needed to be done to reverse the EC's relative economic decline and to respond to the superiority of the United States and Japan in high-technology industries. It was essential for the EC to tap in to the potential of its own market, which had almost as many consumers as the United States and Japan combined. Reducing duplication of effort, encouraging joint research, and removing the final barriers that prevented European companies

223

from doing business in all the member states would reduce costs and improve efficiency and competitiveness. The 1988 Commission-sponsored Cecchini Report argued that completion of the single market could add 5 percent to the Community's GDP, reduce consumer prices by 6 percent, boost EC trade with other countries, save as much as $16–30 billion in border-control costs, and create 2 to 5 million new jobs.[1]

This change of thinking produced the Single European Act. Even though the SEA's much-vaunted goal was to achieve a unified single market by December 1992 and the Act itself represented a quantum leap in that direction, the single market is not yet fully in place. In addition to the many remaining exceptions to the rules introduced by the SEA, one of the most fundamental features of a truly unified market—a single currency—is still missing. As long as there are fifteen national currencies, the fifteen national governments will remain in charge of domestic economic policy, and trade among the member states will be complicated by changes in internal exchange rates.

The Single Market

The 1985 Cockfield White Paper provided the list of specific steps needed to complete the internal market.[2] As discussed in Chapter 4, this list became the basis of the Single European Act of 1986, which came into force in 1987. Its goal was to remove the remaining nontariff barriers to the free movement of people, goods, services, and capital within five years. Those barriers took three main forms: physical, fiscal, and technical.

Physical Barriers

Customs and border checks persisted at the EC's internal frontiers because national governments wanted to control the movement of people (especially illegal immigrants), collect taxes and excises on goods being moved from one state to another, and enforce different health standards. These barriers not only continued to remind Europeans of their differences, thereby posing a psychological block to integration, but they were also a significant economic constraint, a problem compounded by the fact that there was little consistency in these checks. Anyone driving among the Benelux states, for example, simply had to slow down when crossing the border, and customs officials would decide on the spot whether checks were needed. Meanwhile, train travelers could be vetted by customs and police officials, while air travelers went through rigorous security controls.

Barriers to the movement of goods were removed in stages. Despite agreement on the customs union in 1968, most goods were still subject to cross-border checks in the interests of enforcing trade quotas, controlling banned products, collecting taxes, and preventing the spread of plant and animal disease. These checks were costly and time-consuming. The first step in simplifying the process came in 1988 with a decision to move the administrative checks away from internal frontiers by agreeing on common laws as quickly as possible. A second step was taken with the consolidation of paperwork; between 1985 and 1988 more than 130 different forms used by different customs authorities were replaced by a Single Administrative Document,[3] which in turn was almost entirely abolished in January 1993.

One troublesome issue is the control of the drug trade and terrorism. Terrorist groups operating in Britain, France, Germany, and Italy have long had informal links, which have been controllable to some extent because of national frontiers. Removal of border checks would make it easier for these groups to move within the EU. (In a sordid twist on the spirit of the single market, the German Red Army Faction and the Italian Red Brigades cooperated in the attempted murder of a German official at a 1988 meeting of the International Monetary Fund.)

The SEA does not affect the rights of member states to take whatever action they think is necessary to control terrorism, drugs, trade in arts and antiques, or immigration from outside the EU as long as such action does not interfere with trade. At the same time, the member states have agreed to work toward police cooperation (to which end they created Europol in 1993) and toward common measures on visas, immigration, extradition, and political asylum. The goal is not so much to stop terrorists moving from one member state to another as it is to control them at the EU's external borders. This means border controls must be equally effective; in the past, terrorists have found it easier to enter states such as Greece and Portugal than states such as Britain and Germany.

A fast track for the removal of border controls was launched in 1984 by France, Germany, and the Benelux states. Named for the town in Luxembourg near which it was signed, the **Schengen Agreement** is a plan to abolish all border controls among its signatories, a process that has taken longer to agree on than originally hoped. It was not until March 1995 that all customs and passport controls were finally eliminated by France, Germany, Spain, Portugal, and the Benelux states, and every member state except Britain and Ireland was expected to follow suit eventually. Full implementation of the agreement will mean the end of checks at airports for flights among signatory states, the free circulation of non-EU citizens, common rules on asylum, the right of hot pursuit across frontiers, and moves toward a common policy on visas. Britain refused to join the agreement, citing concerns about security, and Ireland could not join because of its customs arrangements with Britain.

Fiscal Barriers

Indirect taxation caused distortions of competition and artificial price differences among the member states and so was a barrier to the single market. All of the member states have a value-added tax, but rates were as low as 12 percent in Luxembourg and as high as 22 percent in Denmark. Excise duties also varied, reflecting different levels of national concern about human health; for example, smokers in France paid nearly twice as much tax on cigarettes as those in Spain, smokers in Ireland paid four times as much, and smokers in Denmark paid six times as much.[4]

As goods moved from one state to another, they had to be controlled so governments could collect VAT and excise duties and prevent fraud and tax evasion. Consumers saw the effects most directly when they tried to take home alcohol, tobacco products, and other consumer items bought duty-free in another country. For example, British visitors to France could buy French wine much more cheaply than they could at home, but they were allowed to take back only limited quantities. Under the SEA, duty-free limits were gradually decreased and then were abolished altogether in January 1993. Agreement was reached in 1991 on a minimum rate of 15 percent VAT (with lower rates on basic necessities such as food), and in 1992 various minimum rates were agreed on excise duties.

Technical Barriers

The EEC had been able to do little to address the persistence of different technical regulations and standards among the member states, which seemed to pose an almost insurmountable barrier to the single market. Most of these regulations were based on different safety, health, environmental, and consumer protection standards, and many seemed petty and inconsequential: different definitions of chocolate that prevented British chocolate from being sold in many other member states, for example, or the insistence by Germans that no beer could be sold in Germany that did not meet local "purity laws." At one level, technical standards were in the interests of consumer safety; at another, they amounted to economic protectionism. The Community had tried to remove technical barriers by developing EC standards and encouraging member states to conform, but this was a time-consuming and tedious task that did little to discourage the common image of interfering Eurocrats.

Three breakthroughs helped to simplify the process:

1. The 1979 Cassis de Dijon decision (see Chapter 9) confirmed that all member states had to accept products from other states that met domestic technical standards. With trade in foodstuffs, for example, the implication was that a member state could not block imports from another member state on the basis of local health regulations.

2. The 1983 mutual information directive required member states to tell the Commission and the other member states if they planned to implement any new domestic technical regulations and to allow the others three months to respond if they felt these regulations would create new barriers to trade.

3. The Cockfield White Paper included a "new approach" to technical regulation: Instead of having the Commission try to work out agreements on every rule and regulation, the Council of Ministers would agree on laws that had general objectives, and detailed specifications could then be drawn up by existing private standards institutes, such as the European Standardization Committee and the European Electrotechnical Standardization Committee (CENELEC).

These three arrangements helped the EC clear many bureaucratic and political hurdles. Progress has been made on regulations for road vehicles, for example, where forty-four directives have been agreed on regarding everything from the brilliance of headlights to the depth of tire treads and limits on exhaust emissions. There is also more agreement on food content, and since 1990 all EU member states have had to print details about nutritional content on packages, following the U.S. model.

There has been less progress in other areas, however. The pharmaceuticals industry (which has $30 billion in sales per year) is still fragmented, although the work of the European Medicines Evaluation Agency should help promote improved coordination. Free trade also continues to be handicapped by technical differences the marketplace is powerless to overcome. For example, television systems are different throughout the EU, obliging manufacturers to make eight different kinds of television sets. Most member states use the German PAL system of TV broadcasting, but the French use their own system, called SECAM. (Both of these are different from the U.S. standard, NTSC.) Similarly, the design of electrical plugs and sockets differs from one member state to another, forcing travelers to take an adaptor with them wherever they go. In 1992, CENELEC announced plans to begin developing a common plug, estimating the total cost of rewiring homes and businesses at $1.2 billion—a figure that will probably prove to be hopelessly conservative.

Differences in professional qualifications constitute another technical barrier. The EU has had to reach agreement on the standardization and recognition of such qualifications, which has not been easy. Although the basic training for most health workers (doctors, nurses, dentists, and so on) was harmonized relatively early, and they were given the right to work in any EC member state, it took seventeen years to harmonize the requirements for architects and sixteen years for pharmacists. Progress was made in 1988 with agreement on the general systems directive, under which member states agree to trust that for some jobs, professional standards in other member states are adequate.[5] The list of mutually recognized professions is growing and now includes accountants, librarians, architects, and engineers; even so, standards still have to be agreed on for nearly eighty more professions. The Commission has published a comparative guide to national qualifications for more than two hundred occupations, helping employers work out equivalencies across the member states.

One of the biggest failures of the EU has been its inability to ease the problem of unemployment, the persistence of which was once described as equivalent to the persistence of poverty in the United States.[6] While U.S. unemployment hovered around 5 percent in 1995 and that in Japan at around 3 percent, EU states had figures ranging from 7 to 9 percent in the Netherlands, Britain, and Germany to 11 to 14 percent in Denmark, France, and Belgium to a high of nearly 24 percent in Spain.[7]

The reason the rates are so high is debatable, but at least part of the problem has been the relative weakness of labor unions and the relative ease with which workers can be laid off. Another factor is the size of the black market in Europe, which makes up as much as 15 to 30 percent of GNP in some states[8] and is all but institutionalized in Italy, where it overlaps with the destructive power of organized crime. The EU has launched a host of retraining programs and is shifting resources to the poorer parts of the EU through various regional and social programs (see Chapters 13 and 14). Although millions of new jobs have been created in the EU since the mid-1980s, nearly half are temporary or part-time, and many are in the service sector. Most are being filled by men and women who are new to the job market, so these jobs have done little to help ease long-term unemployment.

Effects of the Single European Act

The SEA was the most radical of all the steps taken in the process of European integration since the signing of the treaties of Paris and Rome. In addition to accelerating economic integration, it has also had a number of more tangible effects on the lives of Europeans.

Rights of Residence

Since January 1993, any resident of an EU member state has been allowed to live and work in any other EU member state, open a bank account, take out a mortgage, transfer unlimited amounts of capital, and vote in local and European elections. A few restrictions remain, but they are relatively trivial. For example, students are given annual residence permits, and they must be enrolled in college and able to support themselves. Retirees and people of independent means are given five-year renewable residence permits, and those receiving pensions must have proof to that effect so they do not make demands on the social security system of the state in which they are living.

Joint Ventures and Corporate Mergers

European corporations have a long history of transnational mergers, which have produced such giants as Unilever and Royal Dutch Shell (both Anglo-Dutch) and Asea Brown Boveri (Sweden and Switzerland). Despite this, from 1950 to the early 1980s European companies steadily lost markets at home and abroad to competition, first from the United States and then from Japan. (Americans worried about the inroads being made in the U.S. market by foreign auto manufacturers sometimes overlook the other side of the coin; for example, Ford and General Motors together account for nearly one-fourth of the Western European auto market.) With the revival of competitiveness pushed to the top of the EC agenda, the Commission became actively involved in trying to overcome market fragmentation and the emphasis placed by national governments on promoting the interests of often state-owned "national champions." To the delight of the authors of pithy acronyms, the EC also launched new programs aimed at encouraging research in information technology (ESPRIT), advanced communications (RACE), industrial technologies (BRITE), and weapons manufacture (EU-REKA).[9]

Among the more notable joint ventures have been those between Thompson of France and Philips of the Netherlands (high-definition television), between Pirelli of Italy and Dunlop of Britain (tires), between BMW and Rolls-Royce (aeroengines), and among the thirteen member states of the European Space Agency (ESA), set up in 1973 in an attempt to establish European autonomy in space.[10] Since the launch of the first in its series of Ariane rockets in 1979 from Kourou in French Guiana, the ESA has won more than half of the global market for launching commercial satellites,[11] eating into a market long dominated by the United States. Its most notable failure was the attempt to build Hermes—a mini–space shuttle that could compete with the NASA space shuttle—and a space station manned by European astronauts carried into space on board Hermes; the program was abandoned in 1992 on the grounds that it was becoming too expensive.

The single market has helped encourage the growth of new pan-European businesses seeking to profit from the opportunities it offers and looking for the resources to allow them to compete more effectively with the United States and Japan. An unprecedented surge of takeovers and mergers has occurred since the mid-1980s, notably in the chemicals, phar-maceuticals, and electronics industries. In 1984–1985 there were 208 merg-ers and acquisitions in the EC; in 1989–1990 there were 622, and—for the first time—the number of intra-EC mergers overtook the number of na-tional mergers.[12] Recent notable examples include the 1992 purchase by Air France of a 37.5 percent stake in the Belgian airline Sabena, the 1993 takeover of the Dutch aircraft manufacturer Fokker by Germany's Deutsche Aerospace, and the 1994 takeover by BMW of Rover Group, Britain's last mass auto manufacturer. At the same time, though, care has been taken to ensure that the bigger corporations do not develop monopolies and over-whelm smaller businesses, and the EU has developed a controversial com-petition policy to avoid abuses such as price fixing.

Mergers have also raised concerns about sovereignty and independence, as they have in the United States among those concerned about European and Japanese investment. In 1988, for example, the Swiss food group Nestlé tried to take over the British candy maker Rowntree (manufacturer of products such as Kit-Kat). The chair of Rowntree made appeals to na-tionalism, trying to suggest that Kit-Kat was as central to the British na-tional heritage as the union jack and the crown jewels. In fact, Nestlé had already been operating in Britain for 120 years, and its takeover bid ulti-mately succeeded.[13]

A Common Transport System

Markets are only as close as the ties that bind them, and one of the priori-ties of economic policy in the EU has been to build a system of transport, energy supply, and telecommunications that pulls the EU together and pro-motes mobility. Until 1987, the lack of harmonization in the transport sec-tor was one of the great failures of the common market—almost nothing of substance had been done to deal with problems such as an airline industry split along national lines or time-consuming cross-border checks on trucks that led to a black market in fake permits and licenses. Two phenomena have begun to make a difference.

First, there has been a dramatic increase in tourism. Not only is Europe the biggest tourist destination in the world, capturing nearly 60 percent of the world tourist trade, but Europeans are now traveling to each other's

BOX 12.1
European Cooperation and the Aircraft Industry

The possibilities and potential benefits of multinational cooperation among Europeans—and the nature of European economic integration itself—are illustrated by the example of aircraft manufacture. Western Europe was once a major producer of civilian and military aircraft and was home to some of the greatest names in the aircraft industry, including Vickers, Hawker Siddeley, Messerschmitt, de Havilland, and Dassault. But rationalization, competition, and other economic pressures led to mergers and closures, and many of the old manufacturers have become part of massive new national corporations. In Britain, for example, the nineteen aircraft producers of the 1940s had been whittled down to just one, British Aerospace, by 1986.[1] At the same time, the United States and the USSR were producing most of the world's military aircraft, and the civilian airliner market was dominated by Boeing, McDonnell-Douglas, and Lockheed.

One of the earliest European joint ventures in civil aircraft resulted in the Anglo-French Concorde, which was a high-tech product but a commercial disappointment. A less ambitious and much more successful joint venture has been gaining ground since 1970 in the form of Airbus Industrie, a European consortium that has become the only significant competitor in the civil aircraft market dominated by the United States and that has had healthy profits. The Airbus consortium is made up of Aerospatiale of France and Messerschmitt-Bolkow-Blohm of Germany (37.9 percent each), British Aerospace (20 percent), and CASA of Spain (4.2 percent). It produces six different airliners, which together by 1991 had captured 52 percent of the global market in wide-body jets and more than a quarter of the total commercial jetliner market.[2] The United States has criticized Airbus for its heavy reliance on government subsidies, to which Airbus has responded that the subsidies are being repaid as levies and that U.S. manufacturers provide about one-third of the parts for each Airbus.

Europeans have made more modest—but still significant—strides in the market for military aircraft. Individual member states still make competitive products, such as France's Mirage jet fighters and Britain's Harrier jump jets (among the very few foreign-made military aircraft ever bought by the United States), but they are finding it makes better commercial sense to pool resources. The biggest collaboration to date has been the profitable Tornado fighter-bomber (made by the four states involved in Airbus), which played a critical role in the 1990–1991 Gulf War. Another project that has been in the pipeline since 1985 is the European Fighter Aircraft, the deadline for which has been pushed back to the year 2000 (and the name changed accordingly to Eurofighter 2000). The Europeans have also begun to enter the market for military transport aircraft, which is currently dominated by the United States with planes such as the Hercules made by Lockheed. Plans were unveiled in 1994 for a Future Large Aircraft, which may be built by a consortium of the British, French, and German partners in Airbus joined by Alenia of Italy.

Notes

1. *The Economist,* September 3–9, 1994.
2. Axel Krause, *Inside the New Europe* (New York: HarperCollins, 1991), 103.

countries in much greater numbers, which has helped to break down prejudices, made Europeans more familiar with each other, and encouraged greater cooperation in the area of transportation by increasing the demand for cheap and easy access. Tourism now accounts for more than 5 percent of the GDP of the EU.

Second, the rail industry has been revitalized as a cost-efficient and environmentally friendly alternative to road and air transport. The EU hopes to develop a 22,000-mile high-speed train (HST) network connecting Europe's major cities; the building of the $15 billion Eurotunnel under the channel between Britain and France and the construction of a bridge between Sjaelland and Fyn in Denmark have been important steps. France has led the way in new technology with its high-speed TGV (which needs special new track), and Germany has developed its inter-city express (ICE) network (which can use existing track). With trains traveling between 125 and 190 mph (some with coaches finished to luxurious standards), the HST system will cut travel times considerably. Germany even has hopes over the long term of replacing domestic air flights altogether with a system of very high-speed trains (VHSTs), based in part on floating mag-lev technology. Among the possible hurdles to the development of a European HST system are the high costs involved, the fact that most national rail companies are state-owned monopolies that plan in national rather than EU terms, and the tension that exists between centralizing and decentralizing decisionmaking in the EU.[14]

Compared to the rail industry, much work remains to be done in the airline sector. Airlines are still seen as national symbols, and governments are unwilling to do anything that would jeopardize their national carriers. Protectionism reached such a peak in Europe that following the deregulation of U.S. airlines in 1978 it was cheaper to fly from London to Madrid by way of New York than to fly direct. A slow process of deregulation is now underway, and it is inevitable that some of the smaller or less profitable carriers will either close or be taken over, as has happened in the United States. At the same time, the EU is working on the joint administration of air traffic routes and a uniform air traffic control system.

Information and Telecommunications

The mass media play an important role in shaping and determining the extent to which people feel they belong to a community with common interests. The emphasis on localism in the United States, for example, has created media dominated by local newspapers, television, and radio; except for network TV news, public broadcasting, USA Today, and weeklies such as Time and Newsweek, the United States has few national media, which is partly why many Americans are less interested in national and foreign news than they are in local news. By contrast, smaller European countries are dominated by national radio, television, and newspapers—but they remain national rather than European.

The building of European media as a contribution to the creation of a European identity has moved slowly up the EU agenda, but so far it has achieved little. An attempt was made in the mid-1980s to launch a daily European newspaper, the *European,* but it was published in Britain and was in English. The five-nation Europa-TV consortium, which hoped to transmit multilingual TV broadcasts to 5 million homes in the EC, collapsed in 1986 after amassing huge debts.[15] More recently, Euronews was created in 1993 as a multilingual European response to CNN, but it is too early to say how this French-based service will evolve.

The Commission developed a green paper entitled "Television Without Borders" in 1984, and the Cockfield White Paper talked of the need to develop a single market in TV broadcasting, which the Commission saw as an important element of the broader single market project. The Commission subsequently tried to become involved in regulating satellite broadcasting, but the technology was developing faster than it could respond; its involvement was also criticized by several member states who argued that it had no competence in this area.

A major concern for the Commission has been controlling the cultural inroads made by Anglo-American broadcasting and trying to protect the European cinema and electronics industries from U.S. and Japanese competition. A directive was adopted on television broadcasting in 1989, aimed at making sure broadcasters—"where practicable"—used a majority of European programming. Siegfried Magiera has argued that this goes against the European tradition of encouraging cultural interaction with other parts of the world and also against freedom of expression and information.[16] The attempt to impose quotas faces other problems as well: U.S. films and TV shows are more popular on the continent than is much locally produced material, and Europeans do not tend to much like each other's programming (the French, the Germans, and the British, for example, have very different senses of humor); there is also the twin assault of U.S. programming provided by CNN and MTV and Anglo-American programming provided by British satellite companies such as Sky Television and British Satellite Broadcasting.

Toward a Single Currency

Few aspects of European integration have been as controversial as reaching agreement on a single currency, yet few barriers to the creation of a true single market are as fundamental as the existence of fifteen different currencies with fluctuating exchange rates. The issue of currency controls cuts to the heart of sovereignty and independence; a state that gives up control of its national currency effectively gives up control over all significant domestic economic policy decisions. Equally important, a single currency is arguably a prerequisite for a unified system of government.

As discussed in Chapter 4, the EU has tried several times to stabilize exchange rates as a prelude to developing a single currency, but each time it has been derailed by pressures from the global economy (for example, the chaos in foreign exchange markets that unhappily coincided with the launch of the snake in 1971) or by problems experienced by member states in attempting to control changes in the value of their currencies without aggravating inflation and unemployment. These problems have prevented the achievement of economic and monetary union.

Economic union implies agreement on economic policies, which in practice means the establishment of a single market; monetary union implies agreement on a single currency. Whether economic union is a necessary precondition of monetary union or the reverse has long been a bone of contention, but attempts to achieve fixed (or at least stable) exchange rates failed during the early 1970s with the collapse of the snake, thus contributing to the shift of focus to establishment of the single market.

At the heart of EMU is the European Monetary System, launched in 1979. The goal of the system is to set up a zone of monetary stability and to keep inflation in the EU under control by coordinating the economic and financial policies of the member states. It tries to do this through an exchange rate mechanism, which is aimed at reducing the fluctuations of EU currencies relative to each other. Unlike the snake, which was pegged to the U.S. dollar, the ERM is pegged to the European Currency Unit, whose value is calculated on the basis of a weighted basket of European currencies (see Box 12.2). Member states that opted in to the ERM agree to take whatever action they can (adjusting interest rates, for example) to keep their currencies within ± 2.25 percentage points of the central value of their currency against the ECU. If they cannot do so, they have three options:

1. They can negotiate an adjustment of the central rate of their currency in a process known as realignment. There were twelve realignments between 1979 and 1990, mainly because of the revaluation of the German and Dutch currencies against the others. A spate of five realignments came between September 1992 and June 1993 in response to problems in Ireland, Spain, and Portugal.

2. The states can negotiate a wider band within which their currency is allowed to fluctuate. For example, the Spanish peseta, the Italian lira, and the British pound have all been allowed bands of 6 percent

BOX 12.2
The European Currency Unit

The ECU is a unit of account that allows Europeans to measure the relative value of their currencies. It has been used as a means of payment among the central banks of member states and as the core of the ERM, but it is also widely seen as the seed for a future single European currency. (By coincidence, the "ecu" is also the name of a medieval French coin.) Few Europeans were aware of the ECU until the countdown to the creation of the single market, when the number of business transactions in ECUs began to grow. It is now one of the five major "currencies" regularly quoted on the international market (the others are the dollar, the deutsche mark, the yen, and the pound). Against the U.S. dollar, the value of the ECU has fluctuated between 75 cents and $1.40, but in the early 1990s it settled at around $1.20 to $1.30.

The ECU does not yet exist in physical form (except in Belgium and the Isle of Man, which have issued ECU coins for collectors). In 1988, Britain became the first EU member state to issue Treasury bills in ECUs, with the goal of developing an ECU market in London. Travelers can also buy traveler's checks in ECUs for use inside and outside the EU. Luxembourgers can take out a credit card in ECUs; individuals can buy bonds, invest, or—with some banks—take out loans in ECUs; bank accounts can be opened in ECUs in several member states; and even outside states (including Russia) have been using ECUs to finance foreign transactions.

The value of the ECU is calculated on the basis of a basket of currencies, weighted according to the relative size and strength of the participating economies. Although the original agreement was to revise the relative weights every five years, the weighting was frozen in November 1993 (under the terms of Maastricht) at the levels agreed on in 1989:

German deutsche mark	30.53%	Spanish peseta	5.18%
French franc	19.43%	Danish krone	2.53%
British pound	12.06%	Irish pund	1.12%
Italian lira	9.92%	Portuguese escudo	0.785
Dutch guilder	9.54%	Greek drachma	0.77%
Belgian franc	7.83%	Luxembourg franc	0.31%

Tying the EMS to the ECU (instead of to the U.S. dollar, as was the case with the snake) not only gave Europe greater monetary independence from the United States; it also created the seed for a potential future European currency. Because the ECU is more stable than most EU currencies, its availability has also had major short-term benefits for people doing business in Europe.

either way, and Finland negotiated a band of 3 percent either way when it pegged the markka to the ECU in 1991. Changes in the value of the French franc and other currencies against the deutsche mark in July 1993 led to an emergency agreement among EC finance ministers to widen the band for all currencies (except those of

Germany and the Netherlands) to ± 15 percent, leading to fears that the ERM was about to collapse.

3. The states can drop out of the ERM, as Britain did in 1992. Britain has long been ambivalent toward the entire idea of the EMS, an attitude that did nothing to help its claims that London was the financial capital of Europe and that probably contributed to the 1994 decision to site the European Monetary Institute in Frankfurt instead of in London.

EU member states do not have to join the EMS; Portugal and Greece, for example, were long concerned about the stability of their currencies, and Portugal waited until 1992 before it pegged its currency to the ECU. Further, member states can opt in to the EMS, the ECU, or both without opting in to the ERM. Even non-EU states can join the EMS, a move that makes sense for those countries that do most of their trade with the EU—Norway joined in 1990, Finland and Sweden joined in 1991 (although Finland dropped out in 1992), and Cyprus joined in 1992.

The EMS has succeeded where the snake failed, for several reasons: It has allowed member states to better anticipate potential currency divergences and to take preemptive action;[17] it was introduced at a time when EC economies were more closely converged than they had been in 1971; and it is pegged to the ECU rather than to the U.S. dollar, thus giving member states more control over determining its value. There is also a psychological advantage because by binding themselves together, member states are committed to sinking or swimming together. Changes in the health of one of the bigger economies can set off a chain reaction in the others; for example, battles have regularly broken out between France and Germany because the German Bundesbank has frequently changed its interest rates without consulting its European counterparts. Because of the dominating influence of the German economy, this affects interest rates throughout the EU. France has argued that the other EU economies can act as a brake on Germany and stop it from growing too quickly and dominating the rest of Europe.

Opinions are divided about the prospects for the EMS. In the debit column, it has made domestic interest rates in the EU member states more volatile because they have been adjusted more often to help keep national currencies within the bands set by the ERM. Its supporters argue that it has helped Europeans cut their inflation rates, most of which were running at about 2 to 3 percent in January 1995—about the same level as the rate in the United States. But consumer prices in Spain and Italy were growing at more than 4 percent, and fluctuations in inflation rates in comparable non-EMS economies in the period 1980–1990 were little different from those in EMS states.[18] More clearly on the credit side of the ledger, the EMS has helped reduce fluctuations in the relative exchange rates of its members, while exchange rates for currencies outside the EMS have been more volatile.[19] The EMS also helped pave the way for the near completion of the single market program. Most important of all, it has survived.

Debates meanwhile continue about the prospects for a single European currency. Stage one of the Delors Plan called for all EU states to be members of the ERM by 1990, but membership has been both variable and shaky, with Britain joining in 1990 and leaving in 1992, Portugal joining only in 1992, and Greece not joining. (In January 1995, all currencies were in the ERM except those of Britain, Italy, Finland, Greece, and Sweden.) The foundations of stage two were laid in 1994 with the creation of the European Monetary Institute (the precursor to a European central bank), but it still has much work to do. Stage three will mean the permanent fixing of exchange rates as a prelude to a single currency, at which point full authority over European economic and monetary policy would shift to the EU.[20]

Although much of the groundwork for stage three has been laid, problems with the ERM have meant the target date for a single currency is still unresolved. At the July 1995 European Council in Cannes, EU leaders agreed to a target date of 1999 for a single currency, but there were widespread doubts that this was feasible. As these doubts surfaced, the possibility of a two-speed EMU—first raised in 1990 by German Bundesbank president Karl Otto Poehl—became more real. The idea is that states that are not yet ready to lock in to the single currency could do so later. Although the idea was denounced at the time, it was incorporated in the terms of Maastricht, which allows for the possibility of selected "qualified" states going ahead with currency union in January 1999.

Summary and Conclusions

From the beginning, economic integration was seen by many of the founders of the EEC as a means toward the end of political union. The goal of economic integration, for its part, was to be achieved by bringing down the barriers to trade and, more specifically, to the free movement of people, money, goods, and services. The process has roughly followed the stages outlined in Chapter 1: development of a customs union, formation of a common (or single) market, and movement toward economic union as a prelude to political union.

The first of these steps was more or less in place by 1968. Progress was made on the second step, but nontariff barriers continued to stand in the way of a truly unified market and overlapped with concerns about European competitiveness and Eurosclerosis to prompt a conscious decision among the governments of EC member states to again "relaunch" Europe with the Single European Act in 1987. Although this continued to remove barriers, a true single market cannot exist without monetary union. Progress toward that goal—and toward political union—has been made with the EMS, which has soldiered on since 1979 (a major achievement in itself) and has helped tighten the bonds of economic union. Despite the skepticism of the doubters, the EU is now the single biggest market in the world, and it is moving closer to the day when a single currency will be in place and all European economic and monetary policy will be the province of the European Union.

Notes

1. Paolo Cecchini, *The European Challenge: 1992* (Aldershot: Wildwood House, 1988).

2. Commission of the European Communities, *Completing the Internal Market* (the Cockfield Report), COM(85)310 (Brussels: Commission of the European Communities, 1985).

3. Dirk Vantyghem and Jacques Pelkmans, "Border Controls for Goods," in Peter Ludlow et al. (Eds.), *The Annual Review of European Community Affairs 1991* (London: Brassey's, 1991).

4. European Commission figures quoted by Mads Kieler, "Indirect Taxation and Excise Duties," in Ludlow et al., ibid., 46.

5. See Louis H. Orzak, "The General Systems Directive and the Liberal Profession," in Leon Hurwitz and Christian Lequesne (Eds.), *The State of the European Community* (Boulder: Lynne Rienner, 1991).

6. Ralf Dahrendorf, *The Modern Social Conflict* (London: Weidenfeld and Nicholson, 1988), 149.

7. *The Economist,* January 14, 1995.

8. Axel Krause, *Inside the New Europe* (New York: HarperCollins, 1991), 82.

9. Loukas Tsoukalis, *The New European Economy: The Politics and Economics of Integration,* 2d ed. (Oxford: Oxford University Press, 1993), 49–51. Acronyms: ESPRIT (European Strategic Programme for Research and Development in Information Technology), RACE (Research in Advanced Communications for Europe), BRITE (Basic Research in Industrial Technologies for Europe), (EUREKA) (European Research Coordinating Agency).

10. The thirteen members of the ESA in 1995 were Switzerland, Norway, and all of the EU member states except Finland, Greece, Luxembourg, and Portugal. The largest shares of the ESA budget came from France (21.5 percent), Germany (17.2 percent), Italy (11.3 percent), and Britain (4.9 percent).

11. Krause, *Inside the New Europe,* 118.

12. European Commission figures quoted in Tsoukalis, *The New European Economy,* 103.

13. Richard Owen and Michael Dynes, *The Times Guide to the Single European Market* (London: Times Books, 1992), 162–163.

14. John F.L. Ross, "High-Speed Rail: Catalyst for European Integration?" *Journal of Common Market Studies* 32:2 (June 1994), 191–214.

15. Owen and Dynes, *Times Guide to the Single European Market,* 222.

16. Siegfried Magiera, "A Citizen's Europe: Personal, Political and Cultural Rights," in Hurwitz and Lequesne, *The State of the European Community.*

17. Elke Thiel, "Changing Patterns of Monetary Interdependence," in William Wallace (Ed.), *The Dynamics of European Integration* (London: Pinter, 1990), 73.

18. Michele Fratianni and Jurgen von Hagen, *The European Monetary System and European Monetary Union* (Boulder: Westview Press, 1992), 30–31.

19. Ibid., 28.

20. Committee for the Study of Economic and Monetary Union, *Report on Economic and Monetary Union in the European Community* (the Delors Report) (Luxembourg: Office of Official Publications, 1989), 40.

Further Reading

Loukas Tsoukalis. *The New European Economy: The Politics and Economics of Integration,* 2d ed. (Oxford: Oxford University Press, 1993).

A general introduction to the political economy of the European Union that explains how economic integration has happened and with what results.

Peter Ludlow. *The Making of the European Monetary System* (London: Butterworths, 1982).

Although dated, this is a solid study of the politics surrounding the design and launching of the EMS.

Richard Owen and Michael Dynes. *The Times Guide to the Single European Market* (London: Times Books, 1992).

A detailed but accessible guide to the changes arising out of the single market.

Frank McDonald and Stephen Dearden (Eds.). *European Economic Integration* (New York: Longman, 1992).

Written as a college textbook, this is a useful introduction to EU economic integration, with separate chapters on related policy areas from agriculture to the environment.

David Thornton. *Airbus Industrie* (New York: St. Martin's Press, 1995).

A case study of one of the most remarkable and successful examples of European industrial and commercial cooperation that looks at the development, structure, and performance of the Airbus project.

13

Agricultural and Regional Policy

Agriculture sits low on the policy agendas of most industrialized countries and draws much less public attention than, for example, economic or foreign policy. But agriculture is a headline issue in the European Union. It employs just 5 percent of the workforce and accounts for just 3 percent of the combined GDP of the EU, yet it is the biggest, the most expensive, and the most contentious of the policy areas in which EU institutions have become involved. The EU has more powers over agriculture than over any other policy area, it has passed more legislation on agriculture than on any other single policy area, it spends as much on agriculture as on all other policy areas combined, and there is more political activity on agriculture than on almost any other policy area; only the foreign ministers meet more often than the agriculture ministers, for example, and the Commission's directorate-general on agriculture (DGVI) is its second-largest directorate-general.

Agricultural policy also differs from other EU policy areas in two more important respects. First, while barriers are being taken down and markets opened up in almost every area of EU economic activity, agriculture has been heavily interventionist; the EU has taken a hands-on approach to keeping agricultural prices high, thereby drawing criticism not only from within the EU but also from the EU's major trading partners, such as the United States. Second, unlike most other EU policy areas, agricultural policy was built in to the Treaty of Rome, where the commitment to a common agricultural policy was spelled out more clearly than was the case for any other policy area (although the details were only agreed on in the 1960s).

The Common Agricultural Policy aims in part to improve the standard of living of Europe's agricultural communities, a principle that overlaps with another important aspect of EU activities: regional policy. This relates to EU attempts to reduce disparities in wealth among the different parts of the EU and to promote social and economic cohesion. Noble though this goal may be, most economists agree that the free market almost unavoidably contains or promotes social and economic inequalities that have so far defied all attempts to remove them. Cohesion is more an ideal than an achievable objective. Even so, several structural funds have been developed since the early 1970s to shift resources from the wealthier parts of the EU to the poorer regions, to invest in decaying industrial areas and poorer rural areas, to promote employment and equal opportunities, and to improve living and working conditions. These funds include spending under CAP, the European Regional Development Fund, the Cohesion Fund (covered in this chapter), and the European Social Fund and the Social Charter for workers (discussed in Chapter 14). This chapter will look at how agricultural and regional policies work and the effects they have had on European integration.

Agricultural Policy

At the time the Treaties of Rome were being negotiated, agriculture sat high on the agendas of European policymakers. Not only were the disruptions of the war and the memories of postwar food shortages and rationing still fresh in their minds, but agriculture still accounted for about 12 percent of the GNP of the Six and for the employment of about one-fifth of the workforce. Agricultural policy had several unique political and economic implications.

First, agriculture was a key element in the trade-off between Germany and France when the EEC was first discussed. France was concerned that the common market would benefit German industry while providing the French economy with relatively few benefits. France had a large and efficient agricultural sector in the mid-1950s, accounting for 12 percent of GNP and employing about 25 percent of the French workforce—more than was the case in Germany (where agriculture accounted for 8 percent of GNP and 15 percent of the workforce).[1] Concerns that the common market would hurt its farmers encouraged the French government to insist on a protectionist system. Even though this was to prove expensive, even today threats to change the system bring protesting French farmers out in the thousands. The scale of feeling was reflected in the reaction to a plan by Dutch agriculture Commissioner Sicco Mansholt to reform Community agriculture (discussed later in this chapter). When the agriculture ministers met in 1971 to discuss the plan, 80,000 French farmers marched on Brussels, Mansholt was hanged in effigy, cars were burned, and 3,000 police were deployed, one person was killed and 140 injured in the melee that followed.[2]

Second, agricultural prices are more subject to fluctuation than are prices on most other goods, and since Europeans spend about a quarter of their incomes on food, those fluctuations can have serious knock-on effects throughout the economy. Price increases can contribute to inflation, while price decreases can force farmers to go deeper into debt, perhaps leading to bankruptcies and unemployment. The problem of maintaining minimum incomes has been exacerbated by mechanization, which has led to fewer Europeans working in farming. It was argued that subsidies would help encourage people to stay in the rural areas and discourage them from moving to towns and cities and perhaps adding to unemployment problems.

Third, self-sufficiency in food has been a primary factor in determining the direction of agricultural policy. World War II made Europeans aware of how much they depended on imported food and how prone those imports were to disruption in the event of war or other crises. Before the war, for example, Britain imported about 70 percent of its food needs, including wheat from the United States and Canada, beef from Argentina, and sugar cane from the Caribbean. The war made it clear that this reliance on imports was a security problem, so a massive program of agricultural intensification was launched in Britain (and other parts of Europe) after the war, with the result that Britain now imports only about 35 percent of its food needs. The pattern has been similar across the EU, which has experienced a big decline in agricultural imports from outside the EU and a growth in trade among the member states. Although reliance on imports is no longer the factor it once was, the drive to self-sufficiency had a key formative influence on agricultural policy whose effects have not yet gone away.

Finally, although the farm vote in Europe is generally much smaller than it was in the mid-1960s, it is not insubstantial. Across the EU as a whole, the number of people employed in agriculture has fallen from about 25 percent in 1958 to about 5 percent today (compared to 2.3 percent in the United States), but there are wide variations across countries: from less than 2 percent in Belgium and Luxembourg to 4 percent in France, 9 percent in Spain, 12 percent in Ireland, and nearly 20 percent in Greece.[3]

Furthermore, farmers in the richer EU states have traditionally had strong unions working for them. In Britain, for example, the National Farmers Union is a classic example of an insider interest group; it enjoys such a close relationship with the Ministry of Agriculture that most agricultural policy in Britain is made jointly by the ministry and farmers union leaders. At the same time, more than 150 EU-wide agricultural organizations have been formed, many of which directly lobby the EU. Among the most powerful of these is the Committee of Professional Agricultural Organizations, which represents farmers generally on a wide range of issues. Other organizations represent more specialized interests. Not only are farmers a powerful lobby in the EU, but many other people live in rural areas, and there are many rurally based services. Farmers and the residents of small towns and villages add up to a sizable proportion of the population and the vote. No political party can afford to ignore that vote, especially because there is little organized resistance to the agricultural or rural lobbies at either the national or the EU level.

No discussion of EU agricultural policy would be complete without mentioning the special case of France. French farmers account for barely one in twenty-five French workers (or about 0.7 percent of the total EU population), yet they have enormous influence over the French government, which lobbies on their behalf in the halls and corridors of Brussels. This situation helps to underpin the centrality of agricultural spending in the EU budget, causes spillover effects into other EU policy areas, and helps sour EU relations with the United States. Why does the farm lobby have so much influence in French domestic politics?

Much of the explanation lies in the role the countryside plays in the national psyche. Even though three of every four French citizens live in towns or cities, the rural ideal still has a strong nostalgic hold on the sentiments of many, as does the idea that France is still a great power. Italian journalist Luigi Barzini once argued that "foreigners have to remind themselves that they are not dealing with a country that really exists . . . but with a country that most Frenchmen dream still exists. The gap between the two is a large one, but the French indefatigably try to ignore it or forget it."[4] CAP provided a captive market for French agricultural products, and attempts to reform it have always been seen as a direct threat to the rural sector in France. Even urban voters are prepared to defend the rural ideal, which is where the true political significance of the French rural lobby comes into play.

The Common Agricultural Policy

The foundation of agricultural policy in the EU is the misnamed Common Agricultural Policy. The underlying principles of CAP—which were worked out at a landmark conference convened in Stresa, Italy, by Sicco Mansholt in July 1958—are the promotion of a common market in agricultural produce, of "Community preference" (a polite term for protectionism aimed at giving priority to EU produce over imported produce), and of joint financing (the costs of CAP are to be shared equitably across all the member states). The goals set out in the Treaty of Rome included increased agricultural productivity, a "fair" standard of living for the farming community, stable markets, regular supplies, and "reasonable" prices for consumers. In short, all farmers throughout the EU are guaranteed the same minimum price for their produce, regardless of how much they produce and of prevailing levels of supply and demand, and all the member states share the financial burden for making this possible.

The specifics of how CAP would work were agreed on in discussions with the Council of Ministers in the early 1960s. What they agreed on was not so much a common agricultural policy as a common agricultural price support system, which works as follows. Annual prices for all agricultural products are fixed at the meeting of agriculture ministers in the spring (usually April or May). On the basis of discussions and negotiations that have usually been going on since the previous September among the Commission, the Agriculture Council, interest groups, and national governments, the ministers set three kinds of prices:

- Target prices, or the prices they hope farmers will receive on the open market to receive a fair return on their investments.

- Threshold prices, or the prices to which EU imports will be raised if world prices are lower than those in the EU.

- Guaranteed (or intervention) prices, or the prices the Commission will pay as a last resort to take produce off the market if it is not meeting the target price. The EU will buy produce from farmers and place it in storage, thereby reducing the supply and pushing up demand and prices. If prices go above the target price, the EU will sell some of its stored produce until the price has leveled out again, although in practice it has never had to do this because the target prices have always been set high enough to encourage farmers to produce more than the market needs.

This arrangement has become increasingly expensive as EU farmers have produced more and more, exceeding the demands of consumers for commodities such as butter, cereals, beef, and sugar. The EU has been forced to buy the surplus, some of which is stored in warehouses strung across the EU. The rest is sold outside the EU, given as food aid to poorer countries, or "denatured" (that is, destroyed or converted into another product. For example, excess wine might be turned into spirits, which take up less space, or even into heating fuel). The EU has tried to discourage production by subsidizing exports (thereby upsetting other agricultural producers such as the United States) or by paying farmers not to produce food (which has encouraged new golf courses to sprout up in various parts of the EU as farmers convert their land to other uses). The real problem with CAP is the artificially high levels at which prices are set. They are high largely because conservative governments in France and West Germany in the early 1960s wanted to keep the support of farmers.

The costs of CAP are borne by the **European Agricultural Guidance and Guarantee Fund** (EAGGF), which was created in 1962 and has since been consistently the single biggest item in the EU budget (in the late 1980s totaling more than the entire national budgets of either Ireland or Greece[5]). The bulk of funds (about $39 billion in 1993) are spent in the Guarantee Section, which is used to buy and store surplus produce and to encourage

TABLE 13.1 Output Trends in European Agriculture, 1985–1993
(from a base of 100 in 1979–1981; ranked in order of overall increase)

	1985	*1989*	*1993*
Belgium-Luxembourg	101.34	115.49	141.04
Ireland	113.45	109.46	133.08
Denmark	122.43	126.59	131.17
Netherlands	108.00	119.11	122.45
Portugal	105.68	125.81	119.62
Greece	111.66	114.01	118.04
Spain	111.65	119.97	115.00
Austria	108.53	111.23	108.79
Finland	113.07	115.53	107.13
Germany	111.70	117.51	105.73
France	106.57	103.73	105.21
United Kingdom	110.32	109.40	103.44
Italy	101.80	102.52	102.96
Sweden	108.87	102.20	97.91
United States	106.82	125.39	131.68
Japan	107.06	98.78	82.45
World	114.13	122.55	128.49

Source: Food and Agriculture Organization (FAO) of the United Nations, *FAO Production Yearbook 1993* (Rome: FAO, 1994), 41–42.

agricultural exports. Most of the money goes to producers of dairy products (the EU accounts for 60 percent of global dairy production) and the producers of cereals, oils and fats, beef, veal, and sugar.[6] The Guidance Section is one of the three elements that make up the EU's structural funds (discussed later in this chapter), and it is used to improve agriculture by investing in new equipment and technology and helping those working in agriculture with pensions, illness benefits, and other support.

In terms of increasing productivity, stabilizing markets, securing supplies, and protecting European farmers from the fluctuations in world market prices, the Common Agricultural Policy has been a huge success (see Table 13.1). The EU is the world's largest exporter of sugar, eggs, poultry, and dairy products and accounts for nearly 20 percent of world food exports, compared to the U.S. share of 13 percent. Encouraged by guaranteed prices, European farmers have produced as much as possible, with the result that production has gone up in virtually every area and also that the EU now produces far more butter, cereals, beef, and sugar than it needs. The EU is self-sufficient in almost every product it can grow or produce in its climate, including wheat, barley, wine, meat, vegetables, and dairy products. These successes have come partly through intensification and partly from the increased use of fertilizers; EU farmers use nearly 2.5 times as much fertilizer per acre of land as U.S. farmers.

At the same time, member states have tended to specialize in various products, so duplication has been reduced. For example, most of the permanent cropland is now found in the southern states, and most livestock is raised in the northern states. CAP has also helped make farmers wealthier and their livelihoods more predictable and stable; while overall unemployment in the EU has grown, farm employment and incomes have generally remained steady.

Unfortunately, CAP has also created problems. First, EU farmers produce much more than the market can bear. By the early 1970s, the media had begun referring to butter mountains and wine lakes so often that the more gullible visitors to Brussels were asking where they could find these mountains and lakes. In a sense they do exist, because all surplus production is stockpiled throughout the EU, and there are literally warehouses filled with surplus cereal, powdered milk, beef, olive oil, raisins, figs, and even manure.

Second, EU spending on agriculture has increased exponentially, and vast funds are now sucked into the seemingly bottomless pit of agricultural policy. Although the proportion of spending on agriculture has fallen, the absolute amount has grown; about half of all EU expenditure goes to agriculture, and about half of *that* is spent on storage and the disposal of excess food production. The excess produce the EU buys can only be sold at about half of what the EU pays for it, so each year the EU loses about $9 billion on its price support policies—which is more than it spends on its social policies.

To make matters worse, stories of fraud and the abuse of CAP funds abound. The Commission does not have enough staff to ensure that requests for payments are fair, and differences between EU prices and world prices have meant high refunds that provide an irresistible temptation for less honest farmers. The Court of Auditors has regularly criticized the problem of fraud.[7]

Third, CAP has not closed the income gap between rich and poor farmers in the EU. While mechanization and intensification have brought new profits to farmers in the north, those in Ireland, Greece, and Portugal remain relatively poor. To make matters worse, spending on productive northern farmers erodes the support that could be going to less productive southern farmers, thereby undermining attempts to encourage them to stay on the land.[8]

Fourth, CAP spending has drawn EU funds away from other policy sectors. As the London *Times* put it in 1979, CAP "is the cuckoo which is progressively ejecting the other birds—such as the regional and social policy—from the Brussels nest through its voracious appetite for funds."[9]

Environmentalists have been unhappy about the way CAP has encouraged the increased use of chemical fertilizers and herbicides and has also encouraged farmers to cut down hedges and trees and to "reclaim" wetlands in the interests of making their farms bigger and more efficient. Further, CAP has upset consumers forced to pay inflated prices for food despite production that is often surplus to needs; the contradiction between high prices and warehouses filled with stored food has been a major source of public skepticism about the wisdom and benefits of European integration.

As if all this is not bad enough, CAP has distorted world agricultural prices, soured EU relations with its major trading partners, and perpetuated the idea of a protectionist European Union that cannot seem to get its priorities and values straight.

Reforming Agricultural Policy

Several attempts have been made to reform EU agricultural policy, with variable success. The first came at the end of the 1960s when rising concerns about the cost of price supports prompted the Council of Ministers to ask the Commission to look into the problem. Agriculture Commissioner Sicco Mansholt oversaw the drafting of a report on the issue, which was published in December 1968. His recommendations were to encourage small farmers to leave the land and to amalgamate farms into bigger and more efficient units. By the time the Agriculture Council finally met in 1971 to discuss the proposals, they had became bogged down in a web of political problems and were vehemently opposed by small farmers in France and Germany; they slipped down the agenda as currency problems pushed economic and monetary issues up the agenda.

It was left to Britain to take the lead on reform in the 1970s. British domestic policy was the opposite of that of the EC; it gave farmers "deficiency payments" (in other words, compensated them for a loss of income as a result of low prices). This policy still cost the taxpayers money, but not as much as the EU plan. Consumers also enjoyed low prices, and farmers were encouraged to improve their efficiency. Mansholt had tried to win British support for his proposed reforms, but the Heath government did not want to add to the complications over membership negotiations. Margaret Thatcher brought new pressures for change in the early 1980s, although she was concerned less with reforming CAP than with renegotiating British contributions to the EC budget. She argued that Britain was paying far more into the budget than anyone else and demanded reductions, which she won in 1984. In the process, more attention was drawn to the absurdities of agricultural overproduction.

BOX 13.1
The Common Fisheries Policy

Since 1983, the EU has had a Common Fisheries Policy (CFP), the main goals of which have been to resolve conflicts over territorial fishing rights and to prevent overfishing by setting catch quotas. Even though fishing employs just 0.2 percent of the EU workforce, the state of the fishing industry has implications for coastal communities throughout the EU. Disputes over fishing grounds in European waters have occasionally led to bitter confrontations between EU partners and their neighbors. There were, for example, the infamous cod wars between Britain and Iceland in the 1960s over access to fisheries in the North Atlantic. Similarly, in 1984 French patrol boats fired on Spanish trawlers operating inside the Community's two-hundred-mile limit, and more than two dozen Spanish trawlers were intercepted off the coast of Ireland. Spain's fishing fleet was bigger than that of the entire EC fleet at the time, and fishing rights were a major issue in Spain's negotiations to join the EC. Spanish fishing boats became an issue in domestic British politics in 1994 when Euroskeptics in the governing Conservative Party used their presence in traditional British waters as one of their many complaints about the effects of British membership in the EU.

Attempts to resolve competing claims to fishing grounds and to develop an equitable management plan for Community fisheries were bitter and controversial, but they finally resulted in agreement in 1983. The CFP regulates fisheries in four main ways. First, it has opened all the waters within the EU's two-hundred-mile limit to all EU fishing boats, but it gave member states the right to restrict access to fishing grounds within twelve miles of their shores. Second, it prevents overfishing by imposing national quotas (or Total Allowable Catches) on the take of Atlantic and North Sea fish and by regulating fishing areas and equipment (setting standards on the mesh size of fishing nets, for example). Third, it set up a market organization to oversee prices, quality, marketing, and external trade. Finally, it guides negotiations with other countries on access to waters and the conservation of fisheries.

Budgetary pressures pushed CAP reform back to the top of the agenda in 1987–1988. One proposal agreed on at the February 1988 summit of the European Council was to establish maximum guaranteed quantities (MGQs), or quotas beyond which support payments to farmers would be reduced. Pressure for reform was increased by the growing international criticism leveled at CAP as the EC negotiated tariff reductions under the Uruguay Round of GATT (which finally concluded in late 1993) and by the trade embargo imposed by the EC on Iraq in 1990–1991 (which caused a drop in export prices).

In early 1991, Agriculture Commissioner Ray MacSharry took up the banner of reform, warning of the rising volume of stored agricultural produce, which included 20 million tonnes of cereals, nearly 1 million tonnes of dairy products, and 750,000 tonnes of beef (a figure that was growing by 15,000 to 20,000 tonnes per week).[10] MacSharry proposed moving away from guaranteed prices; reducing subsidies on grain by 29 percent, those on beef by 15 percent, and those on butter by 5 percent; and encouraging farmers to take land out of production (the set-aside system, whereby farmers would be compensated for subsidy reductions only if they took 15 percent of their land out of production[11]). All of this predictably earned MacSharry the sobriquet Mack the Knife. Despite the opposition of many farmers and their unions, the proposals were finally approved by the Agriculture Council in May 1992 after eighteen months of talks. Although they initially made CAP more expensive and led to warnings from the Court of Auditors that they heightened opportunities for fraudulent claims from farmers, the changes promised to lead to a medium-term reduction in surpluses, lower food prices for consumers, and—over the longer term—better use of the money spent on CAP.

Regional Policy

The European Union is far from homogeneous; not only are there significant economic and social disparities within most of its member states, but there are disparities from one state to another (see maps on pp. 250–251). The standard measure for comparing differences among countries is to use per capita GDP adjusted for purchasing power parity (PPP, or the purchasing power of each member state currency). On that basis, and expressing the average for the EC as 100, the differences in per capita GDP in 1988 ranged from 121 in Luxembourg to 54 in Greece. Disparities among regions within the member states were even greater, ranging from 182 in Hamburg, Germany, to 48 in Nisia, Greece.[12] Unemployment rates in early 1995 varied from 6.4 percent in Austria to 14.1 percent in Belgium and 23.9 percent in Spain.[13]

In the interests of promoting economic efficiency and social equality, EU priorities have included trying to prevent the persistence of a two-speed Europe and encouraging greater economic and social cohesion by bringing the poorer member states closer to the level of their wealthier partners. Harvey Armstrong outlined four arguments in favor of the EU approach: In theory at least, it ensures that spending is concentrated in the areas of greatest need, it ensures coordination of the spending of the different member states, the member states have a vested interest in the welfare of their EU partners, and without the EU approach economic and social disparities could be a barrier to integration.[14] At the same time, there is an important psychological element: Payments made by the EU to the poorer sections of the member states can help the citizens of those states to see some of the benefits of EU membership.

250

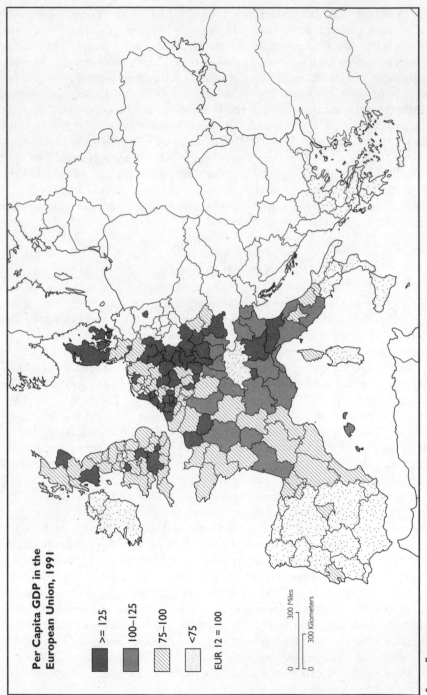

Per Capita GDP in the
European Union, 1991

>= 125

100–125

75–100

<75

EUR 12 = 100

300 Miles

300 Kilometers

0

0

Source: Eurostat.

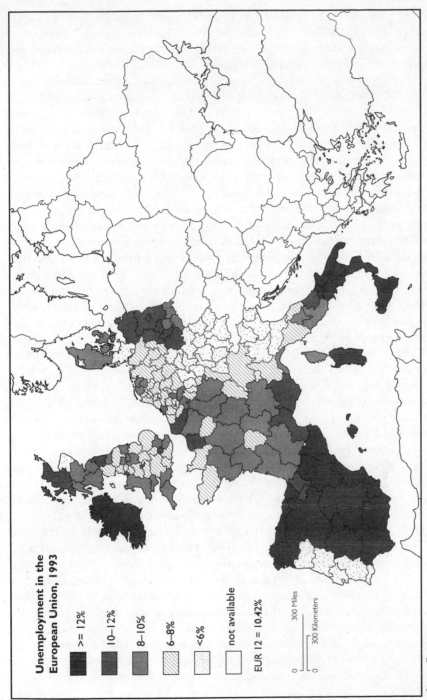

Unemployment in the European Union, 1993

>= 12%

10–12%

8–10%

6–8%

<6%

not available

EUR 12 = 10.42%

300 Miles

300 Kilometers

Source: Eurostat

Very generally, the wealthiest parts of the EU are located in the north-central area, particularly in and around the "golden triangle" formed by London, Dortmund, and Paris. The poorest parts are on the southern and western peripheries: Greece, southern Italy, Spain, Portugal, Ireland, Northern Ireland, and western Scotland. In the mid-1960s, the gap in per capita GDP between the ten richest and the ten poorest regions was 4:1. By 1970 it had fallen to 3:1, but recession and Greek membership had pushed it up to 5:1 by the early 1980s.[15] The EU's marginal areas are relatively poor for different reasons; some are depressed agricultural areas with little industry and high unemployment, some are old industrial areas with out-dated plants, and most suffer relatively low levels of education and health care and have underdeveloped infrastructure (especially roads and utilities).

Individual EU member states have long tried to deal with their own internal problems in different ways. Britain, for example, has designated special Development Areas and has given industry incentives to invest in those areas or to relocate factories. Italy created a Fund for the South to help provide infrastructure and encourage investment in the Mezzogiorno—everywhere south of Rome, including areas so riddled with corruption and so heavily controlled by organized crime that they are effectively independent subgovernments. All the major industrialized states have also tried to address the problem of urban decline in different ways.

The European Coal and Steel Community made provision for grants to depressed areas for industrial conversion and retraining, but the idea of helping depressed regions went against the free market principles of allowing people and money to follow the opportunities. The Guidance segment of CAP included a welfare element in the sense that funds could be used to upgrade farms and farming equipment, improve farming methods, and provide benefits to farmers. Broader regional disparities were not addressed until 1969, when the Commission proposed a common regional policy—including the creation of a regional development fund—but the idea met with little enthusiasm in Germany or France, which were already concerned, respectively, about the costs of CAP and the surrender of more powers to the EC.

Little more was done until the first round of enlargement in the early 1970s, when a complex pattern of political and economic interests came together to make the idea of a regional policy more palatable. Most important, the "rich man's club" of the 1950s (Italy excepted) had been joined by Britain and Ireland, two countries with marked regional problems. Their accession not only widened the economic disparities of the Community but also strengthened Italy's demands for a regional policy. In addition, development funds would make EC membership more palatable to Euroskeptics in Britain. Germany and France also wanted to see Britain settle in to the Community, and Germany was casting an interested eye on Britain as an export market.[16]

The Commission sponsored the 1973 Thomson Report on regional issues, which argued that regional imbalances were a barrier to one of the goals of the Treaty of Rome ("a continuous and balanced expansion" in economic activity), that they threatened to undermine plans for economic and monetary union, and that they could even pose a threat to the common market.[17] Agreement was reached on a **European Regional Development Fund** in 1973, but its launch was delayed until 1975 by the energy crisis of 1973–1974. ERDF spending originally totaled just $1.1 billion (about 5 percent of the Community budget), but it was doubled in 1977 and has grown steadily since then, reaching nearly $10 billion in 1993 (just over 11 percent of the EU budget).

Funds were originally distributed by a system of national quotas that were worked out during the negotiations leading up to the creation of the ERDF. The biggest net beneficiaries were Britain, Ireland, France, and Italy, although the balance changed when Greece, Spain, and Portugal joined. The ERDF was not to be used in place of pre-existing national development spending but was to provide matching grants of—at most—50 percent, supplemented by loans from the European Investment Bank. Requests had to come from the member states, and funds could be spent only on industrial and service-sector projects aimed at creating new jobs or protecting existing ones, on infrastructure related to industry, or in unusual areas such as remote or mountainous regions.

One of the major problems with the way the ERDF and the other structural funds were set up was that the definitions of a "region" and of priority areas were left up to the member states. Each state has a different kind of administrative unit, ranging from the states of Austria and Germany (which have a range of powers independent of those of their respective federal governments) to the *départements* of France and the counties of Britain (which have few independent powers and are governed in very different ways). This means member states have different ideas about how to justify ERDF spending, which has tended to be justified less on the basis of real "need" (however that is defined) than on the basis of the relative political and economic influence member states bring to bear on regional policy negotiations; the structural funds have always carried the danger of promoting pork barrel politics in the European Union.

David Coombes and Nicholas Rees argue that politics enters the equation in at least two ways.[18] First, member states have been reluctant to give the EU powers over industrial development, employment, and social security because doing so would reduce their control over domestic economic policy. Second, member states have been unwilling to transfer powers without the promise of net gains to themselves. They have looked for some kind of compensation and put national interests above European interests. The structural funds have routinely been seen as a way of compensating for the

BOX 13.2
The Mediterranean Debacle

The difficulties of designing structural policies that really work are well illustrated by the record of the Integrated Mediterranean Programmes (IMPs), created in 1984 in an attempt to offset some of the potentially negative consequences of the accession to the EC in 1986 of Portugal and Spain. About 4.1 billion ECU (nearly $5 billion) was to be spent over a seven-year period in Greece, southern Italy, and southern France to make up for the shift of structural funds to Portugal and Spain.

The defects of the IMPs were underlined in a 1990 report by the Court of Auditors and a 1990 resolution by the European Parliament.[1] First, there was minimal coordination of the management of the three different structural funds, which led to an overlap of those funds and the IMPs. Second, the lack of coordination led to planning problems and lengthy delays in agreement on how and where the funds were to be spent. Third, no reliable records were kept on how IMP funds were spent, making it impossible for the monitoring committees to measure the effectiveness of the IMPs or to influence the decisions of the local authorities responsible for implementation. Fourth, all these problems had slowed down the flow of IMP funds, so that by the end of 1989, fewer than one-fourth of the 4.1 billion ECUs set aside had actually been paid out.

The decisionmaking structure of the Commission and all of the political problems associated with trying to impose order, consistency, and equity in the way structural funds are spent make it difficult to see a workable way out of the dilemma. The record of the IMPs also provides insight into the sources of some of the problems with the management of spending under CAP, the ERDF, and the European Social Fund.

Notes

1. For details, see Niall Bohan, "Cohesion and the Structural Funds," in Peter Ludlow et al. (Eds.), *The Annual Review of European Community Affairs 1991* (London: Brassey's, 1991).

uneven distribution of spending under CAP—in that sense, they have become a form of institutionalized bribery.

Another political complication is added by the rise of the nationalist factor in EU politics. As Western European states have integrated at the macro level, there have been growing demands for self-determination at the micro level by cultural regions.[19] The bitter struggles between Catholics and Protestants in Northern Ireland are well-known, as are the on-again/off-again demands of Scottish and Welsh nationalists for independence or devolution. At the same time, there are similar pressures from (among others) Bretons and Corsicans in France, Basques on the Spanish-French border, Catalans in Spain, and Walloons in Belgium. These have long been the domestic affairs of the national governments involved, but European integration, ironically, has given national minorities an opportunity to bypass their governments and to lobby at the European level for a higher priority status, greater self-determination, or both.

Reforms in the late 1970s led to the introduction of a small "nonquota" element in the ERDF (5 percent of the total could be determined by the Commission on the basis of need) and to suggestions that the richer countries should give up their quotas altogether on the grounds that they could afford their own internal development costs. From being a passive recipient of requests for aid, the EC took on a more active approach to addressing the problem of regional disparities. Reforms in 1984 led to a tighter definition of the parts of the EU most in need of help, increased the nonquota segment to 20 percent, and replaced the fixed quotas with minimum and maximum limits. Britain, for example, could receive from 14.5 percent to 19.3 percent, while the maximums for Germany and France were lower (3.4 percent and nearly 10 percent, respectively) and those for Spain and Italy were higher (about 24 percent and 29 percent, respectively). The SEA added a new sense of urgency to the regional issue and argued the need to "clarify and rationalize" the use of the structural funds. More reforms agreed on in 1988 were based on British insistence on reducing spending under CAP and increasing spending under the structural funds to 25 percent of the Community budget by 1993 (in the event, they reached nearly 32 percent of spending).

The EU's regional policy today has the following goals:[20]

- The policy provides help for the poorest regions, described as Objective 1 regions and defined as those in which per capita GDP is at least 25 percent less than the EU average. These regions include Greece, Portugal, Ireland, Northern Ireland, parts of Italy and Spain, and the French overseas *départements*. Germany, Denmark, and the Benelux states receive no funds in this area, although there are plans to include eastern Germany and parts of Belgium and the Netherlands.[21] Objective 1 projects are funded mainly out of the ERDF.

- The second goal is to provide help for Objective 2 areas, defined as those suffering from high unemployment and job losses and industrial decline; these areas are found mainly in the older industrial regions of northcentral Europe and parts of Italy and Spain. These projects are funded primarily out of the ERDF.

- Objectives 3 and 4 are programs aimed at dealing with long-term unemployment and creating jobs for young people. They are funded mainly out of the European Social Fund. Objective 5 focuses on helping agricultural and rural areas and is funded mainly out of the EAGGF.

- In addition, a host of specialized programs have specific objectives, some of which overlap with social policy and all of which have once again provided a field day for the authors of clever acronyms; these include RECHAR (converting coal-mining areas), REGIS (help for overseas regions of the EU), INTERREG (helping border regions prepare for completion of the single market), and PRISMA (aid for infrastructure and business services in poorer regions).[22]

About 80 percent of ERDF spending goes to Objectives 1 and 2, while Objectives 3 and 4 are covered mainly by the European Social Fund and lending by the European Investment Bank, and Objective 5 by spending under CAP. The 1988 reforms were also aimed at improving the efficiency of regional policy by setting up Community Support Frameworks under which the Commission, the member states, and the regions work more closely together to agree on the means for achieving regional development planning goals.

The most recent changes in regional policy came with the Maastricht treaty, under which agreement was reached to set up a Committee of the Regions, designed to allow the regions a greater say in making policy, and also a Cohesion Fund. This fund targets member states with per capita GDPs that are less than 90 percent of the EU average (which includes Greece, Portugal, Spain, and Ireland) and is aimed at helping to compensate these countries for the additional costs of tightening environmental regulations and providing financial assistance for transport projects.

Summary and Conclusions

For years, what critics of the European Community most disliked about European integration was related mainly to its implications for agriculture. The popular image of the EC was inextricably linked with charges of spending and regulation gone mad, of militant French farmers blocking any attempts to undermine their privileged position and bring EC spending under control, and of outrageous food surpluses at a time when many people in the world were starving. The images were not entirely wrong, but they tended to give short shrift to some of the benefits of EC agricultural policy, including increases in production, greater efficiency, and economic boosts to a rural sector that in many parts of the Community had long experienced hardship and occasional poverty.

One of the consequences of the CAP has been to help shift economic resources and political power from the richer to the poorer parts of Europe, a trend that has overlapped with the consequences of EU regional policy. For the EU, regional development has long meant an attempt to help the poorer regions catch up with their richer neighbors, with the utopian goal of encouraging an equitable distribution of the benefits of regional integration. The EU has tended to equate development with growth, but whether quantity and quality go hand in hand has long been debatable. It is also debatable whether the free market can ever entirely eliminate inequalities of opportunity, which is why agricultural and regional policies in the EU have been organized around a kind of grand welfare system based on the redistribution of wealth as a means to encourage equal opportunity. How long it will take to bring the different parts of the EU to the same economic level (assuming this is even possible) remains to be seen.

Notes

1. H. von der Groeben, *The European Community, the Formative Years: The Struggle to Establish the Common Market and the Political Union (1958–66)* (Brussels: European Commission, 1987), 71–72.

2. The *Times* (London), March 24, 1971.

3. Food and Agriculture Organization (FAO) of the United Nations, *FAO Production Yearbook 1993* (New York: FAO, 1994), 19–35.

4. Luigi Barzini, *The Europeans* (London: Penguin, 1983), 124.

5. European Community, *A Common Agricultural Policy for the 1990s* (Luxembourg: Office for Official Publications of the European Communities, 1989), 33.

6. Ibid., 34.

7. Michael Shackleton, *Financing the European Community* (New York: Council on Foreign Relations Press, 1990), 38–40.

8. Anne Daltrop, *Politics and the European Community* (London: Longman, 1987), 175–176.

9. The *Times* (London), December 29, 1979.

10. Debates of the European Parliament, OJ 3-407, July 11, 1991, 282.

11. David P. Lewis, *The Road to Europe: History, Institutions and Prospects of European Integration 1945–1993* (New York: Peter Lang, 1993), 337.

12. Eurostat, *Regions: Statistical Yearbook 1990* (Brussels: Commission of the European Communities, 1990).

13. *The Economist,* January 21, 1995.

14. Harvey Armstrong, "Community Regional Policy," in Juliet Lodge (Ed.), *The European Community and the Challenge of the Future* (New York: St. Martin's Press, 1993).

15. Eurostat, *Basic Statistics of the Community* (Luxembourg: Statistical Office of the European Communities, various years).

16. Stephen George, *Politics and Policy in the European Community* (Oxford: Oxford University Press, 1991), 192–193.

17. Commission of the European Communities, *Report on the Regional Problems of the Enlarged Community* (the Thomson Report), COM(73)550 (Brussels: Commission of the European Communities, 1979).

18. David Coombes and Nicholas Rees, "Regional and Social Policy," in Leon Hurwitz and Christian Lequesne (Eds.), *The State of the European Community* (Boulder: Lynne Rienner, 1991), 209–211.

19. James G. Kellas, "European Integration and the Regions," *Parliamentary Affairs* 44:2 (April 1991), 226–239.

20. Frank McDonald and Stephen Dearden (Eds.), *European Economic Integration* (New York: Longman, 1992), 107–109.

21. Joanne Scott, *Development Dilemmas in the European Community: Rethinking Regional Development Policy* (Buckingham: Open University Press, 1995), 33.

22. For a complete list, see Bohan, "Cohesion and the Structural Funds."

Further Reading

Given all the fuss and expense surrounding CAP, it is surprising how few recent and digestible studies of EU agricultural policy are available. Among them are the following:

John Marsh and Bryn Green (Eds.). *The Changing Role of the Common Agricultural Policy: The Future of Farming in Europe* (London: Belhaven, 1991).

Michael Petit et al. *Agricultural Policy Formation in the European Community* (Amsterdam: Elsevier, 1987).

For a study of the evolution and consequences of regional development policy in the EU, see Joanne Scott, *Development Dilemmas in the European Community: Rethinking Regional Development Policy* (Buckingham: Open University Press, 1995).

14

Environmental and Social Policy

The process of European integration was long motivated by quantity; efficiency, economic expansion, and profit were at the heart of the building of the common market. Although the EEC Treaty mentioned the need for "an accelerated raising of the standard of living," quality was a relatively minor motivating force in the early years of the Community.

By the early 1970s, the emphasis had begun to change. Public reaction in the West decried what was widely seen as uncaring affluence[1] and a shift in favor of promoting quality-of-life issues. The change was exemplified by the rise of the feminist, antiwar, and environmental movements on both sides of the Atlantic. The EC could not avoid becoming caught up in the change, and by the early 1970s it was increasingly involved in promoting both qualitative improvements in the lives of the citizens of its member states and an equitable distribution of the benefits of integration. The 1973 enlargement accelerated that process by widening the gap between the richest and poorest areas of the Community. States with stronger environmental laws and workers' rights were concerned about the flight of industry and jobs to countries with looser standards (the kind of concerns later raised in the United States when Mexico was brought in to NAFTA).

Environmental and social issues have subsequently been high on the EU agenda, with the first proving less controversial than the second. Improvements in environmental quality were driven at first by concerns about the extent to which different standards distorted competition and complicated progress toward the building of a common market. A series of Environmental Action Programmes launched in 1973 provided more policy consistency and direction, and the Single European Act and Maastricht turned the emphasis of policy toward sustainable development and environmental protection as an essential part of "harmonious and balanced" economic growth. The SEA gave the environment legal status as a policy concern of the Community, and both treaties resulted in institutional changes that gave public opinion (through the European Parliament) a greater voice in making environmental policy and that introduced qualified majority voting on most environmental law and policy.

259

Meanwhile, full economic integration also demanded social cohesion, something that was being addressed by the Common Agricultural Policy and the ERDF but that went well beyond the scope of either. The EU began moving into the realm of social policy, a term that covers a multitude of issues but that has been left deliberately vague; it coincides with the equally ambiguous idea of a "people's Europe." Although the outer edges of social policy are fuzzy, the core includes such issues as employment, working conditions, social security, labor relations, education, training, housing, and health. Social issues were addressed by a series of Social Action Programmes launched in 1974, aimed at improving living and working conditions in the EC. There was a social dimension to the SEA as well, and a new and controversial focus on social issues came with the Social Charter of 1989, which pushed the EU further into protecting the rights of workers—an area that is an ideological and a political minefield.

Environmental Policy

Environmental problems do not respect national frontiers. Since the mid-1970s, growing scientific and political awareness of this fact has led to a new emphasis on international responses to such problems as air pollution and the management of shared rivers. But national governments have been slow to take unilateral action for fear of losing comparative economic advantage and have been unwilling to give significant powers to international environmental organizations such as the United Nations Environment Programme, which is underfunded and has no direct powers of coercion.

Regional integration offers a solution to both dilemmas. As states become more dependent on trade and foreign investment and thus break down the barriers to trade, parochial worries about loss of comparative economic advantage become less important. At the same time, different environmental standards can create trade distortions, so national governments may be more inclined to take collective action and to agree on common policies. In the case of the EU, this has already happened; it has been at the heart of the most concerted program ever seen to replace national environmental controls with uniform multinational regulations.

The Treaty of Rome does not mention the environment, and although the EEC agreed on several pieces of environmental law in the 1960s, they came from the drive to build a common market and were incidental to the Community's overriding economic goals.[2] Only in the 1970s did the EEC begin to develop a broader environmental policy. It did this against a background of new public and political interest in the environment, arising out of a combination of improved scientific understanding, several headline-making environmental disasters, new affluence among Western middle classes, and growing concern about quality-of-life issues.[3]

The environmental revolution of the 1960s culminated in the landmark United Nations Conference on the Human Environment in Stockholm, which drew an unprecedented level of political attention to the problems of the global environment. In October 1972, just three months after Stockholm, the EEC heads of government meeting in Paris agreed on the need for an environmental policy, as a result of which the Commission adopted its first **Environmental Action Programme** (EAP) in late 1973. Subsequent Programmes came into force in 1977, 1982, 1987, and 1993.

The first two EAPs were based on taking preventive action and on working against allowing divergent national policies to become barriers to building a common market, a problem noted by the Court of Justice in 1980 when it argued that competition could be "appreciably distorted" without harmonization of environmental regulations.[4] States with weaker pollution laws, for example, had less of a financial and regulatory burden than those without such laws and might attract corporations wanting to build new factories with a minimum of built-in environmental safeguards. The third EAP marked a sea change, with a switch to a focus on environmental management as the basis of economic and social development. For the first time, environmental factors were consciously factored in to other policy areas—notably agriculture, industry, energy, and transport. Environmental concerns were no longer subordinate to the goal of building a common market.[5]

All of these changes took place without amending the EEC Treaty, so EC environmental policy lacked a clear legal basis and was technically unauthorized by the member states.[6] The Community also grew in the 1980s to include Greece, Spain, and Portugal, whose industries were relatively underdeveloped and pollutive and whose environmental standards were relatively weak. The threats these changes posed to the EC's environmental activity were finally addressed by the Single European Act, which gave a legal basis to EC environmental policy, made environmental protection a component of all EC policies, outlined the underlying principles and goals of environmental policy, and included the environment in the list of policy areas subject to the cooperation procedure in the European Parliament.

At the same time, though, the SEA muddied the waters by noting that environmental policy would be based on the principle of subsidiarity: "The Community shall take action relating to the environment to the extent to which the [policy] objectives ... can be attained better at the Community level than at the level of the individual Member States" (Article 130r(4)). This heightened the possibilities of member states challenging EC law by arguing over competence. States with weaker environmental laws could also challenge steps taken by other states to strengthen their laws; the SEA noted that EC measures would not prevent member states from imposing stronger measures of their own but that such measures could not amount to discrimination or a disguised restriction on trade (Article 130T). Arguments over which laws were discriminatory and which were not could go either way. Maastricht helped clarify the issue by making the environment more obviously a priority policy area for the EU, introducing qualified majority voting in the Council of Ministers on most environmental issues (thereby making it more difficult for reluctant member states to avoid toeing the line), and putting the environment on the list of topics subject to codecisions by the European Parliament.

Another boost was given by public support for environmental protection. Eurobarometer polls found that most EC citizens ranked the environment above finance, defense, and employment as an issue of EC concern; that most felt pollution was an "urgent and immediate problem"; and that most agreed that environmental protection was a policy area better addressed by EC states jointly than by member states alone.[7] Meanwhile, green parties won growing support in most member states; thirty green members were returned from seven EC states in the 1989 European Parliament elections (the number fell to twenty-three in the 1994 elections), and by 1995 green members sat in the national legislatures of ten EU member states: Austria, Belgium, Finland, Germany, Greece, Ireland, Italy, Luxembourg, Portugal, and Sweden.

More than 250 new EC environmental controls have now been agreed on, covering everything from environmental impact assessment (1988) to controls on lead in fuel (1978 and 1985), sulfur dioxide and suspended particulates (1980), lead in air (1982), pollutants from industrial and large combustion plants (1984 and 1989, respectively), nitrogen dioxide (1985), and vehicle exhaust emissions (1989). Even so, EU environmental law remains patchy and is regularly criticized by industry and environmentalists alike for lacking coherence. Some of the problems may be addressed by the new **European Environment Agency** (EEA) and the European Environment Monitoring and Information Network, but the EEA is a data-gathering rather than a regulatory agency, lacks direct powers of enforcement,[8] and has an ambiguous relationship with the member states and the other EU institutions.

Although there has been progress on environmental policymaking, the record regarding implementation is less positive. This can be explained in part by the limits on the abilities of the Commission to ensure that member states implement EU law, the long-time lack of a legal basis for EU environmental policy, and the pressure on the Commission to maintain the impetus toward new legislation—all of which have combined to encourage EU policymakers to focus on policy formulation at the expense of implementation.[9] Another problem arises from the differences in the regulatory programs and systems of member states.[10] For example, Greece and Spain have had more infringement proceedings begun against them than most other EU states, mainly because local government in both states is relatively poorly organized and underequipped. Germany and the Netherlands also have weak records on implementation, but both have sophisticated systems of domestic environmental law and thus lack the motivation to fully adapt their own measures to EC requirements. Meanwhile, Denmark has a good record on implementation, helped by high levels of public and official environmental awareness, effective monitoring systems, and the involvement of the Danish parliament in negotiating new environmental law.[11]

The differences in levels of implementation have also been blamed on the lack of financial and technical resources, organizational problems within EU institutions, the fact that most EU law has focused on developing policies rather than on the means for implementation and enforcement, and the failure of the different parties involved in making policy to realize the difficulties in meeting the goals they have set (that is, they are too ambitious). It has been argued that the Commission—through the EEA—should be given the power to carry out inspections and ensure compliance, but this would raise fundamental questions about sovereignty and the "interference" of the Commission in the domestic affairs of the member states. Additionally, effective inspections would demand a huge new staff; even the U.S. Environmental Protection Agency—with a staff of fifteen thousand and a multi-billion dollar budget—is hard-pressed to keep up with everything it is expected to do. For the foreseeable future, the Commission will have to continue to rely on whistle-blowing by interest groups and on cases being brought before national courts and the European Court of Justice.

The Effects of EU Environmental Policies

Despite the varied record on implementation, environmental policy is widely regarded as one of the clear success stories of European integration.[12] EU policies have brought changes where they might not otherwise have come, and agreement on common policies has led to the strengthening of pan-EU institutions and policymaking. The effects of EU policy are particularly notable in three areas.

Harmonization of Standards

The creation of a European single market always ultimately depended on the agreement of common standards, including environmental standards, among the member states. This fact was always implicit in the work of the EEC, was given a boost with the development of the Environmental Action

Programmes, and was finally confirmed with the SEA—under which common standards were adopted on the quality of drinking water, bathing water, water for freshwater fish, levels of various pollutants in water, toxic waste disposal, levels of air pollutants such as smoke and sulfur dioxide, lead in fuel, pesticides, and noise pollution.

Changes in the Policymaking Process

Changes in EU law on the environment have helped to close the gap in the way different member states make domestic policy. For example, unlike either the United States or Germany—both of which rely on enforceable air-quality and emission standards—Britain long relied on flexibility, consensus, consultation, and tailoring standards to meet the circumstances of specific polluters and the local environment. Arguing that government should interfere with industry as little as possible while at the same time trying to placate public opinion, Britain relied on the use of the "best practicable environmental option" to prevent pollution. It also relied on voluntary compliance and on the "good public sense" of industries to implement control measures, rather than using the threat of prosecution.[13] Meanwhile, to make voluntary compliance and the partnership between industry and regulators work, pollution control was shrouded in secrecy.

The combined effect of these approaches was to limit public debate about air and water pollution and to minimize the pressure on government to change the way British pollution-control policy was either made or enforced.[14] EC membership changed this by establishing uniform air- and water-quality standards and pollution-control procedures in Britain for the first time. The need to comply with EC law also made pollution control more overtly a public issue, drew widespread public attention to the parlous condition of Britain's water, and undermined the traditions of secrecy, negotiation, and voluntary compliance. Britain has had to reform and strengthen its pollution-control policies and laws as a result.

The Rise of the European Environmental Lobby

Particularly until the 1970s, most of the pressure for environmental regulation in industrialized countries came from environmental interest groups; they provided the pressure for policy change and also the ideas and the scientific data upon which change was based. Among EC member states, there was initially little inclination for those groups to lobby the Community, because most environmental policy was still made at the national level and the priorities varied from one member state to another. Interest groups have since become much more active, in part because the growing powers of EU institutions have made them a more profitable target for interest group pres-

BOX 14.1
Spillover and the Case of Lead in Fuel

The pace of environmental policymaking in the EU has been set in large part by the tension between "lead" states such as Germany, Denmark, and the Netherlands, which have higher domestic standards, and "lag" states such as Spain, Portugal, and Greece, in which environmental regulation was long seen as a brake on economic development. In the interest of integrating themselves more fully into the European market, the lag states have had to adopt stronger standards than they might otherwise have done, as illustrated by the case of lead in fuel.

Lead was originally added to fuel to improve its performance, but researchers found the lead emitted into the air when fuel was burned posed a serious health hazard. Japan and the United States banned the use of leaded fuel for new cars in the 1970s, while West Germany unilaterally reduced the lead content of its fuel to 0.40 grams per liter (g/l) in 1972, a proportion that allowed the fuel to continue to be used in road vehicles without their engines having to be modified.

The lead content of fuel varied widely across EC member states, and although the 1973 energy crisis made governments less enthusiastic about addressing the lead issue, the Commission—concerned partly about air pollution but mainly about trade distortions—suggested bringing all of the states into line with West Germany by 1976. West Germany then raised the bar by making a second reduction in lead content, to 0.15 g/l. The Commission responded with a 1978 directive requiring member states to reduce lead content to the range 0.40–0.15 g/l.

Further pressure for change came in the early 1980s with the launch in Britain of the Campaign for Lead-Free Air (CLEAR), which used the health argument and won wide public support. Research was also published in West Germany showing that forests were dying from air pollution. (Reducing air pollution from road vehicles can be achieved by fitting catalytic converters to exhaust systems, but they only work with lead-free fuel.) In 1983, both Britain and West Germany proposed to the Commission that lead in fuel be eliminated, albeit for different reasons. The final step came with a 1985 directive mandating the introduction of unleaded fuel throughout the Community by October 1, 1989. Thanks in part to pressure from two of their biggest neighbors, all EU states have switched to unleaded fuel in new vehicles.

---

sure, but also because bodies such as the Commission lack the resources to collect information or enforce laws and thus welcome the input of interest groups. The change was reflected in the opening of new offices in Brussels in the second half of the 1980s by such groups as Friends of the Earth, Greenpeace, and the World Wide Fund for Nature, while many other groups employed full-time lobbyists. The Commission has actively encouraged the participation of Europewide interest groups at almost every stage of policymaking. Although this may slow down the policy process, it also reduces the Commission's workload, provides a ready source of expertise, and helps the Commission monitor the compliance records of member states; interest groups make good whistle-blowers. In 1984, the Commission received only 11 complaints from environmental interest groups, local authorities, MEPs, and private individuals; by 1989, it was receiving more than 450 complaints each year,[15] reflecting the growth in both the number of EC laws and the watchdog functions of interest groups.

Increased access to EU policymakers has led to a more systematic approach to Euro-lobbying among environmental groups and to a clear trend toward approaching domestic environmental problems as EU-wide problems. The complexity of those problems has encouraged domestic groups to work more closely together and to form transnational coalitions, the best-known of which is the European Environmental Bureau (EEB). Founded in 1974 with the encouragement of the Commission, the EEB serves as an umbrella for national interest groups in the EU and acts as a conduit for representing those groups to the EU, particularly the Commission. By 1993, the EEB represented 150 national environmental groups with a combined membership of 23 million.

Although the EU may offer new lobbying opportunities for environmental groups, access is neither guaranteed nor straightforward.[16] First, the agenda-setting process is relatively unstable and unpredictable because EU institutions are still evolving, their briefs and responsibilities are changing, policymaking power is dispersed, and the agenda changes as successive presidencies of the Council of Ministers push their favorite projects to the top of the list. The creation of the European Environment Agency may ease some of these problems.

Second, some powers over policy may have been shifted to Brussels, but many remain with national and local governments, so groups are finding that they have to keep active in several arenas. Although they might be able to play one off against another, doing so stretches their already limited resources and means they often lack the will or the resources to take part in the policymaking process from initiation through to implementation.

Finally, policymaking within the Commission is compartmentalized, with little horizontal coordination. Groups can work with DGXI (Environment) and DGXVII (Energy), but they also need to watch developments in other DGs, where other and perhaps more powerful interest groups representing industry and agriculture may have much more influence.

Regional cooperation among countries promises a more rapid and effective resolution of transnational environmental problems than does any other approach, at least among countries with similar political systems and levels of economic development. Isolated national approaches may be handicapped by fears of a loss of competitive advantage; bilateral or multilateral approaches have worked only when they have been limited to selected issues of mutual concern, such as the management of shared rivers, lakes, or oceans; broader global approaches are handicapped by the increased likelihood of disagreement and deadlock and the lack of competent authorities with the powers to promote and enforce regulation. Given the extent to which the causes and effects of environmental problems do not respect national frontiers, the EU model may provide the *only* effective response to such problems.

Social Policy

Cohesion in the EU has meant investments not only in agriculture, industry, and services but also in social issues such as workers' rights, women's rights, and improved working and living conditions. The poorer economies have been concerned about new competition from economic powers such as Germany, while states with progressive employment laws (such as France) have worried that jobs would be lost to countries with less progressive laws. Social policies are not only a logical outcome of the long histories of welfare promotion in individual Western European states but are also an important part of the drive toward building a single market by ensuring equal opportunities and working conditions. They are also one channel by which the EU can reach each of its citizens and make the implications of European integration more real to them. At the same time, the policies are controversial and have led to some of the most bruising ideological battles the EU has witnessed since its foundation.

Social policy can be broadly defined as policy relating to the rights, opportunities, and benefits provided for potential, actual, or former workers.[17] Relatively little attention was initially paid to issues such as these; even though worker mobility and the expansion of a skilled labor force were important parts of the idea of building a common market, concerns about the competitive implications of different levels of social security payments and labor costs encouraged the Six to avoid addressing social issues head-on during the negotiations leading up to the Treaty of Rome. The treaty was ultimately based on the naive assumption that the benefits of the common market would improve life for all European workers. This was true to the extent that it helped increase wages, but market forces failed to deal with gender or age discrimination, disparities in wage levels, different levels of unemployment, or safety and health in the workplace. The Treaty of Rome made it the Community's business to deal with such issues as free movement of workers, equal pay for equal work, working conditions, and social security for migrant workers, and Article 123 set the goal of creating a European Social Fund that would help promote worker mobility.

In the event, social issues moved down the Community agenda as it concentrated on completing the common market and resolving battles over agricultural policy, and the movement of workers was heavily restricted.

BOX 14.2
Women in the European Union

The position of women in politics and the workforce in the EU is little different (overall) from their relative position in the United States, but the situation varies from one member state to another, giving added significance to EU social policy and the goal of building economic and social cohesion. Very generally, women are in a better situation in progressive northern European states such as Denmark, Finland, and Sweden and are relatively worse off in poorer southern states such as Portugal, Spain, and Greece.

Women make up about one-third of the workforce in the EU. Career options are still relatively limited, proportionately more women than men are employed in part-time jobs, and women are more likely to work in traditionally feminized jobs—such as nursing and teaching—than in management and are also more likely to work in the less well-paid and more labor-intensive sectors of industry.[1] Like their U.S. counterparts, European women are also paid less than men for comparable work—about 80 cents on the dollar. On the credit side of the ledger, about 75 percent of working women are employed in the expanding service sector, every EU member state is legally obliged to provide maternity leave, several member states offer parental leave, and the public provision of child care is improving.

Although the rights of working women were mentioned in the Treaty of Rome (Article 119, for example, establishes the principle of equal pay for men and women), it was not until the EC began to more actively examine social policy in the 1970s that women's issues began to be addressed. The 1974 SAP included the goal of achieving gender equality in access to employment and vocational training, and equal rights at work were promoted by new EC laws such as the 1975 Equal Pay Directive and the 1976 Equal Treatment Directive. Even though direct and indirect gender discrimination is illegal under EU law, however, women still face the same kinds of invisible barriers and glass ceilings in the EU as they do in the United States.

The Single European Act and Maastricht were both concerned more with broad institutional reform than with human rights, and they did little in specific terms to address gender imbalances. Beverly Springer has argued that the single market may actually pose a threat both to the jobs women hold and the laws that protect them. Little was done in the planning stages to anticipate how the changes would affect women, and not all of the proposals made under the SAPs or related Commission White Papers have the force of law; thus compliance is voluntary.[2]

The elitism and gender biases of the EU are exemplified by the obvious imbalances in the staffing of the major EU institutions. The first woman appointed to the Commission was Vasso Papandreou of Greece in 1991 (although five of the twenty commissioners who took office in 1995 were women); there are many more men in the senior bureaucratic positions within the Commission and many more women in secretarial and clerical positions; the 1989–1994 European Parliament had only one hundred women MEPs (just over 19 percent of the total); there has never been a woman on the Court of Justice; and only two women—Margaret Thatcher and former French Prime Minister Édith Cresson—have ever taken part in meetings of the European Council.

Notes

1. Beverly Springer, *The Social Dimension of 1992: Europe Faces a New EC* (Westport, Conn.: Praeger, 1992), 66.
2. Ibid., 72–73.

Restrictions began to be eased so that labor shortages in the larger northern economies could be filled. This led to an influx of immigrants from southern Europe, although most of these came from non-EC states such as Turkey, Yugoslavia, Greece, Portugal, and Spain. There were an estimated 4 million foreign workers in the twelve EU member states by the early 1990s, of which about half came from other EU states (see Table 14.1).

The widening of the gap in economic conditions brought on by enlargement in 1973 pushed social issues back up the agenda, and the first in a series of four-year **Social Action Programmes** (SAPs) was launched in 1974, aimed at developing a plan of action to achieve full employment, improved living and working conditions, and gender equality. A combination of recession and ideological resistance from several European leaders ensured that the words failed to be translated into deeds, but the EEC did establish the European Social Fund in 1974, aimed at helping to combat long-term unemployment and creating jobs and training schemes for young people. Spending under the ESF grew rapidly during the 1980s; the major recipients were Ireland, Portugal, Greece, and Spain (see Table 14.2). The ESF now accounts for about 7 percent of the EU budget (or nearly 6 billion ECUs).

The Single European Act again underlined the importance of social policy by raising questions about the mobility of workers (one of the goals of the SEA was to make it possible for Europeans to live and work wherever they liked in the Community) and bringing up concerns about "social dumping" (money, services, and businesses moving to those parts of the EU with the lowest wages and social security costs). The Commission began promoting social policy more actively, trying to focus the attention of national governments on the "social dimension" of the single market. But economic recession ensured that the SEA initially lacked a social dimension, which encouraged Jacques Delors—a moderate socialist—to launch an attempt in 1988 to draw more attention to the social consequences of the single market.

The idea of a charter of basic social rights had been introduced by the Belgian presidency of the Council of Ministers in 1987, modeled on Belgium's new national charter. The concept was taken up by Jacques Delors in 1989 and was helped by the determination of the socialist government of François Mitterrand to promote social policy during the French presidency of the EC. Germany was also in favor—even though it was led by the moderate conservative government of Helmut Kohl—as were states with socialist governments, such as Spain and Greece. By contrast, the conservative Margaret Thatcher was enthusiastically opposed; she considered it "quite inappropriate" for laws on working regulations and welfare benefits to be set at the Community level and saw the Social Charter as "a socialist charter—devised by socialists in the Commission and favoured predominantly by socialist member states."[18] In the event, the Charter of the

TABLE 14.1 European Union Citizens Living in Another Member State

Nationals of	Belgium 1988	Denmark 1988	Germany 1988	Greece 1987	Spain 1982	France 1988	Ireland 1988	Italy 1988	Luxembourg 1988	Netherlands 1988	Portugal 1988	United Kingdom 1985–1987
B	—	283	17,854	1,233	9,730	50,200	—	3,674	—	22,942	910	—
DK	2,094	—	12,519	1,123	5,451	2,440	—	1,110	—	1,298	348	—
D	24,304	6,320	—	10,693	39,066	43,840	—	24,517	—	39,400	4,133	43,000
GR	19,075	461	274,793	—	606	7,860	—	11,774	—	3,953	51	13,000
E	50,187	875	126,402	906	—	321,440	—	6,841	—	17,578	7,105	30,000
F	92,322	1,853	71,773	6,268	23,599	—	—	17,118	13,200	7,496	2,803	28,000
IRL	1,318	930	8,360	529	684	1,880	—	1,037	—	3,103	199	532,000
I	250,209	2,006	508,656	6,418	13,025	333,740	—	—	—	15,890	1,060	75,000
L	4,948	16	4,542	43	—	3,180	—	223	—	381	26	20,000
NL	60,825	1,763	96,881	2,685	13,821	13,980	—	4,405	20,450	—	1,546	13,000
P	10,554	272	71,068	336	31,012	764,860	—	1,936	32,900	7,766	—	—
UK	21,000	10,096	83,010	16,093	65,318	34,180	—	17,209	—	37,094	7,115	—
EUR 12	536,836	24,875	1,275,858	46,327	202,312	1,577,600	66,400	89,844	—	156,901	25,296	754,000
EUR 12 and in Third Countries	858,650	136,177	4,489,105	155,187	334,935	3,680,100	83,500	407,023	—	591,847	94,453	1,785,000

Source: Commission of the European Communities, A People's Europe (Luxembourg: Office for Official Publications of the European Communities, 1992).

TABLE 14.2   Spending Under the European Social Fund, 1981–1992
(in million ECUs; ranked by spending per capita)

	1981	1984	1987	1990	1992	Spending Per Capita 1992 (ECUs)
Ireland	60.4	131.4	247.4	204.4	298.9	85.40
Portugal	—	—	190.5	69.5	506.0	51.42
Greece	6.6	71.3	151.9	303.2	258.4	25.08
Spain	—	—	311.5	633.9	814.6	20.83
United Kingdom	195.4	610.2	595.1	608.3	676.8	11.62
France	155.3	225.7	406.1	442.9	549.0	9.51
Belgium	15.3	52.1	56.5	51.8	88.9	8.80
Italy	207.1	368.5	539.2	419.5	384.2	6.73
Luxembourg	0.6	0.5	1.7	3.4	2.3	5.89
Denmark	18.5	68.7	31.7	38.3	25.5	4.92
Netherlands	14.3	14.1	52.1	68.8	73.5	4.84
Germany	72.3	63.8	131.6	186.4	326.9	4.04
Total	745.8	1,606.3	2,715.3	3,030.4	4,005.0	11.52

Source: Annual reports of the Court of Auditors; final column: author calculations.

Fundamental Social Rights of Workers (or the **Social Charter**) was adopted at the 1989 Strasbourg summit by eleven of the twelve member states—all but Britain.

The Social Charter brought together all of the social policy goals that had been mentioned throughout the life of the Community, including freedom of movement, improved living and working conditions, vocational training, gender equality, and protection for children, the elderly, and the handicapped, but it was heavy on feel-good goals and light on specifics. An action program listed forty-seven separate measures that needed to be taken to achieve the goals of the Charter, but the challenge of reaching unanimity on social legislation in the Council of Ministers meant very little progress was made on turning principles into law. Britain is usually painted as the major opponent of the Social Charter, but there has been heated debate involving several member states over issues such as working hours, maternity leave, and employment benefits for part-time workers.

Maastricht included a social chapter and provided for more qualified majority voting on social policy, but Britain refused to go along with this chapter. The compromise reached was to exclude Britain from voting in the Council on social issues and for the other eleven member states to form an ad hoc Social Community. Not only do questions remain about the extent to which social goals can be met, but Britain's exclusion splits the EU and undermines the goal of building a true single market.

272

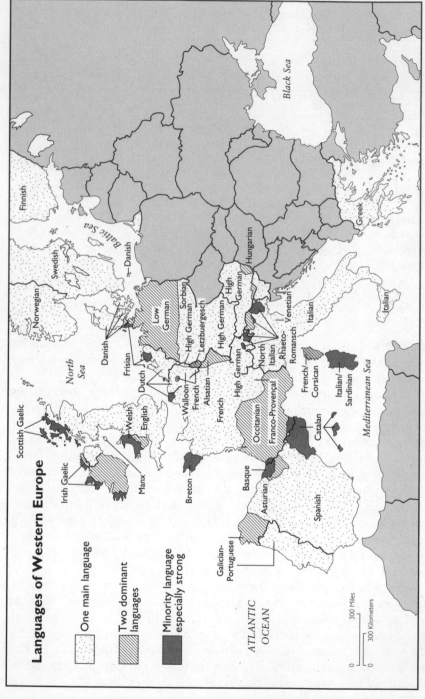

Languages of Western Europe

One main language

Two dominant languages

Minority language especially strong

Source: Based on map in Viktor Keegan and Martin Kettle (Eds.), *The New Europe* (London: Fourth Estate, 1993), p. 92.

Education and Language: Building Worker Mobility

Maastricht made education and youth training a new part of EU activity, allowing the EU to become more involved in encouraging educational exchanges and addressing the knotty problem of language training. Language differences pose a barrier to the free movement of workers, and member states are taking more steps to encourage educational exchanges and training in second and even third languages. These steps include the following:

- ERASMUS, a program to encourage student and faculty exchanges among colleges and universities and to make it easier for students to transfer credits. (Since 1991, degrees or diplomas awarded by any institution of higher education in the EU after three years of study are automatically recognized in all the member states.) More than fifty thousand students have taken advantage of ERASMUS since it was launched in 1987.

- LINGUA is a program that encourages training in second and third languages, TEMPUS is a program to link universities in the United States and Western and Eastern Europe by promoting joint research projects, COMETT is a program that encourages universities and industry to work together on training projects, and PETRA is a program aimed at modernizing vocational training.

The EU now has eleven official languages: Danish, Dutch, English, Finnish, French, German, Greek, Italian, Portuguese, Spanish, and Swedish. Almost all EU business is conducted in English and French, although Germany is eager to ensure that German is not forgotten. One of the consequences of an eastward expansion of the EU will be an increase in the number of Europeans who speak German, which will alter the linguistic balance of power. Almost all secondary school pupils in the EU learn at least one foreign language, but the record varies from one state to another. The British have the worst record, but they have been spoiled by the steady growth of English as the international language of commerce and entertainment and by the fact that a growing number of continental Europeans speak English; more than 90 percent of secondary school pupils in Germany, Spain, the Netherlands, and Denmark learn English as a second language. Meanwhile, only 33 percent of Italian pupils and 23 percent of German pupils are learning French.[19]

The issue of language cuts to the very core of cultural pride and particularly upsets the French, who have done everything they can to stop the perfidious spread of "franglais"—the common use of English words in French, such as *le jumbo jet* (officially *le gros porteur*) and *le fast food* (officially *pret-à-manger*). In an attempt to prevent any one language from winning out over the others, suggestions have been made for all Europeans to learn Esperanto—an artificial language developed in 1887—or even for Latin to be revived. Despite the number of EU employees who work as translators, the publication of every EU document in all eleven official languages, and the attempts by France to stave off the inroads made by English and Anglo-American culture, it seems almost inevitable that English—with the help of U.S. and Japanese business—will continue its steady trend toward becoming the common language of Europe, presenting the French, so to speak, with a fait accompli.

Summary and Conclusions

At the heart of the process of European integration has been a continuing debate about the kinds of policy issues that are best dealt with jointly and those that are best left to the member states. Environmental and social policy provide good examples of the kinds of issues that must be addressed in that debate.

In the case of the environment, there is little question that international cooperation is both desirable and inevitable. Problems such as air and water pollution ignore national boundaries, and there are repeated examples from around the world of one state being a producer of pollution and other states downwind or downriver being the recipients. As construction proceeds on the global economy, a new dimension is added by the barriers different environmental standards pose to trade. There will always be strong ideological disagreements about the extent to which the state should manage natural resources and regulate industry, but there is a strong internal logic to international cooperation on environmental management. A consensus is emerging that holds that the EU has been a progressive force in environmental protection and that European environmental problems are better dealt with at the EU level than at the national or the local level.

Much less agreement is found on the role of the EU in social policy. There is little question that among the foundations of a workable single market are equal pay, equal working conditions, and the provision of the kind of education and training that can help promote worker mobility. But social policy treads on sensitive ideological and cultural toes; conservatives and socialists will never agree on the best way to build a level social playing field, and programs that may be seen as progressive by one member state may be seen as a threat to cultural identity by another.

Notes

1. Ronald Inglehart, *The Silent Revolution: Changing Values and Political Styles Among Western Publics* (Princeton: Princeton University Press, 1977).

2. Daniel P. McGrory, "Air Pollution Legislation in the United States and the European Community," *European Law Review* 15:4 (August 1990), 304.

3. See chapter 3 in John McCormick, *Reclaiming Paradise: The Global Environmental Movement* (Bloomington: Indiana University Press, 1989).

4. *Commission v. Italy* (Case 91/79), in Court of Justice of the European Communities, *Reports of Cases Before the Court*, 1980.

5. Philipp M. Hildebrand, "The European Community's Environmental Policy, 1957 to '1992': From Incidental Measures to an International Regime?" in David Judge (Ed.), *A Green Dimension for the European Community: Political Issues and Processes* (London: Frank Cass, 1993), 20–22.

6. Eckard Rehbinder and Richard Steward (Eds.), *Environmental Protection Policy, Vol 2—Integration Through Law: Europe and the American Federal Experience* (Firenze, Italy: European University Institute, 1985), 19.

7. Quoted in Tamara Raye Crockett and Cynthia B. Schultz, "The Integration of Environmental Policy and the European Community: Recent Problems of Implementation and Enforcement," *Columbia Journal of Transnational Law* 29:1 (1991), 169–191; Commission of the European Communities, *Environmental Policy in the European Community* (Luxembourg: Office for Official Publications of the European Communities, 1990), 21.

8. David A. Westbrook, "Environmental Policy in the European Community: Observations on the European Environment Agency," *Harvard Environmental Law Review* 15:1 (1991), 257–273.

9. Ken Collins and David Earnshaw, "The Implementation and Enforcement of European Community Environment Legislation," in Judge (Ed.), *A Green Dimension for the European Community*, 213; Richard Macrory, "The Enforcement of Community Environmental Laws: Some Critical Issues," *Common Market Law Review* 29 (1992), 347–369.

10. Crockett and Schultz, "Integration of Environmental Policy."

11. Collins and Earnshaw, "Implementation and Enforcement," 219–220.

12. See, for example, Nigel Haigh, *EEC Environmental Policy and Britain*, 2d ed. (Harlow, Essex: Longman, 1990); and David Freestone, "European Community Environmental Policy and Law," *Journal of Law and Society* 18:1 (Spring 1991), 135–154.

13. Eric Ashby and Mary Anderson, *The Politics of Clean Air* (Oxford: Clarendon Press, 1981); and Derek Elsom, *Atmospheric Pollution* (Oxford: Basil Blackwell, 1987).

14. David Vogel, *National Styles of Regulation* (Ithaca: Cornell University Press, 1986), 101.

15. Commission of the European Communities, *Environmental Policy*, 31.

16. Sonia Mazey and Jeremy Richardson, "Environmental Groups and the EC: Challenges and Opportunities," in Judge (Ed.), *A Green Dimension for the European Community*.

17. This definition is based on the one given by Peter Lange, "The Politics of the Social Dimension," in Alberta Sbragia (Ed.), *Euro-Politics: Institutions and Policymaking in the "New" European Community* (Washington, D.C.: Brookings Institution, 1992), 229–230.

18. Margaret Thatcher, *The Downing Street Years* (New York: HarperCollins, 1993), 750.

19. Eurostat figures, quoted in *The Economist,* January 14, 1995.

Further Reading

David Judge (Ed.). *A Green Dimension for the European Community: Political Issues and Processes* (London: Frank Cass, 1993).

A collection of essays on the evolution, nature, and consequences of EU environmental policy.

J. Duncan Liefferink, Philip Lowe, and Arthur Mol (Eds.). *European Integration and Environmental Policy* (London: Belhaven, 1993).

An edited collection of studies on EU environmental policymaking, the global implications of EU policy, and national responses to European environmental integration.

Michael Gold. *The Social Dimension: Employment Policy in the European Community* (London: Macmillan, 1993).

A study of employment policy in the EU and its implications for social policy.

Beverly Springer. *The Social Dimension of 1992: Europe Faces a New EC* (Westport, Conn.: Praeger, 1992).

A look at social policy in the EU, with an emphasis on the underlying goals and possible consequences of the Single European Act.

Sonia Mazey and Jeremy Richardson (Eds.). *Lobbying in the EC* (Oxford: Oxford University Press, 1993).

An edited set of studies on the growth and consequences of lobbying in the EU.

15

Foreign and Security Policy

The crisis set off by the Iraqi invasion of Kuwait in August 1990 dragged European foreign policy into the harsh light of day and found it wanting. Although the Community quickly condemned the invasion, agreed on an oil embargo against Iraq, and supported UN sanctions, its members were torn between taking military action and pursuing a diplomatic response.

Britain strongly favored using force, and Margaret Thatcher apparently played a key role in convincing George Bush of the merits of a rapid counterattack. Britain placed its troops under U.S. operational command, and at the height of the war that followed, its military commitment was second only to that of the United States: 35,000 troops, sixty warplanes, and fifteen naval vessels.

France also made a large military commitment, with 12,500 troops, forty warplanes, and fourteen naval vessels, but it placed more emphasis on a diplomatic resolution. France has long been concerned about keeping good relations with Arab oil producers, placating its 4 million Arab immigrants, and protecting its weapons markets (the only non-Soviet warplanes flown by the Iraqis were French Mirage jets). In the weeks leading up to the allied counterattack in January 1991, France tried to pursue independent peace negotiations with Iraq, hoping to tie a cease-fire to a conference on broader Arab problems.

Germany was constrained by a strong postwar tradition of pacifism, a vocal antiwar movement, and constitutional limits on the deployment of the German military, which could not operate outside NATO states. The war set off a lively debate about what Germany should or should not do; it compromised by sending minesweepers to the Gulf and providing financial support for the war, giving the United States $6.5 billion and Britain $500 million.

Italy made a small naval and air force commitment (ten ships and eight warplanes) and—along with Germany and Belgium—sent fighter-bombers to Turkey to discourage an Iraqi attack. Belgium, Spain, the Netherlands, Denmark, Greece, and Portugal together sent sixteen naval vessels. Out of fear of retribution, however, Belgium refused to sell ammunition to Britain and—along with Spain and Portugal—would not allow its naval vessels to be involved in anything other than minesweeping or enforcing the blockade of Iraq. Luxembourg made a financial contribution, and Ireland maintained its neutrality.[1]

For some, the response to the Gulf crisis emphasized everything that was wrong with the logic behind hopes of building a common European foreign policy. For Jacques Delors, the war provided "an object lesson" on the limitations of the EC;[2] Luxembourg Foreign Minister Jacques Poos complained that the EC response had underlined "the political insignificance of Europe"; Belgian Foreign Minister Mark Eyskens felt the response showed the EC was "an economic giant, a political dwarf, and a military worm."[3] Others felt the crisis had simply caught the Community unprepared and argued that it emphasized the urgency of developing common foreign and security policies to complement and back up the EC's economic power.

In fairness, foreign policy was a latecomer to the agenda of European integration. The Treaties of Rome made no mention of foreign policy, and European integration had long focused on economic goals, although the logic of spillover implied that it would be difficult for the EC to avoid developing common external economic and security policies for long. The task has been complicated by the different national agendas of the member states. The most fundamental division is that between Atlanticists (such as Britain, the Netherlands, and Portugal), who emphasize the importance of their relationship with the United States, and Europeanists (such as France and sometimes Germany), who look more toward European independence. Both Britain and France, meanwhile, have special interests in their former colonies, while Germany has an interest in building links with Eastern Europe. Ireland, Sweden, and Finland want to maintain their neutrality.

Although the Gulf War, the Balkans problem, and other security crises have found the EU unprepared and lacking both political unanimity and military preparedness, the EU *has* made progress toward developing a common foreign policy. As Christopher Hill put it, setbacks have produced renewed efforts at policy cooperation, which has followed a pattern of "peaks and troughs along a gradual upward gradient . . . [and] consensus has become more habit-forming."[4] From a time when the focus of integration was limited mainly to economic issues and Western Europe found itself mainly a bystander in the cold war, the EU has exerted new influence on international political relations.

There has been a steady convergence of positions among the member states on key bilateral relations and external economic relations, helped by the facts that the EU ambassadors to the United Nations meet every week to coordinate their positions and the EU states vote together on about 75 percent of UN Security Council votes (the EU also holds two of the five permanent seats on the Security Council). The development of common positions has often forced the EU to flex its economic muscle to political ends. In 1987, for example, the EC refused to conclude trade agreements with Israel in protest of its policy on Palestinian agricultural exports, it cut all aid to China in 1989 to protest the Tiananmen Square massacre, and it blocked $1 billion in aid to the USSR in 1991 in protest over a crackdown on proindependence groups in the Baltic states.

The EU also coordinates Western aid to Eastern Europe and the former Soviet Union, has become a major supplier of aid to developing countries, and has been a magnet for foreign investment from the United States and Japan. The president of the Commission attends meetings of the G-7 alongside the leaders of the seven most industrialized countries (four of which are member states of the EU). The significance of the EU as an actor on the global stage is reflected in the facts that almost every country in the world has diplomats accredited to Brussels and the EU is treated, for all intents and purposes, as a sovereign state. The Commission, meanwhile, has opened more than 110 overseas delegations.

Foreign Policy Cooperation: From EPC to CFSP

There were several stillborn attempts to build common foreign and security policies in the early years of integration, including the European Defence Community, the European Political Community, and de Gaulle's plans for regular meetings of leaders of the Six to coordinate foreign policy. The 1969 Hague summit not only agreed on enlarging the Community but also encouraged the six foreign ministers to explore the best way of moving toward political unification. They agreed in 1970 to promote **European Political Co-operation**, or cooperation on foreign policy, but this was to occur on a purely intergovernmental basis. Under the Davignon Procedure (named for Etienne Davignon, a senior Belgian foreign ministry official), foreign ministers were to meet at least twice each year—and their senior officials at least four times each year—to coordinate national positions. They eventually began meeting monthly. No new institutions were to be created, although the European Council was launched in 1974—in part to bring leaders together to coordinate policies.

EPC was originally concerned more with *how* foreign policy should be agreed on than with *what* that policy should be.[5] The need to develop common positions was helped by the Conference on Security and Cooperation in Europe (CSCE), officially created with the signing of the Helsinki Final Act in August 1975. Less a body than a process that encourages cooperation on specific "issue areas" (such as science, human rights, and the environment), the CSCE had fifty-two member states in 1995, including the United States, Canada, all of Europe, and the former USSR. EC member

states acted as a group in the CSCE and subsequently consulted with each other on virtually every aspect of foreign policy. They remained reluctant to give up too many of their independent powers, however. EPC was given formal recognition with the Single European Act, which said under Title III that the member states would "endeavour jointly to formulate and implement a European foreign policy." However, this was not incorporated into the founding treaties: EPC remained a loose and voluntary arrangement, no laws were passed on foreign policy, each of the member states could still act independently, and most of the key decisions on foreign policy had to be arrived at unanimously.

The main goal of EPC was to coordinate the foreign policies of the member states on the basis that the EU as a whole could achieve much more than its individual members could do acting independently. The EPC process was overseen by the foreign ministers meeting as the Council of Ministers, with

BOX 15.1
The EU and the Balkans

The outbreak of a civil war on Europe's back porch in 1991 provided another demanding test of the EU's foreign policy capacity. Critics charge that it failed the test, but the crisis forced an accelerated development of EU foreign policy, and—in fairness—the EU was neither politically nor militarily prepared for a crisis of such proportions. Ironically, the fact that the EU has been so strongly criticized by the United States for its weak response suggests how much is now expected of the Union as a political entity. There is another irony in the fact that no other outside actor is as widely trusted as an arbiter, yet the EU lacks the power to impose order on the Balkans.[1]

The creation of Yugoslavia was one of the outcomes of World War I and brought together several independent states whose internal ethnic, religious, and nationalist tensions were kept in check after World War II only by the power of the Tito regime (1944–1980). The end of the cold war brought those tensions into the open, resulting in the June 1991 declaration of independence by Slovenia and Croatia. When Bosnia too seemed about to declare its independence, Bosnian Serbs attacked in April 1992. In May 1993, fighting broke out in Bosnia between Croats and Muslims over historically Croat-controlled territory.

The initial EC position was to try to keep Yugoslavia intact, but under German pressure it recognized Slovenia and Croatia in January 1992, thus undermining its credibility with the Serbs. The EC then tried—without success—to broker cease-fires (sending negotiators such as Lord Carrington and Lord Owen, both former British foreign secretaries). It also sent unarmed monitors to attempt to keep the warring factions apart, imposed sanctions on Serbia, supported an embargo on arms sales to Bosnian Muslims in hopes of reducing hostilities, and contributed most of the UN peacekeeping forces deployed in the area. Ambivalence on both sides of the Atlantic regarding response to the Bosnian civil war led to one of the most serious disagreements that had ever occurred between the United States and its European NATO allies.

Although the Balkans are on Europe's front doorstep, they represent a political quagmire into which the EU has been reluctant to step. Despite the obvious attempts by Serbs to expand Serbia and to eradicate Bosnia's Muslims, the EU was concerned about becoming directly involved in the hostilities and about the implications of Russia's traditional historical ties with the Serbs. At the same time, the EU faced political pressure to address the flagrant disregard for human rights in the conflict and to assuage charges by Muslim states that it was biased. The NATO air strikes against Serbs were dangerous because of possible retaliation against UN peacekeeping forces, nearly three-fourths of which were French and British. Finally, there was little agreement on which of several international actors should provide leadership: the UN, the EU, the CSCE, NATO, or the WEU. Geoffrey Edwards has argued that the EU has shown greater unity over the Balkan crisis than it did over the 1990–1991 Gulf crisis,[2] but the core of that "unity" has been uncertainty about the best action to take.

Notes

1. Christopher Hill, "EPC's Performance in Crises," in Reinhardt Rummel (Ed.), *Toward Political Union: Planning a Common Foreign and Security Policy in the European Community* (Boulder: Westview Press, 1992), 145.

2. Geoffrey Edwards, "European Responses to the Yugoslav Crisis: An Interim Assessment," in Rummel, *Toward Political Union.*

overall leadership coming from the European Council. The Commission was originally excluded from the meetings but is now represented at them all. Continuity was provided by regular meetings of senior officials from all the foreign ministries, and a small secretariat was set up in Brussels to help the country holding the presidency of the Council of Ministers, which tended to provide most of the momentum. Larger and more active states such as Britain and France have had few problems providing that momentum, but policy coordination puts a strain on smaller and/or neutral countries such as Luxembourg and Ireland. The shifting of responsibilities every six months gives each member state its turn at the helm but complicates life for non-EU states, which have to switch their attention from one member state to another and establish contacts with ministers and bureaucrats in fifteen capitals.

One underlying question raised again by the Gulf War was whether common EU policies should extend to defense. Defense had been pushed down the agenda by the emphasis on economic policies, the failure of the European Defence Community, the very different policies and capacities of the member states, the neutrality of member states such as Ireland, and the fact that for many years the main defense issue was security against a Soviet attack—something that fell squarely under NATO's brief. A common defense policy would also be largely meaningless without a European army.

The Maastricht treaty noted that one of the goals of the EU was "to assert its identity on the international scene, in particular through the implementation of a common foreign and security policy which shall include the eventual framing of a common defence policy." The **Common Foreign and Security Policy** became one of three pillars that now make up the European Union, and defense was finally pushed more squarely onto the EU agenda. Although decisionmaking is still loosely structured, the CFSP gives more direction to foreign policy, committing the member states to define and implement a common policy that would "include all questions related to the security of the Union, including the eventual framing of a common defence policy, which might in time lead to a common defence." The goals of the CFSP are very loosely defined, with vague talk about defending "common values" and "fundamental interests," but the CFSP is based around systematic cooperation among the member states, with the European Council agreeing on common positions when necessary.

The EU will continue to work with one arm tied behind its back on foreign policy until it can back up its words with the threat of military force. Together, the fifteen member states amount to a formidable force; they have more than 2 million troops, 22,000 tanks, 21,000 artillery pieces, and 6,300 combat aircraft, which among them make up 85 to 95 percent of the NATO capability in Europe.[6] But there is still relatively little coordination on policy. Some of the obstacles to the development of a European military

BOX 15.2
The Western European Union

The WEU was founded in 1954 in the wake of the collapse of the European Defence Community. It originally consisted of the six members of the ECSC and Britain and was an attempt to help Germany contribute to the defense of Western Europe without taking part in the kind of European army envisioned by the EDC. With the United States playing a key role in Europe's postwar defense, however, the WEU was quickly overshadowed by NATO. As one diplomat put it, the WEU became "a place where you found jobs for retired Italian admirals."[1] But the WEU was revived in 1984 following the failure of a plan to give EPC a security dimension.[2] It passed its first modest test in 1987 when it coordinated minesweeping by its members in the Persian Gulf during the Iran-Iraq War. The 1990–1991 Gulf War stretched the WEU beyond its limits, though, revealing the cracks in the edifices of both the WEU and NATO.

With a secretariat in Brussels (where it was moved from London in 1993) and a ministerial council and consultative assembly in Paris, the WEU hosts biannual meetings of the foreign and defense ministers of its member states, which include Belgium, Britain, France, Germany, Greece, Italy, Luxembourg, the Netherlands, Portugal, and Spain; Ireland and Denmark are observers. As a possible foundation for the development of a true European defense capability, the WEU has several advantages:

- It already exists, so no new organizational machinery is needed.
- It could be used by Europeans to develop their own defense policies independent of the United States.
- It can operate outside its member states (unlike NATO, which is technically limited to the territory of its member states).
- It provides a useful means of building bridges between the EU and its neighbors (Iceland, Norway, and Turkey are associate members).
- Not all EU member states are members of the WEU, so countries such as Ireland, Finland, and Sweden can be members of the EU while preserving their neutrality.

Despite these advantages, opinion is divided over what to do with the WEU. François Mitterrand and Helmut Kohl announced in 1990 that they felt it should be upgraded. Britain agreed but thought it should become the European pillar of, rather than a replacement for, NATO. The WEU's own secretary-general, Willem van Eekelen, felt it was destined in the long-term to be absorbed into the EU.[3] The United States, meanwhile, has been concerned about the implications for NATO,[4] and sees the WEU as complicating attempts to build trans-European security arrangements under the CSCE or NATO's Partnership for Peace program (see Figure 15.1).

Notes

1. *The Economist*, February 2, 1991.

2. Willem van Eekelen, "WEU and the Gulf Crisis," *Survival* 32:6 (November–December 1990), 519–532.

3. *The Economist*, February 2, 1991.

4. Anand Menon, Anthony Forster, and William Wallace, "A Common European Defense?" *Survival* 34:3 (Autumn 1992), 98–118.

FIGURE 15.1 Overlapping Security Alliances in Europe

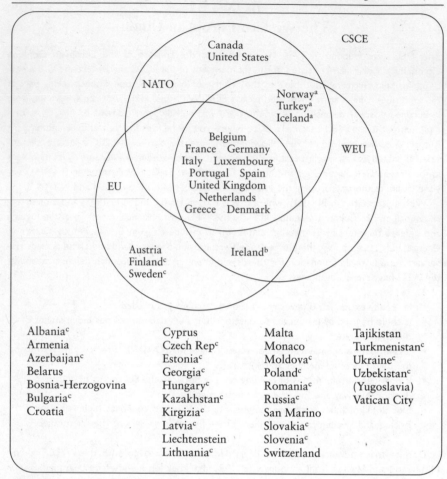

Canada
United States

CSCE

NATO

Norway[a]
Turkey[a]
Iceland[a]

Belgium
France Germany
Italy Luxembourg
Portugal Spain
United Kingdom
Netherlands
Greece Denmark

WEU

EU

Austria
Finland[c]
Sweden[c]

Ireland[b]

Albania[c]	Cyprus	Malta	Tajikistan
Armenia	Czech Rep[c]	Monaco	Turkmenistan[c]
Azerbaijan[c]	Estonia[c]	Moldova[c]	Ukraine[c]
Belarus	Georgia[c]	Poland[c]	Uzbekistan[c]
Bosnia-Herzogovina	Hungary[c]	Romania[c]	(Yugoslavia)
Bulgaria[c]	Kazakhstan[c]	Russia[c]	Vatican City
Croatia	Kirgizia[c]	San Marino	
	Latvia[c]	Slovakia[c]	
	Liechtenstein	Slovenia[c]	
	Lithuania[c]	Switzerland	

[a]WEU associate member.
[b]WEU observer.
[c]Member of the NATO Partnership for Peace program.

were cleared by Maastricht, which also helped revive the long-moribund Western European Union (see Box 15.2). Article J.4 argues that the WEU is an integral part of the EU, that it should "elaborate and implement decisions and actions" of the EU that have defense implications, and that it will be "developed as the defence component of the European Union and as the means to strengthen the European pillar of the Atlantic Alliance."

Another route to the development of a common European military may lie with the **Eurocorps,** created in May 1992 by Germany and France to replace an experimental Franco-German brigade set up in 1990. Headquartered in Strasbourg, the 35,000-member Eurocorps was conceived as a step toward the development of a European army that was to give substance to the CFSP and give the EU an independent defense capability. Germany insists that Eurocorps would complement NATO and that it would be placed under NATO "operational command" in the event of a threat to Western European security, but Britain, the Netherlands, and the United States suspect that France's objective is to displace the U.S. dominance of NATO. Britain would prefer to have Eurocorps operate under the auspices of the WEU, while France apparently prefers to see the WEU and Eurocorps as the seeds of an EU defense wing and to have the WEU eventually merge with the EU.

External Economic Relations

If many questions remain about the EU's military and political power, there are very few about its economic power (see Tables 15.1 and 15.2):

- The EU is the world's largest economic bloc; with just 6.4 percent of the world's population, it accounts for 34 percent of world GDP, 42 percent of imports, and 42 percent of exports.

- Intra-EU trade has grown and now accounts for nearly 60 percent of all EU trade.

- Given that Russia and Eastern Europe account for about 7 percent of EU imports and exports and that there is huge potential for the growth of Eastern European markets, developments in those countries will continue to be critical for the European economy.

- Asia, Africa, and Latin America account for one-third of EU trade, and the rise of newly industrializing countries will increase that pro portion.

The EU is unquestionably an economic superpower, but its external economic policies have caused concern among some of its major trading partners. Article 110 of the EEC Treaty outlined a **Common Commercial Policy** (CCP) based on the principle that the Community would contribute "to the harmonious development of world trade, the progressive abolition of restrictions on international trade, and the lowering of customs barriers." The CCP was not finally put in place until the completion of the single market; meanwhile, the EC's position on global trade negotiations and its focus on internal economic issues had led to talk about a "Fortress Europe," par-

TABLE 15.1 The EU Share of World Trade

	Share of World Imports (%)			Change (%)	Share of World Exports (%)			Change (%)
	1970	1980	1992	1970–1992	1970	1980	1992	1970–1992
European Union	40.8	41.0	42.6	+1223	40.7	37.3	42.1	+1227
EEC[a]	27.1	35.0	39.4		28.3	32.9	38.8	
NAFTA	17.8	16.4	18.8	+1239	19.5	15.4	16.4	+997
United States	13.0	12.6	14.4		13.9	11.3	12.0	
Soviet bloc[b]	10.1	8.2	3.6[c]	+301	14.5	12.1	4.9[c]	+321
Japan	5.8	6.9	6.1	+1237	6.2	6.5	9.1	+1762
Rest of world	25.5	27.5	28.9		19.1	28.7	27.5	
World total	100.0	100.0	100.0	+1172	100.0	100.0	100.0	+1186

[a]Six members in 1970, nine in 1980, twelve in 1992.
[b]Former USSR, Bulgaria, Czechoslovakia, East Germany, Hungary, Poland, Romania, and Yugoslavia.
[c]Figures for 1991.

Source: Calculated from figures in millions of U.S. dollars in United Nations, 1992 International Trade Statistics Yearbook (New York: United Nations, 1993), Special Table A.

TABLE 15.2   The EU in the Global Economy

	Population 1993 (millions)	Share of World (%)	GDP 1991 ($US billion)	Share of World GDP (%)	Per Capita GDP ($US)[a]
Luxembourg	0.39	0.006	9.34	0.04	21,356
Belgium	10.10	0.2	196.87	1.0	17,655
Sweden	8.72	0.1	236.95	1.2	17,541
France	57.70	1.0	1,199.29	6.0	17,386
Denmark	5.18	0.1	130.29	0.7	17,348
Netherlands	15.20	0.3	290.72	1.5	16,648
Austria	7.92	0.1	163.99	0.8	16,566
Finland	5.04	0.1	124.54	0.6	16,522
Germany	80.90	1.4	1,686.56	8.5	16,335
Italy	57.10	1.0	1,150.56	5.8	15,848
United Kingdom	58.20	1.0	978.19	4.9	15,548
Spain	39.10	0.7	482.85	2.4	12,372
Ireland	3.50	0.06	43.59	0.2	11,753
Portugal	9.84	0.2	68.61	0.3	9,115
Greece	10.30	0.2	70.57	0.4	8,237
EU Total	369.19	6.4	6,832.92	34.3	—
United States	258.16	4.5	5,610.80	28.3	22,219
Canada	27.56	0.5	582.01	2.9	20,619
Mexico	88.60	1.5	286.63	1.4	6,917
NAFTA Total	374.32	6.5	6,479.44	32.6	—
Japan	125.90	2.2	3,346.41	16.9	19,042
Russia	148.40	2.6	745.47	3.8	5,012
China	1,222.56	21.2	370.85	1.9	2,982
World Total	5,770.29	100.0	19,822.23	100.0	—

[a]All per capita GDP figures except for Russia are based on purchasing power parity.
Source: Population figures from Economist Intelligence Unit quarterly reports 1994; GDP and per capita GDP figures from United Nations, *Statistical Yearbook 1992* (New York: United Nations, 1994).

ticularly by U.S. political and corporate leaders who were concerned about both the implications of the single market and the EC's unwillingness to cut agricultural subsidies as part of the negotiations under GATT. Some commentators, however, hold that charges of protectionism are unfounded and that the creation of the single market in particular has led to the reduction of both internal *and* external barriers to trade.[7]

All the EU states are members of the World Trade Organization, although negotiations on behalf of the EU have been conducted by the European

Commission. Founded as GATT in 1948, the WTO oversees international negotiations aimed at bringing down the barriers to trade. It has done this through successive rounds of negotiations over a period of several years, the lengthiest and most contentious of which was the Uruguay Round, which opened in 1986. This round began with 92 countries but incorporated 112 by the time it was concluded. The Community had been involved in several earlier rounds of GATT negotiations, but the Uruguay Round was particularly controversial because it was expanded to include agricultural trade, thereby posing a direct challenge to the most protectionist of the Community policy areas.

Led by the United States, the Community's major trading partners insisted on cuts of 90 percent in export subsidies and of 75 percent in other farm support over a period of ten years, charging that such support gave EC farmers an unfair advantage. The EC initially agreed to only a 30 percent cut in farm subsidies and refused to reform the Common Agricultural Policy. After teetering several times on the brink of collapse, negotiations finally achieved a breakthrough in 1992, thanks in part to CAP reforms agreed on by the EC, including production and price reductions and a move away from subsidies to farmers based on production (see Chapter 13). Although the Europeans made concessions on production and subsidies for exports and the Uruguay Round was finally concluded in December 1993, the attitude of the EU toward the negotiations underlined some of its protectionist tendencies and highlighted problems that had emerged from its focus on building the single market without paying due attention to that market's global implications.

Intra-European trade has grown enormously as a result of integration, but the record of EU trade with other parts of the world has been mixed. The United States remains the EU's single-largest trade partner, accounting for about 17 percent of exports and 19 percent of imports, but the balance may change as the United States looks increasingly at building economic ties with the Pacific rim. The ACP program (discussed later in this chapter) has invested in building trade with developing countries, but it has had mixed results, and among them the seventy ACP states account for barely 4 percent of EU trade. India, China, Japan, and Australasia, meanwhile, are more likely to continue building links among themselves; Japan is the second-largest single source of imports to the EU but takes only 5 percent of EU exports. The greatest possibilities lie in Eastern Europe (with more than 125 million consumers and enormous productive potential) and the former USSR (with about 300 million consumers, productive potential, and a wealth of largely untapped natural resources). Building ties with the East and both strengthening and expanding its own internal market are likely to remain the EU's major trade priorities for the foreseeable future.

Relations with the United States

The EU's relationship with the United States has fluctuated as the interests of the two sides have joined and parted. The United States was originally supportive of the idea of European integration, seeing it as a way of building European security as a bulwark against the Soviets and as a means of helping West Germany rebuild. Relations cooled in the early 1960s with Konrad Adenauer's personal dislike of John F. Kennedy and Charles de Gaulle's neuroses regarding Anglo-American relations. They continued to cool as the Europeans disagreed with the United States over Vietnam and Willy Brandt began to make diplomatic overtures to Eastern Europe. Anti-Americanism grew despite the money, personnel, and resources the United States was still committing to the defense of Western Europe.

The collapse of the Bretton Woods system in 1971 marked the beginning of U.S. withdrawal from responsibility for global leadership; the unilateral decision by the Nixon administration to pull the United States off the gold standard also emphasized to many Europeans the U.S. unwillingness to take Europe's position into account. EC economies were rapidly catching up with that of the United States, and the EC was trading less with the United States and more with Eastern Europe. The revival of the European antinuclear movement in the 1980s further strained U.S.-EC relations.

The changing balance was exemplified by the steady withdrawal of the U.S. military from Western Europe with the end of the cold war and by the increasing differences of opinion on policy between the two sides; the EC was slow to criticize the 1979 Soviet invasion of Afghanistan, for example, and West Germany was the only EC member to support the U.S.-led boycott of the 1980 Moscow Olympics. The EC has also been more critical than the United States of Israeli policy in the occupied territories, the U.S. was disappointed by the lukewarm response of some EC members to the Gulf crisis, and the two sides disagreed over policy in the Balkans and over how much to cut farm subsidies during the final stages of the Uruguay Round of GATT negotiations (a disagreement that was symptomatic of the growing economic power of the EC relative to that of the United States[8]).

None of these differences is a surprise, because adjustments such as these would inevitably result from a reassertion of European economic and military influence, the relative decline of U.S. influence, and the recalculation of the balance of power in the vacuum left by the collapse of the USSR. Contacts between the United States and the EC were regularized in 1989–1990 following the call by U.S. Secretary of State James Baker for a new "Euro-Atlantic architecture" of cooperation and the November 1990 signing of a Transatlantic Declaration between the two sides committing them to regular high-level contacts at a time when the United States was becoming concerned about Europe's growing volatility. Biannual meetings now take place between the U.S. secretary of state and EU foreign ministers and between the Commission and members of the U.S. Cabinet; annual meetings also take place between U.S. presidents and the Commission.

Despite policy differences, and despite President Clinton's overtures to the Pacific rim states in the mid-1990s, the interests of the United States and Western Europe continue to overlap at almost every turn. The EU remains a major U.S. ally, the largest market for U.S. exports, the largest destination of U.S. foreign investment, and the largest source of foreign direct investment in the United States. But as economic issues replace military security as the key element in the transatlantic relationship, and as the power of the EU grows and the United States looks increasingly to Latin America and Asia, the United States will need to redefine the balance between prosperity and security and bring economic issues to bear in its relationship with Europe.[9]

Relations with Eastern Europe

EU relations with Eastern Europe and the former Soviet Union have improved so rapidly during the past few years that the EU is now the major source of Western aid for the Eastern bloc, and several East European countries have signaled their hopes of joining the EU. The USSR initially refused to recognize the existence of the European Community but finally acquiesced in the late 1970s. The possibility of trade agreements strengthened during the Gorbachev era, and the collapse of Soviet hegemony forced a rapid reappraisal of the EU's Eastern European policy in the late 1980s, raising the serious prospect (for the first time) of a possible eastward extension of the EU's borders.

A concerted EU response to changes in Eastern Europe was agreed on at the December 1988 Rhodes European Council. Within three months of taking office in January 1989, George Bush was describing Western Europe as an economic magnet that could pull Eastern Europe toward a new commonwealth of free nations, and the United States began to encourage the EC to take responsibility for coordinating Western economic aid to the East. This was formalized at the 1989 G-7 meeting, and the PHARE program was launched in December 1989 to help with economic restructuring in Poland and Hungary (PHARE stands for *Pologne-Hongrie: Actions pour la Reconversion Economique,* but *phare* also means lighthouse in French). PHARE has since been extended to other Eastern European states and to the Baltic states, channeling $600 million to the East in 1990, $940 million in 1991, and $1.2 billion in 1992.[10]

Trade and cooperation agreements have been signed with almost all of the East European states, several billion dollars in loans have been made available by the European Investment Bank, the EU has sent food aid to the East, and several functional programs have been launched to help East European social reform (including help upgrading university departments under the Tempus program). Another step was taken in 1990 with the creation of the European Bank for Reconstruction and Development, which has channeled public money from the EU, the United States, and Japan to help develop the private sector in the East. The Commission now coordinates the aid efforts of the G-24 countries: the EU, what remains of EFTA, and the United States, Canada, Japan, Australia, New Zealand, and Turkey. The EU's leading role in this program has not only helped build EU foreign policy but has also made the EU a major independent actor in the economic and political future of Eastern Europe.

With the end of the cold war, a growing number of requests were made from the East for associate or full EU membership, and irresistible moral pressure was directed toward the EU to open its doors to eastern expansion. Germany (and Chancellor Helmut Kohl) was particularly active in promoting this idea, in part because of its historical links with the East; the Conservative government in Britain also supported eastern expansion, but it did so mainly to slow down the process of integration. The EU signed Europe Agreements (a step beyond associate membership) with Hungary, Poland, and Czechoslovakia in 1991 and association agreements with Romania and Bulgaria in 1992 and 1993, respectively. Prospects are strong for Poland, Hungary, the Czech Republic, and Slovakia to join the EU within the next decade.[11]

Development Cooperation

As the progenitor of—and major participant in—the most active and comprehensive program of colonization in world history, Europe has long had close economic and political links with the South: Latin America, south Asia, and Africa. The end of the colonial era in the 1950s coincided with the beginning of the process of European integration, and the relationship between Europe and its former empires underwent a metamorphosis.

EU development aid policies are based partly on concerns about quality-of-life issues, such as poverty and hunger, but they are also altruistic. The South accounts for 34 percent of EU exports (half again as much as the United States and Japan combined), more than one-fifth of exports from the South go to the EU, and the EU continues to rely on key raw-material imports from the South, such as rubber, copper, and uranium. Development

FIGURE 15.2   The ACP States

AFRICA	Malawi	Bahamas
Angola	Mali	Barbados
Benin	Mauritania	Barbuda
Botswana	Mauritius	Dominica
Burkina Faso	Mozambique	Dominican Republic
Burundi	Namibia	Grenada
Cameroon	Niger	Guyana
Cape Verde	Nigeria	Haiti
Central African Republic	Rwanda	Jamaica
Chad	Sao Tome and Principe	St. Christopher and Nevis
Comoros	Senegal	St. Lucia
Congo	Seychelles	St. Vincent and Grenadines
Djibouti	Sierra Leone	Suriname
Equatorial Guinea	Somalia	Trinidad and Tobago
Ethiopia	Sudan	
Gabon	Swaziland	*PACIFIC*
Gambia	Tanzania	Belize
Ghana	Togo	Fiji
Guinea	Uganda	Kiribati
Guinea Bissau	Zaire	Papua New Guinea
Ivory Coast	Zambia	Solomon Islands
Kenya	Zimbabwe	Tonga
Lesotho		Tuvalu
Liberia	*CARIBBEAN*	Vanuatu
Madagascar	Antigua	Western Samoa

aid now accounts for about 3 percent of the EU budget, adding to the much larger bilateral flows of aid from each of the member states.

The EU aid program takes several different forms. In addition to allowing all Southern states to export industrial products to the EU tariff- and duty-free (subject to some limits on volume), the EU provides food and emergency aid and sponsors development projects undertaken by nongovernmental organizations. The EU has also negotiated a series of cooperative agreements with selected former colonies (mainly non-Asian former colonies of Britain and France). These began with the 1963 and 1969 Yaoundé Conventions (named for the capital of Cameroon where they were signed), which gave eighteen former colonies of the original six EEC member states preferential access to Community markets. The eighteen states in turn allowed the Community limited duty-free or quota-free access to their markets. The process was expanded by the series of **Lomé Conventions** (named for the capital of Togo), which give concessions to seventy African, Caribbean, and Pacific states (the ACP states; see Figure 15.2). The first three Conventions (signed in 1975, 1979, and 1984) each lasted five years; Lomé IV was signed in 1989 to cover the period 1990–2000 and to do the following:

1. Provide financial aid to ACP states under the European Development Fund, mainly in the form of grants for development projects and low-interest loans. The amount available under the fund increased from 7.5 billion ECU ($9.0 billion) under Lomé III to 12 billion ECU ($14.4 billion) for the first five years of Lomé IV.

2. Allow ACP states to export almost anything to the EU duty-free.

3. Provide an insurance fund, called Stabex, for ACP exports. The goal is to offset declines in the value of fifty specified ACP agricultural exports. If prices fall below a certain level, Stabex will make up the deficit. If they go above that level, ACP countries invest the profits in the fund for future use.

Opinions are mixed on the efficacy of the ACP program. On the one hand, it has built closer commercial ties between the EU and the ACP states, and there has been an overall increase in ACP exports to Europe. But oil accounts for a large part of the total export volume, Stabex does not help countries that do not produce the specified commodities, the European Development Fund becomes relatively small when it is divided up seventy ways, and the ACP program excludes larger Southern states (such as India and China) that have negotiated separate agreements with the EU. Additionally, too little attention has been paid to the environmental implications of the focus on cash crops for export, and the program has neither helped address the ACP debt crisis nor really changed the relationship between the EU and the ACP states.[12]

Lomé IV included an attempt to push EU policy in new directions by adding a structural adjustment element to ACP aid; in other words, it now encourages economic diversification in the ACP states rather than simply providing project aid. This has made the EU more like the IMF or the World Bank as a significant financial actor in international economic relations,[13] but whether this will improve prospects for the South remains to be seen.

Summary and Conclusions

The process of European integration has become increasingly extroverted with time. From an era in which it focused mainly on internal economic integration, it has had to look increasingly outward toward building common positions on foreign security and economic policies. The process has steadily gained more consistency and regularity, and it now makes up one of the three pillars that constitute the European Union. But the EU finds itself trying to build a wider base of common foreign, security, and trade policies at a time of great change in the world.

One of the sparks that led to the creation of the EU was the relatively definable security threat posed by the Soviet Union, but that threat has since been replaced by less easily definable economic issues and by the twin dilemmas of how to approach the Balkan crisis and the possible intensification of nationalist pressures in Russia. Which security organization offers the best guarantee of European security: NATO, the CSCE, or the Western European Union? Meanwhile, a global economic system continues to be built under the auspices of the World Trade Organization, and the United States is slowly shifting its economic interest more toward the south and the west. Finally, the wealth and competitiveness of China, India, and other newly industrializing countries continue to grow.

All of these changes make it essential for the EU to more clearly define its own identity and to build the kind of defensive capability and credibility it needs as a new economic superpower.

Notes

1. For details, see the *New York Times,* January 25, 1991; Willem van Eekelen, "WEU and the Gulf Crisis," *Survival* 32:6 (November–December 1990), 519–532; and Scott Anderson, "Western Europe and the Gulf War," in Reinhardt Rummel (Ed.), *Toward Political Union: Planning a Common Foreign and Security Policy in the European Community* (Boulder: Westview Press, 1992).

2. Jacques Delors, "European Integration and Security," *Survival* 33:2 (Spring 1991), 99–109; quote on 99.

3. *New York Times,* January 25, 1991.

4. Christopher Hill, "EPC's Performance in Crises," in Rummel (Ed.), *Toward Political Union,* 135–136.

5. Clive Archer and Fiona Butler, *The European Community: Structure and Process* (New York: St. Martin's Press, 1992), 173.

6. *New York Times,* November 20, 1990; *The Economist,* May 25, 1991.

7. See Dermot McAleese, "The Community's External Trade Policy," in David G. Mayes (Ed.), *The External Implications of European Integration* (Hemel Hempstead: Harvester Wheatsheaf, 1993); and Loukas Tsoukalis, *The New European Economy: The Politics and Economics of Integration* (New York: Oxford University Press, 1993), chapter 9.

8. Michael Smith and Stephen Woolcock, *Redefining the US-EC Relationship* (New York: Council on Foreign Relations Press, 1993), 2.

9. Ibid., 7.

10. Commission of the European Communities, *PHARE: Assistance for Economic Restructuring in the Countries of Central and Eastern Europe; An Operational Guide* (Luxembourg: Office of Official Publications, 1992).

11. Jackie Gower, "EC Relations with Central and Eastern Europe," in Juliet Lodge (Ed.), *The European Community and the Challenge of the Future* (New York: St. Martin's Press, 1993).

12. For a discussion of the problems with the ACP program, see Archer and Butler, *The European Community,* 127–132.

13. Carol Cosgrove and Pierre-Henri Laurent, "The Unique Relationship: the European Community and the ACP," in John Redmond (Ed.), *The External Relations of the European Community* (New York: St. Martin's Press, 1992).

Further Reading

Sir Leslie Fielding. *Europe as a Global Partner* (London: UACES, 1991).

A short and revealing overview by a former Eurocrat of how external policy is made by the European Commission.

Reinhardt Rummel (Ed.). *Toward Political Union: Planning a Common Foreign and Security Policy in the European Community* (Boulder: Westview Press, 1992).

An edited collection of chapters on the different elements of EU foreign and security policy.

Ole Norgaard, Thomas Pedersen, and Nikolaj Petersen. *The European Community in World Politics* (London and New York: Pinter and St. Martin's Press, 1993).

An assessment of the EU's approach to external relations, with chapters on relations with the United States, Japan, Eastern Europe, the former USSR, and the developing countries.

Michael Smith and Stephen Woolcock. *Redefining the US-EC Relationship* (New York: Council on Foreign Relations Press, 1993).

A brief assessment of the causes and possible consequences of changes in relations between the EU and the United States that compares their relative responses to security issues and the global economy.

Enzo Grilli. *The European Community and the Developing Countries* (New York: Cambridge University Press, 1994).

A study of EU policy toward Africa, Asia, and Latin America that analyzes the motives and consequences and discusses the evolution of the relationship between the EU and those regions.

Conclusions: Into the Twenty-First Century

The European Union was born out of the rubble of the most devastating war the world has ever known. It took its first tentative steps in an era divided by potentially fatal ideological tensions but one that also witnessed the end of colonialism and the construction of a global economy. It helped force Europeans to redefine both their place in the world and their attitudes toward one another. It stumbled occasionally, made a few significant breakthroughs, sometimes seemed about to fulfill the prophecies of the skeptics, and at other times left them eating their words. It has not only survived but has grown deeper and wider; in one form or another, the European Union is here to stay.

As Europe approaches the end of the millennium, though, much remains to be done, and there is no certainty about what the EU will become; it is a work in progress. Europeans will be faced with some difficult decisions in the next few years that will either give the EU more definition and permanence or detract from its past achievements. Many of those decisions will come out of the 1996 IGC, convened to give more focus to the direction of the EU in the light of Maastricht and the accession of several Eastern European states. At least eight major issues will be on the agenda as the fiftieth anniversary of the Schuman Declaration approaches.

Institutional Reform

The EU has bred five major institutions and a cluster of subsidiary bodies to deal with specific issues. None of these institutions has been static; all have changed character as the process of integration has evolved, as the demands made on them have grown, and as the relationships among them have been reshaped. More change is to come as "the government of Europe" is given clearer definition:

296

- There will be pressure to make the Commission more responsible and accountable by democratizing the process by which commissioners and the president are chosen and also pressure to rethink its structure as more new member states join the EU.

- There will be a need to reconsider the place of the Council of Ministers and to make its deliberations more open, democratic, and representative; there will be pressure to rethink the Council's system of voting, particularly as the EU expands; the role of the presidency of the EU will also change as membership of the EU grows.

- The powers of the European Parliament will likely grow in the light of increasing demands for accountability, the EP will become more like a true legislature, national political parties will, it is hoped, become more adept at running European election campaigns, and the search for majority parties in the EP will continue; at the same time, the national quotas of seats will need to be recalculated or the EP could grow to more than one thousand members.

- The influence of the Court of Justice will grow in tandem with the breadth and depth of European law.

- The tension between supranationalism and intergovernmentalism will encourage a redefinition of both the role of the European Council and the relationship among the five major institutions.

Addressing the Democratic Deficit

One of the most glaring deficiencies of the European Union is the gap between popular will and the goals of the elites who have made most of the key decisions relating to European integration. As the EU becomes more real to more Europeans and its decisions more strongly affect their lives, popular pressure for more direct input into EU decisionmaking will surely grow. Among the institutions that are ripest for reform are the Council of Ministers and the Commission.

Enlargement

The successes of the European experiment, combined with demands by the leaders of some of its members for eastward expansion, will lead to further enlargement in the next few years. There are twenty-four potential new members: three in Western Europe (Norway, Iceland, and Switzerland), three in the Mediterranean (Malta, Cyprus, and Turkey), twelve in Eastern Europe (including the five states of the former Yugoslavia), and six in what was once the Soviet Union. About half of these states have realistic short- to medium-term possibilities for membership. The next enlargement will most likely focus on states such as Poland, the Czech Republic, Slovakia, and Hungary; this will change the economic, political, cultural, and geographic balance of the Union and make more urgent the need to reform the EU's institutions and decisionmaking processes.

Putting Europeans to Work

High unemployment stands as a constant reminder of one of the most glaring failures of both domestic and European economic policy. Allied to this failure is the disparity in the levels of unemployment among the EU member states, which is highest on the southern and western margins and in the old industrial areas and lowest in the increasingly affluent center. The EU must not only achieve sustained economic growth and create millions of new jobs, but it must also ensure that most of those jobs are created in the areas hardest hit by recession and ensure an emphasis on the kinds of education and training needed to help maintain Europe's competitiveness in the global market.

Building Infrastructure

To give it a solid base from which to compete as a unit in the global market, the EU will need to continue to emphasize the building of European corporate, transport, and communication networks. This will mean anticipating more corporate mergers, building more of a European rail system, opening up the airline system and accepting the inevitability of weaker national carriers going out of business, liberalizing telecommunications, building a European data-transmission network, and creating a European energy generation and supply system.

Building an Economic Union

For many, Maastricht was a treaty too far, and the controversy over its content and implications remains a significant barrier to its full implementation. The most controversial aspect of the treaty was the commitment to a single currency, a goal many skeptics still doubt is possible and that even the most enthusiastic Euro-optimists realize may not be possible by 1999. At one level, a single currency makes eminent good sense as a means to finally completing the single market; at another level, it has already caused some member states severe problems as they have tried to meet the preparatory criteria on inflation, budget deficits, exchange rates, and national deficits, and it promises to cause more difficulties before the issue is finally resolved.

Building a Security Union

As the EU becomes more assertive and confident, its relationship with the United States and its place within NATO will change in a way that will reduce its dependence on the U.S. security blanket and compel it to build a "fourth pillar": common defense policies and a common defense force. The seeds of a security union have already been planted, and the Balkan crisis has emphasized both the policy fault lines in the European military capacity and the urgency of creating the ability to respond to future emergencies. But a security union will not be developed without a resolution of several key problems:

- Policy differences among the EU member states, notably the neutrality of Ireland and Sweden, the independent nature of French foreign policy, and the different spheres of influence and interest of the most powerful member states (Britain and the Commonwealth, France and its former colonies, Germany and Eastern Europe).

- Agreement on the role Germany will play. How long will it take for other Europeans to be comfortable with the prospect of German troops on their soil or of German troops being sent into neighboring trouble spots such as the Balkans?

- Agreement on the relative contributions of the different member states. Will the bigger powers such as Britain, France, and Italy agree to bear the largest share of the burden?

- Agreement on the relationship between the EU and other preexisting security arrangements, notably NATO and the CSCE.

- Agreement on a new balance in the tripartite relationship among the EU, the United States, and Russia. The Balkans debacle has given us a foretaste of the possible implications of a newly reassertive Europe. What effect will Europe's failure to always agree with U.S. foreign and defense policy have on the transatlantic relationship?

Building a Political Union

In a sense, everything that has happened since the Schuman Declaration has been a preamble to the single biggest step the European Union will ever take—the achievement of political union. Such a union is now virtually inevitable, but questions remain about when it will happen, which states will be members, and what form it will take. It may be federal, confederal, or consociational, or it may be an entirely new form of association tailored to meet the needs of what is, after all, a unique situation. It may be a true political union with all members moving together at the same speed, or it may be a multispeed Europe with its members moving toward the same ultimate goal but at a different pace. Some want Europe à la carte, with governments picking and choosing the policies they want to adopt, while others want an equal commitment by every member state.

Whatever form it takes, European political union *will* happen for at least four reasons: The EU experiment has brought peace and prosperity, Europeans have too much in common to allow their differences to act as an insurmountable barrier, Europeans are tied with knots and bonds that are far too complex to be easily unraveled, and European integration has developed an irresistible speed and momentum. The train left the station long ago, and even though the ride may be bumpy, the destination unclear, the design of the engine uncertain, and the relationship among the engineer, the guards, and the passengers still evolving, it is too late for anyone to leave the train without risking severe injury.

This book went to press on the eve of the 1996 IGC, convened to discuss and, it is hoped, to resolve many of the questions about what will happen next with European integration. There have been so many turning points in its history that it sounds trite to say that the IGC promises to be yet another, but it will. At the heart of discussions will be the future character of the European Union and a sharper focus on what Europe will look like in the twenty-first century. Whatever is decided, the IGC will prove to be another milestone on a road that has seen Europe transformed. There can be no turning back.

Acronyms

ACP	African, Caribbean, and Pacific states
APEC	Asia Pacific Economic Cooperation
ARC	Rainbow Group
BEU	Benelux Economic Union
CAP	Common Agricultural Policy
CCP	Common Commercial Policy
CEDEFOP	European Centre for the Development of Vocational Training
CENELEC	European Electrotechnical Standardization Committee
CFP	Common Fisheries Policy
CFSP	Common Foreign and Security Policy
CND	Campaign for Nuclear Disarmament
CoR	Committee of the Regions
COREPER	Committee of Permanent Representatives
CSCE	Conference on Security and Cooperation in Europe
DG	directorate-general
EAGGF	European Agriculture Guidance and Guarantee Fund
EAP	Environmental Action Programme
EBRD	European Bank for Reconstruction and Development
EC	European Community
Ecofin	Council of economics and finance ministers
ECSC	European Coal and Steel Community
ECU	European Currency Unit
EDA	European Democratic Alliance
EDC	European Defence Community
EEA	European Economic Area
EEB	European Environmental Bureau
EEC	European Economic Community
EFTA	European Free Trade Association
EIB	European Investment Bank
EMEA	European Medicines Evaluation Agency
EMI	European Monetary Institute
EMS	European Monetary System
EMU	economic and monetary union
EP	European Parliament
EPC	European Political Co-operation
EPP	European People's Party
ER	European Right

ERDF	European Regional Development Fund
ERM	Exchange Rate Mechanism
ESA	European Space Agency
ESC	Economic and Social Committee
ESF	European Social Fund
EU	European Union
EUL	Group of the European United Left
FDA	Food and Drug Administration
GAC	General Affairs Council
GATT	General Agreement on Tariffs and Trade
GDP	gross domestic product
GNP	gross national product
G-7	Group of Seven
HST	high-speed train
IGC	intergovernmental conference
IGO	intergovernmental organization
IMF	International Monetary Fund
IMP	Integrated Mediterranean Programme
INGO	international nongovernmental organization
IO	international organization
LDR	Liberal, Democratic, and Reformist Group
MEP	Member of the European Parliament
NAFTA	North American Free Trade Agreement
NATO	North Atlantic Treaty Organization
OECD	Organization for Economic Cooperation and Development
OEEC	Organization for European Economic Cooperation
OPEC	Organization of Petroleum Exporting Countries
PES	Group of the Party of European Socialists
PR	proportional representation
SAP	Social Action Programme
SEA	Single European Act
VAT	value-added tax
WEU	Western European Union
WTO	World Trade Organization

Chronology of European Integration

1944	July	Representatives from forty-four countries meet at Bretton Woods, New Hampshire, to plan the postwar global economy
1945	May	Germany surrenders; European war ends
	June	Creation of United Nations
1946	March	Churchill makes his "iron curtain" speech at Fulton, Missouri
1947	March	Announcement of the Truman Doctrine
	June	U.S. Secretary of State George Marshall offers Europe aid for economic recovery
	September	Sixteen countries join the European Recovery Program
	October	General Agreement on Tariffs and Trade signed in Geneva; enters into force January 1948
1948	January	Benelux customs union created
	March	Mutual defense treaty (Treaty of Brussels) signed in Brussels by Britain, France, and the Benelux states
	April	Organization for European Economic Cooperation founded
	May	Congress of Europe held in The Hague
	June	Soviets impose blockade of West Berlin, sparking a year-long airlift of supplies from the West
1949	April	North Atlantic Treaty signed in Washington, D.C.
	May	Council of Europe founded; formalization of division of Germany
1950	May	Schuman Plan published
	October	Publication of plan outlining the European Defence Community
1951	April	Treaty of Paris signed, creating the European Coal and Steel Community
1952	March	Nordic Council founded
	May	The six ECSC members sign a draft treaty creating the European Defence Community
	August	ECSC comes into operation
1953	November	Plans announced for a European Political Community
1954	April	French defeat in Indochina
	August	Plans for European Defence Community and European Political Community collapse

	October	Paris agreement signed, creating the Western European Union
1955	May	Western European Union comes into operation, head-quartered in London
	June	Meeting of ECSC foreign ministers in Messina agrees to take the next step in European integration
1956	October	Soviet invasion of Hungary
	October –December	Suez crisis
1957	March	Treaties of Rome signed, creating Euratom and the European Economic Community
1958	January	Euratom and EEC come into operation
	February	Treaty creating the Benelux Economic Union signed in The Hague
	July	Conference in Stresa, Italy, works out details of Common Agricultural Policy
1960	January	Seven countries sign European Free Trade Association Convention in Stockholm, which comes into force in May
	November	Benelux Economic Union comes into force
	December	OEEC reorganized to become Organization for Economic Cooperation and Development
1961	February	First summit of EEC heads of government
	July	Greece becomes associate member of EEC
	August	Britain, Ireland, and Denmark apply for EEC membership; construction begins on the Berlin Wall
1962	April	Norway applies for EEC membership
1963	January	De Gaulle vetoes British membership in the Community; France and Germany sign Treaty of Friendship and Co operation
1965	April	Merger Treaty signed, establishing a single Commission and Council for the three European Communities
	July	France begins boycott of Community institutions (the "empty chair" crisis)
1966	January	Agreement on Luxembourg Compromise
	May	Britain, Ireland, and Denmark apply for EEC membership for the second time
	July	Norway applies for EEC membership for the second time; Merger Treaty comes into force
1967	December	De Gaulle vetoes British membership in the Community for the second time
1968	July	Agreement on a common external tariff completes the creation of an EEC customs union; agreement on Common Agricultural Policy
1970	June	Membership negotiations opened with Britain, Denmark, Ireland, and Norway; concluded in January 1972
1971	February	Launch of the European exchange rate stabilization system (the snake)

	August	Richard Nixon takes the United States off the gold standard, signaling the end of the Bretton Woods system of fixed exchange rates
1972	September	National referendum in Norway goes against membership in the Community
1973	January	Britain, Denmark, and Ireland join the Community, bringing membership to nine
1974	January	Creation of the European Social Fund
1975	January	Creation of the European Regional Development Fund
	March	First meeting of the European Council in Dublin
	June	Greece applies for Community membership; negotiations open in July 1976
1977	March	Portugal applies for Community membership; negotiations open in October 1978
	July	Spain applies for Community membership; negotiations open in February 1979
1979	March	European Monetary System comes into operation
	June	First direct elections to the European Parliament
1981	January	Greece joins the Community, bringing membership to ten
1984	January	Free trade area established between EFTA and the Community
	June	Second direct elections to the European Parliament
1985	January	Jacques Delors begins his first term as president of the European Commission
1986	January	Spain and Portugal join the Community, bringing membership to twelve
	February	Single European Act signed in Luxembourg
1987	June	Turkey applies to join the Community
	July	Single European Act comes into force
1989	April	Publication of Delors Report on Economic and Monetary Union
	June	Third direct elections to the European Parliament
	July	Austria applies for Community membership
	December	Adoption of the Social Charter by eleven EC member states; rejection of Turkish membership application
1990	June	Schengen Agreement signed by France, Germany, and the Benelux states
	July	Cyprus and Malta apply for Community membership
	October	German reunification brings the former East Germany into the Community
	December	Opening of intergovernmental conferences on economic and monetary union and on political union
1991	December	Treaty on European Union agreed to in Maastricht, signed in February 1992; Europe Agreements signed with Poland, Hungary, and Czechoslovakia
1992	May	France and Germany announce the creation of a thirty-five-thousand-member Eurocorps

	June	Danish voters reject the terms of Maastricht in a national referendum
1993	January	Creation of the single market
	May	Danish voters accept the terms of Maastricht in a second national referendum; Secretariat of WEU moved from London to Brussels
	November	Treaty on European Union comes into force; the European Community becomes one of three pillars of a new European Union
1994	January	Creation of the European Economic Area and the European Monetary Institute
	March	Poland and Hungary become associate members of the EU
	May	Opening of the Channel tunnel linking Britain and France
	June	Fourth direct elections to the European Parliament; public referendum in Austria favors EU membership
	October	Public referendum in Finland favors EU membership
	November	Public referendum in Sweden favors EU membership, but referendum in Norway rejects membership
1995	January	Austria, Sweden, and Finland join the European Union, bringing membership to fifteen
	March	France, Germany, Spain, Portugal, and the Benelux states lift all remaining customs and passport controls

Glossary

This Glossary contains brief definitions of key terms relating to the European Union and the process of European integration.

Acquis communitaire. A concept for which there is no exact translation but that refers to the idea, the concept, or the heritage of the European Union. The literal translation of *acquis* is *experience*. In practice, it is a collective term for all the laws and regulations adopted by the EU.

Assent procedure. An agreement introduced under the Single European Act that states that no new members will be allowed to join the EU without the support of an absolute majority of members of the European Parliament.

Association agreements. Agreements signed between the EU and non-EU states under which those states are given associate membership in the EU, which allows them preferential access to the EU market without being directly involved in EU government or policymaking. See also **Europe Agreements.**

Benelux. A collective term for Belgium, the Netherlands, and Luxembourg.

Bretton Woods system. A plan worked out at a 1944 meeting in Bretton Woods, New Hampshire, among representatives of forty-four countries. Based on U.S. leadership, it was aimed at establishing international management of the global economy, stable exchange rates, low tariffs, and aid to war-damaged economies. The linchpins were the General Agreement on Tariffs and Trade, the International Monetary Fund, and the World Bank.

Codecision procedure. An arrangement under which the Council of Ministers cannot make a final decision on new laws relating to the single market, consumer protection, education, and the environment without giving the European Parliament the opportunity for a third reading.

Cohesion. The goal of ensuring that the development of the European Union closes the social and economic differences between the poorer and richer regions of the Union. In practice, this involves transfers of funds from the richer to the poorer states.

Common Agricultural Policy. A controversial agricultural price support system incorporated in the EEC Treaty that originally supported guaranteed prices to Community farmers for their produce but that has since shifted toward providing compensation for taking land out of production.

Common market. See **Single market.**

Confederalism. An administrative system in which independent political units come together for mutual convenience and cooperate on issues of mutual interest but retain sovereignty and control over their own affairs.

Consociationalism. A system of administration often proposed for small or deeply divided societies that is based on government by a grand coalition, proportional representation for the groups involved, the power of veto for those groups, and the delegation of authority.

Consultation procedure. An arrangement under which the Council of Ministers cannot make a final decision on a new law without giving the European Parliament the opportunity to issue an opinion.

Convergence. The progressive movement of the policies of EU member states toward a common position.

Cooperation procedure. Introduced under the terms of the Single European Act, this is a step up from the consultation procedure. If the opinion of Parliament on a new law runs counter to the position taken by the Council of Ministers, the Council must reach a "common position" (that is, unanimity) and send the revised law back to Parliament for a second reading.

Customs union. An arrangement in which a group of states joins together to abolish all mutual restrictions on trade and to agree on a common external tariff on all goods entering the union from outside. This arrangement tends to increase internal trade at the expense of external trade.

Deepening. The argument that the EU should focus on consolidating integration among existing members before allowing new members to join. Although this seems to contradict arguments in favor of enlargement (see **Widening**), the two are now seen less as alternatives and more as two sides of the same coin.

Democratic deficit. The argument that there is too little of a democratic nature in the way the members of EU institutions (other than the European Parliament) are appointed and too little direct accountability and sense of public responsibility among those institutions—in other words, "the deficit" refers to the gap between the powers given up to EU institutions and the ability of EU citizens to influence those institutions.

Economic and monetary union. The process by which the EU has worked toward the goals of establishing fixed exchange rates, common monetary policies, and a single currency.

Eurocrat. A nickname for EU bureaucrats, particularly those who work in the European Commission.

Europe Agreements. Agreements signed between the EU and selected Eastern European states that allow for gradual movement toward free trade and are increasingly seen as a first step toward eventual EU membership for those states. Agreements with Poland and Hungary came into force in 1994.

European Currency Unit. A unit of account calculated on the basis of a basket of EU currencies that provides an anchor for the **Exchange Rate Mechanism**. Although the ECU does not yet have a physical form, it could be the basis for a future single European currency.

European Political Cooperation. The process by which the EU works toward agreeing on common foreign policy positions.

Eurosclerosis. A term used to describe the apparent lack of growth or progress in European integration during the early 1970s and that has since been used to describe any indications that the members of the European Union are failing to agree.

Exchange Rate Mechanism. An arrangement under which EU member states agree to take whatever action is needed to keep the value of their currencies relatively stable against those of the other EU member states. Seen as a key step in the process of building a single European currency.

Federalism. An administrative arrangement in which central and local levels of government coexist, with independent powers over particular policy areas. For example, the central government might have authority over fiscal and foreign policy, while local government might have independent authority over education, transport, and policing.

Free trade. An arrangement in which the barriers to trade between or among states are either reduced or removed. Because true free trade cannot exist without a single currency and a complete elimination of all the barriers to the free movement of labor, goods, capital, and services, free trade in practice is never totally free.

Functionalism. A theory that argues that states can promote cooperation by working together in selected functional areas (such as the management of coal and steel) and that the ties they build will compel them to cooperate in other areas as well.

Gross national product. The total value of all goods and services produced by a given state, including the value of its overseas investments (gross domestic product is a measure that excludes the latter). The basic measure of the absolute wealth of a state.

Harmonization. The goal of standardizing national legislation in EU member states in the interest of promoting competition and free trade. Involves removing legal and fiscal barriers to competition and free trade.

Intergovernmentalism. The phenomenon by which decisions are reached by cooperation among governments. Usually applied to the Council of Ministers and the European Council. See also **Supranationalism.**

Internal market. See **Single market.**

Luxembourg Compromise. An arrangement worked out in 1966 following a crisis set off by Charles de Gaulle's concerns about the accumulation of powers by the European Commission. The "compromise" allowed member states to veto proposals when they believed their national interests were at stake.

Mutual recognition. Agreement that if a product or service can be lawfully produced and marketed in one EU member state, it should be allowed to be marketed in any other member state.

Neofunctionalism. A variation on the theme of functionalism, which argues that certain prerequisites are needed before functional cooperation can lead to integration and that integration takes place through a process of **spillover:** Cooperation in one area creates pressures that lead to integration in others.

Realism. A theory often described as the "traditional" approach to the study of international relations and that dominated the study of that field in the United States from the 1940s to the 1960s. It argues that states are the major actors in the world system, that world politics is driven by a struggle for power among states, and that states place national interests, security, and autonomy at the top of their agendas.

Schuman Plan. The plan developed by Jean Monnet and Robert Schuman to coordinate the coal and steel industries of Europe. Announced to the public on May 9, 1950, it led to the creation of the European Coal and Steel Community.

Single market. An area within which there is free movement of goods, services, capital, and people. Also known as a common market or internal market. The term can be applied to a single state (such as the United States) or to a group of states that have removed the necessary barriers.

Snake in the tunnel. A mechanism used briefly by the EC in the early 1970s to reduce fluctuations in exchange rates among its national currencies. Member states agreed to keep the value of their currencies within ±1.125 percent of their central value against the U.S. dollar.

Sovereignty. The right to own and control. In relation to states, the term is usually used to connote jurisdiction over a territory, but it can also refer to the rights of one person or group relative to those of another (for example, the sovereignty of the people over government).

Spillover. An element of neofunctional theory that suggests that if states integrate in one area, the economic, technical, social, and political pressures for them to integrate in other areas will increase.

Structural funds. A collective term for the three major regional development funds of the EU: the European Regional Development Fund, the European Social Fund, and the guidance element of the European Agricultural Guidance and Guarantee Fund.

Subsidiarity. A guiding principle by which the EU agrees to take action only in those policy areas that are best dealt with at the EU level rather than at the national or local level.

Supranationalism. A condition in which decisions are made by a process or an institution that is independent of national governments or as a result of accommodations among national governments; those decisions are binding on the subject governments. Often used to describe the work and tendencies of the European Commission but also of the process of European integration. Contrast with **Intergovernmentalism**.

Value-added tax. A form of sales tax used in most European states and applied to any product whose form has been changed through manufacturing, thereby adding value (for example, steel used to construct a car).

Widening. The argument that EU membership should be extended to other European states rather than existing member states giving priority to consolidation among themselves.

Appendix I:
Key Institutions Related to
the EU and Europe

Committee of Permanent Representatives. The meeting place of the permanent representatives of the EU member states to the Council of Ministers. COREPER meets weekly to vet and discuss proposals for new policies and laws submitted by the European Commission and to reduce the workload of the Council of Ministers. Based in Brussels, Belgium.

Committee of the Regions. An advisory body that provides representatives of local government units in the EU with a forum in which they can meet, talk, and give advice on laws and policies to the European Commission and the Council of Ministers. Consists of 220 members appointed by the EU member states for four-year renewable terms. Based in Brussels.

*Conference on Security and Cooperation in Europe. A process (rather than an institution) that grew out of attempts in the early 1970s to promote pan-European cooperation on trade and on civil and human rights. Since 1989 there have been suggestions that the CSCE could form the basis of a new pan-European security organization. It has fifty-two members, including the United States, Canada, Russia, all of Europe, and all of the former Soviet republics. It arranges conferences among its members and has a small secretariat in Prague, Czech Republic.

*Council of Europe. Founded in 1949 by ten Western European states to promote political cooperation and to complement the economic goals of the Organiza-tion for European Economic Cooperation (described later). It remained intergovernmental, however, and has been limited to dealing with issues relating to culture, education, and civil liberties. It has twenty-three members. Based in Strasbourg, France.

Council of Ministers. The primary decisionmaking arm of the EU, consisting of the relevant national government ministers of the member states. In consultation with the European Commission and the European Parliament, it makes the final decisions on adopting or rejecting new laws and policies. Based in Brussels.

---

* Institutions that are not part of the EU system.

Court of Auditors. Founded in 1977, this is the financial watchdog of the EU, charged with auditing EU accounts and ensuring budgetary responsibility. Consists of fifteen auditors appointed by the member states for six-year renewable terms. Based in Luxembourg.

Court of First Instance. A subsidiary of the European Court of Justice, created in 1989 to help ease the growing workload of the higher court. Based in Luxembourg.

Economic and Social Committee. An advisory body that provides employers, workers, and other sectional interests with a forum in which they can meet, talk, and give advice on laws and policies to the European Commission and the Council of Ministers. Consists of 220 members appointed by the EU member states for four-year renewable terms. Based in Brussels.

European Atomic Energy Community. One of the three original European Communities, created in 1958 as a result of the Treaty of Rome. Charged with promoting the integration of the national atomic energy industries of its member states. Based in Brussels, Luxembourg, and Strasbourg.

*European Bank for Reconstruction and Development. An independent development bank created in 1990, with the majority of its capital coming from the EU. Charged with providing loans, encouraging capital investment, and promoting trade, with a focus on Eastern Europe. Based in London.

European Coal and Steel Community. The first of the three original European Communities, created in 1952 as a result of the 1951 Treaty of Paris. Charged with promoting integration of the national coal and steel industries of its member states. Based in Luxembourg with a consultative assembly in Strasbourg. It was superseded by the European Community.

European Commission. The primary bureaucratic and executive arm of the EU, with about 16,500 staff members headed by 20 commissioners appointed for five-year renewable terms by member-state governments. Charged with initiating new laws and policies and overseeing implementation by the member states. Based in Brussels.

European Council. A forum in which the heads of government of the EU member states (or the head of state in the case of France) meet at least twice annually to discuss new policy initiatives and the general direction of the EU. It has no permanent secretariat.

European Court of Justice. The primary judicial arm of the EU, consisting of fifteen judges appointed for six-year renewable terms by the member states. Charged with interpreting the major treaties and resolving disputes between or among member states, EU institutions, corporations, citizens, and other interested parties. Based in Luxembourg.

European Economic Area. An arrangement developed in the early 1990s under which the EC and selected European states outside the EC formed a larger free trade area, with nonmembers adopting many EC principles without being full members. Came into force in January 1994 but lost most of its significance when Austria,

Finland, and Sweden joined the EU in January 1995. It has no permanent secretariat.

European Economic Community. One of the three original European Communities, created in 1958 as a result of the 1957 Treaty of Rome. Charged with building a common market among its member states and promoting the harmonization of their economic policies. Based in Brussels, Luxembourg, and Strasbourg. It largely superseded the ECSC and Euratom and became one of the three pillars of the European Union.

*European Free Trade Association. An alternative free trade area created in 1960 at the urging of Britain, which did not support the implied federalism of the EEC. It originally had seven members, and three more countries eventually joined. All members but Iceland, Liechtenstein, Norway, and Switzerland have since joined the EU. Based in Geneva, Switzerland.

European Investment Bank. An autonomous institution set up in 1958 under the Treaty of Rome to promote development in the poorer areas of the EEC through the provision of loans and guarantees. Governed by the finance ministers of the EU member states, it now also provides loans outside the EU. Based in Luxembourg.

European Monetary Institute. Founded in 1994 as the seed of a possible future European Central Bank. Charged with helping to coordinate the monetary policies of the EU member states and developing a possible future European currency. Based in Frankfurt, Germany.

European Parliament. The primary representative arm of the EU, and one that is slowly winning more of the law-making powers usually associated with a legislature. Consists of 624 members elected directly by EU voters for renewable five-year terms. Charged with discussing and suggesting amendments to EU law before a final decision is made by the Council of Ministers. Based in Strasbourg (plenary sessions), Luxembourg (secretariat), and Brussels (committees).

*General Agreement on Tariffs and Trade. See World Trade Organization.

*Nordic Council. Set up in 1952 to promote cooperation and integration among the Nordic states; Denmark, Iceland, Norway, and Sweden were founder-members, and Finland joined in 1955. Based in Stockholm, Sweden, and Oslo, Norway.

*North Atlantic Treaty Organization. A security organization founded in 1949, consisting of the United States, Canada, thirteen Western European states, and Turkey. Charged with helping to promote the mutual security of its members from external attack, and commits each of its members to take "such action as it deems necessary" to restore and maintain security in the event of an attack on any one member. Under its Partnership for Peace program launched in 1993, NATO is trying to promote security cooperation with Eastern Europe and the former USSR. Based in Brussels.

*Organization for European Economic Cooperation. Founded by sixteen Western European states in 1948 to oversee the administration of funds made available under the Marshall Plan. Envisaged by the United States as the possible seed of a

European economic and political union, it remained purely intergovernmental and was superseded in 1960 by the Organization for Economic Cooperation and Development. Based in Paris.

Western European Union. A security organization founded in 1954 by Britain and the six members of the ECSC. Moribund for most of its life, it took on new vitality with the end of the cold war, although its precise mission—and its relationship with the EU—remains unclear. It has ten full members, two associate members, and two observers. Based in Brussels and Paris.

World Trade Organization. Founded in 1995 to replace the General Agreement on Tariffs and Trade and to continue promoting the reduction and removal of barriers to global trade. GATT was created in 1947 and oversaw several rounds of multilateral negotiations aimed at reducing tariff and nontariff barriers to trade. More a framework for discussions than an institution, it was given greater institutional solidity with the creation of the WTO. Based in Geneva.

Appendix II:
Other Experiments in
Regional Integration

The European Union is the best-known and the most highly evolved example of regional integration among states to date, but it was neither the first nor is it the only such example. This appendix briefly describes some of the more notable past and current experiments in integration in other parts of the world (NAFTA excluded; see Chapter 1).

Latin America and the Caribbean

Latin American Integration Association (LAIA). All eleven independent states in Latin America except Guyana and Suriname are members of LAIA, which was founded in 1980 with headquarters in Montevideo, Uruguay. It replaced the Latin American Free Trade Association (LAFTA), which was founded in 1960 with a twelve-year timetable for eliminating all trade barriers among its members. LAFTA began by negotiating trade liberalization product by product, reaching agreement in 1967 on across-the-board tariff reductions. But its plans were undermined by political upheavals in several member states and by their varied levels of economic development.

LAIA abandoned the goal of a free trade area in favor of bilateral preference agreements that would account for the differences in the levels of economic development of its members. To help achieve this goal, its members were divided into three groups: most developed (Argentina, Brazil, Mexico), intermediate (Chile, Colombia, Peru, Uruguay, Venezuela), and least developed (Bolivia, Ecuador, Paraguay). Cuba has been an observer member since 1986.

The Andean Group. Also known as the Andean Common Market, this group was founded in 1969 as a subgroup of LAFTA with headquarters in Lima, Peru. It originally had six members (Bolivia, Chile, Colombia, Ecuador, Peru, and Venezuela), but Chile left in 1976. Mexico has been a working partner since 1972. The Andean Group promotes mutual development through accelerated economic integration, coordinated regional industrial development, regulation of foreign investment, and a common external tariff. Disputes are resolved by an Andean Judicial Tribunal set up in 1980, with one judge from each country serving a six-year term.

Southern Cone Common Market (Mercosul). Mercosul was founded in 1995 by five LAIA members: Argentina, Brazil, Chile, Paraguay, and Uruguay. Its goal is to abolish tariffs on 85 percent of internal trade and to agree on a common external tariff. Bolivia, Colombia, Ecuador, Peru, and Venezuela have expressed an interest in joining.

Central American Common Market (CACM). CACM was founded in 1960 with headquarters in Guatemala City, Guatemala. Its original goals were to complete a common market by 1965, to attract industrial capital, and to encourage economic diversification. Although it has helped to reduce trade barriers among its five members (Costa Rica, El Salvador, Guatemala, Honduras, and Nicaragua) and has agreed on a common external tariff for many goods, its progress has been undermined by political disagreements and military conflicts in several of its members. It agreed in 1991 to establish a common external tariff by 1993, but this was delayed. In 1993, all of its members except Costa Rica agreed to create a Central American Trade Zone aimed at reducing tariffs on internal trade.

Caribbean Community and Common Market (CARICOM). Founded in 1973 with headquarters in Georgetown, Guyana, CARICOM superseded the Caribbean Free Trade Area (CARIFTA), founded in 1968 by five former British colonies. It has eleven member states: Antigua and Barbuda, Barbados, Dominica, Grenada, Guyana, Jamaica, Saint Kitts and Nevis, Saint Lucia, Saint Vincent and the Grenadines, Trinidad and Tobago, and the British colony of Montserrat. The members have agreed to a customs union with a common external tariff.

CARICOM is helped by the logic of having its mainly small island states pool their resources, but its work began to unravel in the late 1970s because of concern among the poorer members that they were not receiving their fair share of the benefits. In 1981, seven CARICOM members formed their own subregional Organization of Eastern Caribbean States while remaining members of CARICOM. Various target dates for establishing a common external tariff have come and gone with agreement on only selected products.

Southeast Asia

Association of Southeast Asian Nations (ASEAN). Founded in 1967 to replace the Association of Southeast Asia (ASA), which was founded in 1961 by Malaya, the Philippines, and Thailand, ASEAN is headquartered in Jakarta, Indonesia. It was founded by Indonesia, Malaysia, the Philippines, Singapore, and Thailand; Brunei joined in 1985; and membership is likely to spread to Cambodia, Laos, Vietnam, and perhaps Myanmar. From an initial interest in security issues, ASEAN has moved steadily into the areas of economic cooperation and trade, with a view to eventually building a regional economic community. It gained new momentum as a result of the changing balance of power in the region following the Vietnam War and played an important role in ending the Vietnam-Cambodia War. The rapid economic growth of several of its members has given ASEAN new purpose, confidence, and significance.

ASEAN heads of state meet at periodic summits. There are annual meetings of the foreign ministers of member states, and a standing committee conducts business between ministerial meetings. The secretariat is helped by a secretary-general, appointed from one of the member states in three-year rotations.

Asia Pacific Economic Cooperation (APEC). Promoted most actively since 1989 by the United States and Australia, APEC is less an institution than a forum for the discussion of regional economic cooperation among the states of the Pacific rim: the six ASEAN members, Japan, South Korea, China, Taiwan, Hong Kong, Australia, New Zealand, the United States, and Canada. The ASEAN states also set up a Regional Forum in 1994 to open discussions with Russia, China, Vietnam, Laos, and Papua New Guinea.

Sub-Saharan Africa

East African Community (defunct). Founded in 1967 with headquarters in Arusha, Tanzania, this organization promoted joint ventures among its three members (Kenya, Tanzania, and Uganda), such as East African Airways and East African Railways and Harbours, which were inherited from the British colonial era. Beginning with the advantage of a single currency already in place and a lingua franca (Swahili), the Community promoted tariff reduction and free trade, and its wealthiest member—Kenya—provided development assistance for Tanzania and Uganda.

The Community began to collapse as a result of the military coup that brought Idi Amin to power in Uganda in 1970, but it had already been weakened by the perception that Kenya was deriving most of the benefits and attracting most of the foreign investment. It broke up in 1977.

Economic Community of West African States (ECOWAS). Founded in 1975 with headquarters in Lagos, Nigeria, ECOWAS was set up to promote trade, economic cooperation, self-reliance, the harmonization of agricultural policies, and the free movement of people, services, and capital among its sixteen members: Benin, Burkina Faso, Cape Verde, Gambia, Ghana, Guinea, Guinea-Bissau, Ivory Coast, Liberia, Mali, Mauritania, Niger, Nigeria, Senegal, Sierra Leone, and Togo. Its development has been handicapped in recent years by severe political and economic instability in many of its members, notably Nigeria, the dominant regional power.

Central Africa. Several experiments in regional cooperation have been launched in this region, but they have all been undermined by political and economic instability. They include the Organisation Commune Africaine et Mauricienne (OCAM), founded in 1965 with headquarters in Bangui, Central African Republic, which has eight members: Benin, Burkina Faso, Central African Republic, Ivory Coast, Niger,

Rwanda, Senegal, and Togo; the Customs and Economic Union of Central Africa (UDEAC), created in 1976 with six members: Cameroon, Central African Republic, Chad, Congo, Equatorial Guinea, and Gabon; and the Economic Community of the Great Lakes Countries (CEPGL), created in 1976 with three very troubled members: Burundi, Rwanda, and Zaire.

Southern African Development Community (SADC). Founded in 1980, the members of SADC were given common cause by trying to reduce their economic dependence on South Africa and to develop a common transport system that would allow its six landlocked members to bypass South African railroads and ports. Headquartered in Gabarone, Botswana, its leaders meet annually to coordinate their activities. SADC plans, coordinates, and finances a variety of projects in the areas of agriculture, energy, mining, telecommunications, and regional trade. It has twelve members: Angola, Botswana, Lesotho, Malawi, Mauritius, Mozambique, Namibia, South Africa, Swaziland, Tanzania, Zambia, and Zimbabwe. Its prospects for success have been greatly enhanced by the peaceful democratic transition in South Africa, which has an economy that is nearly four times bigger than those of the other eleven SADC states combined. At their August 1995 summit in South Africa, SADC leaders declared their hope of creating a Southern African free-trade area by the year 2000 and even eventually setting up a single currency for the region.

Middle East

With a common heritage, language, and religion and very similar economic bases, the states of the Middle East would seem ripe for economic integration, but to date the region has made only modest progress, mainly because of political disagreements and instability. A Council of Arab Economic Unity was created in 1957; it met for the first time in 1964 and in 1965 founded the Arab Common Market. Membership is open to all twenty-one members of the Arab League, but only five have joined (Iraq, Jordan, Libya, Mauritania, and Syria). The Gulf Cooperation Council was founded in 1981 with headquarters in Riyadh, Saudi Arabia, to promote freer trade and closer economic and defense ties among its six members: Bahrain, Kuwait, Oman, Qatar, Saudi Arabia, and the United Arab Emirates.

Oceania

Most Pacific island states are too small in both area and population, too isolated, and too limited in human and natural resources to function effectively by themselves in the global economy; this fact emphasizes the logic of cooperation and integration. Attempts to encourage cooperation date back to the creation in 1947 of the South Pacific Commission to give advice on social and economic development. The South Pacific Forum was founded in 1971 by Australia, New Zealand, and five independent island states to give a political dimension to the work of the Commission; it was joined in 1973 by the South Pacific Bureau for Economic Cooperation. The Forum is headquartered in Suva, Fiji, and has fourteen members: Australia, Fiji, Kiribati, Micronesia, Nauru, New Zealand, Papua New Guinea, Solomon Islands, Tonga, Tuvalu, Vanuatu, Western Samoa, and two self-governing territories of New Zealand—Cook Islands and Niue.

Appendix III:
Selected Sources of Information

Publishing on the European Union is a growth industry, with the number of new books and journal articles increasing to match both the rapid changes in the powers and significance of the EU and the growing public and political interest in what it is and what it does. The challenge for the researcher and the student lies less in finding material than in wading through all the existing material, keeping up with the torrent of new books and articles pouring onto the market, and mapping out shortcuts to the important sources of information.

This list is not comprehensive. Rather, it is an attempt to outline some of the best and most accessible sources of information on the EU.

Periodicals and News Sources

The Economist. A weekly British news magazine that has stories and statistics on world politics, including a section on Europe (and occasional special supplements on the EU). Contact The Economist, 111 West 57th Street, New York, NY 10019. Tel: (1-800) 456-6086.

Economist Intelligence Unit *Country Reports.* Published by the *Economist,* these are much too expensive for most mortals to afford, but many of the larger research university libraries subscribe to them. Quarterly reports on almost every country in the world provide detailed political and economic news and information.

Journal of Common Market Studies. The best academic journal devoted solely to the EU. Published quarterly, it contains scholarly articles and book reviews and publishes a very useful *Annual Review of Activities* in the EU. Many other academic journals include articles on the EU; the most consistently useful include *West European Politics, International Organization,* and *Parliamentary Affairs.*

Computer Sources

Developments in the electronic delivery of information are moving so quickly that it is impossible to be either comprehensive or current. In addition to the more mainstream sources of news such as America On-Line and Lexis/Nexis, specific information on the EU is available on the following:

World Wide Web (WWW). The European Commission has two servers on WWW. EUROPA provides information on the goals, institutions, and policies of the EU, including data on its history, institutions, and member states; an agenda of events of the Commission and the presidency; and information on EU policies. I'M EUROPE includes full texts of EU treaties and white papers, information on current research, a mailbox for queries and comments, and information on the European Parliament. If you have access to Internet and a WWW browser, use the following URLs:

> Europa: http://www.cec.lu
> I'm Europe: http://www.echo.lu

Also on the Internet, you can connect with two hosts offering both free and paid databases. ECHO—which consists mainly of free databases—includes information on EU archives, research and development projects, scholars doing research on Europe, daily ECU rates, and a directory of European institutions. ECHO can be accessed by telnet at echo.lu (at the login prompt, enter the public password: echo).

EUROBASES includes the full text of press releases from the Commission and the Council of Ministers, weekly summaries of Court actions, speeches by commissioners, the text of the *Official Journal of the European Communities,* and an on-line catalog of the Central Library of the Commission. EU Depository Libraries (see EU Information Centers in North America) have free access to Eurobases, but they have different rules about the extent to which library users can access them. Otherwise, they can only be accessed by users who have paid an annual subscription fee and been issued a password, and there are time use charges. For registration and information on costs, contact Eurobases, Office for Official Publications, 2 rue Mercier, L-2985 Luxembourg. Fax: (352) 2929-42025.

European Union Sources

Virtually all official EU sources are described in Ian Thomson, *The Documentation of the European Communities* (London: Mansell, 1989). It takes him nearly four hundred pages to list all of the sources, so I can do little more than scratch the surface (and add some suggestions of my own). Among the most useful:

Europe. A monthly glossy magazine published by the EU in the United States, containing stories and features on the EU and its member states. Contact Delegation of the European Commission, 2100 M Street NW, Suite 700, Washington, DC 20037. Tel: (1-800) 627-7961.

Eurecom. A free, monthly four-page bulletin of political, economic, and monetary news from the EU, published by the EU office in New York. Contact European Commission, 3 Dag Hammarskjold Plaza, 305 East 47th Street, New York, NY 10017. Tel: (212) 371-3804.

EU pamphlets. The EU publishes a series of short pamphlets on its history, institutions, and policies. Although they are exercises in public relations, many are packed with information, and some are surprisingly honest. All are available free from the EU office in Washington, D.C.: Delegation of the Commission of the European Communities, 2300 M Street NW, Washington, DC 20037. Tel: (202) 862-9500/1/2, fax: (202) 429-1766.

Eurostat News. Published quarterly by the Statistical Office of the European Communities. Contains basic statistical information on the EU, much of which is presented as special issues.

Official Journal of the European Communities. Published daily, this is the official gazette of the EU and is the authoritative source of information on all EU legislation, Commission proposals for new legislation, decisions and resolutions of the Council of Ministers, debates of the European Parliament, new actions brought before the Court of Justice, opinions of the Economic and Social Committee, the annual report of the Court of Auditors, and the EU budget. An index is published monthly, with an annual cumulation.

General Report on the Activities of the European Communities. The major annual report of the EU, with a record of developments in all of the key EU policy areas and key statistical information.

Bulletin of the European Communities. Published monthly, this is the official record of events and policies for all EU institutions. While the *General Report* is a treaty obligation, the *Bulletin* is published by the Commission mainly as a public information service. Contains reports on the activities of the Commission and other EU institutions, along with special feature articles. Supplements contain key Commission documents, including proposed legislation.

Directorate-General Documentation. Every DG in the Commission publishes its own periodicals, reports, and surveys, which are too numerous to list here. Full details can be found in Ian Thomson, chapter 5. One of the most useful of the regular publications is the series of biannual *Eurobarometer* opinion polls published by DGX (Information, Communication, and Culture). These polls have been carried out since 1973, mainly to provide EU institutions and the media with statistics on public attitudes toward European issues and European integration. EU Depository Libraries receive copies of every survey.

Eurostat. An acronym for the Statistical Office of the European Communities, Eurostat is based in Luxembourg and collects and collates many different kinds of statistical information from the EU member states. Much of this material is available on computer on-line services such as CRONOS, REGIO, and COMEXT; all of it is published in the form of yearbooks, surveys, studies, and reports.

Directory of Community Legislation in Force and Other Acts of the Community Institutions. Published annually, with biannual supplements. Lists directives, regulations, and other legislation, as well as internal and external agreements.

EU Information Centers in North America

Most major university and college libraries carry general information on the EU, but some also contain more specialized resources. European Documentation Centers (EDCs) are based in academic institutions, are intended to promote teaching and research on the EU, and receive a wide range of EU publications; Depository Libraries (DEPs) are designed mainly for wider public use and only receive the major publications of the EU; European Reference Centers (ERCs) are collections of basic EU documentation.

United States

All DEPs unless otherwise indicated:

Arizona	University of Arizona, Tucson
Arkansas	University of Arkansas, Little Rock
California	Stanford University, Stanford
	University of California, Berkeley
	University of California, La Jolla
	University of California, Los Angeles
	University of Southern California, Los Angeles
Colorado	University of Colorado, Boulder
Connecticut	Yale University, New Haven
Florida	University of Florida, Gainesville
Georgia	Emory University, Atlanta
	University of Georgia, Athens (EDC)
Hawaii	University of Hawaii, Honolulu
Illinois	Library of International Relations, Chicago
	Northwestern University, Evanston
	University of Chicago
	University of Illinois, Champaign
Indiana	Indiana University, Bloomington
	University of Notre Dame, South Bend
Iowa	University of Iowa, Iowa City
Kansas	University of Kansas, Lawrence
Kentucky	University of Kentucky, Lexington
Louisiana	University of New Orleans
Maine	University of Maine, Portland
Massachusetts	Harvard Law School, Cambridge
Michigan	Michigan State University, East Lansing
	University of Michigan, Ann Arbor
Minnesota	University of Minnesota, Minneapolis
Missouri	Washington University, St. Louis
Nebraska	University of Nebraska, Lincoln
New Jersey	Princeton University, Princeton
New Mexico	University of New Mexico, Albuquerque
New York	Council on Foreign Relations, New York
	New York Public Library, New York
	State University of New York at Albany
	State University of New York at Buffalo
North Carolina	Duke University, Durham
Ohio	Ohio State University, Columbus

Oklahoma   University of Oklahoma, Norman
Oregon   University of Oregon, Eugene
Pennsylvania   Pennsylvania State University, University Park
                            University of Pennsylvania, Philadelphia
                            University of Pittsburgh
South Carolina   University of South Carolina, Columbia
Texas   University of Texas, Austin
Utah   University of Utah, Salt Lake City
Virginia   University of Virginia, Charlottesville
Washington   University of Washington, Seattle
Washington, D.C.   American University (EDC)
                            Library of Congress
Wisconsin   University of Wisconsin, Madison

Canada

All ERCs unless otherwise indicated:

Alberta   University of Alberta, Edmonton
British Columbia   Simon Fraser University, Burnaby
                            University of British Columbia, Vancouver
Manitoba   University of Manitoba, Winnipeg (EDC)
New Brunswick   Université de Moncton, Moncton
                            University of New Brunswick, Fredericton
Newfoundland   Memorial University of Newfoundland, St. John's
Nova Scotia   Acadia University, Wolfville
                            Dalhousie University, Halifax (EDC)
Ontario   Bibliothéque Nationale du Canada, Ottawa (DEP)
                            Brock University, St. Catherine's
                            Carleton University, Ottawa (EDC)
                            Queen's University, Kingston (EDC)
                            Université Laurentienne, Sudbury
                            University of Ottawa, Ottawa
                            University of Toronto, Toronto (EDC)
                            University of Waterloo
                            Wilfred Laurier University, Waterloo
                            York University, Downsview
Prince Edward Island   University of Prince Edward Island, Charlottetown
Quebec   McGill University (EDC)
                            Université de Montréal (EDC)
                            Université Laval, Ste. Foy
                            University of Sherbrooke, Sherbrooke
Saskatchewan   University of Saskatchewan, Saskatoon

Appendix IV:
Summits of European Leaders,
1961–1994

Date	Presidency	Place	Key Agenda Items and Outcomes
Pre–European Council			
Feb. 1961	—	Paris	Appointment of Fouchet Committee on political union
July 1961	—	Bonn	Resolution to hold regular meetings of heads of government
May 1967	—	Rome	Tenth anniversary of Treaty of Rome
Dec. 1969	—	The Hague	Enlargement; new initiatives on monetary union and political cooperation
Oct. 1972	—	Paris	Agreement to complete EMU by 1980 and to work on regional and social policies
Dec. 1973	—	Copenhagen	Called in response to energy crisis
Sept. 1974	—	Paris	Informal meeting to discuss future of EC
Dec. 1974	—	Paris	Decision made to create European Council, hold direct elections to EP
Post–European Council			
1975			
March	Ireland	Dublin	First meeting of European Council; renegotiation of British membership
July	Italy	Brussels	Economic recession; relations with Arab world
December	Italy	Rome	Budget reform; direct elections to EP
1976			
April	Luxembourg	Luxembourg	EMU and EP elections
July	Netherlands	Brussels	Terrorism; fisheries; appointment of Roy Jenkins as president of Commission; agreement on number and allocation of EP seats
November	Netherlands	The Hague	Trade with Japan

1977

March	Britain	Rome	Twentieth anniversary of Treaty of Rome
June	Britain	London	EPC; Middle East
December	Belgium	Brussels	Introduction of a European unit of account; budget contributions

1978

April	Denmark	Copenhagen	Fixed date for first EP elections; discussions of EMS
July	Germany	Bremen	Further development of EMS
December	Germany	Brussels	Launch of EMS; agreement to reform CAP

1979

March	France	Paris	Social policy; employment
June	France	Strasbourg	Energy crisis; first appearance of Margaret Thatcher; beginning of renegotiation of British budget contribution
November	Ireland	Dublin	British budget contribution; Iran and Cambodia

1980

April	Italy	Luxembourg	Convergence; British budget contribution
June	Italy	Venice	EPC; Middle East
December	Luxembourg	Luxembourg	EPC

1981

March	Netherlands	Maastricht	Fisheries; economic and social issues
June	Netherlands	Luxembourg	EPC; economic and social issues; first appearance of François Mitterrand
November	Britain	London	CAP and dairy policy

1982

March	Belgium	Brussels	EPC; twenty-fifth anniversary of Treaty of Rome
June	Belgium	Brussels	EPC; Middle East
December	Denmark	Copenhagen	Early discussions on single market; first appearance of Helmut Kohl

1983

March	Germany	Brussels	Exchange rate realignment
June	Germany	Stuttgart	Agreed need for budget reform; signature of Solemn Declaration on European Union
December	Greece	Athens	Budget reform

1984

March	France	Brussels	Budget reform
June	France	Fontainebleau	British rebate and budget reforms agreed on
December	Ireland	Dublin	Internal market discussions; agreement on membership of Spain and Portugal

1985

March	Italy	Brussels	Agreement on single market by December 1992
June	Italy	Milan	Agreed to call IGC on institutional reform
December	Luxembourg	Luxembourg	Terms of the Single European Act adopted; decision made to hold only two regular annual meetings of European Council

1986

June	Netherlands	The Hague	Chernobyl; South Africa; EPC; single market issues
December	Britain	London	Terrorism; internal security; drugs; asylum

1987

March[a]	Belgium	Rome	Thirtieth anniversary of Treaty of Rome
June	Belgium	Brussels	Opened negotiations on Delors Plan for EMU
December	Denmark	Copenhagen	CAP reform; increases in structural funds

1988

February[a]	Germany	Brussels	Emergency summit to agree on budget reforms
June	Germany	Hanover	Creation of Delors Committee on EMU
December	Greece	Rhodes	Progress report on SEA

1989

June	Spain	Madrid	EMU debated; first stage adopted
November[a]	France	Paris	Emergency summit to discuss events in Eastern Europe
December	France	Strasbourg	Endorsed German reunification; approved creation of EBRD; accepted Social Charter; agreed to establish IGC on EMU

1990

April[a]	Ireland	Dublin I	Agreed on commitment to political union; discussed German reunification

June	Ireland	Dublin II	Agreed to IGC on political union
October[a]	Italy	Rome I	Set timetable for EMU; decision made to create European central bank; final appearance of Margaret Thatcher
December	Italy	Rome II	Opening of IGCs on EMU and political union

1991

April[a]	Luxembourg	Luxembourg	Emergency summit to discuss fallout from Gulf War
June	Luxembourg	Luxembourg	Balkan crisis; discussion of draft Treaty on European Union
December	Netherlands	Maastricht	Agreement on Treaty on European Union and timetable for EMU

1992

June	Portugal	Lisbon	Budget; enlargement; Eastern Europe
October[a]	Britain	Birmingham	ERM crisis; new impetus for Maastricht
December	Britain	Edinburgh	Agreed on opt-out clauses for Denmark on Maastricht; program of meetings of institutions

1993

June	Denmark	Copenhagen	Progress on single market and GATT trade talks; agreed on enlargement to Eastern Europe
October[a]	Belgium	Brussels	Guidelines for implementation of Maastricht; Europol; location of seats of institutions
December	Belgium	Brussels	Implementation of Maastricht

1994

June	Greece	Corfu	Signature of Treaties of Accession on enlargement and treaty of cooperation with Russia; failed to agree on new Commission president
July[a]	Germany	Brussels	Agreement reached on Jacques Santer as Commission president
December	Germany	Essen	White Paper on growth, competitiveness, and unemployment; eastward enlargement

1995

June	France	Cannes	Agreement on creation of Europol; target date of January 1999 set for EMU; aid to Africa

[a]Extraordinary meetings (since 1986).

Source: Based in part on information in Jan Werts, *The European Council* (Amsterdam: North-Holland, 1992).

Selected Bibliography

The number of new books about the EU seems to be growing exponentially, which reflects the growth of public, political, and scholarly interest. Two relatively recent bibliographies are available:

Goehlert, Robert, and Marian Shabaan. *The European Community: Basic Resources* (Bloomington: Indiana University Library, 1993).

Kumcu, Erdogan. *An Annotated Bibliography of the European Community* (Chicago: American Marketing Association, 1992).

The best way to keep up with new publications is to scan the computer catalogs or shelves of your nearest major research university and to check the catalogs of the major publishers with interests in the European Union. In addition to the books listed in the Further Reading section at the end of each chapter in this book, the following titles are also useful sources of information and analysis.

General Introductions and Surveys

Archer, Clive, and Fiona Butler. *The European Community: Structure and Process* (New York: St. Martin's Press, 1992).

Budd, Stanley A. *The European Community: A Guide to the Maze* (London: Kegan Paul, 1989).

Cafruny, Alan, and Glenda Rosenthal (Eds.). *The State of the European Community, Vol. 2: The Maastricht Debates and Beyond* (Boulder: Lynne Rienner, 1993).

Cox, Andrew, and Paul Furlong. *A Modern Companion to the European Community: A Guide to Key Facts, Institutions and Terms* (Cheltenham: Edward Elgar, 1992).

Dinan, Desmond. *Ever Closer Union? An Introduction to the European Community* (Boulder: Lynne Rienner, 1994).

George, Stephen. *Politics and Policy in the European Community*, 2d ed. (Oxford: Oxford University Press, 1991).

Hackett, Clifford. *Cautious Revolution: The European Community Arrives* (Westport, Conn.: Praeger, 1990).

Harrison, David. *The Organisation of Europe* (London: Routledge, 1995).

Hurwitz, Leon, and Christian Lequesne (Eds.). *The State of the European Community, Vol. 1: Policies, Institutions, and Debates in the Transition Years* (Boulder: Lynne Rienner, 1991).

Keohane, Robert O., and Stanley Hoffmann (Eds.). *The New European Community: Decisionmaking and Institutional Change* (Boulder: Westview Press, 1991).

Laffan, Brigid. *Integration and Cooperation in Europe* (London: Routledge, 1992).

Leonard, R. L. *Pocket Guide to the European Community* (London: Economist Publications, 1989).

Lodge, Juliet (Ed.). *The European Community and the Challenge of the Future,* 2d ed. (London and New York: Pinter and St. Martin's Press, 1993).

Nicoll, William, and Trevor C. Salmon. *Understanding the European Community,* 2d ed. (London: Harvester Wheatsheaf, 1993).

Nugent, Neill. *The Government and Politics of the European Union,* 3rd ed. (Durham, N.C.: Duke University Press, 1994).

Ramsey, Anne. *Eurojargon: A Dictionary of EEC Acronyms, Abbreviations and Sobriquets,* 2d ed. (Stamford, Conn.: Capital Planning Information, 1989).

Rhodes, Carolyn, and Sonia Mazey (Eds.). *The State of the European Community, Vol. 3: Building a European Polity?* (Boulder: Lynne Rienner, 1995).

Sbragia, Alberta (Ed.). *Euro-Politics: Institutions and Policymaking in the "New" European Community* (Washington, D.C.: Brookings Institution, 1992).

Evolution

Arter, David. *The Politics of European Integration in the Twentieth Century* (Brookfield, Vt.: Dartmouth, 1993).

Brinkley, Douglas, and Clifford Hackett (Eds.). *Jean Monnet: The Path to European Unity* (New York: St. Martin's Press, 1991).

Burgess, Michael. *Federalism and European Union* (London: Routledge, 1989).

Corbett, Richard. *The Treaty of Maastricht: From Conception to Ratification* (Harlow: Longman, 1993).

Ellwood, David. *Rebuilding Europe: Western Europe, America and Postwar Reconstruction* (London: Longman, 1992).

Gimbell, John. *The Origins of the Marshall Plan* (Stanford: Stanford University Press, 1968).

Heater, Derek. *The Idea of European Unity* (London and New York: Pinter and St. Martin's Press, 1992).

Holland, Martin. *European Community Integration: From Community to Union* (London and New York: Pinter and St. Martin's Press, 1994).

Lipgens, Walter. *History of European Integration,* 2 vols. (London: Oxford University Press, 1981 and 1986).

Marjolin, Robert. *Architect of European Union: Memoirs, 1911–1986* (London: Weidenfeld & Nicolson, 1989).

Milward, Alan S. *The European Rescue of the Nation-State* (London: Routledge, 1992).

Story, Jonathan (Ed.). *The New Europe: Politics, Government and Economy Since 1945* (Oxford: Blackwell, 1993).

Wilson, Kevin, and Jan van der Dussen (Eds.). *The History of the Idea of Europe* (London: Routledge, 1993).

Policies

Adams, William James (Ed.). *Singular Europe: Economy and Polity of the EC After 1992* (Ann Arbor: University of Michigan Press, 1992).

Cahan, Alfred. *The WEU and NATO: Strengthening the Second Pillar of the Alliance* (Washington, D.C.: Atlantic Council, 1990).

Canzoneri, Matthew, Vittorio Grilli, and Paul Masson (Eds.). *Establishing a Central Bank for Europe* (Cambridge: Cambridge University Press, 1992).

Collignon, Stefan, Peter Bofinger, Christopher Johnson, and Bertrand de Maigret. *Europe's Monetary Future: Policy Options* (London and New York: Pinter and St. Martin's Press, 1994).

Crouch, Colin, and David Marquand. *The Politics of 1992: Beyond the Single European Market* (Cambridge: Basil Blackwell, 1990).

Danspeckgruber, Wolfgang (Ed.). *Emerging Dimensions of European Security Policy* (Boulder: Westview Press, 1991).

El-Agraa, Ali M. *The Economics of the European Community*, 3rd ed. (New York: St. Martin's Press, 1990).

Feld, Werner. *The Future of European Security and Defense Policy* (Boulder: Lynne Rienner, 1993).

Fursdon, Edward. *The European Defence Community: A History* (London: Macmillan, 1980).

Giavazzi, Francesco, Stefano Micossi, and Marcus Miller (Eds.). *The European Monetary System* (Cambridge: Cambridge University Press, 1989).

Gros, Daniel, and Niels Thygesen. *European Monetary Integration* (London and New York: Longman and St. Martin's Press, 1992).

Hannequart, Achille (Ed.). *Economic and Social Cohesion in Europe: A New Objective* (London: Routledge, 1992).

Harrop, Jeffrey. *The Political Economy of Integration in the European Community*, 2d ed. (Aldershot: Edward Elgar, 1992).

Holland, Martin (Ed.). *The Future of European Political Cooperation* (New York: St. Martin's Press, 1991).

Ifestos, Panayiotis. *European Political Cooperation: Towards a Framework of Supranational Diplomacy?* (Brookfield, Vt.: Avebury, 1987).

Johnson, Christopher, and Stefan Collignon (Eds.). *The Monetary Economics of Europe: Causes of the EMS Crisis* (London and New York: Pinter and St. Martin's Press, 1994).

Johnson, Stanley P., and Guy Corcelli (Eds.). *The Environmental Policy of the EC* (London: Graham and Trotman, 1991).

Jopp, Mathias, Reinhardt Rummel, and Peter Schmidt (Eds.). *Integration and Security in Western Europe: Inside the European Pillar* (Boulder: Westview Press, 1991).

Nuttall, Simon. *European Political Cooperation* (Oxford: Clarendon Press, 1991).

Thomsen, Stephen, and Stephen Woolcock. *Direct Investment and European Integration* (London and New York: Pinter and St. Martin's Press, 1993).

Wise, Mark, and Richard Gibb. *Single Market to Social Europe: The European Community in the 1990s* (New York: Wiley, 1993).

Member State Case Studies

Pinter Press in London (represented in North America by St. Martin's Press) has published a series of case studies of relations between the EU and individual member states.

Almarcha Barbado, Amparo (Ed.). *Spain and EC Membership Evaluated* (1993).

Bulmer, Simon, Stephen George, and Andrew Scott (Eds.). *The United Kingdom and EC Membership Evaluated* (1992).

Dreyfus, Francois-George, Jacques Morizet, and Max Peyrard (Eds.). *France and EC Membership Evaluated* (1993).

Francioni, Francesco (Ed.). *Italy and EC Membership Evaluated* (1992).

Kazakos, Panos, and P. C. Ioakimides (Eds.). *Greece and EC Membership Evaluated* (1994).

Keatinge, Patrick (Ed.). *Ireland and EC Membership Evaluated* (1991).

Lopes, José da Silva (Ed.). *Portugal and EC Membership Evaluated* (1993).

Lyck, Lise (Ed.). *Denmark and EC Membership Evaluated* (1992).

Schweitzer, Carl-Christoph, and Detlev Karsten (Eds.). *The Federal Republic of Germany and EC Membership Evaluated* (1990).

van Meerhaege, M.A.G. (Ed.). *Belgium and EC Membership Evaluated* (1992).

Wolters, Menno, and Peter Coffey (Eds.). *The Netherlands and EC Membership Evaluated* (1990).

Other member-state case studies include the following:

Brivati, Brian, and Harriet Jones. *From Reconstruction to Integration: Britain and Europe Since 1945* (London and New York: Pinter and St. Martin's Press, 1993).

Bulmer, Simon, and Willie Patterson. *The Federal Republic of Germany and the EC* (London: Allen and Unwin, 1987).

Feld, Werner. *West Germany and the EC: Changing Interests and Competing Policy Options* (New York: Praeger, 1981).

George, Stephen. *An Awkward Partner: Britain in the European Community* (Oxford: Clarendon Press, 1990).

_____ (Ed.). *Britain and the European Community: The Politics of Semi-Detachment* (Oxford: Clarendon Press, 1992).

Kelstrup, M. (Ed.). *European Integration and Denmark's Participation* (Copenhagen: Copenhagen Political Studies Press, 1992).

Lankowski, Carl (Ed.). *Germany and the European Community* (New York: St. Martin's Press, 1993).

Scott, Andrew. *Britain in Europe: An Economic Appraisal* (London and New York: Pinter and St. Martin's Press, 1995).

About the Book and Author

The emergence of the European Union has become one of the defining events of the late twentieth century, changing the way Europeans relate to each other and the way the rest of the world relates to Europe. Already an economic superpower, the EU is now building the foundations of political union among its fifteen member states.

This new text provides a valuable introduction to the institutions and policies of the EU. Clear and succinct, *The European Union: Politics and Policies* is the first text of its kind written specifically for U.S. students and the first to take account of the 1995 enlargement. The author combines description and analysis to provide an accessible guide to a phenomenon that is complex and ever changing and that has growing significance for Europeans and Americans alike.

John McCormick is assistant professor of political science at Indiana University–Purdue University Indianapolis. His teaching and research interests lie in comparative politics, environmental policy, and the politics of the European Union. Among his recent publications are *The Global Environmental Movement*, 2d ed. (1995) and *Comparative Politics in Transition* (1995). Every April, he organizes the Midwest Model European Union in Indianapolis.

Index